W9-BBB-780

DATE DUE

DE 17 '08			
OC 22 '09			
DE 16 '09			
MR 14 '11			

South Asia in
World Politics

Asia in World Politics
Series Editor: Samuel S. Kim

South Asia in World Politics

Edited by Devin T. Hagerty

ROWMAN & LITTLEFIELD PUBLISHERS, INC.
Lanham • Boulder • New York • Toronto • Oxford

ROWMAN & LITTLEFIELD PUBLISHERS, INC.

Published in the United States of America
by Rowman & Littlefield Publishers, Inc.
A wholly owned subsidary of The Rowman & Littlefield Publishing Group, Inc.
4501 Forbes Boulevard, Suite 200, Lanham, MD 20706
www.rowmanlittlefield.com

P.O. Box 317, Oxford OX2 9RU, UK

British Library Cataloguing in Publication Information Available

Library of Congress Cataloging-in-Publication Data

South Asia in world politics / edited by Devin T. Hagerty.
    p. cm.
  Includes bibliographical references and index.
  ISBN 0-7425-2586-4 (cloth : alk. paper — ISBN 0-7425-2587-2 (pbk. : alk. paper)
  1. South Asia—Foreign relations. 2. South Asia—Politics and government. I. Hagerty,
Devin T. II. Series.
DS341.S653 2005
320.954'09'045—dc22
                                    2004022277

Printed in the United States of America

∞™ The paper used in this publication meets the minimum requirements of American
National Standard for Information Sciences—Permanence of Paper for Printed Library
Materials, ANSI/NISO Z39.48-1992.

For Barb

Contents

Part II: International Issue Areas

Acknowledgments

As with many books, it took longer than expected to bring this one from conception to fruition. During a crucial stretch in its preparation, I lost thirty pounds and grew increasingly lethargic. I was ultimately diagnosed with insulin-dependent diabetes, not a happy outcome, but one that can be managed. Between the onset of my illness and its stabilization, I was neither fun to be around nor easy to work with. Still, human nature being what it is, most of my friends, colleagues, and family members feigned obliviousness to my crankiness and treated me with unstinting love.

For their support and fellowship over many months, I would like to thank Mary Ann Bradley, Herb and Ann Hagerty, David and Katherine Bradley, Gene and Nancy Bradley, Rich Hagerty, Sean Hagerty, Shirley Hagerty, Vivian Grace Hagerty, Lou Cantori, Helen Curtice, Andy Flynn Sequeira, Sumit Ganguly and Traci Nagle, Danielle Hamberger, Abul Hassan, Jim and Michele Hentz, Cindy Hody, Brad Moore, Wendy Patriquin, Emma Sellers, and Geoffrey and Jennifer Vaughan. Susan McEachern at Rowman & Littlefield is not only a terrific editor, but she was graciously understanding of my medical problems and has my enduring gratitude.

Of course, only one person bore the full brunt of my fear, anxiety, anger, and puzzlement about my health. Probably only one person could have because my wife, Barbara Bradley Hagerty, possesses what may be a unique combination of qualities: raw kindness, a probing intellect, unflinching integrity, real humility, and the kind of tenacious loyalty usually found only in foxholes. Perhaps the greatest of all Barb's qualities is that she accepts no credit for any of the other ones. I am exceptionally fortunate that she loves me so much, and I lovingly thank her for being by my side every step of the way.

South Asia Chronology

1858	India comes under direct rule of the British Crown after the Indian mutiny.[1]
1885	Indian National Congress founded in Bombay.
1886	Afghanistan's border with Russia demarcated along the Oxus River (now called the Amu Darya).
1887	The Maldives become a British protectorate.
1890	Anglo-Tibetan agreement recognizes British dominance over Sikkim.
1892	Indian Councils Act provides limited Indian role in local administration.
1893	British declare Durand Line as Afghanistan–India boundary.
1894	British expedition to Tibet asserts British-claimed area of influence.
1905	British partition Bengal over widespread public opposition in India.
1906	All-India Muslim League founded in Dhaka.
1907	Britain and Russia agree on spheres of influence in Persia and Asia. Agreement guarantees independence of Afghanistan with foreign affairs under British influence.
1908	Congress declares aim to be a "system of government similar to that enjoyed by the self-governing Members of the British Empire."
1909	Morley-Minto reforms expand Indian role in local government councils.
1911	Partition of Bengal partially rescinded in response to public pressure. Britain declares McMahon Line to be India–Tibet

	boundary in Himalayas. Treaty of Punakha gives Britain control over Bhutan's foreign relations.
1912	Imperial Indian capital moved from Calcutta to Delhi.
1913	Muslim League declares aim to be "self-government suitable to India."
1915	Defense of India Act in World War I mobilizes Indian resources.
1916	Congress and Muslim League jointly advocate Indian self-rule in the Lucknow Pact.
1917	Secretary of State Montagu declares British aim in India to be the "gradual development of self-governing institutions with a view to the progressive realization of responsible government in India as an integral part of the British Empire."
1918–1919	British harshly repress antiregime activities by Indian revolutionaries. April 1919 massacre by British forces kills 379, injures 1,200 in Amritsar.
1919	Montagu-Chelmsford Reforms expand Indian role in provincial administration. Third Anglo-Afghan war ends with Treaty of Rawalpindi. Afghanistan becomes fully independent. Ceylon (today Sri Lanka) National Congress forms to lobby for devolution of political power from Britain to the Ceylonese.
1920	Congress supports Muslim League demand to restore the caliphate.
1920	Congress, under Mohandas Gandhi, adopts policy of noncooperation "by all legitimate and peaceful means" to support demand for self-rule. Congress boycotts legislative assemblies, courts, and British manufactures.
1921	British transform Central Legislative Council in Delhi into a bicameral parliament with some elected members in both houses. Chamber of Princes also created for rulers of the Indian native (princely) states.
1922–1923	Widespread communal violence in India brings new repression and limits cooperation between Congress and the Muslim League. Gandhi suspends noncooperation movement and urges "constructive" steps, like hand-spinning cotton cloth. Gandhi later arrested and sentenced to six-year prison term.
1923	First simultaneous examinations for Indian Civil Service in London and Delhi.
1925	All-India Depressed Classes Association forms to advocate greater electoral reservations for Untouchables and lower Hindu castes.
1928	All-Parties Conference breaks up over communal issues.

1929	Britain concedes that the "natural issue of India's constitutional progress . . . is the attainment of Dominion Status." Congress meeting in Lahore advocates full independence for India. Muslim League's "Fourteen Points" declares conditions for Muslim acceptance of constitutional change in India. Congress boycotts roundtable conference convened by the British to discuss future constitutional arrangements for India.
1930	Gandhi launches mass civil disobedience campaign. Gandhi arrested after leading 241-mile, twenty-four-day march to the sea to protest tax on salt. Large demonstrations across India, as Congress president Jawaharlal Nehru, other senior Congress leaders, and sixty thousand people are imprisoned.
1931	Gandhi and others released; civil disobedience campaign suspended. Congress joins roundtable conference. Britain grants Ceylon limited self-rule and universal franchise.
1932	Communal disagreements doom roundtable conference. Congress resumes noncooperation, boycotting British goods and orchestrating nationwide protests against British policies. Gandhi and tens of thousands of followers are imprisoned. Opposing separate electorates for Untouchables, Gandhi vows to "fast unto death." Gandhi agrees to electoral reservations for Untouchables and ends fast.
1933	Zahir Shah becomes king of Afghanistan.
1935	Government of India Act of 1935 gives almost complete autonomy to provinces. Provides for elections to seats in provincial assemblies and national parliament. Congress again suspends noncooperation as parties prepare to contest elections.
1937	Congress wins majorities in seven provincial assemblies. Forms governments in those provinces and, in 1938, an eighth province.
1937	Burma becomes a colony separate from British India.
1939	World War II breaks out in Europe; Congress governments resign because (British) Government of India declares war without consulting Indians.
1940	Muslim League president Muhammad Ali Jinnah enunciates two-nation theory: Hindus and Muslims are separate nations. League declares its goal to be the creation of Pakistan, a separate state for India's Muslims.
1941	Japan attacks Pearl Harbor. Britain and (British) Government of India declare war on Japan.
1942	Cripps Mission to India offers dominion status or full independence after the war in return for Congress support for the war

	effort. Congress refuses, launches Quit India movement; leaders imprisoned.
1942–1945	Muslim League supports war effort. British-officered Indian army deployed in all wartime combat areas.
1945	Viceroy announces British decision to move India toward self-government.
1945–1946	General and provincial elections held. Muslim League wins overwhelming majority of seats reserved for Muslims. Congress wins large majority of remaining seats.
1946	Hindu-Muslim violence spreads in Bengal, Bombay, Punjab, and Bihar. Three-month British cabinet mission fails to reconcile Congress–Muslim League differences over India's constitutional future. Muslim League reaffirms support for creation of Pakistan, while Congress remains committed to a unified, secular, democratic Indian state.
1947	British announce plan in February for "transfer of power" into "responsible Indian hands" by mid-1948. As communal violence intensifies, British decide in June to partition British India in August.
1947	Pakistan born on August 14. India gains independence on August 15.
1947	Maharaja of Jammu and Kashmir initially hopes for independence, but facing invasion by Pakistan-backed Muslims, accedes to India. Indian army deployed to defend Kashmir. First Indo-Pakistani war begins.
1948	Gandhi is assassinated in New Delhi. Ceylon becomes independent on February 4. Jinnah dies in Karachi. He is succeeded as Pakistan's leader by Liaquat Ali Khan.
1949	Awami League Party established in East Pakistan to campaign for autonomy from West Pakistan. First India-Pakistan war ends. Operative UN resolutions call for the removal of outside forces from Jammu and Kashmir and for the holding of a plebiscite to decide the state's political future.
1950	India adopts a new constitution as an independent, federal republic. India-Sikkim Agreement associates Sikkim with the Indian Union. China invades and absorbs Tibet over Indian protests.
1951	Traditional Rana oligarchy overthrown in Nepal with Indian help; monarchy is restored, and Nepalese Congress Party assumes power. Liaquat Ali Khan is assassinated in Pakistan.
1951–1952	Congress Party wins first Indian general elections.
1953	Muhammad Ali Bogra becomes prime minister of Pakistan.

1954	India–Bhutan treaty affirms Bhutan's independence; requires Bhutan to be "guided" by India on foreign affairs and defense. Pakistan signs mutual security pact with the United States. Chinese foreign minister Chou Enlai endorses Nehru's "Five Principles of Peaceful Coexistence" during Delhi visit.
1955	King Mahendra assumes the throne in Nepal on the death of his father. India is one of the conveners of the Asian-African Conference in Bandung, Indonesia, along with China, Burma, Ceylon, and twenty-three others. Soviet leaders Nikolai Bulganin and Nikita Khrushchev visit India
1956	Pakistan becomes a member of the Baghdad Pact.
1958	Army chief Muhammad Ayub Khan seizes power and declares martial law in Pakistan.
1960	India and Pakistan sign Indus Waters Agreement. Ayub Khan becomes Pakistan's president.
1961	Indian army evicts Portuguese from Goa and other enclaves in India.
1962	Chinese forces defeat Indian army in Ladakh and NEFA. Chinese withdraw to previous positions held on NEFA border.
1964	Indian prime minister Nehru dies; Lal Bahadur Shastri becomes prime minister.
1965	India and Pakistan fight second war over Kashmir. Republic of Maldives becomes independent on July 26.
1966	Prime ministers of India and Pakistan meet at Tashkent under Soviet auspices and commit their countries to seeking a peaceful, bilateral solution of the Kashmir problem. Indian prime minister Shastri dies at Tashkent; Indira Gandhi, Nehru's daughter, becomes prime minister.
1969	Gen. Yahya Khan replaces Ayub Khan as Pakistan's president.
1970	Awami League wins overwhelming election victory in East Pakistan.
1971	Pakistan puts aside election of Awami League government; resulting violence in East Pakistan prompts crackdown by Pakistan army. Civil war follows, leading to East Pakistan's declaration of independence, massive refugee exodus to India, and Indian army intervention. East Pakistani government declares Bangladesh independent on December 16. India signs twenty-year Treaty of Peace, Friendship, and Cooperation with the Soviet Union. Former foreign minister Zulfikar Ali Bhutto becomes Pakistan's prime minister.
1972	India and Pakistan sign the Simla Agreement, pledging to resolve the Kashmir dispute peacefully. Awami League head

	Sheikh Mujibur Rahman becomes Bangladesh's first prime minister.
1973	Bhutto introduces a new constitution establishing Pakistan as an Islamic republic with himself as president. King Zahir Shah is overthrown in Kabul by Mohammad Daud, who establishes a republic with himself as president and prime minister.
1974	Pakistan recognizes Bangladesh. India tests a "peaceful" nuclear device.
1975	Mujibur Rahman becomes president of Bangladesh but is assassinated soon thereafter. Indira Gandhi proclaims a state of emergency in India after being found guilty of electoral malpractice. Civil rights are suspended; opposition leaders are arrested and imprisoned.
1977	Amid widespread unrest, Pakistan army chief Muhammad Zia ul-Haq topples Bhutto, suspends 1973 constitution, and imposes martial law. Indian Congress Party is ousted from power for the first time. Morarji Desai, head of the Janata Party, becomes prime minister. Bangladesh and India reach agreement on sharing eastern waters.
1978	Afghan government overthrown in Communist coup; Islamic resistance begins. General Zia becomes Pakistan's president.
1979	Former Pakistani president Bhutto is convicted of conspiracy to murder and hanged by Zia's government. American Embassy is attacked and set afire in Islamabad, Pakistan. Soviet Union invades and occupies Afghanistan.
1980	Indira Gandhi becomes Indian prime minister again. Sanjay Gandhi, her son, dies in plane crash.
1983	Bangladesh hosts initial foreign ministers' meeting of South Asian Association for Regional Cooperation (SAARC) in Dhaka.
1984	Indian troops storm the Golden Temple in Amritsar. Communal riots erupt in Delhi. Prime Minister Indira Gandhi is assassinated and succeeded by her son, Rajiv.
1985	SAARC heads of state hold first meeting in Dhaka. SAARC formally established by Bangladesh, Bhutan, India, Maldives, Nepal, Pakistan, and Sri Lanka.
1986	Second SAARC summit held in Bangalore, India.
1986–1987	Crisis over India's Brasstacks military exercises brings India and Pakistan to the brink of war.
1987	India deploys peacekeeping troops in Sri Lankan civil war. Third SAARC summit held in Kathmandu, Nepal.
1988	President Mohammad Zia ul-Haq is killed in an airplane crash. Benazir Bhutto elected prime minister of Pakistan. Fourth SAARC summit held in Islamabad, Pakistan.

1988–1989   Soviet Union abandons effort to subdue Afghanistan and withdraws army.

1989   V. P. Singh, leader of the Janata Dal Party, becomes India's prime minister.

1990   Muslim insurgency begins in Indian-administered Kashmir. India withdraws troops from Sri Lanka, having failed to suppress Tamil insurgency. Benazir Bhutto dismissed as Pakistan's prime minister and is succeeded by Nawaz Sharif. Fifth SAARC summit held in Male, Maldives.

1991   Indian prime minister Rajiv Gandhi is assassinated. Congress government launches Indian economic reforms under Gandhi's successor, Narasimha Rao. Sixth SAARC summit held in Colombo, Sri Lanka.

1992   Afghan president Najibullah is ousted from power, killed by opposition forces. Hindu extremists destroy the sixteenth-century Babri Mosque at Ayodhya in Uttar Pradesh, triggering widespread communal riots.

1993   Seventh SAARC summit held in Dhaka, Bangladesh. Nawaz Sharif resigns as Pakistani prime minister and is succeeded by Benazir Bhutto.

1995   Eighth SAARC summit held in New Delhi. India and Pakistan finalize agreement not to attack each other's nuclear facilities.

1996   Benazir Bhutto's second government is dismissed in Pakistan. Nawaz Sharif becomes prime minister in 1997. India and Pakistan celebrate fifty years of independence. Ninth SAARC summit held in Male, Maldives. Indian prime minister I. K. Gujral and Pakistani prime minister Sharif meet, marking the first meeting in four years between the Indian and Pakistani heads of government. Pakistan becomes the first country to formally recognize the Taliban regime in Afghanistan.

1998   BJP forms coalition government in India under Atal Behari Vajpayee. India conducts a series of nuclear explosive tests. Pakistan follows suit. Pakistani military forces secretly occupy territory near Kargil on the Indian side of the LOC in Kashmir. Tenth SAARC summit held in Colombo, Sri Lanka.

1999   Pakistani prime minister Sharif and Indian prime minister Vajpayee meet in Lahore. Two governments issue the Lahore Declaration, a roadmap for conflict resolution. India discovers Pakistani forces near Kargil. Indian military attacks the invaders on India's side of the LOC. Under heavy U.S. diplomatic and Indian military pressure, Pakistan agrees to withdraw its troops. Pakistani prime minister Sharif's government is toppled in a military coup led by army chief Pervez

	Musharraf, who proclaims himself the country's new chief executive.
2000	India marks the birth of its billionth citizen.
2001	Border clashes kill sixteen Indian and three Bangladeshi soldiers. Prime Minister Vajpayee and now president Musharraf hold unsuccessful talks. Operation Enduring Freedom topples Taliban government in Afghanistan. Indian parliament building is attacked by terrorists based in Pakistan. India imposes sanctions on Pakistan, which responds in kind.
2002	Terrorists kill thirty people in raid on Indian army camp in Kashmir. India and Pakistan mobilize one million troops along their common border and the LOC in Kashmir. Crisis abates in autumn 2002. Pakistani general elections result in a hung parliament. Mir Zafarullah Jamali selected as prime minister. Eleventh SAARC summit held in Kathmandu, Nepal.
2003	India and Pakistan agree to resume direct air links and allow overflights.
2004	Twelfth SAARC summit held in Islamabad, Pakistan. Musharraf and Vajpayee agree to restart negotiations, including over the Kashmir dispute. Congress-led coalition wins Indian general elections and forms new government under Prime Minister Manmohan Singh. Indian and Pakistani foreign secretaries meet for the first time in six years. Two sides agree to new confidence-building measures, including the opening of consulates in Mumbai (previously Bombay) and Karachi.

NOTE

1. Sources consulted include BBC News (http://news.bbc.co.uk); W. Norman Brown, *The United States and India, Pakistan, Bangladesh*, 3rd ed. (Cambridge, Mass.: Harvard University Press, 1972); *The Columbia Encyclopedia*, 5th ed. (New York: Columbia University Press, 1993); Robert L. Hardgrave Jr. and Stanley A. Kochanek, *India: Government and Politics in a Developing Nation*, 5th ed. (Fort Worth, Tex.: Harcourt Brace Jovanovich, 1993); *Imperial Gazetteer of India: Afghanistan and Nepal* (Lahore: Sang-e-Meel, 1979 [1908]); Charles H. Kennedy and Craig Baxter, eds., *Pakistan 2000* (Lanham, Md.: Lexington, 2000); Charles H. Kennedy and Rasul Baksh Rais, eds., *Pakistan: 1995* (Boulder, Colo.: Westview, 1995); R. C. Majumdar, H. C. Raychaudhuri, and Kalikinkar Datta, *An Advanced History of India*, 2nd ed. (London: Macmillan, 1953); Francis Robinson, ed., *The Cambridge Encyclopedia of India, Pakistan, Bangladesh, Sri Lanka, Nepal, Bhutan and the Maldives* (Cambridge: Cambridge University Press, 1989); Stanley Wolpert, *A New History of India*, 6th ed. (Oxford: Oxford University Press, 2000).

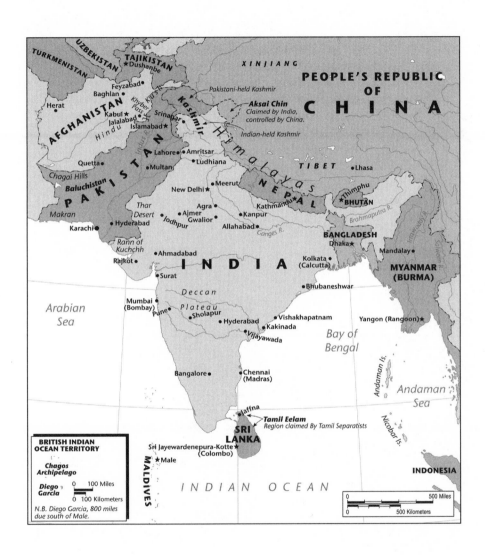

TURKMENISTAN

UZBEKISTAN

TAJIKISTAN
★Dushanbe

XINJIANG

PEOPLE'S REPUBLIC
OF
CHINA

Feyzabad•
Baghlan •

Herat •

AFGHANISTAN

Kabul ★
Jalalabad•
Islamabad★

Khyber
Pass

Hindu

Pakistani-held Kashmir

Aksai Chin
Claimed by India,
controlled by China.

Indian-held Kashmir

Kashmir

Srinagar•

Lahore• •Amritsar
•Ludhiana

H
i
m
a
l
a
y
a
s

TIBET

•Lhasa

Quetta•

Chagai Hills

Baluchistan

Makran

Karachi•

PAKISTAN

Multan•

New Delhi★ •Meerut

Thar
Desert

Agra •
Ajmer•
•Gwalior

Jodhpur•

Kanpur

Allahabad•

Kathmandu★

NEPAL

★Thimphu
★BHUTAN

Brahmaputra R.

Hyderabad•

Rann of
Kuchchh
Rajkot •

•Ahmadabad

•Surat

INDIA

Ganges R.

BANGLADESH
Dhaka★

Kolkata •
(Calcutta)

•Bhubaneshwar

Mandalay•

MYANMAR
(BURMA)

Arabian
Sea

Mumbai•
(Bombay)

Pune•

Deccan

Plateau

•Sholapur

Hyderabad•

•Vijayawada
•Kakinada

•Vishakhapatnam

Yangon (Rangoon)★

Bay of
Bengal

Andaman Is.

Andaman
Sea

Bangalore•

•Chennai
(Madras)

•Jaffna

Tamil Eelam
Region claimed By Tamil Separatists

Nicobar Is.

SRI
LANKA

Sri Jayewardenepura-Kotte★
(Colombo)

★Male

MALDIVES

INDIAN OCEAN

INDONESIA

0   500 Miles

0   500 Kilometers

Introduction: South Asia in World Politics

Devin T. Hagerty

This book is a comprehensive, analytically diverse introduction to the international relations of South Asia, a region encompassing the states of Afghanistan, Bangladesh, Bhutan, India, the Maldives, Nepal, Pakistan, and Sri Lanka. These countries together comprise 23 percent of the world's population. Indians, Bangladeshis, and Pakistanis alone account for 21 percent of all human beings alive today and for 95 percent of all South Asians. The region is geopolitically centered on India, whose territory constitutes 64 percent of South Asia's land area. At least two out of every five Muslims in the world live in South Asia.

SOUTH ASIA AND U.S. FOREIGN POLICY

For much of the last half-century, South Asia has been relegated to the back-burner of U.S. foreign policy interests. While official U.S. attention toward Europe, East Asia, and other areas defined as strategically important has been sustained and proactive, U.S. interest in South Asia has tended to be sporadic and reactive. By and large, the region has gained Washington's steady, high-level notice only during moments of serious international tension:

- In the early 1950s, when the Cold War turned hot in Asia and global bipolarity began to congeal
- From 1962 to 1965, when first China and India, then India and Pakistan, fought major wars
- Throughout 1971, when Pakistani forces engaged in a devastating civil war, and India intervened, defeated Pakistan, and helped to create the new state of Bangladesh

1

- After December 1979, when the Soviet Union invaded and occupied Afghanistan
- Between 1998 and 1999, when India and Pakistan tested their nuclear explosive capabilities and then fought a limited war in Kashmir
- After September 11, 2001, when al Qaeda terrorists, directed by their leaders in Afghanistan, attacked the World Trade Center in New York and the Pentagon outside of Washington, D.C.

In between these moments of international drama, senior U.S. policymakers have often de-emphasized a region that seems somehow destined to suffer deadly conflict after deadly conflict, irrespective of how intensely and sincerely external actors try to temper regional hostilities. The 1990s witnessed the latest and most serious manifestation of this ostrichlike posture, when, after helping the Afghan mujahideen ("holy warriors") chase Soviet forces from their country, the United States essentially turned its back on a part of South Asia—the region's northwestern frontier—that had been wracked by warfare for more than a decade.

Viewed in proportion to Afghanistan's 1978 population of some 15 million people, the carnage of the 1978–1989 phase of the country's long war is staggering: more than 1.5 million Afghans had perished, some 5 million languished in refugee camps in Iran and Pakistan, and millions more had been "internally displaced," that is, driven from their homes and villages by the relentless pounding of Soviet air power. Despite the fact that half of Afghanistan's population had suffered grievously in this last great "battle" of the Cold War, senior-level U.S. policy attention in 1989–1991 shifted precipitously to other "more important" regions: Europe, where the Berlin Wall fell, communism imploded, and the Soviet Union disintegrated, and the Middle East, where Iraq invaded Kuwait, menaced Saudi Arabia, and threatened the free flow of oil on which the United States and its allies depend so heavily.

Tragically, it took a direct, massive attack on the United States in September 2001 to alert Washington to the notion that paying only fitful, desultory attention to one of the world's most volatile regions is a recipe for everyday regional instability, repeated international crises, major and minor wars, and, ultimately, conditions so chronically unsettled that they continue to provide the breeding ground for the greatest threat to American national security in the early twenty-first century: transnational, radicalized Islamic terrorism.

THE VIEW FROM THE ACADEMY

A country's higher-educational priorities, at least in policy-relevant disciplines, tend to reflect its perceived national security interests. In the United

States, the Cold War expansion of U.S. interests around the globe gave rise to "area studies," including "South Asian studies," as interdisciplinary concentrations in American colleges and universities. In the 1950s and 1960s, the federal government funded scores of area studies programs that were intended to train future scholars and policy professionals in the politics, economics, cultures, and languages of regions being newly "discovered" by the United States. Like other area interdisciplines, South Asian studies thrived for a time.

However, in the 1970s and 1980s, financial support for the study of areas viewed as relatively less important, including South Asia, declined considerably. University departments in the social sciences hired fewer area studies experts, and graduate students aspiring to study Africa, South Asia, and other "peripheral" areas of the Third World were encouraged to focus instead on more strategically important parts of the globe. Aspiring scholars who ignored that advice faced an academic job market that in the 1990s was heavily skewed toward candidates with strong "disciplinary" skills, which tended to mean expertise in quantitative methods, formal modeling, game theory, and other ostensibly more "rigorous" methodologies than those employed by area specialists. Partly as a result of this decline in area studies, America awoke on September 12, 2001, to the fact that it was woefully unprepared to understand the very parts of the world that would henceforth generate its chief foreign policy and national security challenges. The news media abounded with stories about how the U.S. intelligence community, with all of its state-of-the-art "national technical means," could eavesdrop on conversations anywhere in the world, but sorely lacked the human capabilities to interpret and analyze the resultant mountains of data that flowed into Washington.

Judging by trends since September 2001, the U.S. foreign policy community has belatedly begun to realize the enormity of its deficiencies in area studies, including South Asian studies. Out of necessities driven by the "global war on terrorism" and the U.S. invasions of Afghanistan (2001) and Iraq (2003), senior U.S. policymakers are now paying more sustained attention to South Asia and other previously neglected regions. Alas, academic priorities turn around as slowly as the proverbial aircraft carrier. While today's professional help-wanted ads are filled with vacant positions for experts in the cultures, languages, politics, and economics of countries from the Mediterranean to the Straits of Malacca, the pre-2001 decline of area studies has rendered the qualified candidate pool quite thin.

University departments have again responded to national priorities and begun to reorient their course offerings toward underemphasized regions like South Asia, but there will be an inevitable time lag before a new generation of South Asianists can move into positions of policy and scholarly influence. This book is a modest effort to ensure that, as increasing numbers of students gravitate toward the study of South Asia, they and their professors will have at hand an introductory overview of the region's international relations and its role in world politics. That there is no such book already available illustrates how neglected South Asia has been in American academia.

WHAT IS SOUTH ASIA?

The concept of a region in international affairs is inherently ambiguous. Numerous characteristics can be invoked to assess the "regionness" of a particular geographical area. These might include strategic dynamics, political alignments, economic interactions, cultural affinities, and language patterns. What appears to be a region in strategic terms may not be one in economic terms. Furthermore, individual scholars will give varying weights to each characteristic of regionness, depending on their own research interests and underlying assumptions about world politics. Adding to this conceptual fluidity is the fact that, although journalists, policymakers, and scholars alike treat regions as if they were static and permanent ("in Western Europe today"), our construction and deconstruction of regions is in reality a much more volatile affair. In sum, regions are ephemeral, intellectual constructs: they wax and wane with changing technological developments, geopolitical events, demographic flows, scholarly fads, and the numerous other dynamics that, taken together, constitute human history.

Conventionally, South Asia has been understood to include, at a minimum, India, Pakistan, Bangladesh, Sri Lanka, Nepal, Bhutan, and the Maldives. These states are the seven members of the South Asian Association for Regional Cooperation, the only significant, formal, regionwide international institution. The logic of this conception rests mainly on the fact that India shares civilizational ties with all six of the other countries, as well as borders with all but the island states of Sri Lanka and the Maldives. Hence, analysts often use "the Indian subcontinent"—or, simply, "the subcontinent"—as a synonym for South Asia. Afghanistan is sometimes included in the roster of South Asian states but is often omitted. The justification for excluding Afghanistan is that it shares neither a border nor strong ethnic and cultural ties with India; indeed, the Khyber Pass has historically been viewed as the major land gateway into South Asia.

This book departs from that logic and treats Afghanistan as an integral part of the region. Although it may once have made sense to treat Afghanistan as lying outside South Asia, the advancing technology of warfare and geopolitical developments over the last twenty-five years have made it impossible to understand South Asian international relations without reference to Pakistan's northwestern neighbor. Not only does Afghanistan share a long border with

Pakistan, but its Pashtun community—40 percent of the population—is closely connected with its ethnic brethren in Pakistan. Always an important foreign policy concern for Pakistani officials, Afghanistan in the late 1970s began to share center stage with India as a top priority for Islamabad. In 1978 a Soviet-supported coup d'état implanted a communist regime in Kabul for the first time. Resistance to the new government developed immediately, as traditionalist Islamic fighters took up arms against what they viewed as an infidel regime. With the country teetering on the brink of all-out civil war in late 1979, the Soviet Union's military forces occupied Afghanistan in an attempt to bring order to Moscow's southern flank. When the United States decided to help the Islamist Afghan resistance battle the Soviets, Washington found a ready strategic partner in Pakistan, which became the conduit for billions of dollars in U.S. training and military assistance for the Afghan mujahideen. That, in turn, had a profound impact on Pakistan's relations with India, which charged throughout the 1980s that Islamabad was using the Afghan conflagration as a rationalization for building up its military capabilities vis-à-vis India.

Since then, Afghanistan has been yet another point of contestation in the Indo-Pakistani rivalry that is at the core of South Asia's international politics. After the Soviet defeat in 1989, Afghanistan reverted to civil war as the fractious resistance groups proved unable to turn victory into peace. Two developments in the mid-1990s brought Afghanistan even more firmly into South Asia's orbit. First, many of the non-Afghan Islamic warriors who had helped their Afghan coreligionists to oust the Soviets ended up drifting eastward to join the ongoing Islamic insurgency in Indian-administered Kashmir. Second, in 1996, Osama bin Laden's al Qaeda terrorist network made common cause with the new Taliban regime in Afghanistan, trading military and financial assistance for sanctuary from Western security and intelligence agencies.

Even prior to 2001, India and Pakistan actively supported opposing sides in the simmering Afghan civil conflict, with Islamabad backing the Pashtun-majority Taliban and New Delhi favoring the various Turkic-speaking factions that were loosely cobbled into the so-called Northern Alliance. The subsequent U.S. war in Afghanistan crippled, but did not kill, the Taliban–al Qaeda condominium, whose bloodied remnants are trying to regroup and to reconstitute the northwestern subcontinent as the epicenter of transnational Islamic radicalism.

WHY IS SOUTH ASIA AN IMPORTANT REGION?

South Asia is one of the world's most dynamic regions. Its biggest country, India, is the world's largest democracy, an aspiring great power, and the globe's second most populous state with 1.1 billion people. India's economy is rapidly growing and modernizing, and its scientific and technological prowess is world-class. India is also a nuclear-weapon state with ballistic-missile capabilities and a growing capacity to project its power around the Indian Ocean littoral. Pakistan and Bangladesh, united as one country until 1971, are the world's sixth and seventh most populous countries, with 151 million and 139 million people, respectively. Among other reasons, Bangladesh and Pakistan are especially significant because they are two of only a handful of Islamic states around the globe with track records as democracies.

South Asia provides the regional context for one of the world's most intractable international disputes, the India–Pakistan conflict over Kashmir. The two countries fought major wars over Kashmir in 1947–1948 and 1965, as well as a limited war there in 1999; the disputed territory was also a battlefield in the Indo-Pakistani war of 1971, which resulted in the creation of Bangladesh out of what had previously been East Pakistan. Furthermore, Kashmir has been the locus of several serious crises between India and Pakistan, crises that have caused increasing international concern as the two countries have emerged as full-fledged nuclear-weapon states. The festering Kashmir dispute fuels an intense conventional and nuclear military competition between India and Pakistan that diverts scarce resources from socioeconomic development, perpetuates human suffering—sixty thousand Kashmiris have been killed since 1989—and all too often threatens to erupt in yet another major war.

As noted above, South Asia's significance in world politics has grown considerably since the al Qaeda terrorist attacks on the United States in September 2001. The subsequent U.S. war in Afghanistan severely damaged the Taliban movement and seems, for the moment, to have limited al Qaeda's ability to use Afghanistan as a sanctuary and base of operations. But after twenty-five years of warfare, the huge task of reconstructing Afghan society and reconstituting the Afghan polity lies ahead. Not only that, India and Pakistan—both allies in Washington's global war on terrorism—are battling their own internal terrorist threats, struggles made exceedingly complex by the politically charged issue of differentiating between terrorists and legitimate seekers of self-determination.

South Asia also provides the context for a wide variety of important political, social, and cultural issues. Politically, India and Sri Lanka have established the region's most stable democracies, but even their experience with democracy has been marked by the occasional lapse into more authoritarian rule. All of the region's other countries have either struggled to institutionalize democracy or failed even to make the effort.

South Asia has also witnessed a number of deadly ethnic conflicts. In addition to Kashmir, these include India's counterinsurgency in the far northeast of the country, Afghanistan's internecine civil war, Pakistan's struggle to contain civil unrest in Karachi's ethnic cauldron, Bangladesh's Chittagong Hill Tracts violence, and Sri Lanka's Tamil insurgency. Most of South Asia's ethnic conflicts have international causes and effects, owing to the postcolonial phenomenon of distinct ethnic groups being artificially divided by international borders. Similarly, the region's uneasy mix of religion and politics has important international dimensions. For example, no account of India–Pakistan relations can afford to ignore the domestic political influence of Pakistan's radical Islamists and India's Hindu-right extremists.

South Asia is also home to a number of pressing international economic dilemmas. Since independence, the region's states have pursued a variety of economic development paths; some have been relatively successful and others less so. More recently, since the Cold War's end, all of South Asia's major states have embraced ambitious economic liberalization programs so as to harness the growth potential of rapid globalization. As elsewhere, the interaction of domestic economies and global markets has created both winners and losers, along with a backlash that seeks to protect traditional cultures against the putatively homogenizing effects of globalization.

SCOPE, METHOD, AND ORGANIZATION

Although *South Asia in World Politics* sits squarely within the political science subfield of international relations, it necessarily strays at times into the companion subfield of comparative politics. Political scientists have long noted that the divide between international relations and comparative politics is an intrinsically artificial one, with causes and effects mingling freely at each level of analysis. The increasing pace of globalization intensifies this erosion of the conceptual wall between international relations and comparative politics, resisting all attempts to explain international outcomes without reference to domestic politics, and vice versa. That having been said, this is a book about South Asia's international relations and its role in world politics, and lines do have to be drawn. Generally speaking, domestic issues are included in this volume if they have a significant bearing on the region's international dynamics. Issue areas included in this category are democratization, economic liberalization, ethnicity and politics, and religion and politics. It also bears reiterating that the book is meant as an introduction to the region—as the first rather than the last word—and as a complement to other, more advanced, readings. Each chapter author has included a brief list of further readings, which may be viewed as something of a starter bibliography on the chapter's subject.

The methodological orientation of *South Asia in World Politics* is purposefully eclectic. While most of the chapters fit easily into the mainstream of what might be termed *area-studies social science*, a few have a narrative drive more common to the humanities than the social sciences. With each step in the volume's long march from concept to idea, it became increasingly clear that imposing some sort of one-size-fits-all analytical framework would render the analysis in each chapter stilted, rather than enrich it. There is, moreover, a considerable amount of substantive overlap between the chapters. This, too, has been intended on the grounds that students beginning their study of South Asia can profit from an appreciation of the different takes individual scholars can have on the same subject areas. Much as we might like to apply a greater degree of conceptual precision to the way we organize the world intellectually, the world is a messy place that often rebels against neat analytical categories.

South Asia in World Politics can be read straight through or consumed more deliberately as a series of stand-alone pieces. The remainder of the book combines actor-specific and thematic chapters, divided into two parts. Part I consists of individual chapters on the foreign relations of the region's three largest states, India, Pakistan, and Bangladesh; a chapter on the international relations and security perspectives of four South Asian "small states," Bhutan, the Maldives, Nepal, and Sri Lanka; a chapter on the reconstitution and reconstruction of Afghanistan; and a chapter on the South Asian interests of the three most important external players in regional affairs, China, Russia, and the United States.

Part II is thematic, covering six broad topics in contemporary South Asia's international relations: (1) the interrelated issues of Kashmir and the Indo-Pakistani nuclear-arms competition; (2) the international dimensions of the region's various ethnic conflicts; (3) the interplay of religion and politics in the subcontinent's international affairs; (4) the regional relationships between democratization and development; (5) the interlocking processes of globalization and South Asian economic liberalization; and (6) the South Asian dimensions of the global U.S. war on terrorism.

I

THE ACTORS AND THEIR INTERESTS

1

India's Foreign Relations

Devin T. Hagerty and Herbert G. Hagerty

On the eve of India's independence day, August 15, 1947, the country's first prime minister said to his compatriots, "Long years ago we made a tryst with destiny, and now the time comes when we shall redeem our pledge, not wholly or in full measure, but very substantially." Jawaharlal Nehru's soaring oratory reflected the bittersweet quality of India's liberation from the British Empire. The Indian nationalist struggle had achieved a monumental victory for the Indian people, but the partitioning of the erstwhile British India into two new states, India and Pakistan, would mar their "tryst with destiny." Violence between Hindus and Muslims had escalated to such horrific proportions in the months leading up to independence that the British government had seen no alternative but to accede to the demand for a separate political homeland for India's Muslims. Nehru noted that "before the birth of freedom we have endured all the pains of labour, and our hearts are heavy with the memory of this sorrow. Some of the pains continue even now." Indeed, as Nehru's words rang out across India, Muslims to India's east and west were celebrating their first day as Pakistanis.[1]

Despite being denied the Muslim-majority areas that became part of Pakistan in August 1947, independent India would be far and away the largest and most powerful country in South Asia. Equally significant was postindependence Indian leaders' firm conviction that they had inherited from the British not only their newfound sovereignty, but also Great Britain's now relinquished role as the manager of regional political affairs. The fundamental goal of New Delhi's grand strategy[2] since 1947 has been to maintain India's hegemony[3] over the aptly named Indian subcontinent. From India's perspective, its size, population, and relative power give it a natural position of regional predominance that conceivably could be undermined only by the intervention of external actors. Thus, the key to India's preferred position in

11

world politics has been to prevent outsiders from establishing a foothold in its region, either directly or indirectly at the behest of India's neighbors. Initially, the chief policy expression of India's grand strategy was the nonaligned stance devised by Nehru in the late 1940s, a posture of siding with neither superpower bloc during the Cold War and instead charting an independent foreign policy course. In Nehru's conception, nonalignment gave India a moral voice in international politics, as well as maximum leverage in its relations with the East and the West. As we shall see below, it was also flexible enough to be modified when security threats arose.

This chapter provides an introductory overview of Indian foreign relations from 1947 to the present. The next four sections discuss the most significant formative influences on India's foreign policy outlook: its anti-imperial ideology, the wrenching experience of Partition, the outbreak of the Cold War and emergence of a bipolar international political system, and New Delhi's desire to establish hegemony over the entire subcontinent, excluding areas that had become part of Pakistan. Subsequent sections trace the evolution of Indian foreign relations in a roughly chronological fashion, paying particular attention to India's relations with Pakistan; its policies toward the main external actors in South Asian affairs, China, the United States, and the Soviet Union/Russia; its development of nuclear-weapons capabilities; and its role in South Asian regional affairs. The chapter concludes with a brief analysis of India's contemporary position in world politics. Although no chapter of this length can be considered comprehensive, every attempt has been made to provide the reader with a historical introduction to the range of issues that will be discussed in subsequent chapters.

INDEPENDENCE

India's emergence as an independent, sovereign state in the late 1940s was the last phase in a decades-long struggle for freedom against the British Empire. Quite naturally, the preindependence, anti-imperial attitudes of India's nationalist leaders carried over after 1947 into the foreign policy perspective of the new Indian state. The struggle against British rule had inspired within India's political elites a profound commitment to controlling their own—that is, India's—national destiny. During more than six decades of agitation for self-rule, they had created an effective mass movement committed to gaining independence from Britain; and, they had accomplished this largely by nonviolent means. The "new" India, led by the extraordinarily popular Jawaharlal Nehru, was resolved to establish a democratic and secular state, based on the rule of law and universal suffrage, and governed under British-type parliamentary institutions. In 1947 Nehru and other Indian leaders saw their coming to power as an important part of a wider anticolonialist revolution against foreign rule. They were determined that their exercise of that power should henceforth always be determined by what they, not outsiders, defined as being in India's interest.

India's experience of nearly three hundred years under British rule affected several aspects of postindependence Indian foreign relations. For India, the imperial era was brought to a culmination in 1947 by the Indian National Congress, which had been founded in 1885 as little more than a polite debating society peopled by well-connected Indians and nonofficial Europeans resident in India. Its purpose was to share ideas and promote reforms, including measures aimed at broadening Indian participation in the British administration. Though unheralded, the birth of the Congress, as it came to be called, occurred amidst a wider awakening of Indian, and especially Hindu, culture and values among Europeans and (what the British described as) India's middle classes. This period also saw the rise of other new organizations in urban Hindu society committed to advancing and improving awareness of traditional Indian values and, in some instances, to reconciling them with European thought. In the world beyond, knowledge about Indian culture was spreading, following linguistic breakthroughs into ancient Indic languages and literature and Indians' own travel abroad. In turn, this growing awareness of India's rich cultural tradition laid the groundwork for increasing political consciousness among Indian elites. Simultaneously, these same Indians were learning about the conventions and institutions of England and Europe through their exposure to the evolving British-Indian institutions, to the English language, and to communications advances.

As the twentieth century dawned, the Congress lobbied for and supported a series of reform acts of the British Parliament aimed at reorganizing the Indian polity, instituting British legal practices, reforming the powers of the (British) Government of India at the local and provincial levels, and granting Indians wider opportunities to play a role in civil administration. Acts of Parliament in 1908, 1919, 1929, and 1935 significantly expanded the role of Indians in many aspects of British Indian administration. Although each of these reforms temporarily calmed Indian discontent with British rule, each one also served to whet the political appetite of new generations of Indians. Thus, London's successive concessions inevitably seemed to fall one step short of what politically active Indians had sought; periodically, too, they were undone by acts of repression. However, there is no doubt that this gradual Indianization of the administration gave Indians valuable experience of governance that enabled them quickly and confidently to assume control of their own state in 1947.

The formation of the All-India Muslim League in 1906 reflected a somewhat later political awakening among Indian Muslims that in the early years of the twentieth century frequently put them at loggerheads with the Congress. A case in point was the aftermath of Britain's 1905 decision to divide Bengal Province, which was strongly supported by the Muslim League and vigorously opposed by the Congress. The partition plan would have been to the advantage of Muslims in the eastern half of Bengal, the part of British India that would become East Pakistan in 1947 and Bangladesh in 1971. In 1916, under Muslim pressure but with the opposition of the Congress, the British fatefully acknowledged this sense of a separate Muslim political interest by agreeing to establish separate electorates for Muslims contending for office under reforms already enacted. During World War I, both the Congress and the League supported the British war effort but were disappointed that this support paid so few dividends in easing the often-heavy British hand.

In economic affairs, Indian nationalists of every stripe had long recognized that British imperial policies served British, not Indian, interests by emphasizing the export of raw materials for a broad spectrum of British industries. They also appreciated the importance of Indian manpower to Britain's overall military capabilities and were justly proud of the accomplishments of the British-officered Indian army on foreign soil in World War I. But they also knew, because of the army's frequent role in support of civil authority in British India, that British imperial imperatives often dictated the deployment of Indians to suppress, even kill, other Indians. Rankling still more was a growing awareness as the war dragged on far from India's borders that this use of Indian manpower, whether in India or abroad, had been undertaken by the British without having sought the approval of any then existing Indian assembly or the consent of a single Indian national.

The war's immediate aftermath saw the emergence of Mohandas Gandhi and his philosophy of nonviolent resistance. Under Gandhi, the Congress stepped up its evolution into a secular, mass-based movement. Also during this period, Congress and Muslim League leaders began to pay more attention to events outside of India, especially to anti-imperialist movements in other dependencies, to the plight of Indians in eastern and southern Africa, and to the progress of the Bolshevik revolution in Russia. In 1920, led by Gandhi, the Congress supported the Muslim League in its condemnation of successful British efforts to prevent the restoration of the Islamic caliphate in Constantinople. But Congress–League cooperation would diminish as the aims of both organizations evolved from advocating selected reforms and expanding the participation of Indians in government toward a demand for independence.

The anticipation of self-rule created a new arena of competition—and ultimately bloodshed—between Hindu and Muslim Indian nationalists. In the 1930s, relations between the Congress and the League considerably worsened. The Congress was heavily Hindu in composition, and the Hindu holy man image projected by Gandhi began to undercut his and his movement's projected secular image among Muslim leaders. This was especially the case as Muslims began to think about the form of an eventual, independent Indian polity in which Muslims would be a permanent electoral minority amidst a much greater Hindu population. The results of provincial elections in 1937 reaffirmed this concern. As Indians moved inexorably toward self-determination, India's Muslim minority grew increasingly anxious about its political prospects in an independent, democratic India. In 1940 these Muslim fears led the League to split with the Congress and to call for an independent nation, Pakistan, to be carved from the Muslim majority areas of British India.

The Congress–Muslim League split continued into World War II and beyond. While the League supported India's role in Britain's war against Germany, Italy, and Japan, the Congress opposed the war effort, even with Japanese troops from Burma threatening northeastern India. In 1942 Congress leaders launched a movement to pressure the British to "Quit India," orchestrating large-scale, but peaceful, noncooperation with the government to dramatize their demand for independence and their denial of Indian support for the war. The "Quit India" campaign resulted in the imprisonment of most senior Congress leaders, which subsequently became a badge of honor when they came to power.

After decades of reluctance to consider full independence for India, interspersed with periodic reforms meeting some minimal Indian desires, a war-weary and weakened Great Britain committed itself in 1946 to Indian independence. Then, having initially announced a target date in 1948, the British suddenly moved the date up to August 1947. This was in large measure because of mounting concern about the likelihood of massive bloodshed in a roiling subcontinent whose leaders were increasingly impatient to assume power. As independence neared, widespread rioting broke out between Hindus and Muslims (and between Sikhs and Muslims).

In retrospect, the Indian independence movement boiled down to a struggle—frequently concerted, but often not—by Muslims, Hindus, Sikhs, and others for control of their own communities' political destinies in consonance with their interpretations of their, and India's, interests. This experience lay behind the postindependence Indian leadership's continuing concerns about foreign influence in India, its embrace of anticolonialist causes in Asia and Africa, and its commitment to a posture of nonalignment in foreign affairs, to be discussed at greater length below. As Prime Minister Nehru phrased India's position,

We will accept any help that comes from outside. But . . . [w]e cannot tolerate interference in our internal affairs or our freedom. . . . We have friendly relations with both the blocs [the Soviet-led East and the U.S.-led West] and yet maintain our freedom. . . . [T]his is the policy best suited for our country and also . . . the only one by which we can serve the cause of world peace.[4]

PARTITION

A second formative influence on India's foreign relations was the messy partitioning of British India into the new states of India and Pakistan. Partition left in its wake an Indo-Pakistani dispute over the political status of the area known as Jammu and Kashmir, today often referred to simply as "Kashmir," a territory roughly the size of Kansas. Kashmir has been the scene of two major wars (1947–1948 and 1965), one limited war (1999), and numerous serious crises between India and Pakistan.

The Kashmir conflict dates back to the months leading up to independence. As the independence date of August 15, 1947, neared, Congress and Muslim League leaders remained divided in their political aims, with the Congress committed to a united, secular, democratic India and the League demanding the creation of a separate, democratic, Islamic nation based on a grouping of provinces where Muslims were a majority. As talks between the Congress, the Muslim League, and the British dragged on with no solution in sight, large Indian cities like Bombay (now Mumbai) and Calcutta were convulsed in Hindu-Muslim violence. When negotiations ultimately failed to produce a compromise and the violence escalated, the British, fearing a bloody, all-out civil war, chose to partition the subcontinent. Parliament passed the Indian Independence Act of 1947, calling for the division of British India into the independent states of India and Pakistan, one avowedly secular, but mainly Hindu, and the other determinedly Islamic.

At independence, the provinces of Punjab in the west and Bengal in the east were partitioned, with territory awarded to Pakistan on the basis of the contiguity of Muslim-majority districts. Pakistan's portion of Bengal was named East Pakistan and was separated by one thousand miles of territory from the Pakistani portion of the Punjab, which was joined with the overwhelmingly Muslim provinces of Baluchistan, the Northwest Frontier Province, and Sindh, plus associated tribal areas adjacent to Afghanistan, to become West Pakistan. In the aftermath of Partition and the British withdrawal in 1947, communal unrest mounted. As an estimated fifteen million Hindus, Muslims, and Sikhs moved east and west across the new borders (Hindus and Sikhs into India, and Muslims into Pakistan), many engaged in a vengeful bloodletting. Estimates of Partition's death toll usually start at one million, and reliable calculations of people wounded and property damaged are impossible to make.

The new governments' agendas were overloaded. Extreme urgency attached to every issue. For leaders on both sides, there was an immediate requirement to assert control over their new domain by affirming borders and restoring domestic order. Efforts at cooperation between the two new dominions, in which civil service and military officers of British nationality still held important posts, failed to stem the tide of violence. Among India's most pressing concerns was the need to stabilize its new eastern and western borders abutting the two "wings" of the new Pakistan. Neither geography nor economic interests sustained these new lines on the map, which were, rather, the product of enmity between Hindus and Muslims, and the communal division was meant to deal with their now national, conflicting ambitions. Along these borders, Partition had left behind a deep-seated residue of anger and distrust, as well as fear on the Pakistani side that India remained unreconciled to Partition and harbored revanchist ambitions. Moreover, the new borders cut across major river and irrigation systems, parts of the five-river complex in the Indus basin, upon which the richest agricultural lands in both dominions depended for water.

In attempting to gain control of its new domain, India's task was larger than Pakistan's because of its greater area and population and its more complex mix of communities. However, India's task was facilitated by the contiguity of its territory, the greater development of its economy, the established administrative divisions within its polity, and the continuing presence of seasoned officials in place. Pakistan lacked much of this but benefited, at least in its western wing, from its smaller size and the greater homogeneity of its population. Even after the massive communal shifts imposed by Partition, tens of millions of Muslims remained in India, and millions of Hindus were left in East Pakistan. Within India, historic schisms rooted in culture, community, and language remained even after the separation of the mostly Muslim areas that became Pakistan. Refugees required comprehensive and immediate assistance, while the legacy of antagonism and mistrust between Muslims and non-Muslims that had characterized the later years of the independence struggle continued to thwart Indian leaders' efforts to consolidate their domestic authority and establish a relationship with the new Pakistan.

Even more daunting was the fact that the territorial award took no account of the status or communal complexion of some 565 princely states that during the colonial period had been governed separately by autocratic Indian monarchs. These states had remained nominally independent, but their rulers had formally acknowledged fealty to the British Crown and were usually kept under watch by a British resident. That link was severed in August 1947 under the terms of the Indian Independence Act. Left to individual monarchs was the crucial decision concerning which of the new countries to join. In the vast majority of cases, accession to either India or Pakistan unfolded smoothly. By early 1948, all but three of the princely states' rulers had come to terms with the inevitable demands of geography, signed accession agreements, and gradually accepted a role in the larger polity.

The smallest of the three recalcitrant princely states was Junagadh, located on the coast of the Arabian Sea and on the new international boundary between the Pakistani province of Sindh and the Indian province of Bombay. Junagadh was governed by a Muslim ruler who initially preferred accession to Pakistan despite his state's longstanding links with the area to the east that had now become India. Finding himself at odds with his mostly Hindu subjects, he signed an instrument of accession with Pakistan. India protested, demanding that he hold a plebiscite to determine his people's will. But the state's Hindu subjects rioted, and the issue was quickly resolved by the Indian army's entry into Junagadh. A 1948 plebiscite confirmed Junagadh's accession to India (where it became part of Saurashtra, which was later absorbed into what is now the state of Gujarat).

More vexed were India's dealings with the other two princes, the Hindu maharajah of Jammu and Kashmir and the Muslim nizam of Hyderabad, a state the size of Minnesota that was deeply embedded within what had become India. Hyderabad was a large and prosperous state with a Muslim ruler and a Hindu-majority population. In January 1947, with Partition still many months off, the nizam had publicly indicated that he would not join India. He reaffirmed this position in July, expressing a preference to remain separate from both India and Pakistan. Days after the end of British rule, the nizam proclaimed the "resumption" of his state's independence. The Indian government objected to the nizam's decision and quickly forced him to desist in his effort. Negotiations on a final settlement continued into 1948 with mounting acrimony, including allegations that the nizam, then one of the richest people in the world, had loaned a substantial sum of money to Pakistan. Fearful of an Indian takeover, the nizam appealed for United Nations intervention, but before the United Nations could act, widespread Hindu-Muslim violence throughout Hyderabad led New Delhi to intervene with its still British-officered army in a widely criticized September 1949 police action. The state was put under Indian military administration, leaving the nizam essentially powerless, but in place. He withdrew his complaint to the United Nations and thereafter acceded to India. Pakistan protested India's actions, but to no avail. The state of Hyderabad was initially kept intact but was eventually dismembered, its territory becoming part of the neighboring Indian states of Andhra Pradesh, Mysore, and what later became Maharashtra in reorganizations of state boundaries in the 1950s.

The status of a third princely state, Kashmir, has not been resolved to this day.[5] In the late summer of 1947, the communal rioting accompanying the independence and partition of India and Pakistan began to spread from Punjab into Kashmir. While Kashmir's Hindu maharaja, Hari Singh, hesitated on the question of accession to either new state, a Muslim revolt erupted in Poonch, in western Kashmir. The Poonch rebels established a provisional government in what they called "Azad Kashmir" ("Free Kashmir"). In October, some two to three thousand armed raiders, mainly Pashtuns from Pakistan's Northwest Frontier Province, crossed the border between West Pakistan and Kashmir, rallying behind the rebels. The government of Pakistan provided material support for the Poonch rebels and their Pashtun allies, who together made fast progress toward the state capital of Srinagar. With his domain on the verge of collapse, and with the support of his popular Muslim prime minister, Sheikh Abdullah, Hari Singh signed Kashmir's accession to India on October 26, 1947. The next day, the Indian government began airlifting troops and supplies to Srinagar, and the Indian army soon drove the insurgents out of the capital.

In January 1948, with a political-military stalemate at hand, India referred the Kashmir dispute to the United Nations. India charged that the invasion by military forces from outside the state had been illegal given Kashmir's accession to India in October 1947. In turn, Pakistani diplomats alleged that India had fraudulently achieved Kashmir's accession. In April 1948 the UN Security Council adopted a resolution calling for the removal of all outside military forces from Kashmir, except for such Indian forces as would constitute the minimum necessary to uphold law and order, and for the subsequent holding of a plebiscite to decide the state's political future. In July, a UN Commission on India and Pakistan (UNCIP) traveled to Kashmir to begin laying the groundwork for a plebiscite. Upon UNCIP's arrival, Pakistan admitted that Pakistan army troops were fighting in Kashmir and that the so-called Azad Kashmiri forces also fought under the operational command of the Pakistan army. The direct involvement of the Pakistan army in Kashmir, suspected but not previously confirmed, represented for UNCIP a material change in the situation. The Kashmir dispute was now understood to be a full-fledged international political conflict, a more serious and potentially much more dangerous affair. In August 1948 UNCIP adopted a resolution calling for an immediate cease-fire and reaffirming the need for a plebiscite. After a period of further negotiations and continued fighting during the autumn, a cease-fire finally went into effect on January 1, 1949.[6]

THE COLD WAR

A third formative influence on India's foreign relations was the cold war political-military confrontation between the United States and the Soviet Union, which rapidly intensified just as India was emerging as a newly independent state. The superpower competition imposed a bipolar structure on international affairs from 1945 until the disintegration of the Soviet Union in 1991. Bipolarity forced virtually every country in the world to make one of three choices: to ally with Washington, to ally with Moscow, or to attempt to remain aloof from the superpower conflict by forging amicable relations with both sides. In the late 1940s and early 1950s, India strove to maintain a position of equidistance between East and West. With a governing elite committed to democracy in political affairs and socialism in economic affairs, India had commonalities with both the United States and the Soviet Union. Some Indian nationalist leaders, including Nehru, had studied in Britain and were steeped in the secular, liberal political traditions of the West. At the same time, most were attracted to the socialist, anti-imperialist policies of the East. Under Nehru, who led India until his death in 1964, New Delhi attempted to chart a "third way" in international affairs, a democratic, socialist path that would, it was hoped, give all Indians a voice in their political system while ensuring that gains from economic development would be distributed equitably across the impoverished population.

As part and parcel of the dramatically escalating global competition between East and West, Moscow and Washington began in the early 1950s to compete for influence among newly emergent, so-called Third World states. Simultaneously, in the colonial domains of several Western European powers, such as the Netherlands East Indies (now Indonesia), French Indochina (now the states of Vietnam, Cambodia, and Laos), and British Malaya (now Malaysia and Singapore), colonial authorities that had been displaced by Japanese forces during World War II tried forcefully to reassert their imperial rule against the armed resistance of indigenous nationalist movements. While Cold War imperatives generally spurred the United States to support its Western European allies, if not colonialism per se, the Soviet Union and its ally as of 1950, the new Chinese Communist regime on India's northern border, sought to embrace and exploit anticolonial independence struggles to their own advantage.

As a recently liberated country, India strongly supported its fellow Third World nationalists, and anti-imperialism became a primary thrust of Indian diplomacy. New Delhi assumed a particularly prominent role at the United Nations in support of self-determination for colonial peoples. India's diplomacy often gave the appearance of siding with the Soviet Union, notwithstanding India's claims of nonalignment. However, this was more the result of India's own experience as a nation recently freed from European rule than any strong sense of affinity with Moscow. Indeed, until Soviet leader Josef Stalin's death in 1953, the Kremlin heaped scorn on India, taking it "as a given that India and other moderate states emerging from colonialism were hopelessly bourgeois and reactionary . . . disparag[ing] Nehru's vaunted nonaligned stance as meaningless and . . . dismiss[ing] Nehru himself as little more than an Anglo-American stooge."[7] Ironically, the U.S. view of India during the early independence years was equally suspicious, especially after New Delhi extended diplomatic recognition to the Communist People's Republic of China in 1949 and subsequently pushed for China's UN seat to be filled by the Beijing regime instead of the Chinese nationalist government on Taiwan. India's leadership role in the Nonaligned Movement (NAM) in the mid-1950s did nothing to quell U.S. doubts about Indian loyalties, especially during the Eisenhower years, when U.S. policymakers adopted the stance that every country was either "with us or against us" in the Cold War.

India's neutral posture during the early Cold War period stood in stark contrast to Pakistan's strategic choices. As the much weaker of South Asia's two largest countries, Pakistan assiduously courted support from outside the region. Postindependence Pakistani leaders believed that many Indian elites were not reconciled to Partition and the creation of Pakistan, and they feared that New Delhi might one day aggressively seek to reincorporate Pakistan into India. In order to prevent that turn of events, Pakistan soon turned to the United States for assistance in narrowing the gap between Indian and Pakistani capabilities. For two reasons U.S. officials were initially reluctant to bring Pakistan into the American strategic embrace. First, they viewed India as a more significant piece in the Cold War chess game with the Soviet Union and worried that close ties with Pakistan would sour relations with New Delhi. Second, during the 1947–1948 Kashmir war, Washington was loath to provide security assistance to either India or Pakistan for fear of it simply being used against the other side.

Gradually, however, Washington yielded to Pakistani blandishments. By 1950 the Kashmir war was over, and it had become unequivocally clear to U.S. decision makers that India would under no circumstances compromise its cherished freedom of action by making a Cold War commitment to the U.S.-led Western bloc. Also, India's accommodating policies with respect to China suggested to American strategists that New Delhi was soft on communism and could not be trusted. To the contrary, Pakistan was willing, even enthusiastic, about siding with the United States and astutely portrayed itself as a strategic asset not only in South Asia but in the Middle East as well. In a successful, groundbreaking visit to America in the summer of 1950, Pakistani prime minister Liaquat Ali Khan maintained that Pakistan "borders on Iran and Afghanistan and has an important situation in relation to the communications to and from the oil-bearing areas of the Middle East." He further stressed that his country's "Islamic ideology" provided religious and cultural links to the Middle East that would "prove a stabilizing factor in Asia." In a calculated contrast with Nehru's rhetoric, Liaquat emphasized both the incompatibility of communism and Islam and the "fighting qualities" of Pakistan's "anti-communist Muslim warriors."[8]

Pakistan's diplomatic efforts finally bore fruit with the advent of the Eisenhower administration, whose secretary of state, John Foster Dulles, championed his vision of a "northern tier" of Middle Eastern states collaborating to contain the spread of Soviet influence. Dulles viewed the northern tier countries—Turkey, Iraq, Iran, and Pakistan—as vital links in a chain of U.S. allies committed to opposing communism. In February 1954 Washington approved Pakistan's latest request for military assistance. Three months later, the United States and Pakistan signed a Mutual Defense Assistance Agreement, according to which Washington would provide military equipment and training to Pakistan's armed forces. Pakistan also joined the Southeast Asia Treaty Organization in 1954 and the Baghdad Pact (later renamed the Central Treaty Organization) in 1955. While India's continuing anticolonial sentiment had dictated that it remain neutral in the Cold War, Pakistan had become America's "most allied ally."

Indian leaders were incensed by the strategic partnership between the United States and Pakistan. Prime Minister Nehru was convinced that one of Washington's motives in enlisting Pakistan into its evolving alliance system was to "check India's power within the region." As he wrote to one of his ministers, "The United States imagine that by this policy they have completely outflanked India's so-called neutralism and will thus bring India to her knees. Whatever the future may hold, this is not going to happen. The first result of all this will be an extreme dislike of the United States in India." Of most long-term significance, the extension of Cold War politics into South Asia militated against the Kashmir settlement envisioned in the relevant UN resolutions. The new U.S. security relationship with Pakistan gave Indian leaders ample justification for their already waning interest in a Kashmir plebiscite. As one historian puts it, "since India was already in possession of the most desirable portion of Kashmir, and since the overwhelming Muslim majority in the state made a vote to join Pakistan the most likely outcome of a fair referendum, a postponement of the plebiscite clearly served India's interests." India's position was bolstered by a warming of relations between New Delhi and Moscow following Stalin's death; in 1955, the Soviet Union endorsed the Indian position on Kashmir, thereby ensuring that Moscow's UN Security Council veto would henceforth prevent the international community from imposing a Kashmir solution contrary to India's interests.[9]

SECURING INDIA'S FRONTIERS

A fourth shaper of India's foreign relations was its dogged insistence on gaining influence over those portions of the subcontinent's landmass that had not been hived off during Partition. Most of India's periphery consists of natural boundaries: the Himalayan mountain range, the Arabian Sea, and the Bay of Bengal. Partition had settled India's eastern and western borders with Pakistan. Still to be resolved were the nature of India's relations with three neighboring polities south of the Himalayas, the status of two European outposts on the subcontinent, and a dispute with China over competing claims to territory.

With the glaring exception of the China issue, all of these matters were resolved relatively easily. Soon after independence, New Delhi tried to persuade France and Portugal to give up their centuries-old possessions in India. Diplomacy worked with the French, who ceded Pondicherry, Karikal, Yanaon, Mahe, and Chandernagor to India without incident. Portugal, however, resisted giving up its colonial possessions, Goa, Daman, and Diu, and India ultimately resolved the standoff through military action in 1961. To the north, India and Bhutan signed a 1949 treaty by which India assumed what had previously been Britain's control of Bhutanese foreign affairs in exchange for New Delhi's explicit recognition of Bhutan's sovereignty.[10] In Nepal, India assisted in the 1950 overthrow of a hereditary oligarchy and the 1951 restoration of the monarchy by the Nepalese Congress Party, which was allied ideologically with the Indian Congress. Although Nepal was nominally nonaligned during the Cold War, India strongly influenced Nepalese affairs, especially foreign policy. In 1951 India and Sikkim signed a treaty defining Sikkim as a protectorate in which India would exercise "full rights over defense, foreign affairs, and communication," making Sikkim little more than a vassal state.[11]

India's most serious territorial and border challenges have concerned China. India and China have been natural competitors in Asia since they emerged as large, modern, postcolonial states in the late 1940s. Both are ancient civilizations with extraordinarily rich cultures. Both were compelled to submit to foreign masters during the age of imperialism. Both were then reborn in the first half of the twentieth century as the culmination of nationalist movements that inspired millions of people around the developing world. Once free of foreign domination, India and China pursued starkly different political-economic development paths, which in turn provided competing models for scores of newly independent Third World countries. China's Mao Zedong touted his brand of revolutionary communism as the one true path for new states. In contrast, Nehru promoted his third way to socioeconomic development, which earned him Chinese propagandists' scorn as the "running dog" of Western imperialism. When assessing their country's status in the hierarchy of nations, postindependence Indian decision makers have for more than half a century reflexively cast their gaze at China for purposes of comparison.

In the late 1940s, both the Chinese and Indian governments faced the challenge of securing the sovereignty and territorial integrity of their sprawling, heterogeneous countries. The "new" India and China found that they had an immediate disagreement about the contours of their border in two main areas: the Aksai Chin Plateau, bordering Tibet, Xinjiang, and Ladakh (part of Indian-controlled Kashmir), and along the Himalayan frontier in the northeastern subcontinent. Taken together, the total area of these disputed territories is roughly the size of Alabama. India's postindependence policies with respect to Bhutan, Nepal, and Sikkim, described above, were aimed primarily at shoring up India's dominance in regions bordering China. Meanwhile, Beijing pursued a characteristically more forceful solution to the problem of Tibet's political future by invading and occupying the territory in October 1950. In May 1951 Tibet became a "national autonomous region" of China, nominally under the traditional authority of the Tibetan Buddhist leader, the Dalai Lama, but actually ruled by Beijing. In response, New Delhi lodged a formal protest against China's "aggression" but also realized that, as a practical matter, India could do little to overturn Chinese control of Tibet. In sum, the 1949–1951 period saw both India and China asserting their authority over the parts of their shared Himalayan frontier that they now viewed as lying within their respective spheres of influence.

Once that had been accomplished, the two Asian giants, preoccupied with internal development and wider Cold War priorities, engaged one another in a mutual peace offensive. The two countries' leaders exchanged repeated visits, during which they proclaimed a new era of pan-Asian cooperation. In 1954 Beijing and New Delhi signed a treaty in which India formally recognized Chinese sovereignty over Tibet. More expansively, the treaty's preamble contained the Panch Sheel ("five principles"): (1) respect for each other's sovereignty and territorial integrity, (2) nonaggression, (3) noninterference in each other's internal affairs, (4) equality and mutual benefit, and (5) peaceful coexistence. On paper, if not in practice, the Panch Sheel became a template for peaceful cooperation among developing countries, celebrated, for example, at the 1955 Bandung (Indonesia) Conference of twenty-nine African and Asian states. Out of Bandung grew the Nonaligned Movement, formed to promote economic development, oppose colonialism, and resist bipolarity's incursion into every part of the globe, which held its first official meeting in Belgrade in 1961.

Despite these expressions of neighborly solidarity, Sino-Indian relations soured in the late 1950s. Although the 1954 treaty was supposed to settle the issue, Beijing and New Delhi continued to bicker over Tibet. Ignoring the principle of noninterference, Nehru allowed Tibetan nationalists to wage an anti-Chinese independence struggle from India. In 1956 the U.S. Central Intelligence Agency (CIA) began a covert operation in support of the Tibetan resistance. The CIA operation, run from Indian territory and assisted by Taiwanese agents, posed a direct challenge to China. In March 1959 a revolt erupted in the Tibetan capital of Lhasa, and Beijing violently suppressed the insurgents. The Dalai Lama and thousands of his followers fled to India, where New Delhi granted them political asylum. From 1959 to 1962, Sino-Indian relations chilled. Border probes and skirmishes increased; negotiations failed. In October to November 1962, China launched stinging attacks across the disputed border, soundly defeating the ill-equipped and outmanned Indian defenders. Then, as suddenly as it had started, the Sino-Indian war ended. Having conclusively demonstrated its military superiority, China unilaterally withdrew its forces.

Events in the late 1950s and early 1960s dramatically reshuffled the South Asian geostrategic cards. Toward the end of President Dwight D. Eisenhower's second term in office, his administration had already begun to take a more even-handed approach to South Asian affairs. India had emerged as a leader of the fledgling Nonaligned Movement and as a noncommunist Asian power whose diplomatic influence, especially in the Third World, outweighed its material capabilities. Washington was coming to the gradual realization that it had tilted too far toward Pakistan in the early 1950s. Simultaneously, Pakistan itself had begun to chafe at its dependence on the United States and started to diversify its diplomatic ties, courting both the Soviet Union and China. Meanwhile, a significant, although still not public, rift was developing between Moscow and Beijing, with the Soviets increasingly warming toward India. This reinforced the increasing overlap of interests — mutual enmity toward India — between China and Pakistan, which had previously had luke-warm relations.

In the immediate aftermath of China's 1962 military offensive, the United States and Great Britain rushed transport aircraft, antitank weapons, and small arms to a stunned and desperate India. Meanwhile, Pakistani leaders provocatively stoked Indian fears of a two-front war against China and Pakistan. After the war was over, China mounted a diplomatic campaign to isolate India. As if to highlight Indian intransigence on the border issue, Beijing rapidly concluded territorial settlement agreements with Burma, Nepal, and Pakistan. With India's security vulnerabilities having been painfully exposed by the Chinese attack, Washington and London managed to persuade a reluctant, but weakened, Nehru to enter into bilateral discussions with Pakistan over Kashmir. Five rounds of desultory talks produced no progress on Kashmir, in part because Pakistan and China in March 1963 "settled" their own territorial dispute in an agreement that "gave" China some two thousand square miles of Kashmir. Indian leaders were furious, maintaining that Pakistan had, in effect, illegally negotiated away Indian territory. Sino-Pakistani relations grew increasingly close in the early 1960s as China provided its new ally with tanks, fighter aircraft, and other military equipment. The two countries also aligned their diplomatic postures, with China adopting Pakistan's position on Kashmir and Pakistan adopting China's on Taiwan.[12]

TWO MORE WARS WITH PAKISTAN

In 1965 India and Pakistan went to war over Kashmir for the second time. India's 1962 humiliation, its rapidly increasing military power (thanks in part to aid from the United States and Great Britain, as well as to a tripling of India's defense spending), and political discontent in Indian-controlled Kashmir itself combined to convince Pakistani leaders that they had only a brief window of opportunity to strike preventively and wrest the territory away from New Delhi. At the very least, an aggressive Pakistani policy could keep Kashmir on the boil by forcing India back to the negotiating table. In the summer of 1965, Pakistan infiltrated thousands of armed guerrillas across the 1949 cease-fire line in a clumsy attempt to spark a rebellion among Kashmiri Muslims. New Delhi responded with its own invasion of Pakistan-controlled Kashmir, capturing several key mountain passes. On September 1, Pakistani armor crossed the cease-fire line in southern Kashmir and inflicted heavy losses on Indian forces. Faced with the possible loss of a vital road connecting the state capital, Srinagar, with India proper, New Delhi responded with a dramatic offensive across the India–Pakistan border in Punjab. The invading Indian forces outfought their Pakistani counterparts and halted their attack on the outskirts of Lahore, Pakistan's second-largest city. By the time the United Nations intervened on September 22, Pakistan had suffered a clear defeat.

Disgusted with this latest turn of events in South Asia and preoccupied with the escalating U.S. war in Vietnam, the Johnson administration had, on September 8, imposed an arms embargo against both India and Pakistan. Also, in the war's aftermath, President Johnson "directed that the United States adopt a lowered profile in the subcontinent and pursue more limited policy objectives there."[13] In the first manifestation of this new orientation, Washington stepped aside and allowed the Soviet Union to convene a successful peace conference at Tashkent in January 1966.

Six years later, India and Pakistan fought another war. The 1971 conflict grew out of a Pakistani civil war that had erupted in March of that year. The root cause of Pakistan's civil strife was the severe polarization that had emerged between the eastern and western wings of the country since independence, which in the late 1960s led to increasingly aggressive Bengali separatism and a correspondingly repressive response by the Punjabi-dominated Pakistani state. As the fighting in East Pakistan escalated in the spring of 1971, the Pakistan army resorted to extreme brutality, causing millions of Bengali refugees to seek safety in India. By May, the refugees were arriving in India at a rate of sixty thousand per day.[14] Faced with severe pressures from the Bengali refugees and tempted by the prospect of permanently erasing a two-front security threat from Pakistan, New Delhi decided to support the secessionists' aspirations for their own state of Bangladesh ("land of the Bengalis").

In April, the separatists issued a declaration of independence and formed a government-in-exile on Indian soil. New Delhi also set up training camps for the Bengali guerrillas on Indian territory near the East Pakistan border and assisted the insurgents in their operations across the border. In July the Indian government decided on a war to liberate Bangladesh. By the fall, New Delhi was deploying artillery, tanks, and air power in support of guerrilla operations in East Pakistan. In late November India "launched simultaneous military actions on all of the key border regions of East Pakistan, and from all directions, with both armored and air support." Having planned a December 6 offensive to capture the East Pakistani capital of Dhaka, Indian leaders were "greatly relieved and pleasantly surprised" when Pakistan initiated preemptive air strikes against Indian air installations on December 3. When the Indian army finally did invade on December 5, it made rapid progress. Dhaka fell on December 16, and Bangladesh was born.[15]

By 1972 South Asia's strategic landscape had again been fundamentally altered. India's victories over Pakistan in two wars had to a great extent overcome the lingering humiliation of India's 1962 defeat at the hands of China. Indeed, the limits to Sino-Pakistani cooperation were laid bare in both the 1965 and 1971 wars. In both cases, Beijing dutifully condemned Indian "aggression," gave Pakistan diplomatic, military, and economic support, and vaguely promised to intervene if India threatened Pakistan's very survival. However, the Chinese also made it clear to Pakistan that they would not shed blood on its behalf. Beijing's assistance was useful but limited; although China was resolved that Pakistan would survive as a state that could help to contain Indian influence, China would not invest enough of its scarce resources to turn the South Asian tide in Pakistan's favor.

One reason for Chinese restraint in 1971 was that the Nixon administration was quietly pursuing an initiative to jump start official U.S. relations with China. In July, National Security Advisor Henry Kissinger secretly visited Beijing for talks that would pave the way for President Nixon's dramatic 1972 "opening" to China. Kissinger had flown to China from Pakistan, where the government had assisted his clandestine travels. When the trip became public, the Indian government, along with many others, was shocked. New Delhi clearly could not expect support from Washington if a war with Pakistan induced Chinese intervention against India. In their own dramatic counterstroke, New Delhi and Moscow announced in August 1971 that they had signed a limited security pact, thereby formalizing the strategic partnership that had developed between them in the late 1950s and 1960s. By 1972, then, two broad coalitions had emerged in South Asian international affairs, with Pakistan, China, and the United States on one side and India and the Soviet Union on the other.

In July 1972 India and a weakened Pakistan signed the Simla Agreement, which turned the Kashmir cease-fire line into a line of control (LOC) and stipulated that New Delhi and Islamabad would settle their political differences peacefully through bilateral negotiations or any other mutually acceptable means. Simla essentially froze the international dimension of the Kashmir conflict; moreover, the power asymmetry between India and the rump Pakistan after 1971 was such that Islamabad was in no position to challenge the status quo. Indian Kashmir was also relatively quiet. Tranquility in Kashmir coincided with what one scholar calls "the logic of the American approach to South Asia in the mid-1970s—that is, the desire not to be bothered with a region that had consistently proved more troublesome than profitable."[16]

NUCLEAR WEAPONS

Events in the 1970s and early 1980s injected a new issue into the war-scarred Indo-Pakistani relationship: nuclear weapons. By this time, India had long been pursuing nuclear-weapons capabilities, primarily through indigenous research and development, but with substantial infusions of foreign technology. In doing so, New Delhi's fundamental strategic aim was to give itself the option of building nuclear weapons in short order should India's security predicament eventually warrant such a move.

India's gradual nuclearization from the 1940s to the 1970s was motivated by a number of factors. Domestically, what one analyst has called a "strategic enclave" of "research establishments and production facilities"[17] pushed Indian political leaders along the nuclear path for both national security and prestige purposes. Scientists and engineers within this strategic enclave created the vital technological foundation for Indian nuclear prowess, providing India's nuclear program with inexorable momentum even as successive political leaders demonstrated a profound ambivalence about India's becoming a nuclear-weapon state.

Internationally, Indian leaders' main concern for most of this period was with China, India's chief competitor for power and prestige in Asia. As discussed above, China trounced India in a 1962 border war. Soon thereafter (1964), China tested its first nuclear explosive device and thereby joined what would become the exclusive nuclear-weapon club established by the Nuclear Non-Proliferation Treaty (NPT) in 1970. The NPT effectively conferred legitimacy on a small group of nuclear-weapon states whose membership was frozen at five: the United States, the Soviet Union, the United Kingdom, France, and China. When the door to this club slammed shut in 1970, India found itself on the outside, consigned to remaining a nuclear have-not or becoming an illegitimate nuclear-weapon state. By the early 1970s, neither status was acceptable to Indian leaders, who had taken close note of three menacing developments in the eventful year of 1971: President Nixon's opening to China in July, the October seating of China in the UN General Assembly and Security Council, and the December movement of a U.S. aircraft carrier task force toward the Bay of Bengal during the third Indo-Pakistani war. In 1972 Indian prime minister Indira Gandhi authorized the building of a nuclear explosive device, and in 1974 she gave the final go-ahead for India's first nuclear test.[18]

AFGHANISTAN

The December 1979 Soviet invasion of Afghanistan posed difficult challenges for Indian foreign policymakers. On one hand, the Soviet Union was by then India's main ally, providing much of the Indian armed forces' advanced weaponry on concessionary terms. On the other hand, New Delhi deplored any direct extension of Cold War conflict into South Asia because it threatened India's dominant regional position, both by injecting superpower military forces into regional affairs and by augmenting Pakistan's military capabilities, as in the 1950s. In 1981 Indian defense planners' worst fears were realized with the resurrection of the U.S.-Pakistani strategic partnership, which had been dormant since the early 1960s. Soon after the Soviets occupied Afghanistan, President Carter ordered a clandestine CIA operation to supply U.S. aid to the anti-Soviet resistance that would become the agency's largest covert operation since the Vietnam War. Pakistan became the vital conduit for that assistance. When the Reagan administration arrived on the scene in 1981, it promptly agreed to a $3.2 billion military and economic assistance package for Islamabad that suddenly vaulted Pakistan into the highest reaches of U.S. aid recipients—in league with Egypt, Israel, and Turkey. Although Indian leaders protested that the new infusion of U.S. military assistance would set off an arms race and destabilize the region, their arguments were undercut by the fact that India itself had in May 1980 procured $1.63 billion of top-of-the-line Soviet weaponry on exceedingly generous terms.

In retrospect, Pakistan's reemergence as a frontline state in the Cold War had a surprisingly limited impact on Indo-U.S. relations. Although the Indian government refused publicly to condemn Moscow's brutalization of Afghanistan, Indian leaders were privately and acutely distressed by their ally's behavior, and they quietly conveyed their discontent to the Kremlin.

How could New Delhi sustain its position as a champion of Third World interests while its superpower patron was systematically devastating a small neighboring country? Also, as the information-technology revolution gathered steam, Indian leaders had begun to perceive that their economic relations with the stagnating Soviet Union were of limited utility. New Delhi wanted to "grow" its economy in electronics, computers, and telecommunications, areas where Washington could be much more useful than Moscow.

India began to explore new cooperation with the United States in the early 1980s. Momentum accelerated when Rajiv Gandhi succeeded his mother, Indira Gandhi, as prime minister in 1984. The younger Gandhi was a former airline pilot, enamored of high technology and responsive to the developmental possibilities of economic liberalization. With the Reagan administration eager to isolate the Soviet Union, U.S. officials had their own incentives to pursue a warming of relations with New Delhi. The first significant breakthrough in Indo-U.S. affairs was a May 1985 memorandum of understanding in science and technology that removed India from the U.S. list of "diversion-risk" countries, paving the way for increased investment and technology transfer.

RELATIONS WITH PAKISTAN

The 1970s was a decade of relatively peaceful relations between New Delhi and Islamabad. The Simla Agreement had essentially frozen the Kashmir dispute, at least for the time being. Moreover, the asymmetry in power between India and Pakistan after 1971 was so great that Islamabad was in no position to challenge the regional status quo. This changed in the 1980s. The primary bone of contention was each side's claim that the other was meddling in its internal ethnic disputes. Particularly important early in the 1980s was Pakistan's support for the Sikh insurgency that was raging in the Indian border state of Punjab.[19] In 1981 the Akali Dal, the main Sikh political party, launched a sustained agitation against the Indian state. Sikh leaders hoped to resolve certain longstanding disputes, including the status of Chandigarh, which had been the capital of both Punjab and the neighboring state of Haryana since the old state of Punjab was linguistically reorganized in 1966.

As negotiations between Sikh leaders and Indira Gandhi's government failed to bear fruit, the Sikh political movement descended into militancy. With the violence escalating, Sikh insurgents turned the Golden Temple in Amritsar, Sikhism's holiest shrine, into a sanctuary and base of operations. Some called for the creation of Khalistan, an independent Sikh state. In June 1984 the Indian army launched Operation Bluestar, an assault on the Golden Temple and other Sikh temples where militant leaders had taken refuge. Perhaps a thousand people were killed in the three-day siege. The

Indian Home Ministry claimed that the Sikh insurgency had been a prelude to the creation of Khalistan, supported by "neighboring and foreign powers," which would have "crippled the armed forces in any future confrontation across the borders." In October 1984 Indira Gandhi was murdered by two Sikh members of her personal security detail. In the assassination's aftermath, some twenty-seven hundred Sikhs were slaughtered in Delhi's worst violence since Partition.[20]

In the meantime, Pakistan had its own concerns about Indian cross-border meddling. Islamabad accused New Delhi of fomenting violence in the southern Pakistani province of Sindh, which had seen a huge influx of migrants since independence. The first wave of settlers consisted of *muhajirs* ("refugees") from India, who fueled the growth of Karachi, Pakistan's largest city. Later settlers included Punjabis and, especially during the Afghanistan war, Pakistani Pashtuns and Afghans of various ethnicities. Sindhi nationalism had grown in the 1970s as a response to what ethnic Sindhis felt was their increasing subordination to outsiders. In 1983 a coalition called the Movement for the Restoration of Democracy launched violent protests against the military regime of Gen. Zia ul-Haq. This agitation took on a sharp regionalist tone, with Sindhis demanding greater provincial autonomy, reduced disparities in economic development, a more equitable distribution of federal government funds, and increased representation in the military and civil services. In the summer of 1983, thousands of Sindhis engaged in a "rural mass movement," the first of its kind in the country's short history.[21] When the insurgents began to carry out armed attacks against property, infrastructure, and Pakistan army forces, the Zia government smashed the rebellion with thousands of troops and helicopter gunships.[22] Throughout the early 1980s, Islamabad vociferously accused Indian operatives of aiding and abetting the violence in Sindh.

Another element of Indo-Pakistani conflict emerged in April 1984, when Indian military forces were deployed on the Siachen Glacier in northern Kashmir, just south of China's Xinjiang Province. Pakistani forces soon followed suit, and sporadic battles have been fought between the two sides from June 1984 to the present. The glacier measures some one thousand square miles of territory in the Karakoram mountain range, much of which lies at elevations above twenty thousand feet. Because both India and Pakistan claim all of Kashmir as their own, each country also claims complete control over the glacier, which makes the Siachen Glacier dispute a subset of the larger Kashmir dispute. Competing claims over the glacier itself have their roots in the vagueness of the 1949 agreement demarcating the cease-fire line between India and Pakistan after the first Kashmir war. When the line was drawn, roughly forty miles of the boundary leading up to the Chinese border was left undelineated because the area "was considered an inaccessible no-man's land." The issue remained unresolved by the Simla Agreement of 1972, which had replaced the cease-fire line with the new LOC without addressing the matter of the undrawn boundary. On the Siachen Glacier, more casualties have been inflicted by fierce weather conditions than by enemy fire.[23]

The 1980s also witnessed the steady maturation of Indian and Pakistani nuclear-weapons capabilities.[24] In 1981 Prime Minister Indira Gandhi "claimed that India and 'the rest of the world' knew that Pakistan was developing the capacity to build nuclear weapons and would soon explode a nuclear device. She said this might prompt India . . . to explode another nuclear device of its own."[25] Although press reports throughout the early 1980s speculated that both countries were making preparations for a nuclear test, one prescient analyst raised the possibility that Pakistan had "given up the idea of aping India by actually detonating an underground nuclear device and has instead opted for the Israeli strategy of reaching, or letting the world believe it has reached, a high level of nuclear technology without actually staging a nuclear test."[26] This analysis proved to be correct. By 1984 it was clear that even if Pakistan did not test a nuclear explosive device, it would still hedge its bets by quietly developing all of the capabilities necessary to keep its options open.

Predictably, Pakistan's evident nuclear strides sparked a renewed Indian debate about how to respond. Just before her death in October 1984, Indira Gandhi called Islamabad's recent progress in developing nuclear weapons a "qualitatively new phenomenon in our security environment," one which added a "new dimension" to Indian defense planning.[27] By the middle of 1985, Mrs. Gandhi's son and successor, Rajiv, admitted that in light of Pakistan's nuclear progress, India was reconsidering its own commitment not to build nuclear weapons.[28] In June 1985 Rajiv Gandhi was quoted as saying that Pakistan was "very close" to building a bomb; as for India, he said, "In principle we are opposed to the idea of becoming a nuclear power. We could have done so for the past 10 or 11 years, but we have not. If we decided to become a nuclear power, it would take a few weeks or a few months."[29] Four months later, Rajiv Gandhi said, "Pakistan has either already got the bomb or will get one in a matter of months and may not even need to test it."[30] In October 1985 a high-level U.S. delegation failed to convince the Indian government that Islamabad's nuclear program was not as far along as New Delhi feared. As Rajiv said, "The U.S. seems to believe that Pakistan has not got the enriched uranium yet. We believe they have."[31] The next month, the Indian foreign minister charged that Islamabad had enough weapons-grade uranium for three to five atomic bombs.[32]

This was the strategic backdrop for the first major crisis of South Asia's nuclear era. In autumn 1986 a series of Indian military exercises called "Brasstacks" began a spiral of competitive mobilization between India and Pakistan. The final phase of the maneuvers was South Asia's largest-ever military exercise, comparable in scale to North Atlantic Treaty Organization maneuvers in Europe during the Cold War. The hypothetical scenario underlying Brasstacks was a Pakistani invasion of India to bring about the separation from India of the troubled states of Kashmir and Punjab. By January 1987, both countries' military forces were on alert, with Indian and Pakistani armored formations poised near sensitive areas along the international frontier, including the very tense Indian state of Punjab. Just as quickly as it began, though, the crisis abated. By the end of January, Islamabad and New Delhi began negotiating over the withdrawal of troops from border areas, and in early February the two sides agreed to a phased demobilization of forces that was implemented over the next few months.[33]

REGIONAL AFFAIRS

In the meantime, there were important developments in India's relations with the region's smaller countries. In 1980 Bangladesh's president proposed that the South Asian states (except Afghanistan) establish a forum for multilateral cooperation. India had historically resisted such efforts, fearing that New Delhi's neighbors might use a regional organization collectively to oppose Indian interests. Indian leaders preferred to deal with individual—and weaker—South Asian states on a bilateral basis, so that India's advantages in power could ensure outcomes consistent with New Delhi's interests. However, by the 1980s, India had grown secure in its position of regional predominance; Indian foreign policymakers had come to view the prospect of multilateral cooperation as a means by which India could more effectively influence regional affairs, as well as gain diplomatic credit for adopting a more conciliatory posture. New Delhi's willingness to participate paved the way for the creation of the South Asian Association for Regional Cooperation (SAARC) in 1985. SAARC's main goals are "to promote the welfare of the peoples of South Asia and to improve their quality of life," as well as "to accelerate economic growth, social progress and cultural development in the region." Importantly, from India's perspective, the SAARC charter declares that "decisions at all levels shall be taken on the basis of unanimity" and that "bilateral and contentious issues shall be excluded from the deliberations." The SAARC countries have met at twelve summits since 1985. Dramatic achievements have been few, but SAARC has provided a useful forum for informal interaction.[34]

India also acted decisively in the late 1980s to reaffirm its commitment to excluding external actors from encroaching on its regional management role. In the most robust example of this policy, India took the lead in trying to put an end to the escalating Sri Lankan civil war, which was sparked in July 1983 by the eruption of violence between Sri Lanka's Sinhalese-dominated government and Tamil insurgents. Under the terms of a 1987 Indo–Sri Lankan peace accord, the Indian army was charged with enforcing a "cessation of hostilities" between Tamil militants and the Sri Lankan army. In exchange, the Colombo government agreed to respect New Delhi's regional management role and to refrain from allowing extraregional powers to intervene in the conflict. Unfortunately for New Delhi, its fifty thousand peacekeepers soon found themselves involved in heavy fighting against battle-hardened Tamil guerrillas in the dense jungles of northern and eastern Sri Lanka. By the time the Indian army left Sri Lanka in 1990 at the request of the Colombo government, eleven hundred Indians had died in their country's longest war.[35]

THE POST–COLD WAR ERA

The international system was fundamentally transformed between 1989 and 1991. The toppling of the Berlin Wall, the "velvet revolutions" in Eastern Europe, the reunification of Germany, and the disintegration of the Soviet Union were successive political earthquakes whose global aftershocks rumble even today. Every state in the world has faced the necessity of adapting to the sudden end of bipolarity and the emergence of a new, unipolar international order. This transition has been all the more challenging for New Delhi because it has come at a time when India itself has been undergoing its own social, economic, and political revolutions.[36] Historians will likely remember the 1990s as the decade when the so-called Nehruvian consensus, based on secularism, socialism, and nonalignment, breathed its last.

As the twenty-first century began, India's economy and political system looked much different from what they had a decade earlier. Politically, the most dramatic developments have been the decline of the Congress Party and the rise of the Bharatiya Janata Party (BJP), or Indian People's Party. The BJP rose to prominence on a wave of Hindu nationalist sentiment loosely referred to as *Hindutva*, a concept with no literal translation into English, but which connotes an enhanced sense of "Hinduness" or "Hindu-consciousness."[37] The growth of *Hindutva* in Indian political life has increasingly filled the political vacuum left by the Congress system's decline (see note 19). Under Indira and Rajiv Gandhi, a weakening Congress morphed into a party less staunch in its commitment to secularism and more willing to exploit intensifying Hindu nationalism for political gain. Thus, it was the Congress itself that legitimized the resort to religious sentiments and symbolism that previously characterized the tactics of only marginal opposition parties. Unable to remain above the communal fray, India's once-dominant party effectively abdicated its role as the watchdog of secularism.

Meanwhile, developments such as the burgeoning Sikh movement for Khalistan, the Indian army's 1984 intervention in Punjab, Indira Gandhi's subsequent assassination, and the reemergence in the mid-1980s of Muslim political discontent in Kashmir created something of a siege mentality in the so-called Hindi heartland; one commentator noted, "Hindus throughout north India are wallowing in . . . a 'majority's minority complex.' Militant Hindu groups are invoking a conspiracy of anti-Hindu forces at home and abroad, which are posed as threats to the Indian nation but are actually excuses for reasserting upper-caste Hindu dominance over uppity Sikhs, Muslims, and lower castes."[38]

These trends led for the first time in the 1980s to an emotionally charged competition for the allegiance of India's Hindu majority. Starting with the election of 1989, the BJP has tapped into Hindu angst with increasing effectiveness. In the 1984 national elections, the BJP won only two seats in the Lok Sabha, India's lower house of parliament. That number increased to eighty-six in the BJP's breakthrough election of 1989. Ten years later, the BJP won 182 seats and its National Democratic Alliance a total of 299—respectively, 33 percent and 55 percent of the 545 Lok Sabha seats. BJP-led governments ruled India from 1998 until May 2004, when the BJP's electoral coalition was defeated and a Congress-led coalition took power.

The 1990s also witnessed the beginnings of a profound Indian economic transformation, which is discussed at greater length in chapter 11. For the first four decades after independence, the Indian economy had been organized along socialist lines, with the government favoring policies intended to distribute India's scarce wealth evenly over policies that might achieve higher growth rates but result in widening economic disparities. For Nehru and his economic policymakers, this meant that the Indian economy would require strong centralized planning, a large public sector in most basic industries, and tight government control over the private sector. Indian industry was protected by high tariff walls that over the years prevented Indian manufactured goods from reaching sufficient quality to be competitive on world markets. Foreign investment in and ownership of Indian companies was strictly controlled. So tight was the government's control of private economic activity that it earned the disparaging moniker "license raj" or "permit raj" (*raj* means "rule" in Hindi). With equal measures of sadness and derision, many economists prior to the 1990s came to refer to the "Hindu rate of growth," an appreciable but plodding—by developing country standards—3 percent per year.

Although the Congress government of Rajiv Gandhi began to make some liberalizing reforms in the 1980s, it took a severe balance-of-payments crisis in 1991 to convince New Delhi that the Indian economy required drastic restructuring. Since then, successive governments headed by both major parties, the Congress and the BJP, have liberalized foreign investment and foreign exchange rules, substantially lowered tariffs and nontariff barriers to trade, overhauled India's fiscal and monetary policies, and significantly reformed the country's financial sector. India's overall economic perform-ance has distinctly improved in the last decade, with average growth rates roughly double those of the prereform era. Inflation has been lowered, and foreign investment has skyrocketed, albeit from a very low baseline. India's foreign currency reserves are now substantial, and the country enjoys a small current account surplus.

RELATIONS WITH PAKISTAN

As the 1990s began, the end of the Cold War had serious repercussions for South Asian international relations. The 1989 Soviet withdrawal from Afghanistan had erased the rationale for a U.S.-Pakistani strategic partner-ship, which quickly gave way to Islamabad's continued development of nu-clear weapons as the issue of foremost concern for U.S. policymakers. India's relationship with the Soviet Union also suffered. When Soviet leader Mikhail Gorbachev's liberalizing reforms plunged the Soviet economy into depres-sion, the Kremlin was compelled to alter the concessionary terms under which it had pursued its economic and military ties with allies during most of the Cold War. India's trade with the Soviet Union, previously conducted in ru-pees, was shifted to a more conventional commercial footing, and the terms of Soviet military sales also grew less attractive. More broadly, the emergence of a unipolar international system rendered the notion of nonalignment, the chief pillar of Indian foreign relations for decades, a relic of the past.

Regionally, the late 1980s saw the reemergence of Muslim discontent in Kashmir, which soon sent Indo-Pakistani relations into another tailspin. In the late 1980s, agitation against the central government in New Delhi had grown among Kashmiri Muslims. After the 1972 Simla Agreement, discussed above, the Indo-Pakistani dispute over Kashmir was dormant, although both sides continued to press their claims to the territory. New Delhi maintained that Kashmir was an integral part of the Indian Union, its status as such legit-imized by both its incorporation into the Indian constitution and decades of democratic Kashmiri political activity within the Indian federation. Islam-abad disagreed: sovereignty over Kashmir remained contested, its status un-resolved according to either the operative UN formula or the more direct Indo-Pakistani talks envisioned by the Simla signatories.[39]

The decline of India's Congress system had disastrous consequences for political stability in Kashmir. In 1983 state assembly elections, the predomi-nantly Muslim National Conference Party had won a convincing victory by sweeping the heavily Muslim Vale of Kashmir, while the Congress fared well only in predominantly Hindu Jammu. The next year, the Congress ousted the National Conference chief minister (the state's head of government, analogous to the prime minister at the national level), Farooq Abdullah, Sheikh Abdullah's son. This bloodless coup ignited a cycle of political degeneration that further alienated Kashmiri Muslims from the Indian Union. In anticipation of new state elections in 1987, Prime Minister Rajiv Gandhi insisted that the National Conference join the Congress in an electoral alliance and subsequent governing coalition. Farooq Abdullah accepted and was elected chief minister once again. The 1987 elections were demonstrably rigged,[40] and the new government proved to be corrupt and inefficient. By 1988 political estrangement blended with economic angst to produce a critical mass of alienated Kashmiri Muslims. Antigovernment agitation erupted in the form of sporadic violence and organized strikes. Militants set off bombs in Srinagar, and security forces, judges, and other government officials became murder targets. By 1989 Islamic militants in the Vale of Kashmir were in open rebellion, heralding a secessionist insurgency that continues today.[41]

The escalating subconventional war between Indian security forces and the Kashmiri insurgents, who were increasingly supported by Pakistan, radically worsened Indo-Pakistani relations. With the Afghanistan war winding down, the newly invigorated Pakistan army rechanneled its energies and military muscle toward the so-called freedom fighters struggling against Indian rule in Kashmir. The escalating war between Indian security forces on one side, and Pakistan-supported insurgents on the other, gave the two governments their first compelling reason to shed blood since the Bangladesh war two decades earlier. Early in 1990 the Kashmir fighting evolved from a primarily civil conflict into an international crisis that brought India and Pakistan dangerously close to major war. New Delhi and Islamabad placed their military forces on high alert and issued bellicose threats suggesting that war was imminent. Some analysts believe that during the 1990 crisis Pakistan readied its nuclear weapons for deployment; others discount that view. Either way, the first Bush administration was sufficiently alarmed that it dispatched Deputy National Security Advisor Robert Gates to the region for talks with both governments. The Gates intervention helped to calm tempers on both sides of the border.[42]

NUCLEAR TESTS

For most of the 1990s, New Delhi and Islamabad avoided crossing any nuclear Rubicons, preferring instead to refine their nuclear-weapons and delivery capabilities quietly. The prevailing perception in both capitals seemed to be that even these nonweaponized capabilities would deter the other side from aggression. However, India turned out to be less content than Pakistan with this adolescent nuclear standoff. While Islamabad's nuclear program is purely the product of strategic concerns about India, New Delhi, as always, plays on a larger field. As one scholar wrote in 1999, the Cold War's end had for India "resulted in the loss of a critical counterweight to the Chinese threat: the security guarantee implied in the 1971 treaty with the Soviet Union disintegrated with the Soviet collapse."[43] Moreover, as another analyst argued, the structural "shift from bipolarity to unipolarity has only been complemented by a second external reality: discomforting changes in the regional environment centered on, among other things, the rise of a new great power, China." This author captured the essence of New Delhi's thinking in the late 1990s: "The growth of China's economic power, its continued nuclear and conventional military modernization, and its increasing influence in various areas of strategic relevance to South Asia, all combine to forebode serious Indo-Chinese military-strategic competition down the line."[44]

National security imperatives and the strategic enclave's lobbying ultimately bore fruit when India stunned the world by conducting a series of nuclear explosive tests on May 11 and 13, 1998. A few weeks later, and despite considerable external pressure, Islamabad followed suit. Long after they had become de facto nuclear-weapon states, India and Pakistan came out of the closet and declared themselves to be full-fledged, de jure nuclear-weapon states. India's foreign minister described his government's thinking: "Nuclear weapons remain a key indicator of state power. Since this currency is operational in large parts of the globe, India was left with no choice but to update and validate the capability that had been demonstrated 24 years ago in the nuclear test of 1974."[45]

But why in 1998, after twenty-four years of restraint? Here, domestic politics enter the equation. Indian leaders had considered nuclear tests at several points from 1974 to 1998. Each time, decision makers decided that the costs of such a course would outweigh the benefits. But no previous government had staked its political life on restoring India to greatness, at least not to the extent that the BJP had in campaigning during the 1998 national election. As party president L. K. Advani said on the stump, "the BJP rejects the notion of nuclear apartheid and will actively oppose attempts to impose a hegemonistic nuclear regime. We will not be dictated to by anybody in matters of security and in the exercise of the nuclear option."[46] If, once in office, the BJP-led government had decided against nuclear tests, Indian voters would have viewed it as another in a succession of vacillating coalition governments that had come to characterize the national political scene in the mid-1990s. In post-Nehruvian India, few votes are to be found in a posture of nuclear dovishness.

THE KARGIL WAR[47]

Within a year of the 1998 nuclear tests, India and Pakistan fought their most violent military clashes since 1971. In the late 1990s, it had seemed as if the insurgency against the Indian state was waning. Indian officials estimated that the number of committed separatists had declined in a few years from between five and ten thousand to roughly twenty-five hundred.[48] Alas, peace was fleeting. One important factor was the transnationalization of the Islamic insurgency. As a U.S. analyst wrote in 1999,

> For five years now, the rebels with clout have been cut from the same cloth: based in Pakistan, trained in Afghanistan, and motivated by pan-Islamic fundamentalism rather than Kashmiri nationalism. Their ranks filled with Punjabis and Pashtuns, Afghans and Arabs, many of the fighters wage war on behalf of a people whose language they do not even speak.[49]

Unbeknownst to the Indian government, by the spring of 1999 hundreds of well-armed infiltrators had dug in along a 140-kilometer stretch of Himalayan ridges, some 5 to 15 kilometers on the Indian side of Kashmir's LOC. The intruders' positions overlooked National Highway 1A, the only decent road between Srinagar and Leh, and thus the only ground supply route to Indian military forces manning the border between Ladakh and China. The Pakistan army supported the invaders, who in May destroyed an Indian ammunition dump outside Kargil.[50] Outraged, the Indian government responded decisively. Special forces personnel were dropped onto high ridges by helicopter. Army soldiers equipped with howitzers, rocket launchers, and heavy mortars launched attacks supported by helicopter gunships.[51] Soon thereafter, Indian ground-attack aircraft began to pound the intruders' positions.[52] Indian leaders also ordered their armed forces to prepare for war all along the Indo-Pakistani border. According to one account, "elements of the Indian army's main offensive 'strike force' were loading tanks, artillery, and other heavy equipment onto flatbed rail cars." In addition, U.S. officials say retrospectively, "armored units intended for offensive use were leaving their garrisons in Rajasthan . . . and preparing to move."[53] By the end of June, Indian "mechanized and artillery divisions [had] advanced to forward positions all along the border in Gujarat, Rajasthan, Punjab, and Jammu and Kashmir." The Pakistan army was making similar preparations along the Punjab frontier.[54]

As the crisis escalated, the diplomatic maneuvering intensified. In late-May talks between senior U.S. and Indian officials, the United States reportedly agreed to deal firmly with Pakistan; in return, India pledged not to cross the LOC or otherwise escalate the fighting.[55] President Clinton called the Indian and Pakistani prime ministers on June 14–15, urging both sides to resist widening the conflict.[56] As casualties mounted, though, New Delhi's patience wore thin, and a senior Indian official informed Washington that India might be compelled to escalate its operations.[57] Deeply concerned about this prospect, Clinton sent the commander in chief of the U.S. Central Command, Gen. Anthony Zinni, to Islamabad. Zinni pressured Pakistani leaders to end the Kargil operation[58]; in response, he received assurances that the insurgents would be withdrawn from the Indian side of the LOC.[59] New Delhi's resolve to eject the infiltrators from its side of the LOC, Indian military successes on the ridges of Kargil, and pressure from the United States ultimately convinced Islamabad to call off its misadventure. Some eleven to twelve hundred Indians and Pakistanis died in the 1999 Kargil war.[60]

SEPTEMBER 11, DECEMBER 13, AND THE 2001–2002 INDIA–PAKISTAN CRISIS

After a brief period of relative peace, large-scale carnage returned to Kashmir on October 1, 2001, less than three weeks after the al Qaeda attacks on the World Trade Center and the Pentagon. Terrorists from the Pakistan-based Jaish-e-Muhammad ("Muhammad's Troops") attacked the Kashmir Legislative Assembly in Srinagar, killing thirty-eight people.[61] Then, on December 13, Jaish-e-Muhammad and Lashkar-e-Taiba ("Army of the Pure"), another Pakistan-based terrorist group, attacked the Indian Parliament in New Delhi, leaving fourteen dead.[62] The audacious strike at the heart of India's government, far from Kashmir's peaks and valleys, dealt a blow to Indian society not unlike that of September 11 in the United States. New Delhi responded by deploying the Indian army to border positions; putting its combined military forces, including those in Kashmir, on high alert; severing road, rail, and air links with Pakistan; and recalling its high commissioner from Islamabad. Ultimately, India moved roughly half a million soldiers, including three armored strike corps, to the parts of Punjab, Rajasthan, and Gujarat bordering Pakistan.[63] Islamabad responded by mobilizing its own armor and three hundred thousand Pakistan army troops to the adjacent border areas of Punjab and Sindh.[64]

India's strategy was partly aimed at inducing Washington to urge Islamabad to stop supporting cross-border terrorism, a posture bolstered by President Bush's post–September 11 doctrine of targeting terrorists and the states that support them. In response to U.S. pressure, Pakistan's leader, Gen. Pervez Musharraf, pledged that Pakistan would crack down on terrorism in Kashmir.[65] Alas, Musharraf proved unwilling or unable to clamp down completely on Pakistan's terrorists, who in May 2002 attacked an Indian military base in Jammu, killing thirty-four people and setting off a full-blown crisis.

While Indian prime minister Atal Behari Vajpayee warned the Indian army to "prepare for a 'decisive battle,'" Musharraf strongly implied that "if India insists on launching all-out war to attack Pakistan's support for Kashmiri militants, Pakistan is prepared to go nuclear."[66]

Once again, Washington scrambled to prevent war in South Asia. In June 2002 Deputy Secretary of State Richard Armitage traveled to Islamabad, where he elicited a promise from Musharraf to "end cross-border infiltration permanently."[67] All in all, India's army chief estimated that militant crossings declined by about half from 2001 to 2002.[68] Although the immediate crisis faded in June, the Indo-Pakistani troop buildup lasted until October, when India announced that it would withdraw its forces from the border with Pakistan. Despite the fact that India and Pakistan nearly fought a major war in the summer of 2002, the conflict grinds on.

INDIA IN CONTEMPORARY WORLD POLITICS

Since 1947 India has consistently pursued a grand strategy of preventing extraregional powers from unduly influencing South Asia's international politics. Indian foreign policy has had two fundamental goals: to ensure what India regards as its natural hegemony in the region and to safeguard the integrity of the Indian Union. During the first phase of independent India's foreign relations, from 1947 to 1962, New Delhi pursued what might be termed *true nonalignment*; that is, it attempted to have friendly relations with all three of the most important external powers, China, the United States, and the Soviet Union. True nonalignment was shattered by the 1962 Chinese attack, which laid bare India's weaknesses and the perils of going it alone in world politics.

From 1962 to 1991, India followed a policy of what we might term *tilted nonalignment*. For several years immediately after the China war, India relied on the United States and Great Britain in attempting to enhance its defense capabilities. Then, as Washington drew back from South Asia with the onset of the 1965 Indo-Pakistani war, India allowed itself to become more dependent on the Soviet Union to meet its security needs. In 1971 with another India–Pakistan war looming, New Delhi gained an extra measure of reassurance by formalizing its security relationship with Moscow.

With the end of the Cold War and the collapse of the Soviet Union in 1991, the notion of nonalignment lost its meaning. As during the 1947–1962 period, India has tried in recent years to navigate the shoals of world politics by maintaining amicable ties with the same three external powers: a rapidly strengthening China, a weakened Russia, and a globally hegemonic United States. What has changed relative to forty years ago is that India is a significantly more powerful actor in international relations. As table 1.1 shows, India's economy today is the world's fourth largest, accounting for nearly 5 percent of global economic output. Although India's per capita gross domestic product (GDP) of $2,600 places it only 156th out of 231 entries in the CIA's *The World Factbook*,[69] its continuing economic liberalization and fast-growing consumer market have attracted a great deal of international interest, especially compared with the early postindependence years, when imports and foreign investment were tightly restricted.

In terms of its defense capabilities, India today is an established nuclear-weapon state. Although the 1999 Kargil war demonstrated that nuclear weapons may not deter Pakistan from continuing to stoke the insurgency in Indian-controlled Kashmir, it also showed that neither side is willing to escalate the conflict beyond Kashmir into India and Pakistan proper. Indian nuclear weapons also make a Chinese invasion of India exceedingly unlikely. In conventional terms, New Delhi deploys a large, well-trained army, a capable, relatively modern air force, and a growing, but modest, navy. More specifically, Indian military forces along the frontier with China are considered to be among the world's best mountain divisions, with little resemblance to the Indian army that was routed in 1962. As table 1.2 shows, Indian military spending ranks eleventh in the world.

As always, India's most pressing challenges concern socioeconomic development. According to the UN Human Development Index (HDI), which combines life expectancy at birth, adult literacy, school attendance, and per capita GDP, India ranks 127th out of 175 entries. On the positive side, India's HDI has steadily increased over the last three decades: it was 0.416 in 1975, 0.443 in 1980, 0.481 in 1985, 0.519 in 1990, 0.553 in 1995, and 0.590 in

Table 1.1.   Gross Domestic Product (Purchasing-Power-Parity Method), 2002 Estimates

Economy	Dollars (millions)
World	49,000
1 United States	10,450
2 China	5,989
3 Japan	3,651
4 India	2,664
5 Germany	2,160
6 France	1,558
7 United Kingdom	1,528
8 Italy	1,455
9 Russia	1,409
10 Brazil	1,376

Source: CIA World Factbook, 2003.

Table 1.2. Military Spending

Economy		Dollars (thousands)	Date
1	United States	276,700	NA
2	China	55,910	FY02
3	France	46,500	2000
4	Japan	39,520	FY02
5	Germany	38,800	2002
6	United Kingdom	31,700	2002
7	Italy	20,200	2002
8	Saudi Arabia	18,300	NA
9	Brazil	13,408	NA
10	Korea, South	13,094.3	FY02
11	India	11,520	FY02
12	Australia	11,390	FY02

Source: CIA World Factbook, 2003.

2001, an overall increase of 42 percent. In comparison, China today ranks 104th, with an HDI of 0.721, an increase of 38 percent since 1975.[70]

In more qualitative terms, India's foreign policy has, as one scholar notes, "grown up."[71] In previous decades, New Delhi's protests against external influence in South Asia were often so shrill as to belie its claims to be the regional hegemon. As India's power has grown, its diplomacy has matured, and its rhetoric has moderated. New Delhi's responses to the issues of the day exhibit a confident, measured tone that was missing even ten years ago. Nowhere is this more evident than in India's relations with the United States, which have improved considerably since the mid-1990s. The BJP's 1998 gamble that India's long-term prestige would grow after New Delhi declared itself a nuclear-weapon state seems to have paid off. The Indian nuclear tests caused only a brief furor, and Indo-American relations today are as strong as they have ever been. In this context, it is instructive to compare India's relatively calm reaction to the post–September 11 renewal of the United States–Pakistan security partnership with Nehru's outrage at the first U.S.-Pakistani strategic embrace fifty years ago.

India's relations with China and Russia are also on a relatively even keel today. Sino-Indian ties had been gradually warming since 1988, until senior Indian officials justified their 1998 nuclear tests by claiming that Chinese nuclear weapons posed a serious threat to India. Despite the short-term harshness of China's response to that charge, Sino-Indian relations continue their slow, upward trajectory, even though conflicting boundary lines remain formally unreconciled. New Delhi and Moscow have their typically solid relationship, with Russia helping to meet Indian defense needs and Indian military purchases providing Russia with a scarce source of hard currency.

India's relations with Pakistan are rockier, but even here one can discern a glimmer of hope. Prime Minister Vajpayee and President Musharraf met in January 2004 and agreed to start a negotiating process over the issues dividing New Delhi and Islamabad, including Kashmir. High-level talks resumed in June after the Congress-led coalition took office under Prime Minister Manmohan Singh. Although little progress has been made on the Kashmir dispute, the two sides have agreed to a number of diplomatic and confidence-building measures, including the planned reopening of consulates in Karachi and Mumbai. The obstacles to Indo-Pakistani rapprochement are daunting, but bilateral dialogue and revitalized diplomatic relations are improvements over the sorry state of India–Pakistan affairs as recently as 2002.

India's improved relations with China, Pakistan, Russia, and the United States are interrelated in a way that reflects well on Indian diplomatic prowess. Unlike in previous decades, all of the major extraregional actors in South Asian affairs support India's position on Kashmir, that the conflict should be resolved bilaterally on the basis of the Simla formula. Russia has always been solidly on India's side concerning Kashmir, but the same cannot be said for the United States and China. Both Washington and Beijing have made it much clearer in recent years that they will not support in any way Pakistani efforts to alter the status quo unilaterally. This can be counted as a substantial success for Indian diplomacy, as well as further testament to the emergence of India as a leading middle power in world affairs.

NOTES

1. The quotations are from Nehru's speech to India's Constituent Assembly, New Delhi, August 14, 1947. For the complete text, see the *Norton Anthology of English Literature*, Norton Topics Online, available at www.wwnorton.com/nael. Independence and Partition are discussed at length below.

2. If military strategy is the "art of distributing and applying military means to fulfill the ends of policy" (B. H. Liddell Hart, *Strategy*, 2nd rev. ed. [New York: Praeger, 1967], 335), then grand strategy is the art of using all of a state's means—military, diplomatic, covert, economic, and so forth—for this purpose. Grand strategy is the "modern equivalent of what was, in the seventeenth and eighteenth centuries, called *ragione di stato* or *raison d'état*. It is the rational determination of a nation's vital interests, the things that are essential to its security, its fundamental purposes in its relations with other nations, and its priorities with respect to goals." (Gordon A. Craig and Felix Gilbert, "Reflections on Strategy in the Present and Future," in *Makers of Modern Strategy: from Machiavelli to the Nuclear Age*, ed. Peter Paret [Princeton, N.J.: Princeton University Press, 1986], 869.) Grand strategy is as much a peacetime as a wartime preoccupation, which makes it an ideal conceptual lens through which to view India's foreign relations over time. The essence of grand strategy is its long-term nature and its imperviousness to the everyday events of international politics and even changes in government. Grand strategies evolve only in response to fundamental transformations in the context of international politics, such as the world wars or the end of the Cold War.

3. *Hegemony* has become something of a loaded term in the academic study of international relations. Our usage here conforms to the more neutral, literal definition of hegemony as "leadership or predominant influence exercised by one state over others." *The American College Dictionary* (New York: Random House, 1970), 561.

4. From a 1949 speech, quoted in Stanley Wolpert, *Nehru: A Tryst with Destiny* (New York: Oxford University Press, 1996), 448.

5. This section draws from a longer discussion of the Indo-Pakistani conflict over Kashmir: Devin T. Hagerty, "U.S. Policy and the Kashmir Dispute: Prospects for Resolution," in *The Kashmir Question: Retrospect and Prospect*, ed. Sumit Ganguly (London: Frank Cass, 2003), 89–116.

6. In the portion of Kashmir that remained in Indian hands, a 1956 vote in the constituent assembly endorsed the state's integration into India.

7. Robert J. McMahon, *The Cold War on the Periphery: The United States, India, and Pakistan* (New York: Columbia University Press, 1994), 46.

8. Devin T. Hagerty, "The Development of American Defense Policy toward Pakistan, 1947–1954," *Fletcher Forum* 10, no. 2 (Summer 1986): 217–42.

9. McMahon, *Cold War on the Periphery*, 172, 34, 219–20.

10. Bhutan was admitted to the United Nations in 1971.

11. Francis Robinson, *The Cambridge Encyclopedia of India, Pakistan, Bangladesh, Sri Lanka, Nepal, Bhutan and the Maldives* (Cambridge: Cambridge University Press, 1989), 239. Sikkim has since been incorporated into the Indian Union.

12. This paragraph draws on Hagerty, "U.S. Policy and the Kashmir Dispute," 96, and Devin T. Hagerty, "China and Pakistan: Strains in the Relationship," *Current History* 101, no. 656 (September 2002): 286.

13. McMahon, *Cold War on the Periphery*, 334.

14. Richard Sisson and Leo E. Rose, *War and Secession: Pakistan, India, and the Creation of Bangladesh* (Berkeley: University of California Press), 152.

15. Rose and Sisson, *War and Secession*, 142–44, 210–15.

16. Thomas P. Thornton, "U.S.-Indian Relations in the Nixon and Ford Years," in Harold A. Gould and Sumit Ganguly, *The Hope and the Reality: U.S.–Indian Relations from Roosevelt to Reagan* (Boulder, Colo.: Westview, 1992), 104.

17. Itty Abraham, "India's 'Strategic Enclave': Civilian Scientists and Military Technologies," *Armed Forces and Society* 18, no. 2 (Winter 1992): 233.

18. For details, see George Perkovich, *India's Nuclear Bomb: The Impact on Global Proliferation* (Berkeley: University of California Press, 1999), 161–89.

19. Both the Punjab crisis and the subsequent Kashmir crisis (discussed below) had their roots in a structural transformation of Indian politics during Indira Gandhi's rule (1966–1977 and 1980–1984). The most salient changes included the increasing centralization of power in New Delhi, the decline of political, judicial, and administrative institutions at every level of government, and the consequent evolution of an institutional vacuum increasingly filled by populist and religious demagoguery of a decidedly unsecular tone. Collectively, these developments have become known as the decline of the Congress system. For more detailed analysis, see Paul R. Brass, *The Politics of India since Independence* (Cambridge: Cambridge University Press, 1990), and Atul Kohli, *Democracy and Discontent: India's Growing Crisis of Governability* (Princeton, N.J.: Princeton University Press, 1988).

20. Robert L. Hardgrave Jr. and Stanley Kochanek, *India: Government and Politics in a Developing Nation*, 5th ed. (Fort Worth, Tex.: Harcourt Brace Jovanovich, 1993), 152–60; Paul R. Brass, "The Punjab Crisis and the Unity of India," in *India's Democracy: An Analysis of Changing State-Society Relations*, ed. Atul Kohli (Princeton, N.J.: Princeton University Press, 1988), 169–213; Salamat Ali, "The 'Hidden Hand,'" *Far Eastern Economic Review*, June 28, 1984, 14.

21. Mary Anne Weaver, *Pakistan: In the Shadow of Jihad and Afghanistan* (New York: Farrar, Straus and Giroux, 2002), 71–3.

22. Owen Bennett Jones, *Pakistan: Eye of the Storm* (New Haven, Conn.: Yale University Press, 2002), 120.

23. This paragraph draws heavily on Robert G. Wirsing, *Pakistan's Security under Zia: The Policy Imperatives of a Peripheral Asian State* (New York: St. Martin's, 1991), 143–94.

24. Pakistan's nuclear program dates back to the 1950s, when the country's leaders began to explore the idea of using nuclear energy for civilian purposes. Within a decade, however, military priorities had supplanted civilian ones in the nuclear thinking of Pakistani leaders. The chief proponent of a Pakistani nuclear bomb was then foreign minister Zulfikar Ali Bhutto, who argued in the wake of the 1965 humiliation by India that Pakistan needed a nuclear equalizer. The 1965 war had revived serious concerns about Pakistan's long-term security, especially given the country's lack of strategic depth. Moreover, as Bhutto began to mount his own challenge to President Ayub Khan's rule, he perceived that nuclear nationalism would be an effective way to rally Pakistan's masses behind him. Pakistan's nuclear aspirations were further fueled by the 1971 Bangladesh war; in 1972, given the huge asymmetry that had emerged in Indian and Pakistani military capabilities, now President Bhutto ordered Pakistan's own strategic enclave to begin developing nuclear arms. Pakistani leaders apparently believed that "a small nuclear program would enable the Pakistanis to do in nuclear terms what their ground and air forces could not do in conventional terms: threaten to punish any Indian attack so severely that consideration of such an attack would be deterred from the outset." U.S. Defense Intelligence Agency, "Operational and Logistical Considerations in the Event of an India-Pakistan Conflict." Report DDB-2660-104-84, December 1984, 2.

25. Michael Richardson, "Arms and the Woman," *Far Eastern Economic Review*, September 25, 1981, 20.

26. Dilip Bobb, "Sinister Nuclear Strategy," *India Today*, November 15, 1981, 119.

27. Leonard S. Spector, *Going Nuclear* (Cambridge, Mass.: Ballinger, 1987), 78.

28. Richard P. Cronin, *The United States, Pakistan and the Soviet Threat to Southern Asia: Options for Congress* (Washington, D.C.: Congressional Research Service, 1985), 28.

29. Maynard Parker, "Rajiv Gandhi's Bipolar World," *Newsweek*, June 3, 1985; and Spector, *Going Nuclear*, 78.

30. Spector, *Going Nuclear*, 270n21. Gandhi's remark about testing was a reference to credible reports that China had given Pakistan vital nuclear-weapon-design information.

31. Patricia J. Sethi and John Walcott, "The South Asia Two-Step," *Newsweek*, November 4, 1985, 42; William Stewart and Ross H. Munro, "An Interview with Rajiv Gandhi," *Time*, October 21, 1985, 50.

32. "Foreign Minister Speaks in Parliament on Pak Nuclear Bomb," confidential cable from the U.S. Embassy in New Delhi to the Secretary of State, no. 28599, November 1985.

33. For a longer discussion, see Devin T. Hagerty, *The Consequences of Nuclear Proliferation: Lessons from South Asia* (Cambridge, Mass.: MIT Press), 91–116.

34. SAARC can be accessed through its website at www.saarc-sec.org.

35. Devin T. Hagerty, "India's Regional Security Doctrine," *Asian Survey* 31, no. 4 (April 1991): 351–63.

36. Space constraints prohibit a comprehensive discussion of these upheavals in Indian society. Recent political and economic changes, which have had a greater impact on India's foreign relations than the social convulsions permeating Indian society, will be discussed below. For a brief, introductory overview of India's social revolution—the rise of the Backward castes, the increasing assertiveness of *Dalits* and tribals, the disaffection and consequent activism of Muslims—see Achin Vanaik, "Hostile Intentions," *Red Pepper* (London), October 1997 (available online at www.tni.org). For an in-depth treatment, see Francine R. Frankel, Zoya Hasan,

Rajeev Bhargava, and Balveer Arora, eds., *Transforming India: Social and Political Dynamics of Democracy* (New Delhi: Oxford University Press, 2000).

37. This notion has been described by one scholar as the belief that "India is composed of an essentially Hindu society. Therefore the state should reflect the values and ambitions of the Hindus, just as Western states reflect the values and ambitions of their Christian population, the Muslim states reflect Islam, and Israel embodies the values and aspirations of Jews. The Hindu revitalists argue that India must act in the world as a Hindu civilization-state. Non-Hindus are welcome to live in India, but only if they accept the fundamentally Hindu nature of the country." Stephen Philip Cohen, *India: Emerging Power* (Washington, D.C.: Brookings, 2001), 119–20.

38. Emily MacFarquhar, "Push Comes to Shove: A Survey of India," *The Economist*, May 9, 1987, p. 6 of the survey.

39. In point of fact, many Pakistanis question the very legitimacy of the Simla Agreement. A top-level Pakistani official, by then out of government, told one of the authors in 1998 that Simla had for all practical purposes been dictated to Pakistan at gunpoint and was therefore irrelevant to resolution of the Kashmir conflict.

40. Inderjit Badhwar, "A Tarnished Triumph," *India Today*, April 15, 1987, 76–78; Inderjit Badhwar, "Farooq under Fire," *India Today*, September 15, 1987, 42–47.

41. Most estimates put the number of deaths in Kashmir at more than 60,000 since 1989.

42. Devin T. Hagerty, "Nuclear Deterrence in South Asia: The 1990 Indo-Pakistani Crisis," *International Security* 20, no. 3 (Winter 1995/1996): 79–114.

43. Sumit Ganguly, "India's Pathway to Pokhran II: The Prospects and Sources of New Delhi's Nuclear Weapons Program," *International Security* 23, no. 4 (Spring 1999): 167.

44. Ashley Tellis, quoted in Neil Joeck, "Nuclear Developments in India and Pakistan," *Access Asia Review* 2, no. 2 (July 1999): 20.

45. Jaswant Singh, "Against Nuclear Apartheid," *Foreign Affairs* 77, no. 5 (September–October 1998): 44.

46. John Zubrzycki, "Hindu Nationalists Aim for Nuclear Arsenal," *The Australian*, February 4, 1998.

47. This account of the Kargil conflict draws on Devin T. Hagerty, "Kashmir and the Nuclear Question Revisited," in *Pakistan 2000*, ed. Charles H. Kennedy and Craig Baxter (Lanham, Md.: Lexington, 2000), 90–4.

48. John F. Burns, "In Brinkmanship's Wake, All Quiet on the Kashmir Front," *International Herald Tribune*, June 16, 1998.

49. Jonah Blank, "Kashmir: Fundamentalism Takes Root," *Foreign Affairs* 78, no. 6 (November–December 1999): 42.

50. John Lancaster, "US Defused Kashmir Crisis on Brink of War," *Washington Post*, July 26, 1999.

51. Harinder Baweja and Ramesh Vinayak, " Peak by Peak," *India Today International*, June 14, 1999, 17–21.

52. Michael Fathers, "On the Brink," *Time*, June 7, 1999, 48–49.

53. Lancaster, "US Defused Kashmir Crisis."

54. Raj Chengappa, "Will the War Spread?" *India Today International*, July 5, 1999, 14–17.

55. Raj Chengappa, "Face-Saving Retreat," *India Today International*, July 19, 1999, 16.

56. Raj Chengappa, "On High Ground," *India Today International*, June 28, 1999, 25.

57. Chengappa, "Face-Saving Retreat," 17.

58. Chengappa, "Will the War Spread?" 14.

59. Lancaster, "US Defused Kashmir Crisis."

60. Christopher Kremmer, "Outsiders Stoke the Flames of War," *Sydney Morning Herald*, June 26, 1999; "Pakistan Urges Fresh Peace Talks with India," *Reuters*, July 12, 1999.

61. K. Alan Kronstadt, "Pakistan–US Relations," *Issue Brief*, Congressional Research Service, Washington, D.C., October 28, 2002, 9.

62. For background on these groups, see Jessica Stern, "Pakistan's Jihad Culture," *Foreign Affairs* 79, no. 6 (November–December 2000): 115–26.

63. John Lancaster, "Pakistan to Follow India in Removing Troops from Border," *Washington Post*, October 18, 2002.

64. John Lancaster, "India to Remove Some Forces from Border with Pakistan," *Washington Post*, October 17, 2002. The oft-quoted figure of one million Indian and Pakistani soldiers facing off against one another included troops in Kashmir.

65. President Pervez Musharraf's Address to the Nation, January 12, 2002, available at www.pak.gov.pk/President_Addresses.

66. Steve Coll, "Between India and Pakistan, A Changing Role for the US," *Washington Post*, May 26, 2002.

67. Rahul Bedi and Anton La Guardia, "Pakistan Steps Back from Brink," *Daily Telegraph*, June 8, 2002.

68. "Infiltration of Terrorists into J&K Down by Half: Army Chief," *Hindustan Times*, November 8, 2002.

69. At www.odci.gov/cia/publications/factbook (accessed April 22, 2004).

70. See "Human Development Indicators 2003," available at http://hdr.undp.org/reports (accessed April 22, 2004).

71. Sumit Ganguly, "India's Foreign Policy Grows Up," *World Policy Journal* 20, no. 4 (Winter 2003/04).

FURTHER READING

de Bary, William Theodore, ed. *Sources of Indian Tradition.* New York: Columbia University Press, 1998.

Cohen, Stephen Philip. *India: Emerging Power.* Washington, D.C.: Brookings Institution Press, 2001.

Frankel, Francine R., et al., eds. *Transforming India: Social and Political Dynamics of Democracy.* New Delhi: Oxford University Press, 2000.

Ganguly, Sumit. *Conflict Unending: India–Pakistan Tensions since 1947.* New York: Columbia University Press, 2001.

Garver, John. *Protracted Contest: Sino-Indian Rivalry in the Twentieth Century.* Seattle: University of Washington Press, 2001.

Hagerty, Devin T. *The Consequences of Nuclear Proliferation: Lessons from South Asia.* Cambridge, Mass.: MIT Press, 1998.

Hodson, H. V. *The Great Divide: Britain, India, Pakistan.* Karachi: Oxford University Press, 1997.

McMahon, Robert J. *The Cold War on the Periphery: The United States, India, and Pakistan.* New York: Columbia University Press, 1994.

Mohan, C. Raja. *Crossing the Rubicon: The Shaping of India's New Foreign Policy.* New York: Palgrave Macmillan, 2004.

Perkovich, George. *India's Nuclear Bomb: The Impact on Global Proliferation.* Berkeley: University of California Press, 1999.

Watson, Francis, and Dilip Hiro. *India: A Concise History.* London: Thames and Hudson, 2002.

Wirsing, Robert G. *Kashmir in the Shadow of Nuclear War: Regional Rivalries in a Nuclear Age.* Armonk, N.Y.: M. E. Sharpe, 2003.

Wolpert, Stanley. *Nehru: A Tryst with Destiny.* New York: Oxford University Press, 1996.

2

Pakistan's Foreign Relations

Peter R. Lavoy[1]

Pakistan is sometimes accused of not having a complete, multidimensional foreign policy. All of Pakistan's relationships with foreign governments and international bodies are believed to revolve around its competition with one state: its immediate neighbor and long-time foe, India. This rivalry is said to hinge on a single dispute over the former princely state of Kashmir, the political status of which India and Pakistan have argued and fought over since their emergence as independent states in 1947. This accusation is only partially correct. Political and military competition with India is the centerpiece of Pakistan's foreign policy, and the Kashmir dispute lies near the heart of Pakistan's raison d'être and its competition with secular, but predominantly Hindu, India. But Pakistan's foreign policy is much more complex. Pakistan's unique history and its diverse population also influence its conduct of relations abroad.

Pakistan came into being as a democratic homeland for the Muslims of South Asia in August 1947, when the British ended their imperial rule of the Indian subcontinent. It was the first state in the world created in the name of Islam. Because of this founding ideology, and also because Islam is an international political interest, as well as a domestic, religious-communal matter for Pakistan, which has one of the world's largest Muslim populations, the promotion of Islamic values and ties abroad has been a key element of Pakistan's foreign policy. Believing that Pakistan's pro-Western policies and its nonradical outlook on Islam would have a moderating influence on other Islamic nations, the United States has encouraged Pakistan in its cultivation of strong foreign relationships throughout the Islamic world.

Although Pakistan's population is almost entirely Muslim, it is divided into five main ethnic/linguistic groups: Punjabis, Sindhis, Pashtuns, Baluchis, and *muhajirs* (the Indian Muslims who migrated to Pakistan when the Indian subcontinent was partitioned in 1947), all of whom share some identity and allegiance with groups in neighboring countries. The British created Pakistan's borders without regard to the traditional boundaries of local ethnic or tribal groups. Thus, Pakistan seeks in its foreign relations to prevent foreign states and social movements from stimulating or supporting separatist tendencies within its ethnically and tribally divided population. This chapter describes how Islamic nationalism, ethnic fragmentation, and the competition with India all shape Pakistan's approach to foreign policy and its most important international relationships.

COMPETITION WITH INDIA

As discussed in chapter 1, antipathy between Pakistan and India dates back to August 1947, when Britain partitioned its empire in India into two independent states. Partition had its roots in the political competition that marked the Indian independence struggle prior to 1947. As the likelihood of independence drew near, Mohammed Ali Jinnah and the Muslim League concluded that only a separate, democratic state in which Muslims would be a majority could protect Muslim interests in South Asia. Although predominantly Hindu, the leadership of the Indian National Congress under Jawaharlal Nehru (a secular-minded Hindu) sought the creation of a single state committed to a secular, democratic approach to government and opposed the creation of Pakistan. Faced with the prospect of increasingly bloody conflict between Hindus and Muslims, the British decided to form two independent states out of their former imperial domain.

More than one million migrants died during Partition, and many of the religious minorities remaining behind were treated poorly.[2] This poignant experience and the associated feelings of victimization remain a powerful influence on Pakistan's identity and its approach to the outside world to this day. Bitter memories of Partition are still etched in the minds of older Pakistanis, and even the young hold strong views because of jingoistic accounts passed down through state-controlled educational texts and the popular media. Many Pakistanis fear that Indians still reject the two-nation theory that led to Partition and ultimately will seek to undo Partition by reabsorbing Pakistan into India. New Delhi's support for the creation of Bangladesh, which had been the east wing of Pakistan, in 1971[3] reinforced the perception that elements of the Indian government, especially right-wing Hindu nationalists, want to reunify the Indian Empire under Indian control, or at least to turn Pakistan into a subservient protectorate.

By contrast, many Indians believe that Pakistan justifies its existence by vilifying India and therefore cannot live in peace with its stronger and more populous and prosperous neighbor. Partition's bitter legacy thus makes the

Indo-Pakistani relationship one of the world's most intractable rivalries. Moreover, because both India and Pakistan are vulnerable to communal and linguistic/ethnic fragmentation, each side lives in fear that the other will exploit its social cleavages to undermine the legitimacy of the state. This is the larger context in which bilateral disputes play out.

The specific dispute that has caused three out of four India–Pakistan wars and is a continuing source of tension was also a product of Partition, described in chapter 1. At independence in 1947, the princely states were not covered by the communal award of Partition. Kashmir, which had a Muslim-majority population but a Hindu ruler (or maharajah), shared borders with the two new nations. The Pakistani government coveted Kashmir to complete its identity as a homeland for the region's Islamic population, so when tribal Muslim militants from Pakistan's Northwest Frontier Province sought to "liberate" Kashmir from the maharajah's control, the Pakistan army rushed in to assist them. Coming under intense pressure from the invaders, the maharajah signed an instrument of accession with India. Unwilling to lose Kashmir, lest other religious and ethnic groups inside India press for their own autonomy, India sent in its armed forces to crush the tribal rebellion. War then broke out between India and Pakistan. When the fighting ended in 1948, Kashmir was divided, leaving India with the larger share of the state, including the picturesque Vale of Kashmir. Since then, Pakistan has tried various methods, from diplomacy to the direct use of force, to wrest the remainder of Kashmir from Indian control, but to no avail.

For the past fifteen years, a violent insurgency has ravaged Kashmir with Pakistan's support. Pakistan portrays it as a freedom movement, and India calls it state-sponsored terrorism by Pakistan. The truth probably lies somewhere in between these perspectives. Having claimed the lives of tens of thousands of Kashmiris, and more than once bringing India and Pakistan to the battlefield, the Kashmir issue has become an unstable, emotionally charged source of nuclear danger, now that both India and Pakistan have nuclear weapons.[4]

The Kashmir dispute is perilous because no matter how dangerous the threat of nuclear war has become, India and Pakistan appear unable to resolve the issue. Pakistan has welcomed either direct negotiations with India or third-party mediation, but New Delhi has refused to go along with what it sees as a Pakistani ploy to embarrass India and politicize what India deems to be a domestic or, at best, a bilateral issue. Concerned outsiders have over the years proposed several promising frameworks to bring India and Pakistan to the negotiating table, but neither country has been sincerely willing to abandon its hard-line position. The threat and actual use of force have been the dominant forms of "dialogue" between India and Pakistan on the Kashmir dispute, at least until very recently, when India and Pakistan agreed to reopen discussions. Historically, in order to compete politically and militarily with its stronger neighbor, Pakistan has turned to various sources of external support, most notably, the United States, China, Saudi Arabia, and, most recently, North Korea.

PAKISTAN'S ON-AGAIN, OFF-AGAIN
FRIENDSHIP WITH THE UNITED STATES

Pakistan's need for outside assistance to offset the perceived threat posed by India has made the United States Pakistan's most important foreign partner from the time of Partition to the present. During the Cold War, the U.S. government was eager to bring Pakistan into its network of regional security alliances. In 1954, for example, U.S. president Dwight D. Eisenhower considered South Asia to be "a major battleground in the cold war" and viewed Pakistan's membership in a regional anticommunist defense pact as "most desirable."[5]

Pakistani leaders had slightly different motivations for allying with the United States. They needed economic and military assistance, as well as political support in their competition with India. Although their security interests were not identical, they were compatible enough for the United States and Pakistan to sign a Mutual Defense Assistance Agreement in May 1954. A year later, Pakistan joined two of Washington's three most important regional defense alliances, the Southeast Asia Treaty Organization (SEATO) and the Baghdad Pact, which in 1958 evolved into the Central Treaty Organization (CENTO).[6] Between 1955 and 1965, Washington provided Pakistan with more than $700 million in military grant aid. U.S. economic assistance to Pakistan between 1947 and 2000 reached nearly $11.8 billion.[7]

Pakistan would have preferred to be the main focus of U.S. attention in South Asia, but the United States has always sought to have as close, or even closer, ties with India. In fact, balancing relations with India and Pakistan always has been an acute policy challenge for the United States. During the Cold War, the United States treated Pakistan as an important ally in the struggle against communism and supported it with plentiful military and economic aid, which India considered as a threat to its own security. During his visit to the White House in December 1956, Indian prime minister Jawaharlal Nehru privately told President Eisenhower that the very creation of Pakistan presented real problems for India and that he "never accepted the theory of the organization of states along religious lines."[8] He said that Pakistan's receipt of U.S. military assistance and its entry into SEATO and the Baghdad Pact compounded India's security problems by strengthening Pakistan's military capabilities, as well as its hard-line approach on Kashmir and other bilateral disputes.

Today, India opposes U.S. support to Pakistan on similar grounds. New Delhi believes that close U.S. ties to Pakistan, and especially U.S. security assistance to the Pakistan army, indirectly encourage Pakistan's strategy of "state-sponsored terrorism" against India.[9] Nevertheless, then as now, the United States pursued a relatively even-handed approach to relations with the two major powers of South Asia.

The Eisenhower administration tried to resolve this dilemma by pursuing one course of action for Pakistan and a separate track for India. Viewing Pakistan as a linchpin in its collective-security strategy and as a "moderating influence on the extreme nationalism and anti-Western attitudes of the Arab states," Washington continued the policy of military assistance and regional security planning with Pakistani leader Ayub Khan, who had engineered a bloodless military coup in 1958.[10] Nehru, an "utterly impractical statesman" in the view of U.S. secretary of state John Foster Dulles,[11] adamantly refused to enter into any U.S. collective-security scheme. Thus, the American strategy for India focused on strengthening that nation's democratic government and its mixed economy as counterweights to Chinese communism and as models for other developing nations in Asia. The key instruments in this strategy were economic and technical assistance, with an emphasis on projects and programs having the maximum potential to help India achieve its second five-year economic plan.

From 1960 through the late 1980s, the United States had on-again, off-again relations with Pakistan, even though the Pakistani military remained a strong bulwark against communism in South Asia. President John F. Kennedy favored a closer relationship with India and also sought to reduce Pakistan's military dependence on the United States. When Pakistan and India went to war in 1965, the United States suspended military assistance to both sides, a move that hurt Pakistan more because of its much greater dependence on U.S. support. When civil war erupted in East Pakistan in 1971 and soon triggered another India–Pakistan war, the United States again suspended aid to each country. But this time, Washington applied tremendous pressure to discourage New Delhi from attacking West Pakistan after its armed forces had prevailed in the east. U.S. president Richard Nixon not only wanted to protect his anti-Communist ally, he also valued the role Pakistan had played in the secret efforts of his National Security Advisor, Henry Kissinger, to establish diplomatic relations with Communist China. It was through the prism of this opening to Beijing, and simultaneous American maneuverings against Moscow, that Nixon and Kissinger viewed developments in South Asia in the early 1970s.[12]

In the mid-1970s, Pakistan sought to respond to India's 1974 "peaceful nuclear explosion" by seeking its own nuclear-weapons capability. This created a serious new challenge in its relations with the United States, which still has not been overcome. Washington resumed limited military assistance to Pakistan in 1975, but President Jimmy Carter suspended aid again in April 1979 because of Islamabad's construction of a covert uranium-enrichment facility at Kahuta. After the Soviet Union invaded Afghanistan in December 1979, the United States once again viewed Pakistan as a frontline state in the struggle to block Soviet expansionism and thus de-emphasized the nuclear factor in bilateral relations. In September 1981 President Ronald Reagan provided Pakistan with a $3.2 billion, five-year economic and military aid package. Pakistan became the primary conduit for U.S. arms supplies and covert support to the Afghan mujahideen.[13]

Despite the restoration of U.S. military aid and close security ties, many in Washington, especially in Congress, remained concerned about Pakistan's nuclear-weapons program. Because of mounting evidence that Pakistan had embarked upon a crash program to develop nuclear weapons, in 1985, the Pressler Amendment was added to the U.S. Foreign Assistance Act, requiring the president to certify to Congress that Pakistan does not possess a nuclear explosive device during the fiscal year for which aid is to be provided. This amendment represented a compromise between those in Congress who wanted to terminate aid to Pakistan because of evidence that it was continuing to develop its nuclear program and those who wished to reward Pakistan for its vital role in resisting the Soviet occupation of Afghanistan.[14]

After the Soviets pulled out of Afghanistan in 1989, Pakistan's continued nuclear progress again became the focus of U.S. policy attention. In October 1990 President Bush declined to certify that Pakistan was not in possession of a nuclear device; in other words, the United States cut off most economic and all military assistance to Islamabad. Also mandated under the Pressler Amendment was the suspension of all deliveries of major military equipment. Most notably, this resulted in the cancellation of some seventy-one F-16 fighter aircraft ordered by Pakistan in 1989.[15] As a consequence, Islamabad refocused its efforts toward nuclear-capable missile-delivery systems and promptly set out to conclude missile-assistance deals with China and North Korea.

PAKISTAN'S SUPPORT FOR OPERATION ENDURING FREEDOM

Al Qaeda's September 11, 2001, attacks against the United States fundamentally altered Pakistan's relations with the United States. The second Bush administration's campaign to destroy the Taliban as a haven for terrorist networks with global reach and to eliminate the al Qaeda network had a particularly dramatic impact on Pakistan, which had been the Taliban's strongest ally. Pakistan had helped the Taliban consolidate power in

Afghanistan in the mid to late 1990s. Viewing the Taliban as a friendly, if fanatical, regime that could stabilize Pakistan's often unruly Pashtun population and also provide much-needed "strategic depth" in Pakistan's military competition with India, Pakistani leaders were loath to see the return of instability, and possibly hostility, to their western flank. But faced with intense pressure from the United States, President Pervez Musharraf agreed to break relations with the Taliban, provide basing and overflight permission for U.S. and coalition forces, deploy a large number of troops along the Afghanistan border in support of Operation Enduring Freedom (OEF), and provide intelligence support to the international antiterrorism coalition. When he announced this controversial policy reversal on Afghanistan in a September 2001 speech to the nation, President Musharraf indicated that any other decision could have caused "unbearable losses" to the security of the country, the health of the economy, the Kashmir cause, and to Pakistan's strategic nuclear and missile assets.

While Pakistan's mainstream political parties generally supported the government's decision to join the international coalition against terrorism, the country's Islamist groups and parties were outraged. About two dozen religious parties, including the powerful Jamaat-e-Islami, which earlier had cooperated with the Musharraf government, came together under the umbrella of the Pak-Afghan Defense Council and launched a nationwide campaign to oust Musharraf. Strikes and street demonstrations occurred throughout the country, American flags were burned, several people were killed, and much property was destroyed. Truckloads of Pakistani extremists also traveled to Afghanistan to fight with the Taliban against the antiterrorism coalition. However, none of these actions managed to incite the Pakistani population against the government or persuade President Musharraf either to reverse his policies or to step down.

The Bush administration has provided strong support for President Musharraf and his government's efforts to maintain internal stability and implement much-needed political and economic reforms while assisting coalition forces in the war on terrorism. At the same time, Washington has been criticized for not providing the kind of economic and military assistance required to help Pakistan shore up its crippled economy and modernize its oft-sanctioned armed forces, which are about half the size of India's.[16] In reality, the economic benefits Washington already has provided to Pakistan are substantial: the United States waived all the sanctions imposed against Pakistan after its May 1998 nuclear tests and General Musharraf's October 1999 coup, rescheduled some of Pakistan's $38 billion external debt, and provided over $2 billion in economic support and security assistance, including a $600 million Economic Support Funds grant, over $30 million in agriculture support, and $75 million in foreign military financing.

Washington has not yet offered the kind of military-assistance package that many observers had expected (including renewed F-16 fighter aircraft sales) because it has not wanted to aggravate the Indo-Pakistani military standoff that seethed for most of 2002 and also because it wished to work out mutually agreeable requirements for the forthcoming arms transfers. However, U.S. under secretary of defense for policy Douglas Feith, who led a forty-four-member U.S. Defense Cooperation Group (DCG) team to Pakistan in late September 2002, affirmed that the Bush administration would soon restore military assistance and arms sales "to boost Islamabad's military capabilities."[17] The DCG, which met for the first time since 1997, also agreed on other important steps to enhance bilateral defense ties, including new military education and training exchanges, military exercises, and enhanced cooperation in countering terrorism.[18] In June 2003 President George W. Bush pledged to seek a five-year, $3 billion aid package for Pakistan to begin in 2005.[19]

CHINA: A RELIABLE ALLY

China and Pakistan forged a close relationship in 1960, a remarkable feat considering that Pakistan was an active participant in the U.S.-led system of anticommunist alliances. The United States had put strong pressure on Pakistan to oppose Communist China on all fronts, but when Washington moved closer to India in the late 1950s, Pakistani leaders reached out to Beijing (and, to a lesser extent, Moscow), in part to reduce their dependence on the United States. Beijing responded favorably to these overtures. "After the formation of SEATO in 1954," Chinese prime minister Zhao Enlai revealed several years later, "the Pakistan Government often declared to the Chinese Government that its participation in that organization was not for the purpose of being hostile to China and would not prejudice Pakistan's friendship for China."[20] The Chinese understood that Pakistan's main interest in aligning with the West was to gain support for its military competition with India. Thus, Pakistan and China established a stable friendship around a common concern about India. Although the Chinese refused Pakistan's request for direct support on the Kashmir dispute, Zhao did affirm that "China accepted the existence of the Kashmir dispute and hoped that it would be settled peacefully."[21]

After boundary tensions intensified between India and China in 1960, Pakistani leader Ayub Khan became concerned about the threat Communist China posed to Pakistan's northern areas. But he also saw this as a golden opportunity to settle Pakistan's own border issues with Beijing and to enlist Chinese support to help it induce Indian concessions on Kashmir.[22] In early 1961

Pakistani and Chinese diplomats began negotiations over the demarcation of the border in Pakistan-controlled Kashmir. In May 1962 they announced a provisional boundary agreement. Although this pact was not supposed to prejudice the eventual settlement of the Kashmir dispute, the Indian government protested China's recognition of Pakistan's control of Gilgit, Hunza, and Baltistan districts in northern Kashmir.[23]

Indian officials became even more upset when Chinese and Pakistani officials finalized a boundary agreement in March 1963. Pakistan ceded more than two thousand square miles of Kashmir's territory to China in this pact. Foreign Minister Zulfiqar Ali Bhutto declared to Pakistan's National Assembly in 1963 that Pakistan could now rely on Chinese assistance in the event of another India–Pakistan war. "If India were in her frustration to turn her guns against Pakistan," Bhutto stated, "the international situation is such that Pakistan would not be alone in the conflict."[24] From this point onward, Indian defense planners would have to take Chinese political support and even the possibility of Chinese military intervention into consideration in their efforts to deal with Pakistan.

China has been a major arms supplier to Pakistan since the 1960s. It has helped Pakistan establish several factories for manufacturing arms and provided aircraft and other weapons systems. In the 1980s and 1990s, Pakistan turned to China for assistance in developing nuclear weapons and ballistic missiles. It is now known that in the early 1990s China secretly delivered thirty-four M-11 short-range ballistic missiles to Pakistan, an act that led the United States to impose sanctions on Chinese entities. In 1993 the Clinton administration determined that China again had transferred to Pakistan prohibited M-11 missile technology (not complete missiles) and imposed trade sanctions on one Pakistani and eleven Chinese entities (including government ministries and aerospace companies). Although China is not a member of the Missile Technology Control Regime (MTCR), Beijing has indicated that it will abide by the export restrictions of that regime. Nonetheless, numerous reports in the Western media concern China's continued support for Pakistan's missile program, including for Pakistan's new Shaheen-1 short-range ballistic missile and its Shaheen-2 medium-range ballistic missile.[25]

China's support for Pakistan's nuclear-weapons program appears to have been just as substantial. Although media reports of Chinese assistance to Pakistan in the design and testing of nuclear explosive devices have not been confirmed, U.S. government officials have indicated that Beijing has transferred critical technologies and industrial components for Pakistan's uranium-enrichment program. In particular, leaked U.S. intelligence reports alleged that in the mid-1990s China sold ring magnets, a special industrial furnace, and high-tech diagnostic equipment to Pakistan, all of which Islamabad required to produce weapons-grade uranium and to convert this material into nuclear explosives. Pakistan and China have denied these reports, and the U.S. government decided not to levy sanctions after it reached a 1996 under-standing with China about future nuclear-export controls. Even after China pledged in 1996 not to "provide assistance to unsafeguarded nuclear facili-ties," new allegations surfaced of Chinese help in the construction of an un-safeguarded plutonium-production reactor at Khushab. Although China has acted as a moderating force on Pakistan's foreign policy—for example, urg-ing Pakistan to withdraw its forces from Indian-held Kashmir after Pakistani soldiers occupied dozens of mountain posts on India's side of the Kashmir line of control in the 1999 Kargil conflict—its support for Pakistan's strate-gic-weapons programs cannot be denied.[26]

NORTH KOREA: A FRIEND IN NEED

Apart from Saudi Arabia, discussed below, North Korea is the other country that Pakistan has turned to for limited support in its military competition with India. Although Pakistan and North Korea have no meaningful political or ideological ties, their relations date back over thirty years to the period when then prime minister Zulfiqar Ali Bhutto sought to reduce Pakistan's reliance on the United States and improve its relations with the socialist world. In the past, Islamabad and Pyongyang engaged in a very limited conventional arms trade and then worked together closely during the Iran-Iraq war, when they both provided assistance to Iran. Their recent strategic cooperation appears to have been initiated by Pakistan in the early 1990s as part of its effort to build a missile force after the termination of U.S. aircraft deliveries under the Pressler Amendment.

With the short-range M-11 missiles already in its inventory, Pakistan sought a longer-range missile capable of delivering nuclear warheads to major India cities, such as New Delhi and Mumbai. The North Korean No Dong, flight-tested in 1993, was well suited to Pakistan's needs. Western analysts assess that Pyongyang transferred components or possibly even complete missile-assembly sets for one to two dozen of the liquid-propellant, fifteen-hundred-kilometer range, nuclear-capable missiles.[27] After allegations appeared in the Western me-dia in October 2002 that Pakistan had paid for these missile deliveries with as-sistance to North Korea's then secret uranium-enrichment program, Pakistani of-ficials insisted that they paid cash for whatever missile aid they received from Pyongyang. Islamabad also has denied providing any nuclear assistance to North Korea, a claim that subsequently has been disproved as a result of the late 2003 and early 2004 revelations about illicit nuclear-technology transfers to Iran, Libya, and North Korea by the notorious Pakistani nuclear official, Abdul Qadeer Khan.

MUSLIM NATIONALISM

The unique circumstances that brought Pakistan into being continue to play an important role in shaping its national identity and foreign relations. Preindependence Indian Muslims sought self-determination and an end to European rule. Whereas this expression took the familiar form of territorial, linguistic, and racial nationalism seen among other Islamic peoples, Indian Muslims were just as eager to prevent the more numerous Hindus from replacing the British as their political masters. So Pakistan was established as an independent nation-state for South Asian Muslims to govern themselves. Muslim nationalism became much more than a nationalist ideology; over time, it became a rallying cry for Islamic solidarity and Muslim causes all over the world.

In the years following Pakistani independence, the government earned international respect for its promotion of Islamic causes, such as the national-liberation struggles of Algeria, Indonesia, Libya, Morocco, and other Muslim nationalist groups in Africa and Southeast Asia. However, Pakistan's sometimes amateurish efforts to be seen as a leader of the Islamic world upset some countries that saw themselves as more fitting international leaders or that did not place as much political emphasis on Islam as a political force. For example, King Farouq of Egypt, who generally had emphasized Arab nationalism over political Islam, made fun of Pakistan's tendency to equate Islam with its own national independence. Even though Pakistan lobbied aggressively in the United Nations for Indonesian independence, Indonesia's first president, Soekarno, turned out to be more supportive of Jawaharlal Nehru's India because of their common attachment to secularism and nonalignment. After Nehru died in 1964, though, Soekarno moved away from India and supported Pakistan in the 1965 India–Pakistan war. Just seven days after that war ended, Soekarno was removed from power, and his successor, Suharto, broke ties with Communist China and distanced Indonesia from Pakistan.

Pakistan enjoyed good relations with Iran and Turkey, and at U.S. urging joined together with these countries and with Iraq to form the Baghdad Pact, a security grouping that became CENTO after Iraq's withdrawal. While Pakistan benefited from this alliance, especially in the form of military assistance from the United States, the Baghdad Pact created serious tension in Pakistani relations with Saudi Arabia, which had a dynastic feud with Iraq and a separate rivalry with non-Arab Iran. In an important sense, this period witnessed the failure of Pakistan's idealistic policy of Islamic internationalism. Competing national interests among Muslim nations were too intense for the common bond of religion to resolve them or render them meaningless. Nevertheless, in 1964 Pakistan, Iran, and Turkey strengthened their political and economic collaboration in a regional arrangement called the Regional Cooperation for Development (RCD), an organization that was renamed the Economic Cooperation Organization (ECO) in 1984 after the RCD was disbanded in 1979 with the overthrow of Shah Muhammad Reza Pahlavi's government in Iran. Today, there are new strains in Pakistan's relationships with Turkey, Iran, and Saudi Arabia.

TURKEY

Pakistan has no serious dispute with Turkey, but the latter's self-identification as a secular, European country and its close relations with Israel have increased the distance between the two countries, especially in recent years. As the dominant political institutions in their respective nations, the Turkish and Pakistani armed forces have much in common and cooperate closely in military training and education. However, while the Turkish army takes a dim view of all manifestations of Islamic orthodoxy, Pakistani army leaders have been willing to cooperate with, and sometimes eager to cultivate, domestic Islamic political parties and social movements. With the gradual rise in violence committed by political activists and terrorist organizations in the name of Islam, this tension between Pakistan and Turkey has grown.

In the realm of foreign relations, the fall of the Soviet Union has turned Turkey and Pakistan into respectful competitors for influence in Central Asia. Because it shares ethnic origins with the six new Islamic states of Central Asia, Turkey has sought to play a leading role in this region. However, Pakistan, too, has tried to increase its influence in this region, which historically has been the source of significant security threats to South Asia.[28]

Pakistan and Turkey have had even more disagreement over the fate of Afghanistan. Turkey, like the states of Central Asia, was troubled by the rise of the Taliban and the potential for Islamic fundamentalism to spread throughout the area. Because of its own security compulsions, the Pakistan government helped bring the Taliban to power and was their greatest supporter before turning against them under heavy American pressure after the terrorist attacks of September 2001. Today, Pakistan and Turkey, along with Iran, India, the United States, and several other countries, are jockeying for influence in the ongoing struggle to shape Afghanistan's political future.

IRAN

Iran has played a very important role in Pakistan's foreign policy, not only because it is a neighbor but also because of its close historical, ethnic, religious, and political ties with the people of Pakistan. In addition, a stable Pakistan–Iran relationship is crucial for Islamabad because of its military competition with India. In the event of another India–Pakistan war, a hostile Iran could require Islamabad to draw its troops from the Indian front to defend the western border with Iran, a development that could spell disaster for Pakistan's defense planners. Iran also has valued defense cooperation with Pakistan, which during the 1950s and 1960s had a larger military and a slightly more advanced defense industry. Pakistan also served as a valuable non-Arab Muslim ally in Iran's age-old rivalry with the Arab world. As Iran amassed tremendous wealth in the oil boom of the 1970s, the power balance shifted decidedly in favor of Iran. The shah treated Pakistan as a junior partner. Although the shah's condescending attitude ruffled the feathers of Pakistani political leaders and diplomats, relations remained relatively stable while the shah was in power, in part because the Pakistani government needed all the support it could get in its intense rivalry with India.

The Iranian revolution had a major impact on Pakistani-Iranian relations. Iran's new revolutionary leaders placed Islam at the forefront of their internal as well as international behavior. This approach had a certain appeal in Pakistan, which became the first country to recognize the new Iranian revolutionary government. However, Tehran generally did not return Pakistan's many expressions of friendship. The revolutionary regime distrusted Pakistan because of its former ties to the shah and its ongoing relationship with Iran's nemesis, the United States. Iran, which is predominantly a Shia Muslim nation, also objected to the manner in which Pakistan treated its Shia minority population and began playing an active role in support of the Shia cause inside Pakistan. In order to counter Iran's growing regional power, Saudi Arabia, a conservative Sunni nation, increased its own support to Pakistan's majority Sunni population. The result has been a dramatic increase in sectarian tensions inside Pakistan, which often have erupted in violence. Today, Pakistan seeks to reduce Iranian interference in its internal affairs and also inside Afghanistan, where the two countries support opposing powers, all while trying to maintain correct and cooperative relations with Tehran for diplomatic and strategic reasons.

SAUDI ARABIA

Along with the United States and China, Saudi Arabia is Pakistan's closest and oldest friend. Relations with the Saudi monarchy have not always been smooth, but they extend deeply into the religious, political, economic, and defense spheres. As the custodian of Islam's two holiest cities, a generous provider of many of Pakistan's mosques and religious schools, and a source of income for tens of thousands of visiting Pakistani workers, Saudi Arabia has won the appreciation and respect of the Pakistani people. However, government-to-government relations have been less stable, especially in the early years.

Saudi Arabia and other Arab nations welcomed Pakistan's formation in 1947, but the idea of partition along religious lines was anathema in most other Muslim lands where nationalism, not Islam, was the salient political issue and unifying force. Muslim nations in the Middle East, which had their own divisions and rivalries, also resented Pakistan's attempts to unify the world's Islamic population. As noted above, Pakistan's entry into the Baghdad Pact aggravated Saudi Arabia because of the Riyadh government's enduring rivalries with Iraq and Iran. In a 1955 broadcast, the Saudi government–operated Radio Mecca called Pakistan's act "a stab in the heart of the Arab and Muslim states."[29] Pakistan's decision to join the U.S.-backed security grouping also upset more radical Arab states, such as Egypt, which opposed any relationship with Israel's protector, the United States.

When Pakistan experienced a downturn in relations with the United States in the late 1950s and early 1960s, it moved to diversity its foreign relations, cultivating a friendship with China and restoring ties with the Arab world. These efforts paid off. Saudi Arabia lent Pakistan seventy-five military aircraft in the 1971 war with India, and Jordan sent another ten planes. Pakistan placed even greater emphasis on relations with the Muslim world under the leadership of Zulfikar Ali Bhutto. Although Bhutto's socialist leanings (and extravagant lifestyle) initially disturbed the conservative Saudis, relations improved after he hosted the second Islamic Summit in February 1974, visited Saudi Arabia four times, and in 1976 lavishly hosted a visit of Saudi Arabia's King Khalid, who subsequently financed the King Faisal Mosque and Islamic Center in Islamabad.[30]

Bhutto also established a strong economic relationship with the Saudi kingdom. Since the early 1970s, more than two million Pakistanis have gone to work as doctors, pilots, soldiers, and policemen, as well as in other occupations, in Saudi Arabia and the other Persian Gulf monarchies. Saudi Arabia and neighboring Muslim countries have become the largest market for Pakistani exports. Oil remittances exceeded $2 million annually from Saudi Arabia, the United Arab Emirates (UAE), and other Middle Eastern countries at the end of Bhutto's reign. With the stabilization of oil prices, much of the Saudi aid has dried up, but thousands of Pakistanis still work in the gulf and send their earnings home to their families in Pakistan. The loss of remittances caused by the 1991 Persian Gulf War was a serious problem for Pakistan, but the situation improved after the war.

In the past, Pakistan assisted in the defense of several Arab states, supplying both officers and enlisted troops. When Zulfiqar Ali Bhutto was Pakistan's leader, ten thousand Pakistani soldiers were deployed to Saudi Arabia alone; many more were sent to Kuwait, Iraq, Oman, the UAE, and Libya. Under Bhutto's successor, Gen. Zia ul-Haq, the number of Pakistani troops sent to the Middle East was doubled. In exchange, these wealthy Arab countries financed many of Pakistan's arms purchases from the United States and Europe. Pakistan's relations with Saudi Arabia and the Persian Gulf states became strained during the 1990–1991 crisis in the gulf. Although a member of the U.S.-led international coalition, Pakistan played only a limited role, sending a force of eleven thousand troops to "protect" religious sites in Saudi Arabia. Moreover, during the conflict a vocal segment of public opinion in Pakistan called for the ouster of the Kuwaiti monarch and approved of Saddam Hussein's resistance against the United States. To make matters worse, Pakistan's army chief, Gen. Mirza Aslam Beg, also expressed support for Iraq, resulting in further embarrassment for the government of Benazir Bhutto. Following the first Gulf war, Pakistan undertook diplomatic efforts to restore its relationships in the region. In addition, many Pakistani expatriate workers returned to their jobs, and cooperative defense training activities resumed. As a result, Pakistan largely restored its position as an influential player in the Middle East.

Today Saudi Arabia no longer depends on Pakistan to counter the threats posed by Israel, Iran, and Iraq, but Saudi-Pakistani defense ties have grown in new areas. Pakistan continues to train and conduct joint exercises with the Saudi, UAE, Kuwaiti, Bahraini, and Qatari militaries. In 2001 Saudi Arabia and Pakistan initiated a joint project to manufacture light arms and ammunition. In 2002 Saudi Arabia provided nearly $400,000 to support Pakistan's military research and development. Beyond this conventional military cooperation, there have been unconfirmed media reports that Saudi Arabia (together with Libya) financed a large part of Pakistan's nuclear-weapons and missile programs.[31]

There are also unconfirmed reports that Pakistan at some time might cooperate to help Saudi Arabia replace its aging arsenal of Chinese-supplied CSS-2 ballistic missiles and possibly provide nuclear warheads to go along with a new generation of missiles.[32] However, as long as the United States maintains close ties with both Pakistan and Saudi Arabia, these countries are not likely to engage in any military behavior that would seriously jeopardize their friendship with Washington. But if the United States were to pull away from Pakistan or Saudi Arabia, cooperation on strategic weaponry between the two cannot be ruled out. President Pervez Musharraf stated in June 2002, "When Pakistan faces any problem, Saudi Arabia is the first shelter to which Pakistan turns." If the United States is no longer willing to support Pakistan in its perennial competition with India, Saudi Arabia might attempt to play such a role.

ETHNIC FRAGMENTATION

Apart from seeking support for its abiding competition with India and trying to gain influence in the Islamic world, the other major factor that has
shaped Pakistan's international relationships over the years has been the
need to discourage outside parties from exacerbating Pakistan's deep internal divisions. Already noted above is Islamabad's heightened interest in reducing Saudi and Iranian support for the country's Sunni and Shia Muslim
populations, which in the past has triggered widespread sectarian unrest and
violence.

Of even greater concern to the Pakistani government is maintenance of the
unity of Pakistan's diverse ethnic groups. After all, ethnic fragmentation
played a major part in the dismemberment of the country in 1971. Probably
the greatest fear of Pakistan's current leadership is a repeat of the centrifugal
process that led to the loss of East Pakistan. Three major ethnic groups exist
under the domination of the Punjabi government and military elite: Sindhis,
Baluchis, and Pashtuns.[33] Each of these groups has pressed for increased autonomy at one time or another in Pakistan's history. As a result, much of Pakistan's current foreign policy is oriented toward preventing the revival of
these separatist impulses.

SINDHUDESH AND INDIA

Ethnic tensions in the province of Sindh first appeared at the time of Partition,
when thousands of Indian Muslims moved to the city of Karachi and surrounding urban areas. These *muhajirs*, most of whom spoke Urdu, a language
not spoken in the part of British India that became Pakistan, maintained their
own customs and refused to learn the Sindhi language. Because the migrants
were often better educated and wealthier than the local population, ethnic tensions flared over the competition for jobs and other precious resources. Sindhi
resentment and discontent intensified when Urdu was made the national language of Pakistan, the federal capital was relocated from Karachi to the new
city of Islamabad, and Zulfiqar Ali Bhutto, Sindh's most famous politician,
was ousted in a bloodless coup, then tried and executed by his handpicked
army chief, Gen. Zia ul-Haq. Separatist sentiments peaked in the early 1980s
when the Sindhi Movement for the Restoration of Democracy, chafing under
Zia's dictatorship, demanded greater provincial autonomy and more equitable
distribution of federal funds, jobs, and other resources. In the 1990s, the rivalry between Sindhi and *muhajir* groups turned violent and claimed over
five thousand lives.[34]

Islamabad generally has handled Sindhi separatist demands and Sindhi-*muhajir* violence as domestic law-and-order matters. However, Pakistani defense planners are aware that India could fan ethnic tensions in Sindh as part of an overall military campaign to destabilize the country and possibly to separate Sindh from the rest of Pakistan. It was with this threat in mind that Gen. Khalid Kidwai, director of Pakistan's Strategic Plans Division, the military organization created in 1999 to oversee the development and employment of nuclear weapons, told a pair of Italian researchers that Pakistan might resort to the use of nuclear weapons "if the very existence of Pakistan as a state is at stake." General Kidwai identified four conditions in which nuclear use might be contemplated, one of which was if "India pushes Pakistan into political destabilization or creates a large-scale internal subversion in Pakistan."[35] The Pakistan leadership's sensitivity to the reemergence of Sindhi separatism is a subtle, but important, military consideration in its relationship with India.

BALUCHISTAN AND IRAN

Baluchistan, Pakistan's poorest and most rugged province, was the scene of a violent separatist struggle in the 1970s. Baluchistan occupies more than half of Pakistan's land area, but it has the smallest population of any province. Tensions were sparked by Prime Minister Bhutto's attempt to wrest power from local tribal leaders, who for ages had exercised authority in the very traditional region regardless of who held power to the east, the Mughals, the British, or the Pakistanis. Although Bhutto sent in one hundred thousand Pakistani soldiers to subdue the secessionists, stability did not return to Baluchistan until Bhutto's successor, Gen. Zia ul-Haq, restored the authority of the region's tribal leaders.

Complicating matters during the Baluch separatist struggle was the attempt by local tribal leaders to link up with neighboring Baluch tribes in Iran to form an autonomous region cutting across the Iran–Pakistan border. Although the Shah of Iran refused to grant the Baluch tribes autonomy inside his own country, he did threaten Bhutto that unless Pakistan cooperated on other bilateral matters, he would provide assistance to Baluch separatists inside Pakistan. Perhaps even more disconcerting to Islamabad was the covert campaign initiated by the Soviet Union to support the Baluch secessionist movement.[36] Although Pakistani forces have gained greater control over Baluchistan as part of their cooperation with the U.S. military to track down elusive Taliban and al Qaeda terrorists in this area, the possibility that the Tehran government might again try to incite Baluch separatist feelings cannot be ruled out and remains a key concern in Pakistan's foreign relations with Iran.

PASHTUNISTAN AND AFGHANISTAN

The movement for an independent nation of Pashtunistan has been by far the most difficult ethnic challenge for Pakistani authorities to control. It predates Pakistan's independence and is intimately related to the tribal loyalties of the Pashtun people, who are scattered across Pakistan's Northwest Frontier Province and in the southern and western regions of Afghanistan. Pashtun nationalist sentiments were kindled in 1893, when the British drew the Durand Line, arbitrarily dividing the Pashtun tribes between Afghanistan and what was then British India. The rulers of Afghanistan, who were predominantly Pashtun, objected to what they considered to be a confiscation of a vital part of their domain. Consequently, successive Afghan governments have sought to stir up tribal loyalties and press for Pashtun autonomy across the Durand Line, which now demarcates the Pakistan–Afghanistan border.[37]

Pashtun separatism died down during the 1980s when the Soviets occupied Afghanistan and Pakistan assisted the mujahideen effort to oust them. It remained quiet in subsequent years when tribal warlords fought each other for control over Afghanistan. Viewing the chaos across the border as an opportunity to exert its influence and prevent the Pashtun issue from reemerging, the Pakistani government, through the military's Inter-Services Intelligence (ISI) directorate, helped bring the Taliban to power in the mid-1990s and backed their struggle to assert control over the entire fragmented country. Although the Taliban were becoming increasingly difficult to manage, Pakistan continued to support them until September 11, 2001, and the subsequent U.S. war in Afghanistan.

Today Pakistan's influence in Afghanistan is considerably diminished. Although Pakistan's leadership supports the American-led effort to restore unity and stability to Afghanistan, it fears that if that country again disintegrates, it will have to deal not only with renewed calls for the creation of a Pashtun homeland but also with the reality of Iranian and Indian intervention to bring anti-Pakistan elements to power in Afghanistan. Such a development would pose grave political problems for Islamabad. It also could present Pakistan's defense planners with the unenviable challenge of having to fight a two-front war in the event of another military conflict with India. For these reasons, Pakistan's foreign relations with Afghanistan are perhaps every bit as important to Islamabad as those with India, the United States, China, Iran, and Saudi Arabia.

CONCLUSION

Pakistan's political and military competition with India is the centerpiece of its foreign policy, but it is by no means the only concern that influences Islamabad's relations with the outside world. Pakistan's unique history as a homeland for the Muslims of South Asia and its diverse ethnic and sectarian population also have shaped its conduct abroad. Because Pakistan has always felt vulnerable to its much larger neighbor to the east, a country that never fully accepted the two-nation theory that led to the creation of Pakistan, Pakistani political and military leaders have looked to the West, and the United States in particular, for support in their strategic rivalry with India. However, when Western support was not forthcoming, or when it failed to meet the expectations of Pakistan's leadership, Islamabad has turned to other countries for diplomatic and military assistance, most notably, China, Saudi Arabia, and North Korea. These relationships in turn have complicated Pakistan's ties with the West. Although Pakistan's foreign relations are sometimes perceived in the West as troublesome, and occasionally even dangerous, it is clearly in the political and military interest of the United States and other Western powers to maintain strong bilateral ties with Pakistan.

NOTES

1. The author alone is responsible for the information and views contained in this chapter. They do not represent the positions of the Naval Postgraduate School or the U.S. Department of Defense.

2. Stanley A. Wolpert, *A New History of India*, 6th ed. (New York: Oxford University Press, 1999), 348.

3. For a comprehensive history of the Bangladesh conflict, see Richard Sisson and Leo E. Rose, *War and Secession: Pakistan, India, and the Creation of Bangladesh* (Berkeley: University of California Press, 1990).

4. For a longer, more detailed treatment of the Kashmir conflict, see Victoria Schofield, *Kashmir in Conflict: India, Pakistan and the Unending War* (London: I. B. Tauris, 2003).

5. U.S. National Security Council (NSC), "U.S. Policy toward South Asia," NSC 5409, February 19, 1954, 1, 5. Digital National Security Archives (DNSA), no. PD0039.

6. SEATO and CENTO are now defunct; but Washington's other regional security alliance, the North Atlantic Treaty Organization (NATO) continues to modernize and expand.

7. K. Alan Kronstadt, "Pakistan–U.S. Relations," *Issue Brief*, Congressional Research Service, September 3, 2003, 1.

8. Dwight D. Eisenhower, "Memorandum of Conversations with Prime Minister Nehru of India," December 17–18, 1956, 8, Declassified Documents Reference System (DDRS), no. CK3100184553.

9. Peter R. Lavoy, "Fighting Terrorism and Avoiding War in South Asia: The Indo-Pakistani Situation," *Joint Forces Quarterly* no. 32 (Autumn 2002): 27–34.

10. NSC, "U.S. Policy toward South Asia," NSC 5701, January 10, 1957, 5. DNSA, no. PD00492. See also Dennis Kux, *The United States and Pakistan, 1947–2000: Disenchanted Allies* (Baltimore: Johns Hopkins University Press, 2001), 51–85.

11. Minutes of June 1, 1953, NSC meeting, in U.S. Department of State, *Foreign Relations of the United States, 1952–54*, vol. 9, pt. 1 (Washington, D.C.: U.S. Government Printing Office, 1986), 147.

12. President Nixon told Joseph Farland, the U.S. ambassador to Pakistan, that he was deeply troubled by the prospect of an Indian-Pakistani war "not only for its intrinsic tragedy and danger but also because it could disrupt our steady course in our policy toward China." Henry Kissinger, "President's Meeting with Ambassador Joseph Farland," memorandum for the President's file, July 28, 1971, document no. 18, contained in *The Tilt: The U.S. and the South Asian Crisis of 1971*, National Security Archive Electronic Briefing Book No. 79, ed. Sajit Gandhi, December 16, 2002, available at www.gwu.edu/~nsarchiv/NSAEBB/NSAEBB79.

13. Kux, *The United States and Pakistan*, 256–57.

14. Kronstadt, "Pakistan-U.S. Relations," 2.

15. In December 1998, the United States finally put the F-16 dispute to rest by agreeing to pay Pakistan $324.6 million from the U.S. Treasury Judgment Fund and to supply Pakistan with $140 million in goods, including agricultural commodities. Kronstadt, "Pakistan-U.S. Relations," 2.

16. India has a 2:1 advantage in manpower, armor, artillery, and combat aircraft; it has an even greater advantage in naval vessels and aircraft. See Anthony H. Cordesman, "The Asian Conventional Military Balance in 2002: South Asia," Center for Strategic and International Studies, February 26, 2002, available at www.csis.org/burke/mb/index.htm.

17. "U.S. to Restore Military Aid Soon," *The News International* (Islamabad), September 28, 2002.

18. The DCG met again in September 2003 and agreed to a new series of military-to-military exercises and training activities to "broaden and deepen existing bilateral military cooperation, and provide new opportunities to gain greater interoperability and familiarization." Joint Statement on U.S.-Pakistan Defense Consultative Group, September 24, 2003, available at www .defenselink.mil/releases.

19. White House Office of the Press Secretary, "Bilateral Multi-Year Assistance: U.S. and Pakistan," June 24, 2003, available at www.state.gov/p/sa/rls.

20. *Pakistan Times*, April 11, 1963.

21. Cited in Rosemary Foot, "Sources of Conflict between China and India as Seen from Beijing," in *Mending Fences: Confidence and Security-Building Measures in South Asia*, ed. Sumit Ganguly and Ted Greenwood (Boulder, Colo.: Westview, 1996), 61.

22. Roger Hilsman, director, State Department Bureau of Intelligence and Research, to Secretary of State Dean Rusk, "The Five-Fold Dilemma: The Implications of the Sino-Indian Conflict," memorandum, November 17, 1962, 23, DDRS, no. CK3100373873.

23. For background, see W. M. Dobell, "Ramification of the China–Pakistan Border Treaty," *Pacific Affairs* 37, no. 3 (Autumn 1964): 283–95, and Pervaiz Iqbal Cheema, *Pakistan's Defence Policy, 1947–58* (New York: St. Martin's, 1990), 54–57.

24. Cited in Dobell, "Ramification of the China-Pakistan Border Treaty," 291.

25. Shirley A. Kan, "China and Proliferation of Weapons of Mass Destruction and Missiles: Policy Issues," *Congressional Research Service Report*, August 8, 2003.

26. Kan, "China and Proliferation of Weapons of Mass Destruction and Missiles."

27. Sharon A. Squassoni, "Weapons of Mass Destruction: Trade between North Korea and Pakistan," *Congressional Research Service Report*, May 7, 2003.

28. Shahid M. Amin, *Pakistan's Foreign Policy: A Reappraisal* (Karachi: Oxford University Press, 2000), 130–1.

29. S. M. Burke, *Pakistan's Foreign Policy: An Historical Analysis*, 2nd. ed. (Karachi: Oxford University Press, 1990), 204.

30. See Stanley Wolpert, *Zulfi Bhutto of Pakistan* (Oxford: Oxford University Press, 1993).

31. According to documents produced in 1994 by a prominent defector from the Saudi government, Riyadh had financed much of Pakistan's nuclear-weapons program up to that point. In return, Pakistan reportedly agreed to come to Saudi Arabia's aid with nuclear weapons if the

gulf kingdom were ever attacked with nuclear weapons. See GlobalSecurity.org, "Saudi Arabia Special Weapons," available at www.globalsecurity.org/wmd/world/saudi.

32. Richard L. Russell, "A Saudi Nuclear Option?" *Survival* 43, no. 2 (Summer 2001): 69–79.

33. The *muhajirs*, the Urdu-speaking Indian Muslims who migrated to Pakistan at the time of Partition, are the country's fifth major ethnic group; but they are not discussed here because they have never sought to separate from Pakistan and form their own nation.

34. For background, see Craig Baxter, Yogendra K. Malik, Charles H. Kennedy, and Robert C. Oberst, *Government and Politics in South Asia*, 5th ed. (Boulder, Colo.: Westview, 2002), 216–19, and Charles Kennedy, "The Politics of Ethnicity in Sindh," *Asian Survey* 31, no. 10 (October 1991): 938–55.

35. See Paolo Cotta-Ramusino and Maurizio Martellini, "Nuclear Safety, Nuclear Stability and Nuclear Strategy in Pakistan," *Concise Report of a Visit by Landau Network—Centro Volta*, January 21, 2002, available at http://lxmi.mi.infn.it/~landnet.

36. For background, see Selig S. Harrison, *In Afghanistan's Shadow: Baluch Nationalism and Soviet Temptations* (Washington, D.C.: Carnegie Endowment for International Peace, 1980).

37. For background, see Leon B. Poullada, "Pushtunistan: Afghan Domestic Politics and Relations with Pakistan," in *Pakistan's Western Borderlands*, ed. Ainslee T. Embree (Delhi: Vikas, 1977, 1985), 126–51.

FURTHER READING

Amin, Shahid M. *Pakistan's Foreign Policy: A Reappraisal.* Karachi: Oxford University Press, 2000.

Baxter, Craig, Yogendra K. Malik, Charles H. Kennedy, and Robert C. Oberst. *Government and Politics in South Asia.* 5th ed. Boulder, Colo.: Westview, 2002.

Bennett Jones, Owen. *Pakistan: Eye of the Storm.* New Haven, Conn.: Yale University Press, 2002.

bin Sayeed, Khalid. *Pakistan: The Formative Phase, 1947–1948.* Karachi: Oxford University Press, 1992.

Burke, S. M. *Pakistan's Foreign Policy: An Historical Analysis.* 2nd ed. Karachi: Oxford University Press, 1990.

Cheema, Pervaiz Iqbal. *Pakistan's Defence Policy, 1947–1958.* New York: St. Martin's, 1990.

Cohen, Stephen P. *The Pakistan Army.* Berkeley: University of California Press, 1984, 1998.

Kux, Dennis. *The United States and Pakistan, 1947–2000: Disenchanted Allies.* Baltimore: Johns Hopkins University Press, 2001.

Schofield, Victoria. *Kashmir in Conflict: India, Pakistan and the Unending War.* London: I. B. Tauris, 2003.

Sisson, Richard, and Leo E. Rose. *War and Secession: Pakistan, India, and the Creation of Bangladesh.* Berkeley: University of California Press, 1990.

Wolpert, Stanley. *Zulfi Bhutto of Pakistan.* Oxford: Oxford University Press, 1993.

3

Bangladesh's Foreign Relations

Craig Baxter

Professor Muhammad Shamsul Huq, a former foreign minister of Bangladesh, has used as a subtitle to his book *Bangladesh in International Politics*[1] the phrase "The Dilemmas of the Weak States." Bangladesh is indeed weak by any measure, be it economic, military, or political development. Further, this weakness is accentuated by its location next to India, a country that is often unfriendly and at odds with its weaker neighbor, whose land boundary is almost entirely with India. Shamsul Huq has also contributed a general statement of the goals of Bangladeshi foreign policy.

> The cornerstone of Bangladesh foreign policy lies in three basic objectives: (1) consolidation of our hard won independence and national spirit; (2) safeguarding our sovereignty and territorial integrity; and (3) securing the much needed international cooperation in the task of national reconstruction and development. To reduce these basic policy objectives, we endeavoured to seek friendship of all countries including our neighbouring countries. Our efforts in this direction were governed by these principles: (1) recognition of the sovereign equality of all states; (2) respect for territorial integrity; and (3) non-interference in the internal affairs of other states.[2]

Any country, newly independent or not, might well put forward these sentiments. The question here is how well these were followed and, if followed, what the outcomes have been.

INDEPENDENCE

Bangladesh became independent on December 16, 1971, when the occupying Pakistan army surrendered to the Indian army (see chapter 1 for background on the war). Interestingly, the surrender was taken by the Indian local commander and not by the Bangladeshi liberation force, the Mukti Bahini. This has led to speculation that India's goal when it entered the conflict at the end of November[3] was primarily the defeat of Pakistan and only secondarily the liberation of Bangladesh. A defeat of its historic enemy would presumably weaken Pakistan, although this is also questionable, as, except for the Bangladesh case, conflict between India and Pakistan has been almost entirely in the west.

When the Pakistan army began its crackdown on March 25, 1971, the political leader of East Pakistan, Sheikh Mujibur Rahman of the Awami League, was arrested, along with others, and the army assaulted the faculty residences and dormitories of the University of Dhaka and other educational institutions, causing many deaths and, at the same time, spurring the resistance of East Pakistanis.[4] A group of political leaders from the Awami League escaped to Mujibnagar, a border town, and later to Calcutta to set up a provisional government of Bangladesh. Although India permitted the group to function, it did not grant formal recognition. Maj. Ziaur Rahman (later general and president) proclaimed the independence of Bangladesh on March 26 as he spoke from a radio station in Chittagong, claiming the authority of Mujib.

Supporters of Bangladesh were not inactive in the international scene. Most prominent of those visiting abroad and trying to gain support for Bangladesh was Justice Abu Sayeed Chowdhury.[5] He had been in Geneva attending a session of the UN Commission on Human Rights and could say clearly that the rights of East Pakistanis had been violated by the refusal of the leaders of Pakistan to recognize the victory of the Awami League in the national election held in December 1970 and January 1971. He visited a number of countries and won the sympathy of the public, if not always of the governments involved.

He was not alone. I have had personal experience, with the Bengali staff of the Pakistan embassy in Washington and the mission to the United Nations in New York. The Pakistani ambassador in Washington, Agha Hilaly, eventually relieved three senior Bengali officers and replaced them with transfers from West Pakistan. One of the Bengali officers involved, A. M. A. Muhith, later a finance minister, has written on the American position.[6] It was not only in Washington and New York that defections took place; they occurred in many other diplomatic missions. Defections also took place from the army. Ziaur Rahman would become the most noted of these, but many joined the Mukti Bahini from the military, as did others from paramilitary and police forces. Many civilians rallied as well.

AFTER THE SURRENDER

Recognition. Relief. Rehabilitation. Reconstruction. These key words governed the immediate needs of the newly formed government under the leadership of Mujibur Rahman, who was released by Pakistan and allowed to return to Dhaka. He arrived there on January 10, 1972, to an enormous reception. The provisional government had named him president, but he expressed his preference for a parliamentary system and became prime minister, with Abu Sayeed Chowdhury becoming the ceremonial head of state.

India had recognized the Bangladesh government on December 12, 1971, as the Indian army began its campaign against the Pakistan army in East Pakistan.[7] This was significant as it made it clear to the emerging Bangladeshis and to the world that India had entered the conflict to help Bangladesh gain independence from Pakistan. Bhutan, following as it must the foreign policy actions of India, gave its recognition the following day. A number of smaller countries, most of them within the Soviet bloc, followed suit during the month of January. The Soviet Union, which had signed a security treaty with India in 1971, recognized Bangladesh on January 25. As Bangladesh desired to enter the Commonwealth of Nations, recognition by the United Kingdom on February 2 set that process in motion; however, Pakistan, at that time a Commonwealth member, would greatly delay Bangladesh's recognition. Muslim states, as Pakistan's fellow members of the Organization of the Islamic Conference (OIC), delayed recognition. The ranks were broken when both Malaysia and Indonesia granted recognition on February 25, but the Arab states acted much more slowly. Iraq was the first to act on July 8, 1972.

Pakistan was to host the second summit meeting of the OIC in February 1974. The second largest Muslim state, Bangladesh, was not invited to attend. As the group gathered in Lahore, several heads of state from the Arab world, especially King Hussain of Jordan, put pressure on the Pakistani prime minister, Zulfiqar Ali Bhutto, to invite Sheikh Mujibur Rahman to attend. Bhutto yielded, and Bangladesh was invited. In fact, Mujib was flown by a special aircraft from Dhaka to Lahore. Pakistan recognized the independence of Bangladesh on February 22, 1974. Iran and Turkey, which had held back, along with Pakistan, recognized Bangladesh on the same day.

The United States delayed, although it maintained an office in Dhaka and was very active in relief supplies. The Awami League and Bangladeshis at large saw the United States as an ally of Pakistan. Nixon was not favorably disposed toward India and especially not toward Indira Gandhi.[8] The incident that was (and to an extent still is) in the Bangladeshi mind is the movement of an American aircraft carrier from the area of the Strait of Malacca into the Bay of Bengal during the 1971 war. Henry Kissinger has explained this movement as "ostensibly for the evacuation of Americans but in reality to give emphasis to our warnings [to India] against an attack on West Pakistan." He added, "we recognized the Indian occupation of East Pakistan as an accomplished fact."[9] Needless to say, many Bangladeshis did not buy this explanation when it was published eight years later. The United States ultimately recognized Bangladesh on April 4, 1972.

Bangladesh was heavily damaged during the conflict and, among other things, suffered from a lack of food and medicine. Many countries immediately began relief efforts both bilaterally and in cooperation with international organizations. Rehabilitation and reconstruction, most often with international assistance, often took the form of grants and later, frequently, that of loans, usually at concessionary rates. This will be discussed further below.

RELATIONS WITH NEIGHBORS

Bangladesh has but two neighbors whose territories abut its own: India and Burma (Myanmar). It is almost surrounded by India, with which it shares a 4,053-kilometer (2,518-mile) border. The remainder of the boundary is with Burma, with which it shares a 193-kilometer (120-mile) border, and the Bay of Bengal, which forms 580 kilometers (360 miles) of its border. While there have been contentious issues with Burma that will be noted below, relations with India have been most troublesome and seemingly irresolvable. Matters of concern with India include the division of the waters of the Ganges River, the land boundary, the sea boundary, Indian allegations of the use of Bangladeshi territory by Pakistan's Inter-Services Intelligence (ISI) and rebellious groups from the northeastern states of India, and the presence, according to Indian government statements, of some sixteen million illegal Bangladeshi immigrants in India.

It has been said that Mujib took a fawning approach toward India, looking to be the thankful person for the help of India and of Mrs. Gandhi. This attitude, according to some Bangladeshis, was evident in the Indo-Bangladeshi Treaty of 1972, a twenty-five-year agreement on friendship and cooperation.[10] The treaty has been defined as a quid pro quo exacted by India in return for the withdrawal of Indian troops from the Chittagong Hill Tracts. Indeed, after the assassination of Mujib on August 15, 1975, relations deteriorated as Bangladesh began to raise the issues discussed below. The treaty of 1972 was not renewed in 1997, a step on which both the government and the opposition agreed. If it is not contradictory, relations can now be described as correct but strained.

GANGES WATERS, FARAKKA BARRAGE

In a 1983 discussion of the foreign relations of Bangladesh, I suggested facetiously that

> the best solution for the foreign policy problems for Bangladesh . . . would be
> to take a gigantic saw and cut the nation loose from the subcontinent floating it

into a safe position somewhere in the Indian Ocean. However well this might meet the difficulty Bangladesh faces in being a small country almost completely surrounded on its land sides by a very much larger country, it would, were it possible to do so, leave the nation surrounded instead by unusable water. And it is water, a blessing and a curse for Bangladesh, that is its single most important foreign policy issue.[11]

Obviously, this is not a viable solution. But solutions that might seem viable to outside observers and that have been proposed by Bangladesh have been denied by an obstructionist, indeed bullying, India. Bangladesh has the misfortune to live next to an elephant and one that is cantankerous. India's position on the Ganges appears to be that it is the upper riparian, and it will do with the water whatever it pleases. The Indians decided to erect a barrage on the Ganges just upstream from the East Pakistan–India border at a place called Farakka. The purpose was to divert water down a canal to the Bhagirathi River and the Hooghly River to reduce salinity in the Hooghly and to augment the river's flow to reduce the buildup of silt that was endangering the use of Calcutta as a seaport. Bangladesh maintains that it needs the water withdrawn during the low-flow season (April and May especially) to irrigate land in the Khulna division and to reduce salinity in that area. It should be noted that during the high-flow period the waters of the Ganges exceed the needs of either country and in some years cause floods in both.

The concept of a barrage is not a new one. In the first decade of the twentieth century, British engineers proposed such a diversion of the Ganges as the reduction of the flow of the Bhagirathi was measurable. Historically, the principal distributary of the Ganges was the route of the Bhagirathi and Hooghly and their channels. In the later part of the sixteenth century, siltation diverted the flow eastward to the present distributaries of the river in what is now Bangladesh and which are often labeled on maps as "the mouths of the Ganges."

Bangladesh has proposed that a plan be drawn that would take in the waters of the entire Ganges basin (less the southern tributaries) rather than simply the flow of the river at the border. The Bangladeshi concept is that there are three, not simply two, states involved, as a number of major tributaries of the Ganges arise in Nepal. The proposal is simply that dams be built on some or all of the tributaries rising in Nepal that could both store and regulate the flow of the Ganges and generate hydroelectric power, much of which could be sold to power-short India (and perhaps Bangladesh), earning Nepal foreign exchange. India, in response to this seemingly practical, if initially costly, proposal, maintains that a third party should not be involved in what it deems a bilateral issue. Nepal has expressed cautious interest, recognizing that a considerable amount of land would be taken as reservoirs.

India proposes that water be drawn from the Brahmaputra and conveyed by a link canal to the Ganges just below Farakka. The model for this was the highly successful Indus Basin Project that followed the 1960 treaty between India and Pakistan on the division of the waters of the Indus basin. Two things make this model impractical for Bangladesh. First, much of the land traversed by the link canals in Pakistan was sparsely inhabited, so the question of re-settlement was minimal. The link canal contemplated by India would displace several million people in a country in which resettlement is difficult, if not impossible, as there is no "empty" land. Second, all of the link canals in Pakistan began and ended in Pakistani territory. This would not be the case in a Brahmaputra–Ganges link canal. It would start in Indian territory and end in Indian territory. Bangladesh would not be prepared to place the faucets at each end in the hands of another country. Engineers have said that the project is possible from their point of view, but this does not consider the political and resettlement issues.

On May 16, 1974, the two prime ministers, Sheikh Mujibur Rahman and Indira Gandhi, declared that the Farakka Barrage would not be commissioned until the two sides arrived "at a mutually acceptable allocation of the water available during the periods of minimum flow in the Ganges."[12] Nonetheless, without an agreement with Bangladesh, India began the operation of the bar-rage in 1975. When the Indira Gandhi government was replaced by one headed by Morarji Desai, negotiations between the two governments began in earnest, and an agreement on the sharing of the water came into effect in 1978.[13] It was a five-year agreement and was renewed once in 1983 to run un-til 1988. It then took another eight years before a new agreement was made in 1996. This treaty specifies maximum withdrawals by India and minimum availability to Bangladesh in ten-day segments from January 1 to May 31 each year.[14] However, the Bangladeshis still feel they have been shortchanged as projects that require more water, such as the Ganga–Kobadak project ben-efiting primarily Khulna division, cannot be carried out. Also, the decreased flow of the Ganges in Bangladesh also harms the Sundarbans, an international environmental site shared with India.

A recent proposal by India, however unlikely its costly implementation may be, is to divert water throughout much of the country to transfer water from sur-plus areas to deficit areas through an enormous series of link canals. Among the diversions would be "a fourth of the water of the Brahmaputra River through a 12,500 km maze of canals to irrigate 34 million hectares of land."[15] To say that this plan, if ever undertaken, would starve Bangladesh is putting it mildly.

LAND BOUNDARY

There are two aspects of the land boundary problem. The first is the demar-cation of the boundary in general, a task that should not be difficult considering the extensive surveying done by the British. The Radcliffe Commission, which delimited the boundaries in the 1947 partition of British India into India and Pakistan, gave thorough directions as to how the land was to be divided. Interestingly, there have been no significant complaints between India and West Pakistan. There were, of course, complaints about the borders for political reasons, but not about demarcation. The border with East Pakistan/Bangladesh was and is a matter for disagreement, despite the signing by Bangladesh and India of an agreement on May 16, 1974, that details the procedure for a settlement.[16]

In an article entitled "A Neighbourhood of Trouble," *India Today* discusses the problem along with those of other neighbors.[17] In an interview with Foreign Minister Yashwant Sinha, the article raises the issue of sanctuary to opponents of India (see below). The author concludes, "Sort out the border delineation in favour of Bangladesh and make trade concessions; deal firmly with illegal immigrants and carry [out] covert strikes on militant bases." It is doubtful if the Indian government would carry out the suggestions in the first clause, but action on the second clause might conceivably be taken.

The second aspect of the land boundary is the matter of exclaves and enclaves in each country's territory. This results partly from the divided territory ruled by the then princely state of Cooch Behar (Indian princely states are discussed in chapter 1), now incorporated into West Bengal as a district, as well as from realignment of land from shifts in stream channels. *The Economist* states that there are 161 parcels whose status has not been resolved.[18] The more important, although not at all large, segment is the Berubari Enclave, which is Bangladeshi but cut off from Bangladesh proper. In 1992 an area known as Tin Bigha (literally, "one acre," as three *bighas* are equal to one acre) was transferred by India to Bangladesh to permit access to Berubari. Indian officials have not always honored the transfer, and disputes have arisen. Other specks on the map also exist.

SEA BOUNDARY

There also are two facets of the dispute with India over the sea boundary. The first results from the provisions of the international agreement on the law of the sea. States that are at the head of sea indentations, such as the Bay of Bengal, are awarded but small areas of the adjacent sea. Bangladesh claims a territorial zone of twelve nautical miles, the standard for all states with sea coasts.[19] Within this zone the state controlling the zone may regulate all economic and transportation activity.

The difficulty, as Bangladesh sees it, comes in the category of the exclusive economic zone. Bangladesh claims the normal two hundred nautical miles, but this conflicts with the exclusive economic zones of India and Burma. The question is additionally complicated by Indian ownership of the Andaman and Nicobar islands in the Bay of Bengal. The Law of the Sea Treaty, signed in 1982, is quite clear on what is to be done when states are separated by less than four hundred nautical miles of sea: there must be a sep-arate agreement between or among the concerned states. The exclusive eco-nomic zone provision gives the states having such a zone rights to the re-sources of the continental shelf in the zone, such as oil, gas, and minerals. If the continental shelf extends beyond two hundred nautical miles, the rights to the resources end at the two-hundred-nautical-mile limit. With the discovery of extensive natural gas resources, some of them off shore, Bangladesh wishes to have an "equitable" settlement with India and Burma. The recent discovery of gas off the shore of Andhra Pradesh in India has heightened Bangladeshi interest.

The second issue concerns the emergence of a new island in the Bay of Ben-gal on the border of India and Bangladesh. The coast of the Bay of Bengal is dotted with islands that have been formed, in many cases over the centuries, by the silt carried in the distributaries of the Ganges–Brahmaputra–Meghna river system. Known as chars, many of these islands are inhabited although they are often devastated by the cyclonic storms that arise in the bay. The island in ques-tion is known as South Talpatty Island to Bangladesh and New Moore Island to India. It lies at the mouth of the Hariganga River, a distributary of the Ganges, and is uninhabited. Bangladesh has proposed that the flow of the Hariganga be analyzed to determine whether the flow into the bay is primarily on the east or west side of the island. If it is on the west, the island should belong to Bangladesh; if on the east, it should go to India. While this would appear to be a rational solution, India has refused to accept it. If the island were recognized as Bangladeshi, it would make a slight difference in the calculating of the terri-torial waters.[20]

INDIAN CHARGE THAT BANGLADESH IS HARBORING TERRORISTS

India has charged that Bangladesh has become a safe haven for rebel groups in many of the northeastern states of India including Tripura, Nagaland, and Assam.[21] Those from Assam include the Bodo tribals, who also have training areas in southern Bhutan. Not surprisingly, Bangladesh denies the charge. The borders between these Indian states, especially Tripura, and Bangladesh are mountainous and forested so that patrolling the boundaries is difficult. Further, in some cases people have affinities on each side of the border, no-tably in the Chittagong Hill Tracts, a district in which Bangladesh has faced rebellion that it claimed India was abetting.[22]

India has also accused Bangladesh of harboring fugitive members of al Qaeda and the Taliban and of permitting the use of its territory by Pakistan's ISI. In an interview with Raj Chengappa of *India Today*, Foreign Minister Yashwant Sinha said, "We would like to continue our friendship and cooperation with Bangladesh. . . . We have been assured by Bangladesh that it would not permit its territory to be used for activities against India." Sinha went on to say that India has shared information with Bangladesh on this subject.[23] It seems that Bangladesh does not knowingly permit anti-Indian activities, but as already noted, the border is so porous that full control of passage is all but impossible to achieve.

ILLEGAL BANGLADESHIS IN INDIA

India claims that there are more than sixteen million Bangladeshis living in India and that Bangladesh should take them back. An *India Today* map[24] gives the number to the last digit of such persons living in each state, from 14 in Kerala to 7,650,123 in West Bengal. The source given for the map is the Home Ministry. This raises a question: if numbers can be given with such precision, why cannot the persons allegedly represented by the numbers be found and deported? A case that made international news in early February 2003 involved 213 persons who were described as itinerant snake charmers from Bangladesh attempting to cross into India. Apparently, they were planning to perform in the West Bengal towns of the Cooch Behar and Jalpaiguri districts, thereby earning money in India, a practice forbidden to undocumented foreigners. India determined that they were Bangladeshis as they were said to be carrying Bangladeshi electricity bills and receipts. This prompted *The Economist* to ask, "what use have itinerant snake-charmers for electricity, let alone bills?" The group, Muslims who in their profession also worship the Hindu snake goddess, were denied entry.[25]

Indian deputy prime minister and home minister L. K. Advani stated at the time of the snake charmers' being turned back, "Bangladesh should recognize illegal immigration from her soil and take the people back."[26] There is no doubt that a substantial number of people from Bangladesh have illegally entered India. Many have established businesses and professions. It is not at all strange that people will cross borders, legally or illegally, if there is opportunity for economic improvement or to join family members already in the targeted country. This is demonstrated by immigration to the United States, both legal and illegal, as well as to most European countries. It seems to be a fact of life, and the process of rounding up illegals is difficult. India will find it no different.

GAS EXPORTS TO INDIA

Bangladesh has an enormous stock of natural gas that far exceeds its own requirements for many years. There is also a strong likelihood that additional gas fields will be developed both on land and offshore. The latter, of course, heightens the issue of the sea boundary discussed above. A report prepared by Petrobangla and the U.S. Geological Survey in 2001 estimated the recoverable reserves of gas to be 32.1 trillion cubit feet (TCF), of which 23.3 TCF were onshore and 8.8 TCF were offshore.[27] Further discoveries have presumably raised that figure. Principal domestic uses of natural gas are the manufacture of ammonia-urea fertilizers, domestic uses in major cities, and electricity generation. With the increasing availability of gas, the total usage within the country will clearly increase. This obvious assumption led to opposition to exports to India during the government headed by Sheikh Hasina Wajid (1996–2001). Although the Khaleda Zia government has been in office since 2001, that government's views are not yet clear. In the opinion of many involved in gas production and of those who study the economics of the industry, Bangladesh should export gas to energy-short West Bengal and beyond in India.[28] There are two methods for export. The means India is likely to prefer would be to pipeline it to a terminal in West Bengal. The other possibility is to generate electricity in Bangladesh using gas, then to transmit the power to India. A combination of the two might also be used. Employment opportunities would be generated during the construction of either a pipeline or an electrical transmission line, but the latter would be more likely to maintain employment opportunities.

It must, however, be noted that India and Iran have explored gas transmission from Iran. The two have agreed to look into bypassing Pakistan via an under sea route. Turkmenistan, Afghanistan, and Pakistan have an agreement to transmit gas from Turkmenistan through Afghanistan to Pakistan. Pakistan has offered to extend the line to India and has said that such extension would help make the system profitable. Burma also has an interest in transmitting gas to India for which a route across Bangladesh would be more practical than a difficult northern route that would go direct from Burma to India. India has also been looking into transmission of gas from Tripura across Bangladesh to West Bengal. One can be certain that negotiations on one or more of the possible means for India to obtain more gas will be ongoing.

BURMA (MYANMAR)

The border between India and Burma has been delineated, although it is in territory difficult to patrol. As already noted, the question of the sea boundary remains on the agenda of Bangladesh. The most pressing issue between Burma and Bangladesh has to do with the Muslims in Arakan (now Rakhine) Province in Burma. The Muslims are known as Rohingyas, a term derived from an ancient name of Arakan, Rohang. About 40 percent of the population of the province is Muslim.[29] The historical connections between Arakan and adjacent Chittagong are many. The Chittagong area was first ruled by a Buddhist king of Arakan in the ninth century, passed to Muslim rulers, returned to the Arakanese in the sixteenth century, became Mughal territory a century later, and became part of the British Empire in 1760. A few years later, in 1784, Arakanese independence ended when Arakan was conquered by the Burmese. Many Buddhist Arakanese fled to Chittagong, where they are known as Maghs. The Muslim Rohingyas claim descent from Arab and Persian traders who navigated to the Arakanese coast as early as A.D. 900.[30]

Oppression, as seen by the Rohingyas, caused about two hundred thousand of them to flee Burma and go to Bangladesh as refugees principally in the Cox's Bazaar District of the Chittagong region in early 1978. They came across the border that is the Naaf River at the southern tip of Bangladesh. With the assistance of the UN High Commissioner for Refugees (UNHCR) and other international organizations, most of this group was repatriated, beginning later in 1978. However, conditions in Burma depreciated in the eyes of the Rohingyas in 1992, and perhaps 270,000 fled to Cox's Bazaar. Again UNHCR assisted, and most of the Rohingyas have been repatriated.

OTHER SOUTH ASIAN COUNTRIES

In discussing relations with other South Asian countries, obviously those with Pakistan are most important, those with Nepal and Bhutan are of importance, and those with Sri Lanka and the Maldives are of minimal importance. The binding of the South Asian states together is seen in the South Asian Association for Regional Cooperation (SAARC), a concept first posed by President Ziaur Rahman.

Pakistan withheld recognition of Bangladesh until February 22, 1974, and, as has been noted, extended it then only under pressure from other Islamic states attending a meeting of the OIC in Lahore. Pakistan used the veto of China to keep Bangladesh from membership in the United Nations until the new state was admitted in September 1974. To Pakistan, Bangladesh remained a rebellious province. Initially, Pakistan stated that it would break diplomatic relations with any state that recognized Bangladesh. This policy soon became impractical as state after state did so anyway. High commissioners were exchanged in 1976, and relations have become what can be called normal. Heads of state and of government have exchanged visits, and such practical matters as air routes and trade have been regularized.

Two issues remain important and seemingly intractable. The first of these is a Bangladeshi demand that the financial assets of Pakistan be divided through a mutual agreement. The result is hardly unexpected: what assets were in East Pakistan are now Bangladeshi and what assets were in West Pakistan are Pakistani. On the other hand, there was an agreement in 1975 on the division of the external debt of Pakistan. Bangladesh nationalized the assets held by private citizens of Pakistan, most notably the now closed Adamjee Jute Mill in Narayanganj, the then largest jute mill in the world. Pakistani banks were nationalized. It can be said that the loss of West Pakistani managers meant that many enterprises were run less well.

The second issue is that of Urdu speakers living in Bangladesh, who are generally known as Biharis because at Partition in 1947 many fled Hindu India, mostly from Bihar, to East Pakistan rather than to West Pakistan like the vast majority of refugees. The loss of West Pakistani employers affected many Biharis as they were often employed by these enterprises. A program by UNHCR to transport Biharis to Pakistan has only been minimally successful. As Urdu speakers the Biharis would prefer to go to Karachi where there is a large community of Urdu speakers, but the potential growth of the Urdu community there and in Hyderabad is opposed by the Sindhi population in the province named after them (see chapter 2 for a discussion of immigration-related political violence in Sindh). As a result many of the Biharis remain in camps and in separate areas in and near Dhaka, often living in squalid conditions with few sources of income. They have also been the subject of anti-Bihari actions by both government forces and private groups. In February 2003 a large number of Biharis were evicted from the Mirpur relief camp and their dwellings burned.[31]

Questions remained about Bangladeshis who were detained in Pakistan, non-Bengalis in Bangladesh who opted for repatriation to Pakistan, and prisoners of war held by India. Many in the first two categories were government officials who were, in effect, stranded; some were Bengali military personnel who had been relieved of duty in Pakistan and were detained. Among the prisoners, Bangladesh wanted to try 195 for war crimes. Indian prime minister Indira Gandhi and Pakistani president Zulfiqar Ali Bhutto met in Simla and signed an agreement on July 2, 1972, intended to restore relations between the two countries to the status quo prior to the arising of the Bangladesh issue and to provide a means for the peaceful settlement of disputes.[32] India and Bangladesh decided to separate the question of prisoners of war from the question of Pakistan's recognition of Bangladesh's independence. Following the Simla Agreement, further talks between Bangladesh, India, and Pakistan led to an agreement on August 9, 1974, to implement the return of Bangladeshis from Pakistan, Pakistanis from Bangladesh, and prisoners of war from India to Pakistan. Bangladesh agreed that the 195 accused war criminals would also be returned to Pakistan and the charges dropped.[33]

Nepal and Bhutan, as upper riparians of the Ganges–Brahmaputra–Meghna basin, are important to Bangladesh and its proposals for the augmentation of the flow in the basins during low-flow periods. Bhutan, taking foreign policy direction from India, was the second state to recognize Bangladeshi independence, and Nepal followed very quickly.

SAARC

SAARC was a concept initiated by Ziaur Rahman in 1980. So long as there existed tensions between Bangladesh and Pakistan, especially over the question of recognition, as well as distrust between India and Pakistan, the idea of regional cooperation was distant at best. The Simla Agreement put at least some light on relations between India and Pakistan, and Pakistani recognition of Bangladesh opened the door for Ziaur Rahman. He discussed his idea during official visits to India, Pakistan, Nepal, and Sri Lanka and put his plan forward in letters to the heads of government of each of these countries as well as the Maldives and Bhutan. The assassination of Ziaur Rahman on May 30, 1981, ended his pursuit of the concept, but it was carried forward by his successor, Abdus Sattar.

Meetings began at the level of foreign secretaries in 1981 and 1982 and were raised to the level of foreign ministers in 1983. These meetings delineated the areas in which cooperation among the member states could be expected. India insisted that bilateral matters not be discussed in the framework of SAARC. Areas for cooperation, it was agreed, would include agriculture, rural development, telecommunications, meteorology, and health and population activities, that is, those areas in which serious bilateral disagreement was not likely to arise. Meanwhile in Bangladesh a military coup had deposed Sattar and Hussain Muhammad Ershad became president on March 24, 1982. With Ershad as host, the heads of government met in Dhaka on December 7–8, 1985, to sign the agreement forming SAARC.[34]

The organization has held regular meetings, but it is difficult to say it has accomplished much. SAARC is not the European Union or even the Organization of American States. Some steps have been taken to form a South Asian Preferential Trade Association (SAPTA) as the road to an eventual South Asian Free Trade Association (SAFTA), but little has been accomplished toward either of these goals. The 2002 meeting held in Kathmandu was marred by hostility between India and Pakistan, although Pakistani leader Gen. Pervez Musharraf moved at least to shake hands with Indian prime minister Atal

Behari Vajpayee. The 2003 session was scheduled for Islamabad in January, but Vajpayee refused to attend, and the meeting was postponed. It was finally held in Islamabad in January 2004.

OTHER COUNTRIES

Bangladesh has diplomatic relations, resident and nonresident, with a large number of countries, but its most important relations outside the South Asia region are with the United States, the European Union, the Islamic states, Japan, China, and Russia.

Relations with the United States got off to a rocky start as a result of the movement of the carrier *Enterprise* into the Bay of Bengal and the delay in granting Bangladesh formal recognition, which came finally on April 4, 1972.[35] Despite the lack of formal recognition, the United States began very quickly to send assistance to the ravaged country. American economic assistance, both in grants and loans, has been very large, although in recent years it has been exceeded by assistance from Japan. There are no significant issues outstanding between the two countries. There has been some investment by American firms, especially in banking and in gas and oil exploration. The United States is also a major market for the burgeoning Bangladeshi garment industry.

Substantial assistance has also been forthcoming from the states of the European Union and from bodies directly connected to it. As with the United States, the relationships are primarily in the field of economic development. The European Union has also been a major export market for the garment industry. Japan has been particularly generous with its assistance to Bangladesh. A number of Japanese commercial and industrial companies have invested in Bangladesh, taking advantage of the lower wage costs there. With the Western states and Japan, relations have been based most heavily on economic issues, primarily economic assistance and secondarily on trade. Bangladesh has been one of the major recipients of economic development and food assistance since it gained independence, not only from states but also from international agencies. Some of this takes the form of grants, but most is in loans. This has created an external debt problem that could become unmanageable. The external debt in 1998 was more than $16 billion, or 22 percent of the country's gross domestic product.[36]

Relations between Bangladesh and China began with difficulty as a result of the close relations between China and Pakistan. At the request of Pakistan, China regularly used its veto power on the UN Security Council to block the membership of Bangladesh in the United Nations. With the recognition of Bangladesh by Pakistan, the Chinese dropped the use of its veto and Bangladesh was admitted to the United Nations on September 17,

1974. Shamsul Huq speculates that in addition to the close China–Pakistan relationship, China was concerned about the separation of Bangladesh for "domestic compulsions stemming from the 'Taiwan factor' and the problems in Tibet."[37] Relations have since been cordial and based principally on trade and cultural matters.

The Soviet Union, which had signed a security treaty with India in 1971 as the conflict in East Pakistan was underway, followed the lead of its ally and recognized Bangladesh on January 25, 1972; the other members of the Soviet bloc in turn followed suit (except for Bulgaria, which had done so thirteen days earlier). The perceived leftist leaning of the Mujib regime caused some to think that the Soviet Union exercised considerable influence over Bangladesh. The Soviet Union offered a large number of scholarships to Bangladeshi students, and one writer notes that the "pro-Moscow parties . . . became stronger during this period of the early 1970s," but adds that "there was a suspicion that Russia was engaged in destabilising the country."[38] Bangladesh did expel some Soviet diplomats for exceeding their mission. The Soviet Union supplied a squadron of MiG aircraft in 1972, and Russia sold another squadron in 2001, although it is unclear what use Bangladesh has for them. Russia has supplied technical assistance, but its own economy is weak, and it is not now able to send significant economic assistance.

INTERNATIONAL ORGANIZATIONS

Bangladesh is a member of a host of international organizations. Some of these are truly international in that membership is drawn from the world at large. Others are regional, such as SAARC, discussed above. Others in this category include the Economic and Social Commission for Asia and the Pacific and the Asian Development Bank. Others require specific qualifications, such as the (British) Commonwealth of Nations.

One organization that has specific requirements is the OIC. Based in Jeddah, it was organized in 1971. Bangladesh was denied membership until after it was recognized by Pakistan at the insistence of a majority of the members of the OIC. The organization operates loosely to put forward causes that have an Islamic bearing. It does not differentiate between Sunni and Shia Muslims. Conferences are held regularly that not only discuss matters of importance but also give leaders of Islamic countries an opportunity to become better acquainted. It also sponsors the Islamic Development Bank, which provides loans for economic development in less developed Islamic states including Bangladesh.

In the broader international scene, membership in what might be described as the parent organization, the United Nations, is a basis for membership in the organizations associated with the United Nations. Bangladesh was admitted to the United Nations on September 17, 1974, after the ending of the Chinese veto. It has twice been elected a member of the Security Council, and in 1986 the then foreign minister of Bangladesh, Humayun Rashid Chowdhury, was elected president of the General Assembly. Bangladesh is a member of all of the organizations associated with the United Nations, including the specifically financial bodies such as the World Bank, the International Monetary Fund, and the International Development Association. In addition, it belongs to bodies that are programmatic, such as the World Health Organization, the Food and Agricultural Organization, the International Labor Organization, and the UNHCR. Bangladesh is an active member of the Non-aligned Movement (NAM) and attended the 2003 session held in Kuala Lumpur. On what might be described as the economic side of NAM, it is a member of the Group of 77. As such, it supports the idea of a new international economic order.

CONCLUSION

In international relations, the root of Bangladeshi activity is primarily economic. Political issues have generally been settled with diplomatic recognition and with the opening up of the opportunity for membership in international organizations following the withdrawal of the Chinese veto on UN membership. Even the problems with India are often economic, such as the disputes over the division of the Ganges waters and the demarcation of the sea boundary. Perhaps even the question of illegal residents in India who are Bangladesh nationals can be seen as economic as Bangladesh would be overwhelmed by the forced return of sixteen million (to use India's enumeration) people. Possible negotiation with India on the export of natural gas is an economic issue, as it would earn a substantial amount of foreign exchange if it were carried out. Bangladesh, to echo Shamsul Huq's subtitle, is a weak state. It is no longer, in the phrase attributed to Henry Kissinger, an "international basket case," but it is a state that needs, even requires, continued economic assistance. Hence its relations with the world will be based on that premise.

NOTES

1. Muhammad Shamsul Huq, *Bangladesh in International Politics: The Dilemmas of the Weak States* (New Delhi: Sterling, 1993).
2. Quoted in Fakhruddin Ahmed, *Critical Times: Memoirs of a South Asian Diplomat* (Dhaka: University Press, 1994), 207.

3. There has never been stated an official date for the entry of Indian forces into the conflict, although India had been training and equipping Mukti Bahini forces for several months before its forces entered what was then formally East Pakistan.

4. This chapter is not intended to enter into a description of the conflict. For an interesting study of the effect of the conflict on a citizen, see Jahanara Iman, *Of Blood and Fire,* trans. from the Bengali by Mustafizur Rahman (Dhaka: Academic Publishers, 1990).

5. Chowdhury had also been vice chancellor of the University of Dhaka and would be president of Bangladesh from January 1972 to December 1973 and foreign minister briefly in 1975.

6. A. M. A. Muhith, *American Response to Bangladesh Liberation War* (Dhaka: University Press, 1996).

7. There was also limited conflict between India and Pakistan on the western front begun by an air attack by Pakistan.

8. During the time that I served as acting consul general in Lahore, Nixon stopped in Lahore en route to Islamabad from New Delhi. In a private conversation he described Mrs. Gandhi as a "most difficult woman."

9. Henry Kissinger, *The White House Years* (Boston: Little Brown, 1979), 905.

10. The text is contained in Harun ur Rashid, *Indo-Bangladesh Relations: An Insider's View* (New Delhi: Har-Anand, 2002), appendix 1.

11. Craig Baxter, "Bangladesh: Problems without Powers," paper given at the Twelfth Annual Conference on South Asia, University of Wisconsin, November 5, 1983.

12. Quoted in Harun ur Rashid, *Foreign Relations of Bangladesh* (Varanasi, India: Rishi, 2001), 69.

13. Text is in ur Rashid, *Indo-Bangladesh Relations*, appendix 5.

14. Text is in ur Rashid, *Indo-Bangladesh Relations*, appendix 6.

15. See *India Today*, January 20, 2003, 20–24.

16. Text is in ur Rashid, *Indo-Bangladesh Relations*, appendix 4.

17. Raj Chengappa, *India Today*, February 10, 2003, 38–45.

18. *The Economist*, February 8, 2003, 42.

19. The Bangladesh position on the sea boundary is contained in an act of Parliament dated April 13, 1974. The text of the act is in ur Rashid, *Indo-Bangladesh Relations,* appendix 3.

20. The text of a white paper on the South Talpatty Island, prepared by the Bangladesh Ministry of Foreign Affairs on May 26, 1981, is contained in Shamsul Huq, *Bangladesh in International Politics*, 341–53.

21. In early British times, the district of Comilla was known as Tippera, while the princely state was known as Hill Tippera. The area that is now Comilla was incorporated into the Mughal province of Bengal in 1733 and then into British territory as British control expanded in the early nineteenth century. One of the tribes resident in the Chittagong Hill Tracts is known as the Tripura.

22. See Mizanur Rahman Shelley, ed., *The Chittagong Hill Tracts of Bangladesh: The Untold Story* (Dhaka: Centre for Development Studies, Bangladesh, 1992), and Ameena Mohsin, *Chittagong Hill Tracts, Bangladesh: On the Difficult Road to Peace* (Boulder, Colo.: Lynne Rienner, 2003).

23. *India Today*, February 10, 2003, 40.

24. *India Today*, February 17, 2003, 19.

25. See *The Economist*, February 8, 2002, 42, and *India Today*, February 17, 2003, 18–20.

26. *India Today*, February 17, 2003, 20.

27. National Bureau of Asian Research at www.nbr.org/regional_studies/Bangladesh/ (accessed February 25, 2003).

28. A report prepared in October 1999 by the Centre for Policy Dialogue that supports exportation can be found at www.cpd-bangladesh.org/report14.pdf (accessed February 25, 2003).

29. ur Rashid, *Foreign Relations of Bangladesh*, 114–15, 285.
30. Shamsul Huq, *Bangladesh in International Politics*, 131.
31. *Dawn*, February 27, 2002.
32. For a study of the Simla Conference, see Imtiaz H. Bokhari and Thomas Perry Thornton, *The 1972 Simla Agreement: An Asymmetrical Negotiation* (Washington, D.C.: Foreign Policy Institute, The Johns Hopkins University School of Advanced International Studies, 1988).
33. The text of the memorandum recording the meeting and signed by the three foreign ministers (Kamal Hossain for Bangladesh, Swaran Singh for India, and Aziz Ahmed for Pakistan) is contained in ur Rashid, *Indo-Bangladesh Relations,* appendix 2. The release of the 195 prisoners is referred to in paragraph 15.
34. A brief history and documents relating to SAARC up to the time of publication are contained in Abul Ahsan, *SAARC: A Perspective* (Dhaka: University Press, 1992). Ahsan, a Bangladeshi diplomat, was the first secretary general of SAARC and opened the secretariat in Kathmandu.
35. According to a chart in Shamsul Huq, *Bangladesh in International Politics,* 358–60, the United States was the fifty-fifth state to recognize Bangladesh, following almost all of the European Union members and most of the Commonwealth.
36. World Bank, *World Development Report, 2000/2001*, Table 21, 314.
37. Shamsul Huq, *Bangladesh in International Politics*, 166.
38. ur Rashid, *Foreign Relations of Bangladesh*, 180.

FURTHER READING

Ahmed, Fakhruddin. *Critical Times: Memoirs of a South Asian Diplomat.* Dhaka: University Press, 1994.
Baxter, Craig. *Bangladesh: From a Nation to a State.* Boulder, Colo.: Westview, 1997.
Baxter, Craig, and Syedur Rahman. *Historical Dictionary of Bangladesh.* 3rd ed. Lanham, Md.: Scarecrow Press, 2003.
Bhardwaj, Sanjay. *Bangladesh-U.S. Relations: From Cooperation to Partnership.* Delhi: Kalinga, 2002.
Crow, Ben, and Alan Lindquist. *Sharing the Ganges: The Politics and Technology of River Development.* Thousand Oaks, Calif.: Sage, 1994.
Dixit, J. N. *Liberation and Beyond: Indo-Bangladesh Relations.* Delhi: Konark, 1999.
Hazarika, Sanjoy. *Rites of Passage: Border Crossings, Imagined Homelands, India's East and Bangladesh.* New Delhi: Penguin, 2000.
Khan, Zillur Rahman, ed., *SAARC and the Superpowers.* Dhaka: University Press, 1991.
Maniruzzaman, Talukder. *Politics and Security of Bangladesh.* Dhaka: University Press, 1994.
Momen, Nurul. *Bangladesh in the United Nations: A Study in Diplomacy.* Dhaka: University Press, 1987.
Rashid, Harun ur. *Foreign Relations of Bangladesh.* Varanasi, India: Rishi, 2001.
———. *Indo-Bangladesh Relations: An Insider's View.* New Delhi: Har-Anand, 2002.
Shamsul Huq, Muhammad. *Bangladesh in International Politics: The Dilemmas of the Weak States.* New Delhi: Sterling, 1993.
Shamsul Huq, Muhammad, and Chowdhury Rafiqul Abrar. *Aid, Development and Diplomacy: Need for an Aid Policy.* Dhaka: University Press, 1999.
Sharma, Sarbjit. *U.S.-Bangladesh Relations: A Critique.* New Delhi: UBS Publications, 2001.
Tajuddin, Muhammad. *Foreign Policy of Bangladesh: Liberation War to Sheikh Hasina.* New Delhi: National Books, 2001.

4

South Asia's Small States in World Politics

Swarna Rajagopalan

There is more to South Asia than India, Pakistan, Kashmir and nuclear weapons, poverty in Bangladesh, and ethnic conflict in Sri Lanka.[1] This chapter considers the international relations and security perspectives of each of South Asia's four smaller states and highlights the points of their engagement with India, the region's preeminent state, with other South Asian states, and with the rest of the world. While the first is the best-known context, each of these countries has its own view of what matters and has sought to engage and further those interests on its own terms.

WHAT IS SMALL? IDENTIFYING SOUTH ASIA'S SMALL STATES

In a region where states are of continental size and house hefty proportions of the global population, the term *small state* begs definition. Next to India, there are only a handful of states in the world that do not seem small in terms of population and size. By convention, the term *small state* is used to describe a state with a population of one million or less.[2] However, smallness is relative. South Asian states vary widely on those dimensions, but India's proportions exacerbate that variation. So let us remove India from our consideration of the question, what is small? With populations of over one hundred million, both Pakistan and Bangladesh qualify as large states, and so we may designate the remaining states—Sri Lanka, Nepal, Bhutan, and the Maldives—as small states by virtue of having populations under one hundred million, and in the case of two of them, under one million (see the appendix to this chapter). It should be noted that one of them, Nepal, is slightly larger geographically than Bangladesh, which houses around six times Nepal's population! The differences between the four countries designated here as "small" are

89

significant, both in physical and political terms. Sri Lanka, for instance, has been a significant player in the global arena as a founding member of the Nonaligned Movement in the same way as India has. However, it is possible to find points of comparison between the four states.

India provides the first source of comparison. It is one of the inescapable realities of life in South Asia that India lies at its center in every way imaginable. Its massive landmass lies at the physical center of the subcontinent. Every South Asian state, except Afghanistan and the island nations, borders India, and practically none of the others share borders. Indians have ethnic kin (or some ethnic ties) in every other state, and the lines between the states have remained just porous enough to maintain those ties. In turn, each South Asian state (other than the Maldives) views India through the lens of these shared relationships, with all their attendant common pride and their histories of troubled interactions.[3] In the worldview and security calculus of each of these states, India casts a long and often unpleasant shadow. On the positive side, India has helped each of the smaller states of South Asia with development projects, as well as when they have needed security assistance. The Chukha hydroelectric project in Bhutan and India's quick response at the time of the Maldives 1988 coup are examples of this positive role. What lingers, however, is the image of India as a hegemon with a sanctimonious streak. India's assistance to secessionist movements in Pakistan and Sri Lanka— discussions of its motivation apart—and its military intervention in both cases, its part in domestic Nepali politics and its willingness to cut off Nepal's transit rights, and its annexation of Sikkim in 1976 are the best-known examples of its will and ability to intervene in the affairs of its neighbors.

Geographical circumstances further allow us to make paired comparisons. Sri Lanka and the Maldives are the two island states of South Asia. Bhutan and Nepal are its landlocked, mountain states, both sandwiched between India and China (through Tibet). Although the issue is beyond the scope of this chapter, the Maldives and Bangladesh also share concerns about global warming and rising ocean levels.

Finally, in the last decade, no part of the region has been exempt from the globalizing trend that has facilitated the flow of weapons, drugs, money, and militancy across frontiers.[4] That the situation in Afghanistan allowed the rise of training camps that exported terror and arms bazaars along the Pakistani border, we all now know. The Afghanistan–Pakistan–Kashmir connection is also well-known. Links between militant groups there and those in India's northeast have also been reported. The Tamil Tigers are said to have been training some of the northeastern groups and the Maoists in Nepal. Sri Lankan Tamil militants seeking a safe haven for their activities engineered the 1988 coup in the Maldives. If the larger states of South Asia have provoked, assisted, and paid for such political activities, the smaller states have been unable to remain immune. Nepal's Maoists and others in South Asia formed the Coordination Committee of Maoist Parties and Organizations of South Asia (CCOMPOSA) in July 2001. Bhutan's southern reaches have been a safe haven for several of the militant groups operating in Assam. The Maldives' distant atolls remain vulnerable to militant and mercenary attacks. In short, the vulnerability of the small states is exacerbated in this situation.

Roberto Espindola states that small developing states have three alternative courses of action in international relations: neutrality and nonalignment, regional security arrangements, and Finlandization (or relying on larger powers to protect them).[5] The South Asian states analyzed here have adopted each of these tactics to some extent. All four states are nonaligned, and Nepal specifically speaks of neutrality and of being a zone of peace. All are members of the South Asian Association for Regional Cooperation (SAARC), which, in spite of not having explicit collective-security arrangements, does seek to create a secure regional environment through frequent contact and confidence building. Finally, through treaty arrangements or by request at times of crisis, all four states have called on India's support in political, diplomatic, economic, and military terms. Espindola's three alternatives are not mutually exclusive but mutually reinforcing and balancing. The next part of this chapter is devoted to a country-by-country survey of each one's worldview, security perceptions, and key international relationships and initiatives.

LANDLOCKED STATES: NEPAL AND BHUTAN

Bhutan and Nepal are South Asia's landlocked Himalayan states, with mountains and foothills making up their terrain. Both of these attributes have certain implications for their worldview and their security perceptions, and they certainly constrain their choices. The UN Office of the High Representative for the Least Developed Countries, Landlocked Developing Countries and Small Island Developing States (OHRLLS), which advocates the interests of states with special needs, identifies "lack of territorial access to the sea, remoteness and isolation from world markets and high transit costs"[6] as the major constraints faced by landlocked states. Another problem faced by landlocked states is that of access to the resources of the sea and seabed.[7] However, in the case of developing countries, that is not as pressing an issue as that of transit.

Landlocked states are heavily dependent on the states that can provide them with access to the sea, and they respond to this dependence in two ways. The first is by accommodating the transit state, and the second is by placing transit states in a competitive position.[8] For both Nepal and Bhutan, India is the only feasible transit state. India surrounds them on three sides, and to the north of both lies Tibet. Furthermore, since in both cases, population, production, and market centers are located on the southern foothills of the Himalayas, transit access through China would entail traversing very difficult terrain. The OHRLLS website points out that unlike the landlocked countries of Europe, most developing countries are very far from the sea and are not surrounded by developed markets. They tend to be commodity exporters whose products are expensive due to high cost and sometimes unreliable transportation and communication links through the transit state.

Mahnaz Ispahani uses the term *tyranny of terrain* to capture the extent to which geography limits a state's choices.[9] Historically, landlocked states have either been neutral like Switzerland or buffer states like Afghanistan during the imperial age. Defined as the outer frontier of neighboring coastal states, their foreign policy autonomy is considerably limited. Indian prime minister Nehru described Nepal, Sikkim, and Bhutan in exactly such terms. The relationship between these countries is asymmetrical, and in 1976 Sikkim was absorbed into the Indian Union following political upheavals within the state.

Kautilya's *rājamandala* ("circle of kings"), depicted most often as concentric circles of polities, might well illustrate a landlocked state's relationship with its neighbors.[10] The natural animosity between a polity and those on its frontiers compels it to seek alliances with those whose relationships with its antagonists are equally (and similarly) hostile. In the case of both Nepal and Bhutan, the relationships with India and China are fraught. By virtue of its relative size, Nepal's foreign policy conforms more closely to the Kautilya model than does Bhutan's. While Nepal is constrained by its transit dependence on India, it has tried to leverage its relationship with each of its neighbors in its relationship with the other. Making common cause with India's other South Asian neighbors, most of whom have grievances against India, has been easier. Bhutan's relationship with China is haunted by the Chinese annexation of Tibet. In the aftermath of that event, Bhutan's relationship with India has been very close, but in Bhutan's gradual opening to the region and the world, we can discern the *rājamandala* at work.

Dick Hodder, writing about landlocked developing states, describes their situation as "double dependency."[11] First, they depend on others by virtue of location. Second, they are in dependent relationships by virtue of being peripheral states in the global political economy. To this, in the context of mountain states, we may add a third source of dependency. The "triple dependency" of Nepal and Bhutan is a function of their terrain, which limits the land available for cultivation, clusters population in certain areas, and, as mentioned earlier, limits their choice of transit state. It also makes some border areas impossible to monitor and exacerbates regional differences within the state. Both of these have important political and security consequences for the two states discussed in this section.

For all its smallness and remoteness, Bhutan has a well-defined sense of identity and, consequently, a well-considered worldview. The Bhutanese polity—Druk-Yul to give it its Bhutanese name—was founded in the early 1600s when Tibetan dissidents broke away and asserted their independence from Tibet's prevalent Buddhist hierarchy and secular authorities. The first element of Bhutanese identity comes from the Mahayana Buddhist sect that came to dominate its cultural, spiritual, and political landscape, even fashioning the last: the Drukpa sect. The second comes from the distinctive political institutions that evolved in Bhutan in subsequent decades—distinct from the other Himalayan kingdoms. Since the late 1980s, this national identity has been articulated in very specific ethnolinguistic terms. The dialect, diet, and dress of the western and central parts of Bhutan are taken as the national standard, and to be Bhutanese, according to the *driglam namzha*, or traditional code, is to speak Dzongkha and to wear the *gho* and *kira* on formal occasions. This has been enforced as law since the late 1980s, along with laws that deny citizenship to foreigners marrying Bhutanese.[12]

The external interests of the Bhutanese elite were oriented at first to warding off Tibetan campaigns in the north and west and to creating and maintaining tributary relationships with the kingdoms of the plains areas along their southern borders, like Cooch-Behar and the Assam Duars.[13] Accepting Bhutan's suzerainty, these areas offered a steady source of revenue to the Bhutanese, funding military efforts in the north. In the late eighteenth century, transformations on both fronts began to alter Bhutan's foreign policy approach. In the north, China–Tibet alliances, then greater Chinese influence in Lhasa, made Bhutan wary. In the south, the British expansion into northern Bihar and Assam posed a direct challenge in this Bhutanese sphere of influence. Bhutan and Britain went to war twice, first in 1772–1773 over Cooch-Behar and then in 1865 over the Assam Duars. The net result of these two encounters was a shrinking of both Bhutanese influence in and revenues from the area and minimal concessions from the India–Tibet trade in which Bhutan had a long-time interest. Faced with the reality of being sandwiched between two much larger forces, the Bhutanese elite chose isolation as a means of ensuring their survival. To the British, whose Indian holdings now verged on Bhutan, this was perfectly acceptable. Indeed, it was consistent with what they sought in buffer states. Their 1910 treaty with the new *druk-gyalpo*, Ugyen Wangchuk, recognized him as such in return for his accepting their guidance in matters relating to foreign policy. When India became independent, it entered first into a standstill agreement whereby all the old treaty obligations would continue, and then in 1949 a new treaty was negotiated on terms more favorable to Bhutan. The treaty recognized Bhutan's independence and conceded its territorial claims in return for its acceptance of India's guidance in matters of foreign policy.

When the Chinese occupied Tibet in 1950, isolation and neutrality seemed less than realistic. While sympathetic, Bhutan had to face two new realities: the prospect of hundreds of Tibetan refugees flooding Bhutan and changing its delicate demographic balance and the prospect of China's territory extending along its northern and western borders. Its response was to seal the Tibet border, allowing refugees to use Bhutan only as transit to India. The first consequence of this was to rupture old trading contacts between Bhutan and Tibet. Second, it drew Bhutan closer to India, diplomatically and economically. Finally, it increased Bhutan's strategic importance. The special relationship between Bhutan and India has diplomatic and economic dimensions. As previous paragraphs indicate, it is underpinned by, first, the historical legacy of the Anglo-Bhutanese wars and the 1910 treaty with British India and, second, the 1949 Indo-Bhutanese Treaty. India sponsored Bhutan's entry into the United Nations system, and since then, Bhutan has joined several international organizations and movements, including the Nonaligned Movement. Perhaps the most important dimension of the economic relationship between the two states is the provision of trade and transit access to landlocked Bhutan. In addition to its ports, India has built a road across the narrow strip of its territory that separates Bhutan and Bangladesh, thus providing an alternative access route to the state. India has also played a key role in Bhutan's development plans, providing generous funding and technical expertise. Cooperation between the states has included joint projects like the hydroelectric plant at Chukha, the setting up of basic infrastructure such as roads and postal services, and the training of Bhutanese civil and military officials in India.[14] The hydroelectric projects have underscored the interdependence of the two economies since India is the major purchaser of surplus energy produced by Bhutan's plants. For the most part, Bhutan's foreign policy is consistent with India's, although they are not necessarily identical.

A new issue has emerged in Bhutan's relationship with India, that of the United Liberation Front of Assam and National Democratic Front of Bodoland militants who have used the porous border to escape from the Indian army and to establish bases and training camps in Bhutan's southern reaches. This is intrinsically problematic; however, when you consider the presence of refugee camps in the same part of Bhutan, the problem becomes much more troubling. The late 1980s marriage, citizenship, and national-identity policies have made refugees of thousands of Nepalese living in Bhutan. Bhutanese authorities claim that not everyone in the camps actually lived in Bhutan—UNHCR camps have a higher standard of living than areas around them and draw attention. Moreover, reminiscent of the Afghan camps in Pakistan, over the years children are born into refugee households that do not know other realities. Finally, the camps have become a base for prodemocracy dissident activity against the present Bhutanese establishment. In these circumstances, the close proximity of militant bases and camps poses a fundamental security threat. In a path-breaking monograph, Aruni John identifies several prevailing factors that make it possible and appealing for Lhotshampa youth to take up militancy.[15] Bhutan does not have the military capability to take on the militants and fears reprisals. It sees joint operations with India as pointless and has tried to negotiate with the militants to shut down their camps. While it is possible that as India and the present rebels themselves come to terms, the militants will shut down the camps and move out, Bhutan's innate vulnerability to future territorial incursions by other militant groups fighting in India stands revealed.

The refugee crisis precipitated by Bhutan's national-identity and citizenship policies has strained Bhutan's relationship with Nepal. Nepal has had to contend with the arrival of several thousand refugees by way of India. India has its own Gorkha community that in the 1980s fought for and won its own district in West Bengal. Some Lhotshampa leaders express their protest in terms of seeking help from fellow Nepalese and also in antimonarchical and anti-Drukpa terms. This underscores the notion that land-hungry Nepal could develop expansionist tendencies, whether or not this is realistic. Nepal also retains an interest in the welfare of its émigré community. Negotiations between Bhutan and Nepal for over a decade have yielded no resolution. The stumbling block appears to be the question of how to categorize the people in the refugee camps, with Bhutan insisting on identifying those with criminal records and those it says emigrated voluntarily, facing Nepalese opposition.[16] Never close, Nepal–Bhutan relations have been greatly strained by this crisis.

Bhutan has close relationships with other South Asian countries. It was a founding member of SAARC and has been an active participant in the organization's meetings and projects. SAARC has played an important part in reducing Bhutan's isolation further (with the establishment of air and telecommunication links, for instance) and also in diversifying its external relationships. Bhutan was the second country, after India, to recognize Bangladesh, and growing trade ties have brought them closer. It maintains a neutral stance on all India–Pakistan disputes, abstaining where it cannot vote with India at the United Nations on these matters.[17] Bhutan hosted the India-mediated 1985 talks between the Sri Lankan government and the leaders of Tamil militant groups. Rajesh Kharat quotes the Bhutanese weekly, *Kuensel*: "Bhutan is emerging as an 'Eastern Geneva,' a venue for peace-making efforts in South Asia."[18]

Bhabani Sen Gupta identifies development as the first aim of Bhutan's foreign policy.[19] Moving from an early dependence exclusively on India, Bhutan has been diversifying its sources of development assistance. In keeping with the decades-old commitment to development balanced with cultural and ecological conservation, Bhutan has expanded its engagement with the world through participation in the United Nations system and other multilateral groupings. Bhutan now receives assistance from Denmark, Japan, and the Asian Development Bank, among other sources, even though it does not maintain residential representation in most countries. SAARC, too, helps Bhutan meet this objective. It gives Bhutan access to the region's food reserves, to technical assistance, to collaborative exploration of its mineral resources, and to the region's burgeoning middle-class tourist market.[20] The terms and manner of Bhutan's engagement with the world reflect its will to preserve its national identity, both politically as a sovereign state and culturally as a reflection of its religion and customs, even as it develops its resources, human and natural.

The history of Nepal's interactions with the outside world suggests a dialectic between a national self-image that accords to Nepal the rightful domination of the Himalayan region and the state's geographical reality of being sandwiched between India and China. The two threads converged to reinforce Nepal's determination to remain independent and sovereign; however, in acting on its expansionist impulse, Nepal had to literally walk a fine line between the rulers of the Indian plains and the Chinese or Tibetans, all of whom laid claim to the same regions. In the years after its unification by Prithvi Narayan Shah, Nepal's ambitions brought it into conflict with China and Tibet between 1788 and 1792, with the Sikhs in 1809, with the British between 1814 and 1816, and with the Tibetans between 1854 and 1856. A treaty with China called upon Nepal to send gifts to the Chinese emperor every five years, a practice that continued for several decades.[21]

However, Nepal's other reality is that India and China are not equidistant from it physically, economically, or culturally. Its main population centers lie in the Terai, which is an extension of the Gangetic plains. Therefore, it is easier to get goods and supplies to and from India than Tibet, and it would be irrational to seek maritime access through Chinese rather than Indian ports. Therefore, notwithstanding the theoretical idea of being sandwiched between two powers with the option of leveraging one relationship against the other, Nepal is much more dependent on India.

The establishment of British paramountcy in the plains checked Nepal's southward ambitions. The Treaty of Sugauli was signed in 1816 between the British East India Company and Nepal.[22] Nepal had to cede some of its territories, including newer acquisitions, to the British and to Indian princes like those in Awadh and Sikkim; this strengthened British India's northern frontier. Disputes between Nepal and Sikkim were particularly to be referred to British arbitration, which would be binding on Nepal. Nepal could no longer hire Europeans or Americans in its service. Diplomatic relations were established, although the British were not to interfere in court affairs. The British resident would report back on matters of security concern. The treaty also reserved for the British the right to recruit Nepalese soldiers into the British Indian army. The Shah rulers and the Ranas saw remaining on good terms with the British as important. For the latter, it was a way to ensure both the survival of their own regime and the independence of Nepal.[23] In 1923 a second treaty was signed by Britain and Nepal, which recognized the independence of Nepal while stipulating that Nepal would consult British India on matters relating to defense and foreign affairs.

The departure of the British from India in 1947 might have been an opportunity to redefine the India–Nepal relationship. For the Ranas, it was not clear whether India's new democratic leaders would choose to support the new Nepali Congress and intervene in Nepali politics. The new Indian leadership, however, inherited British geopolitical ideas, and Nehru's statement identifying the Himalayan kingdoms as an important line of defense is quoted often to illustrate that.[24] A standstill agreement was signed between India and Nepal, stating that relations between the two states would continue on the basis of the 1923 treaty, pending the negotiation of new terms. The departing colonial power, its successor state, and Nepal also renegotiated the terms on which Nepalese (Gurkha) soldiers would henceforth be recruited. This remains an important tie between the three countries. Under the Tripartite Memorandum of Agreement signed in 1947, the majority of the Gurkha regiments in the British Indian army went to the Indian army, with the British retaining about four regiments.[25] The deployment of Gurkhas by the two foreign armies is conditional; they may not be deployed against Nepal, against other Gurkhas, or against Hindu or other unarmed mobs.[26]

In 1950 China annexed Tibet. With this, the security of India and Nepal became mutually interdependent. The Treaty of Peace and Friendship between the two countries was signed in June 1950. India needed to ensure Nepal's neutrality vis-à-vis China and the Rana regime did not wish to antagonize the Indian leadership, which was predisposed toward democratization. The treaty assures mutual friendship, communication, and security between the two states. It also established a free market between the two states to assure the movement of people and goods. This treaty is criticized both because it was signed with an undemocratic government (the Ranas) and also because, in the long run, it has placed Nepal at a disadvantage in economic and political terms. In 1951 the Ranas were overthrown and the monarchy was restored along with some semblance of democratic institutions. In 1959 King Mahendra dismissed an elected Nepali Congress government and drew criticism from India for it. This underscored the resentment felt by many Nepalese after the conclusion of the Indo-Nepali treaty. The Nepali Congress was seen as being pro-India, allowing its activities to be depicted as India-sponsored and the monarch's anti-Nepali Congress positions to be depicted as assertions of sovereignty. Thus, notwithstanding

India's own intentions and actions, it was always implicated in Nepalese politics. During this phase, the king moved away from the close relationship with India to seek ties also with China and Pakistan.[27]

In this most complicated relationship, certain issues are particularly difficult. The first is the question of trade and transit. As Nepal has sought to diversify its contact with the world, India has used the negotiations and renewal of mutual trade and transit agreements to show its disapproval. It has done so by failing to renew the treaty and by granting less access than the Nepalese ask for but more than is required by international law.[28] In 1988, to India's consternation, Nepal bought a large number of defensive and offensive weapons from China. In 1976 three trade and transit agreements were signed between India and Nepal that expired in March 1989. India responded to the Nepalese arms purchase by sealing thirteen out of fifteen transit points between the two countries. Failure to renew the treaty served as an effective economic blockade of Nepal. Nepal's attempt to appeal to other powers for help yielded little fruit, and popular frustration with the regime that had allowed this crisis to develop facilitated the second democratic transition in Nepalese history. The trade and transit treaty was finally renewed with new provisions that gave primacy to India's security concerns. Nepal assured India that it would not use its policy of equidistance to the detriment of India's security. Consultations would precede important defense agreements made by either side. The *status quo ante* April 1, 1990, was restored, removing the work-permit requirement placed on Indian citizens in Nepal and opening all fifteen transit points. Since then, renewal has been fairly routine, but the memory of the 1989–1990 crisis remains fresh.

India's technical and economic assistance to Nepal has also come under criticism. The projects funded, their design, and the choice of technologies are all criticized by some Nepalese as better suited to India's interests and needs than the needs and local conditions in Nepal.[29] Further, the free access of Indians to work and property in Nepal is seen as unfair. Although Nepalese enjoy the same access in India, Indians are seen as pressing their existing advantages further. In all, if arrogance marks Indian attitudes to Nepal, then petulance characterizes the Nepalese response to India.

How does Nepal get along with the rest of South Asia? The only other South Asian state with which Nepal's relations are strained is Bhutan. Bhutan's summary disenfranchisement of Bhutanese of Nepali origin, or Lhotshampas, is the primary cause of this strain, although the two states have never been as close as their common circumstances might suggest. Thousands of refugees live in camps in the south of Bhutan, and still others have fled to Nepal via India, which is unwilling to host them in light of its own northeastern problems. Nepal has sought ties with Pakistan as a means of balancing India. Bangladesh shares Nepal's concerns about water management, and two transit routes through India actually lead Nepali goods to Bangladeshi ports.

> Today SAARC is high on the agenda of Nepal's foreign policy, the parallel of which is King Birendra's proposal for declaring Nepal a Zone of Peace. Both can be called twin strategies—one for the consolidation of Nepal's political independence from both China and India, and the other (SAARC) aims at reducing Nepal's economic dependence on India.[30]

In the last two decades, SAARC has become Nepal's safest option when it comes to adding ballast to its dealings with India. SAARC headquarters, along with the attendant regional nongovernmental organizations, are located in Kathmandu. If Thimphu can claim to be the region's Geneva, then Kathmandu is its Brussels. SAARC holds for Nepal the hope of increased interdependence with the rest of the region to offset its dependence on India. Nepal sees several of the issues important to it, trade and water for instance, as better addressed in a regional, multilateral setting because these in fact involve more than two states. Water management in the Gangetic basin, for instance, involves Nepal, India, and Bangladesh.

King Birendra mooted the zone-of-peace idea in his coronation speech in 1975. It was an idea that found easy support among many countries, but conspicuously absent from their number has been India. Bhutan also has not endorsed this idea. What does Nepal mean by asking to be recognized as a "zone of peace"?[31] Its seven-point action plan (1982) tells us, as follows:

1. Nepal will adhere to peace, nonalignment, and peaceful coexistence with all.
2. It will not use force in any way threatening to other countries.
3. It will seek peaceful settlement of all disputes.
4. Nepal will not interfere in the internal affairs of other states.
5. It will not permit activities on its soil that are hostile to other states supporting this proposal and seeks reciprocity in this matter.
6. It will continue to honor its treaty obligations.
7. It will not enter into military alliance or allow foreign bases and seeks reciprocity in this matter.

These are the basic principles enshrined in the UN Charter and the founding principles of the Nonaligned Movement, of which Nepal is a member. India's lack of support, which renders the proposal meaningless, is attributed to many factors. India does not like to reassess its security-threat perception unduly.[32] It does not think it feasible, given an open border, to promise not to permit activities on its soil that are hostile to Nepalese regimes. Once in India, Nepalese enjoy the same constitutional rights as Indians.[33] India states that it is not clear whom Nepal considers a threat in this proposal, and it will not entertain a redefinition of the special relationship between the two countries.[34] In conclusion, India looms large in Nepal's attempt to find itself a place in the world. In some ways friendship with India is a guarantor of that place, and in others India is its most real threat. The truth lies between those two perspectives. As a major tourist center and through its participation in SAARC, Nepal has made itself much less peripheral than its size and location might determine. While it does not seem likely that Nepal will revert to its earlier expansionist agenda, given its internal conflicts and external constraints, the memory of its ambitions lingers in the Himalayan region. Nepal's quest depends now on the success of SAARC and SAARC's ability to rekindle old regional flows and interdependence in new ways.

ISLAND STATES: THE MALDIVES AND SRI LANKA

Island states vary greatly in terms of geology, size, distance covered, and population. Sri Lanka and the Maldives, both in this category, exemplify this. Indian Ocean states both, the first is much larger than the second, and it is only in the context of South Asia that it would be considered a small state. The island of Sri Lanka is close to and a fragment of the Indian continental plate system. The Maldives are an archipelago of atolls (raised coral reefs) comprising more than twelve hundred islands that spread out over 800 kilometers north to south and 130 kilometers east to west. Only two hundred of the islands are inhabited.

Small island states, especially archipelagic states like the Maldives, face special constraints to development and security.[35] We might summarize these as economic constraints stemming from size and a limited resource base, ecological vulnerabilities, and a tendency to depend on outside help. Writing of small island developing states, Farah Faizal states, "the remoteness of these islands in many cases, their maritime features, their insularity and their environmental fragility add to the wider concept of security problems faced by developing countries."[36] While these are more evident in the case of the Maldives, Sri Lanka demonstrates another quality David Lowenthal ascribes to insular states, the critical importance of maintaining intergroup cooperation. Absence of such cooperation opens the door to outside intervention, which is something that small states particularly fear.[37] In this age of globalization, small island states are susceptible on new fronts. Global trade in oil and the transportation of hazardous waste for disposal in other countries leaves them open to the consequences of shipping accidents that might pollute their waters and disrupt the marine life they depend on. Their dependence on tourism opens other gaps in their security. First, as travel modes and routes become more vulnerable as targets in conflict, tourism is bound to suffer. Second, the experience of the Caribbean islands in the age of European explorations can more easily be replicated in this age of fast-spreading diseases. Fluctuations in global commodities markets (like that for tuna) and close-knit financial networks drag hitherto isolated states into the rough and tumble of the world economy. Finally, for archipelagic states, it is even harder to monitor the comings and goings of nontraditional actors like terrorists and drug traders, who might use outlying islands.

Historically, the Maldives have had regular contact with the outside world: they feature in South Asian folklore; they are mentioned by outside travelers and writers like Ptolemy, Alberuni, and Ibn-Batuta; Islam found its way to the Maldives as had Buddhism before it; and the migration of Indians, Sri Lankans, Southeast Asians, Arabs, and Persians created the Maldivian nation.[38] The Maldives had trading relations with India and Sri Lanka, exporting cowrie shells, coir, coconuts, amber gris, and tortoise shell, and importing rice from Sri Lanka in exchange for dried fish.[39] In fact, it was an important staging post on sea routes from Pacific Asia to Africa. Insofar as the Maldives have a traditional adversary, it would be the Mapillas from the southwest (Malabar) coast of India.[40] Further, the Maldives for a while paid tribute to the ruler of Cannanore on India's Malabar coast, and this transferred somewhat to Sri Lanka's colonial rulers as they took their turn: the Portuguese, Dutch, and British. The Portuguese occupied the northern part of the Maldives for fifteen years. On occasion, the European rulers of Sri Lanka, which was called Ceylon until the name was changed to Sri Lanka in 1972, provided the Maldives with protection against the Mapillas. The Maldives formally became a British protectorate in 1887, ceding to the British the right to control defense and foreign relations as well as the right to install and recognize the sultan of the Maldives. (The British, however, did not maintain an official presence in the Maldives until the 1960s.) During this period, trade contacts between the Maldives and the South Asian mainland rose steadily.

The Maldives formally gained independence in 1965, and the nation adopted its current republican constitution in 1968. However, the continued presence of a British base at Gan compromised Maldivian independence until 1976. With the independence of Ceylon in 1948 and the British military presence in Trincomalee and Colombo's Katunayake airport being terminated in 1956, an agreement was signed in the same year that allowed them to use Gan Island as an air force base for a hundred years. The Gan base issue highlights five important security concerns.

1. First, as an island state and also as a developing country emerging from protectorate status, credible assertions of autonomy and independence are important to the Maldives.

2. In a regional environment where the hegemonic power (India) frowns on extraregional military presences in its sphere of interest, and other states have proposed a nuclear-weapon-free zone (Pakistan), a zone of peace (Nepal), and making the Indian Ocean a zone of peace (Sri Lanka), allowing the British base to remain at Gan would have been impolitic. The Maldives, as South Asia's smallest state, must temper its assertions of independence with some understanding of the regional climate.

3. As is common in atoll states, remoteness within the state fostered separatist sentiments in three southern atolls, including Addu, where the Gan base was located.[41] The British military presence fueled these sentiments and led the Maldivian government to suppose that the British were encouraging the separatists. It is no less important for the Maldives than it is for any other state to preserve its territorial integrity, and the Addu problem was resolved in the state's favor ultimately.

4. The Gan base underscored a common problem created by foreign employers in the context of any developing state. Salary disparities between what the British base would pay and what the residents of the southern atolls might otherwise earn in their traditional occupations further alienated them from the Maldives economy and polity. Measures to deal with this only made matters worse.[42]

5. The strategic importance of the Maldives has only grown since the second half of the twentieth century. The superpowers vied for bases in the Indian Ocean that would give them access to the littoral states of Asia, Africa, and Australia. The location of the Maldives, and of Gan specifically, is ideal as a base from which to conduct both surveillance and military operations. Even with the end of the Cold War, the war on terror and the centrality of the Indian Ocean base of Diego Garcia to that effort underscore the potential of the Maldives. While this provides the state with some international leverage, it also increases its vulnerability to the pressure of really large states.

While the issue of allowing military bases allowed us to identify five important concerns, this is hardly an exhaustive consideration of the foreign policy imperatives of the Maldives. Foremost on that nation's agenda is that the international community should acknowledge the special security needs of small states and guarantee their protection. This stems from the Maldives' many experiences with coups d'état. Since the state attained independence in 1968, there have been attempted coups in 1980, 1983, and 1988.[43] The 1980 coup was the first time mercenaries were hired to stage a coup.[44] The 1988 coup was by far the most ominous attempt to overthrow the Maldivian government, in which two Colombo-based Maldivian dissidents joined forces with about eighty mercenaries from the Tamil militant group, the People's

Liberation Organisation of Tamil Eelam (PLOTE). Indian intervention foiled the attempted coup, giving chase to fleeing mercenaries and their hostages. One of the captured Maldivian dissidents stated that the coup had been funded by PLOTE in order to gain a secure base for their struggle against the Sri Lankan state.[45] It is possible, however, that that was merely a quid pro quo for PLOTE assistance to the dissidents. After the 1988 coup, the Maldives raised the issue of the protection of small states at the UN General Assembly. A resolution was adopted recognizing their vulnerability and advising that they should be assisted as needed. Since that 1989 resolution, the Maldives has organized workshops and initiated debates on the question at each international forum of which it is a member.

The 1988 coup is portentous beyond the Maldives. In the present international situation, where weak state control has time and again permitted violent nonstate actors to avail themselves of the power vacuum to establish safe havens, bases, and training camps, the vulnerability of an archipelagic state like the Maldives to conflicts waged elsewhere increases many fold. Although landlocked, Afghanistan is very much a hinterland state of the Arabian Sea, lying just to the north of the Maldives. By the government's own admission, it is not possible to secure all the islands of the state equally. What precludes a repetition of the 1988 scenario, this time from the north? This vulnerability of the Maldives becomes, in this climate of collective resolve, the vulnerability of all states.

Global warming is another issue where the resolve of the rest of the world has dramatic consequences for the Maldives. It is expected that global warming will cause sea levels to rise about three-quarters of a meter, which would wipe out the Maldives altogether, but a smaller rise could also be very destructive.[46] The Maldivian government has understandably been very active in keeping this issue alive in international forums like the Global Conference on the Sustainable Development of Small Island Developing States (1994).

The Maldives's closest relationship, traditionally, has been with Sri Lanka. Sri Lanka is the Maldives's main trading partner, and it was to Colombo that the Maldives government turned in the colonial period, seeking protection or assistance. Sri Lankans work and vacation in the Maldives, and Maldivians work, study, and vacation in Sri Lanka. However, since India helped foil the coup in 1988, Indo-Maldivian relations have grown close, and India has become a major donor of technical and financial assistance to the Maldives. The Maldives also have good relationships with Pakistan and Bangladesh, with Islam underscoring the ties in both cases. Bangladeshi workers have also found their way to jobs in the Maldives, adding a contemporary economic dimension to the relations between the states. For the Maldives, as with other small South Asian states, natural (through Islam, for instance) and cultivated (through SAARC, for instance) affinities with all other states must be balanced so that the relationship with India remains positive. This can be a very delicate matter, even beyond the South Asian context.

While Maldivian Islam is moderate, the island state has not been immune to the waves of radical Islamic movements that are sweeping the globe. Like many other states, the Maldives must walk that tightrope between traditional moderation, the impulse to modernize, and the pressure generated by this groundswell. With close ties to both Arab and non-Arab Islamic states, in today's international relations climate where the clash of civilizations thesis meets Thomas Hobbes and Hans Morgenthau with disastrous results, states like the Maldives are called on to make diplomatic choices that reflect their affinities as much as their constraints. The Maldives have joined the Non-aligned Movement, the Commonwealth of Nations, and the Organization of the Islamic Conference in the last three decades. It has been a member of SAARC since the latter's inception. Like the other small states of the region, it views SAARC as providing an opportunity for its own development, as well as for the amelioration of the regional security environment. It has twice hosted SAARC summit meetings, and at its initiative, 1992 was observed as the SAARC Year of the Environment.

In spite of its limited resources, the Maldives have taken membership in the international system seriously and contributed in three significant ways. First, as an active member of SAARC, the Maldives, along with Nepal and Bhutan particularly, have helped keep the organization alive, notwithstanding the very acrimonious disputes that flare up from time to time between India and the other three members. Second, the Maldives have consistently raised the question of small-state security, forcing attention to an issue that at this particular moment could acquire great significance. Finally, the role played by the Maldives in highlighting the impact of global climate change has provided perspective to debates on sustainable development and definitions of human security. After all, if a country can simply be swallowed by the rising ocean tides, all other discussions of defense, trade, and diplomatic relations are really rather futile!

By most measures, and in any region outside South Asia, Sri Lanka would not be a small state. At the very least, its record of international engagement and initiative would place it in a different category. By virtue of its long coastline and proximity to the subcontinental mainland, Sri Lanka has never been isolated from the rest of the world. The island served as an entrepôt between Africa and Asia, having trading contacts with imperial Rome and Greece, as well as kingdoms in Africa, Persia, Byzantium, Southeast Asia, and China.

Historically, the island's most prominent and influential interactions were with the peoples and states of the subcontinental mainland. Centuries of migration, commercial interactions, and intermarriage created a composite culture on the island with three or four distinctive ethnolinguistic groups. Over the centuries, while not mutually exclusive, the Tamil communities have come to be associated with the northern areas while the Sinhalese are associated with other parts; this separation is underscored by the north's proximity to the South Indian home of many of the armies that would maraud, and occasionally settle to rule, large parts of the island. The history of repeated confrontation between Tamils from India and the people of the island resonates both in the rhetoric of contemporary ethnic relations in Sri Lanka as well as in Sri Lanka's relationship with India.

Colonialism affected Sri Lanka more profoundly than it did other parts of South Asia. Three European powers successively sought to assert their paramountcy over the island. First, the Portuguese arrived, establishing themselves on Sri Lanka's west coast and then seeking to spread their influence into the hinterlands. They remained on the island from 1619 to 1663. The Dutch, en route to their future stronghold, the Dutch East Indies, arrived around 1658 and remained until 1796. Their presence in peninsular India was challenged by the Anglo-French rivalry, and when they lost their mainland holdings altogether, they also ceded Ceylon to the British, who initially ruled it as part of Madras Presidency. In 1802 Ceylon became a Crown colony, and thence the British expanded and consolidated their administration, unifying the island under their flag until 1948. For the first time, the maritime territories and the Kandyan kingdom were brought together in a unitary arrangement, designed to disenfranchise the powerful Kandyan aristocracy.

Ceylon's insular nature and size ensured the near-total penetration of its space and culture by the colonial powers. This period saw the development of port cities like Galle, Colombo, and Trincomalee, which became pivots for the large-scale movement of peoples and goods across the global reaches of the British Empire. Apart from those western powers that sought political control over Ceylon, there was also a significant missionary presence, mostly American, concentrated in northern Ceylon. The missionaries established the island's first English schools and colleges in the north, giving northerners an edge in modern education and, therefore, eligibility for government and university employment that they would retain into the first decades after independence.

Like India and Pakistan, Ceylon chose to remain within the British Commonwealth, and it signed a defense pact with Britain. One of the early achievements of the Commonwealth, the Colombo Plan, which remains one of the leading Afro-Asian initiatives for technology transfer and development assistance, was launched in 1950. The fact that Ceylon adopted the Soulbury Constitution, a legislative enactment presuming the continuing validity of British laws and customs, in the same year as it became independent, retaining this as its basic law until 1972, also cemented its postcolonial relationship with Britain.

Sri Lanka also participated in the San Francisco Peace Conference in 1951, making a plea for compassion and forsaking vengeance.[47] The country was also in the forefront of the Asian initiatives that led to the Bandung Conference in 1955 and, later, to the Nonaligned Movement. As a founding member of the latter movement, Ceylon enjoyed great prestige in the developing world. The success of its basic-needs development strategy contributed to this prestige as, unique in South Asia, the strategy yielded excellent results in the spheres of education and health. In 1971 Sri Lanka proposed the creation of a zone of peace that would encompass the Indian Ocean, its islands, and littoral and hinterland states and that would be recognized by the major powers. It also sponsored the related resolution in the UN General Assembly. Sri Lanka has been a member of SAARC since its inception.

Sri Lanka has good relationships with all the other countries of South Asia, with educational, cultural, and economic ties growing over time. However, its most important bilateral relationship is with India, notwithstanding the many reservations Sri Lankan writers on international relations express about India's motives and actions. This centrality is underscored by the fact that research for this chapter on Sri Lanka's foreign policy revealed more writing on the India–Sri Lanka relationship than any other topic.[48] While India's relationship with this neighbor has also had its problematic moments, on the whole they have been resolved amicably. Four issues in particular have plagued this relationship.

First, chronologically speaking, came the question of the Tamils brought to Ceylon by the British to provide labor for their tea and coffee plantations. In 1948 the new Ceylonese state deprived them of citizenship, leaving them stateless. Several rounds of negotiations worked out specific formulae for their repatriation, leaving thousands still stranded in the plantation districts. Second, the demarcation of maritime borders between the two countries has led to disputes over the possession of Kachchathivu in the Palk Strait. As the strait is rich in marine life, the real victims of this dispute are fishermen, who are arrested upon straying into the wrong waters. Notwithstanding the 1976 agreement between the states, the question continues to be raised from time to time, especially on the Indian side.[49] Third, the tendency of many Indians to regard South Asia as lying within India's proper sphere of influence is irksome to Sri Lanka. India has regarded with disfavor any attempt by Sri Lanka (and its other neighbors) to enter into close strategic relationships with other states. It sees these relationships as threatening to its security. Sri Lanka has sought close relationships with Britain and the United States, and, since the outbreak of the ethnic conflict, with Pakistan and Israel, but this has not been acceptable to India.

Finally, the issue of ethnic conflict has dominated the India–Sri Lanka relationship in recent years. From India's point of view, the floods of Tamil refugees, the prospect of other powers' intervening, and the political pressures created by the people of Tamil Nadu constitute adequate grounds for concern about this internal conflict. The view from Sri Lanka is not as simple. For some Sri Lankans, especially those in the Sinhalese majority, the presence of fifty million Tamils across the straits makes it hard to think of compromise on the question of national identity. India's part in arming and training the Tamil militants is well documented,[50] but events following the Indo–Sri Lankan Accord (1987) first embittered Sri Lanka and then, after the assassination of Rajiv Gandhi, India. In recent years, in spite of its continuing stakes in the Sri Lankan situation, India's participation in the conflict and the peace process has been low-key. India's role in the escalation of the conflict is of a piece with historical Indian interventions that remain vivid in the Sri Lankan collective memory. While India's involvement in the conflict was abhorrent to Sri Lanka (as the reverse would have been), its unwillingness to host peace talks or to mediate has also been regarded with dismay. This ambivalence is illustrated by the fact that after he was sworn in, in April 2004, one of Mahinda Rajapakse's first acts as the new Sri Lankan prime minister was to seek Indian assistance to settle the problem. His party is allied with the party that most violently opposed the Indian intervention in the late 1980s. India, unwilling to appear directly involved, has not hesitated to actively cooperate with the Sri Lankan forces to provide training, functional assistance, and intelligence.

A basic problem in South Asian international relations is illustrated by this dimension of the India–Sri Lanka interaction—these are states whose peoples are organically connected but politically divided by lines that are only arbitrarily designated internal or international at particular historical moments. States, reflecting the reactions of their people, must respond to each other's internal politics, but, respecting international law, they cannot in fact do so.

Beyond India and South Asia, Sri Lanka's most important international efforts in the last few years have involved an effort to win support for its war with the Liberation Tigers of Tamil Eelam (LTTE), a secessionist militant group. It has tried to get the LTTE banned, and it has tried to counter the propaganda and fund-raising efforts of that organization. Since the December 2001 cease-fire, it has attempted to win support for the peace process and reconstruction assistance from the international community. Norway has been the chief mediator, and Thailand, Germany, Sweden, and Norway have hosted sessions of the talks between the government and the LTTE. Norway's role has, however, been contentious within Sri Lankan political circles, and debates over the Norwegians' impartiality have slowed down the peace process.

All of India's neighbors, except possibly Bangladesh, make some effort to distance themselves from the South Asian heartland. Pakistan and the

Maldives have built strong connections with the Islamic world, and Nepal and Bhutan have tried to balance their relationships with India and China. Sri Lanka has tried to join the Association of Southeast Asian Nations (ASEAN), but as it does not meet the geographical criterion for membership, this has not been possible.

THE SMALL STATES OF SOUTH ASIA IN WORLD POLITICS

Size, location, and resource limitations have not deterred the four small states discussed in this chapter from being proactive in the international arena. Undeterred also by the shadow India casts over their universes, they have asserted their individuality and their own strategic interests at some risk. Combining the three policy alternatives identified by Espindola, they have maximized their agency in an international system in which they are deeply disadvantaged. All four states are members of the Nonaligned Movement. All of them are members of major international groupings other than the United Nations, for example, the Commonwealth of Nations in the instance of the Maldives and Sri Lanka. All of them are active members of SAARC and use that forum to influence the regional political agenda. All four states have also demonstrated a willingness to rely on India's support in critical matters—Nepal and Bhutan for access to the sea, the Maldives during the 1988 coup attempt, and Sri Lanka in the late 1980s—even though India's expanding presence in their politics is an important security concern for each. Since the founding of SAARC, all four states have built ties with other regional actors to counter or offset this dependence on India, but with varying success.

The two island states seem to have had more success at distancing themselves from India than the two landlocked states. The Maldives are the least identified with India anyway, lacking physical closeness and having the most tenuous of cultural ties. Sri Lanka operated very much as an equal partner until the Indian intervention in its internal conflict, but given its high international profile, it is not as vulnerable to the vagaries of its relationship with India as the other states. The two landlocked states are literally in a bind on this score! They can go nowhere past India, and wherever they go, there India is. It seems as though in the context of smallness, being landlocked adds to vulnerability, while some of the vulnerability of island states is offset by their physical separateness and their maritime contacts with others. This chapter shows that while size and location limit choices, they do not have to strip a state of agency. The four states of South Asia discussed here offer this morsel of hope to states similarly or otherwise condemned to insignificance in realist readings of international relations.

NOTES

1. I would like to thank Farah Faizal for her careful reading of an earlier version of this chapter and especially for her invaluable insights (and corrections) on the Maldives section.

2. For a fuller discussion of smallness, see Sangeeta Thapliyal, *Mutual Security: The Case of India–Nepal* (New Delhi: Lancer, 1998), 5–6.

3. To some extent, the inclusion of the Maldives in the South Asian Association for Regional Cooperation (SAARC) undercuts the Indocentric quality of the region, but not significantly given India's size and strategic reach.

4. See, e.g., *South Asia Terrorism Portal*, at www.satp.org; Farah Faizal, "Maldives," in "Security Problems of Small Island Developing States: With Special Reference to the Indian Ocean," Ph.D. dissertation (Hull: Hull University, 1996); Deepak Thapa, "Erosion of the Nepali World," *Himal South Asia* (April 2002), available at www.himalmag.com/2002/april/essay.htm (accessed March 13, 2003); Aruni John, *Potential for Militancy among Bhutanese Refugee Youth*, RCSS Policy Studies 15 (Colombo: Regional Centre for Strategic Studies, 2000).

5. Roberto Espindola, "Security Dilemmas," in *Politics, Security and Development in Small States*, ed. Colin Clarke and Tony Payne (London: Allen and Unwin, 1987), 75–78.

6. Office of the High Representative for the Least Developed Countries, Landlocked Developing Countries and Small Island Developing States (OHRLLS), "Landlocked Developing Countries (LLDCs)," 2002, available at www.un.org/special-rep/ohrlls/lldc/default.htm (accessed February 2, 2003).

7. Martin Ira Glassner, "Resolving the Problems of Land-lockedness," in *Land-locked States of Africa and Asia*, ed. Dick Hodder, Sarah J. Lloyd, and Keith McLachlan (London: Frank Cass, 1998), 198.

8. Thapliyal, *Mutual Security*, 20–21.

9. Mahnaz Ispahani, *Roads and Rivals: The Political Uses of Access in the Borderlands of Asia* (Ithaca, N.Y.: Cornell University Press, 1989), 2.

10. Kautilya, *The Arthashastra*, trans. L. N. Rangarajan (New Delhi: Penguin, 1987), 559–63.

11. Dick Hodder, "Conclusions," in *Land-locked States of Africa and Asia*, 210.

12. Syed Aziz-al Ahsan and Bhumitra Chakma, "Bhutan's Foreign Policy: Cautious Self-Assertion?" *Asian Survey*, 33, no. 11 (November 1993): 1,049–51.

13. The historical review in this section draws on the detailed narrative in Leo Rose, *The Politics of Bhutan* (Ithaca, N.Y.: Cornell University Press, 1977), 55–105.

14. Bhabani Sen Gupta, *Bhutan: Towards a Grass-root Participatory Polity* (New Delhi: Konarak, 1999), 141.

15. John, *Potential for Militancy*.

16. Smruti S. Pattanaik, "Nepal-Bhutan Bilateral Talks and Repatriation of Bhutanese Refugees," *Strategic Analysis* 22, no. 10 (January 1999), available at www.ciaonet.org/olj/sa/sa_99pas01.html (accessed March 1, 2003).

17. On matters relating to nonproliferation and disarmament, Bhutan has on occasion voted in opposition to India's position at the UN. See Rajesh Kharat, *Bhutan in SAARC* (New Delhi: South Asian Publishers, 1999), 27–29.

18. Kharat, *Bhutan in SAARC*, 56.

19. Sen Gupta, *Bhutan*, 130.

20. Kharat, *Bhutan in SAARC*, 85–87.

21. Kumar B. Bhatta, "Sino-Nepalese and Indo-Nepalese Relations: A Comparative Study," *The People's Review,* online edition, November 21–27, 2002, available at www.yomari.com/p-review/2002/11/21112002/view2.html (accessed March 2, 2003).

22. Thapliyal, *Mutual Security,* 18–20.

23. Lok Raj Baral, *The Politics of Balanced Interdependence: Nepal and SAARC.* New Delhi: Sterling Publishers, 1988, 17.

24. Baral, *The Politics of Balanced Interdependence,* 22–23.

25. Baral, *The Politics of Balanced Interdependence*, 19.

26. See both Baral, *The Politics of Balanced Interdependence,* 19, and Thapliyal, *Mutual Security*, 38, for a discussion of this provision.

27. Partha S. Ghosh, *Cooperation and Conflict in South Asia* (New Delhi: Manohar, 1989), 125–26.

28. Thapliyal points out that India is not a signatory to either the Convention on Trade and Transit to Landlocked Countries or the Law of the Sea Convention governing transit rights. Thapliyal, *Mutual Security*, 136.

29. See, e.g., Dipak Gyawali and Ajaya Dixit, "How Not to Do a South Asian Treaty," *Himal South Asian* (April 2001), available at www.himalmag.com/apr2001/essay1.html (accessed March 2, 2003).

30. Baral, *The Politics of Balanced Interdependence,* 66.

31. Baral, *The Politics of Balanced Interdependence*, 31–32.

32. Baral, *The Politics of Balanced Interdependence*, 32.

33. S. D. Muni, quoted in Baral, *The Politics of Balanced Interdependence,* 33.

34. Baral, *The Politics of Balanced Interdependence,* 34.

35. Anthony Dolman, "Paradise Lost? The Past Performance and Future Prospects of Small Islands Developing Countries," in *States, Microstates and Islands*, ed. Edward Dommen and Philippe Hein (London: Croom Helm, 1985), 41–42. See also François Doumenge, "The Viability of Small Intertropical Islands," in *States, Microstates and Islands*, 102–13.

36. Farah Faizal, "Smallness and Security of SIDS," in *Security Problems of Small Island Developing States*, 11.

37. David Lowenthal, "Social Features," in *Politics, Security and Development in Small States*, eds. Colin Clarke and Tony Payne (London: Allen and Unwin, 1987) 40–41.

38. Urmila Phadnis and Ela Dutt Luithui, *Maldives: Winds of Change in an Atoll State* (New Delhi: South Asian Publishers, 1985), 1–5. See also, Thor Heyedahl, *The Maldives Mystery* (London: Adler and Adler, 1986).

39. Phadnis and Dutt Luithui, *Maldives*, 16.

40. The following is reconstructed from Phadnis and Dutt Luithui, *Maldives*, 17–19.

41. Faizal, "Maldives," 122–23.

42. Phadnis and Dutt Luithui, *Maldives*, 30–31.

43. Hideyuki Takahashi, "Maldivian National Security—and the Threats of Mercenaries," *The Round Table*, 1999, no. 351, 436.

44. Farah Faizal, personal communication, March 13, 2003.

45. Ravinatha Aryasinha, "Maldives, Sri Lanka and the 'India Factor,'" *Himal South Asian* (March 1997): available at www.himalmag.com/97mar/cov-mal.htm (accessed February 15, 2002).

46. "Not sinking but drowning," *The Economist*, May 11, 2000, available at www.economist .com/PrinterFriendly.cfm?Story_ID=333841 (accessed December 9, 2001).

47. K. M. de Silva, *Regional Powers and Small State Security* (Washington, D.C.: Woodrow Wilson Center Press, 1995), 39.

48. For instance, three out of nine chapters in Shelton U. Kodikara, ed., *South Asian Strategic Issues: Sri Lankan Perspectiv*es (New Delhi: Sage, 1990), relate to the India–Sri Lanka relationship, as do seven out of nineteen chapters in P. V. J. Jayasekera, ed., *Security Dilemma of a Small State, Part One* (New Delhi: South Asian Publishers, 1992). K. M. de Silva's *Regional Powers and Small State Security* is subtitled *India and Sri Lanka, 1977–1990.*

49. One person who has regularly sought to highlight this issue is Professor V. Suryanarayan of the University of Madras. See his book *Kachchativu and the Problems of Indian Fishermen in the Palk Bay Region* (Madras: T. R. Publications, 1994).

51. The most commonly cited source is Rohan Gunaratna, *Indian Intervention in Sri Lanka: The Role of India's Intelligence Agencies* (Colombo: South Asian Network on Conflict Research, 1993).

FURTHER READING

Aryasinha, Ravinatha. "Maldives, Sri Lanka and the 'India Factor,'" *Himal South Asian* (March 1997), available at www.himalmag.com/97mar/cov-mal.htm.

Aziz al-Ahsan, Syed, and Bhumitra Chakma, "Bhutan's Foreign Policy: Cautious Self-Assertion?" *Asian Survey* 33, no. 11 (November 1993).

Baral, Lok Raj. *The Politics of Balanced Interdependence: Nepal and SAARC.* New Delhi: Sterling Publishers, 1988.

de Silva, K. M. *Regional Powers and Small State Security.* Washington, D.C.: Woodrow Wilson Center Press, 1995.

Faizal, Farah. "Maldives." In "Security Problems of Small Island Developing States: With Special Reference to the Indian Ocean." Ph.D. Dissertation, Hull University, United Kingdom, 1996.

Ghosh, Partha S. *Cooperation and Conflict in South Asia.* New Delhi: Manohar, 1989.

John, Aruni. *Potential for Militancy among Bhutanese Refugee Youth*, RCSS Policy Studies 15. Colombo: Regional Centre for Strategic Studies, 2000.

Kharat, Rajesh. *Bhutan in SAARC.* New Delhi: South Asian Publishers, 1999.

Kodikara, Shelton U. *Foreign Policy of Sri Lanka.* 2nd ed. New Delhi: Chanakya, 1992.

Phadnis, Urmila, and Ela Dutt Luithui. *Maldives: Winds of Change in an Atoll State.* New Delhi: South Asian Publishers, 1985.

Rose, Leo. *The Politics of Bhutan.* Ithaca, N.Y.: Cornell University Press, 1977.

South Asia Terrorism Portal, available at www.satp.org.

Thapliyal, Sangeeta. *Mutual Security: The Case of India–Nepal.* New Delhi: Lancer, 1998.

APPENDIX

Comparative Area and Population Figures for South Asian and Select Non–South Asian States, 2000.

	Territory (sq. km.)	Population (millions)
Within South Asia		
India	3,300,000[6]	1,002[1]
Pakistan[9]	796,100	141.5
Bangladesh[4]	144,000	133.4
Nepal[8]	147,200	23.5
Sri Lanka[10]	65,610	19.6
Bhutan[5]	47,000	0.828
Maldives[7]	300	0.282

	Territory (sq. km.)	Population (millions)
Beyond South Asia		
China	9,560,000[3]	1,265.8[1]
USA	9,629,090[2]	285[2]
Russia	17,075,400[2]	145.6[2]
France	551,500[2]	59[2]

Sources:
1. Asia and the Pacific in Figures, UN Economic and Social Commission for Asia, Statistics Division, at www.unescap.org/stat/statdata/apinfig.htm (accessed February 1, 2003).
2. Trends in Europe and North America, *2001 Statistical Yearbook of the UN/ECE*, www.unece.org/stats/trend/trend_h.htm (accessed February 1, 2003).
3. "China," *Britannica Student Encyclopedia*, Encyclopædia Britannica Online, at http://search.eb.com/ebi/article?eu=294398 (accessed February 1, 2003).
4. Bangladesh Data Profile, World Bank Group, at http://devdata.worldbank.org/external/CPProfile.asp?SelectedCountry=BGD&CCODE=BGD&CNAME=Bangladesh&PTYPE=CP (accessed February 1, 2003). Population figures are for 2001.
5. Bhutan Data Profile, World Bank Group, at http://devdata.worldbank.org/external/CPProfile.asp?SelectedCountry=BTN&CCODE=BTN&CNAME=Bhutan&PTYPE=CP (accessed February 1, 2003). Population figures are for 2001.
6. India Data Profile, World Bank Group, at http://devdata.worldbank.org/external/dgprofile.asp?RMDK=82602&SMDK=1&W=0 (accessed February 1, 2003). Population figures are for 2001.
7. Maldives Data Profile, World Bank Group, at http://devdata.worldbank.org/external/CPProfile.asp?SelectedCountry=MDV&CCODE=MDV&CNAME=Maldives&PTYPE=CP (accessed February 1, 2003). Population figures are for 2001.
8. Nepal Data Profile, World Bank Group, at http://devdata.worldbank.org/external/CPProfile.asp?SelectedCountry=NPL&CCODE=NPL&CNAME=Nepal&PTYPE=CP (accessed February 1, 2003). Population figures are for 2001.
9. Pakistan Data Profile, World Bank Group, at http://devdata.worldbank.org/external/CPProfile.asp?CCODE=PAK&PTYPE=CP (accessed February 1, 2003). Population figures are for 2001.
10. Sri Lanka Data Profile, World Bank Group, at http://devdata.worldbank.org/external/CPProfile.asp?SelectedCountry=LKA&CCODE=LKA&CNAME=Sri+Lanka&PTYPE=CP (accessed February 1, 2003). Population figures are for 2001.

5

The Reconstitution and Reconstruction of Afghanistan

Devin T. Hagerty and Herbert G. Hagerty

Afghanistan is a dry, craggy, landlocked country roughly the size of Texas. Much of the country's territory consists of steep mountains or barren deserts, and a mere 12 percent of the total land area is arable. Afghanistan's place in world politics today is heavily influenced by its history as an important corridor of commerce and conquest between Europe, Persia, and Central Asia, on one hand, and South and East Asia on the other. Rarely in its frequently turbulent history has Afghanistan been governed as a unified polity under the control of its resident population; indeed, during much of the country's history, it has been administered as part of the territory of one of its neighbors.

Afghanistan's current boundaries reflect the borders of its nineteenth-century neighbors: imperial Russia to the north, Persia (now Iran) to the west, and the British Indian Empire and its affiliated protectorates to the east and south. The population of Afghanistan, estimated today at approximately twenty-five million, is at once overwhelmingly Muslim (84 percent Sunni, 15 percent Shia) and exceedingly diverse, reflecting the linguistic, tribal, and ethnic identities of neighboring Islamic populations. Persian-speaking Hazaras live near the Iranian frontier; Tajiks, Uzbeks, and Turkmen speak the tongues of the former Soviet Central Asian republics Tajikistan, Uzbekistan, and Turkmenistan; and Pashtuns, Baluchis, and others communicate in the Indic languages of Pakistan. About 40 percent of Afghans are Pashtuns, 25 percent are Tajiks, 20 percent are Hazaras, and 6 percent are Uzbeks. Afghans speak some seventy distinct languages and dialects. This polyglot Afghan population is united only by the fact that Islamic practices permeate every aspect of daily life.

Afghanistan's recent history has been a tortured one. War has raged in the country for much of the last twenty-five years, first between a Soviet-supported Marxist regime and a nascent Islamic resistance movement (1978–1979), then between the Soviet Red Army itself and the increasingly potent Afghan resistance (1979–1989), then between various Afghan factions themselves (1989–1996), then between the emergent Taliban regime and northern opposition forces (1996–2001), and lastly between a U.S.-led coalition and the Taliban (2001). With the toppling of the Taliban government in November 2001, the process of reconstitution and reconstruction has begun, but chronic violence continues between a bewildering variety of political factions, each with its own well-armed militia and its own parochial view of what Afghanistan's political future should look like.

Through it all, the Afghan people have suffered to a degree almost unimaginable. One credible account estimates that more than 1.5 million Afghans have been killed in the fighting.[1] Another source puts the figure at two million.[2] Some five to six million more have lived as refugees in neighboring Pakistan and Iran. Those classified by the United Nations as "internally displaced people" (i.e., residents forced to flee their homes owing to the violence raging around them) numbered more than one million at the time of the Taliban's defeat in 2001.[3] Innumerable Afghans, certainly many hundreds of thousands, have been maimed in the world's most heavily land-mined territory.

Following the 2001 U.S.-led military victory in Afghanistan, the international community pledged to put back together an Afghan entity that in recent years had ceased to be a country in any meaningful sense. This will entail a long-term process of integrating into a functional state what had for all intents and purposes become a semipermanent battlefield, occupied by a variety of heavily armed ethnic groups, tribes, clans, and warlords. The task is enormous. It will require the reconstitution of Afghanistan into a polity where the interests of all these groups can be protected, the reconstruction of an economy that lay in ruins as of late 2001, and the rebuilding of an Afghan society that offers a modicum of material well-being and opportunity in a country where the life expectancy is forty-four years, one in four children dies before the age of five, and 70 percent of the population is undernourished.[4]

This chapter examines the ongoing process of reconstituting and reconstructing Afghanistan in the context of a historical introduction to the country. The next three sections trace the political history of Afghanistan up until the Soviet invasion of 1979, during the Soviet war from 1979 to 1989, and in the post-Soviet era from 1989 to 2001. Subsequent sections analyze the Afghan rebuilding process in two broad areas: politics and security, and economics and society. The issue of security is crucial because the prospects for Afghanistan's political and economic rebirth are dependent on whether or not reform-minded Afghans and their international backers can create a peaceful, stable order to replace decades of warfare and political tumult. The chapter's final section assesses how far Afghanistan has progressed along the road to stability, as well as the likelihood that it can soon rejoin the international community as a fully sovereign, democratic country.

HISTORY

Afghanistan's political history has been marked by periods of domination by one of its neighbors, interspersed with frequent periods of chaotic internal struggle among local leaders seeking to advance their own regional or tribal interests, often with the support of confreres beyond Afghan frontiers. Important exceptions have been relatively short periods during which a dynamic leader, usually arising in eastern Afghanistan, extended his influence further afield. Perhaps the most famous and influential of these was Mahmud, a Turk in the city of Ghazni in southeastern Afghanistan, who in the first millennium established a domain with enduring historic importance that stretched eastward across the Indus River as far as Delhi, westward into Persia as far as Isfahan, and northward across the Oxus River (known today as the Amu Darya) into Central Asia.

In the eighteenth century, Ahmad Shah Durrani, a Pashtun from the Abdali clan, came to power in Kabul and established an empire in Afghanistan that also encompassed portions of the Indus valley to the east, including the Punjab and Kashmir. Durrani's imperial rule was relatively short-lived, and his nineteenth-century heirs came increasingly under British influence. London's main concern was to maintain Afghanistan as a neutral buffer between czarist Russian power in Central Asia and the British Raj fleshing out its control westward in the Indian subcontinent. Thus, in the second half of the nineteenth century, Afghanistan was embroiled in the so-called Great Game, a competition between the Russian and British empires for influence in Central Asia. Between 1873 and 1887, Russia and Britain reached agreement on the details of the border between Afghanistan and Russia, and the British negotiated with Kabul another series of agreements that essentially placed Afghanistan under British protection. In 1893 the British unilaterally drew the boundary between British India and Afghanistan. Called the Durand Line, it ran mainly along a relatively low mountain chain separating the Indus River valley from Afghanistan. This division had the effect of separating a substantial number of Pashtun tribes from their kinsmen in Afghanistan by what had become, to them, a largely irrelevant international border.

The British role in Afghanistan was further strengthened in 1907 when Russia, weakened by its defeat in the 1904–1905 war with Japan, negotiated an agreement with the British that spelled out spheres of influence in Asia. The agreement acknowledged Afghanistan to be an unchallenged sphere of

British influence. The later Durrani rulers in Kabul were successful in negotiating virtual "independence" agreements with the British in 1919 and 1921,
setting the stage for Afghanistan's emergence in modern times as a national
state. From 1933 to 1973, the country was governed by the final Durrani heir,
King Zahir Shah, providing Afghanistan with one of its longer periods of governmental continuity.

After World War II, Afghanistan was widely accorded the status of a sovereign, independent state, with seats in the United Nations and other international fora. However, beneath the veneer of a modern-style royal government,
Kabul's writ over the entire country was often quite limited. The authoritarian regime dealt harshly with challenges to its authority, especially by non-
Pashtun groups. At the local level, governors appointed by Kabul exercised
considerable autonomy, often in league with regional or tribal warlords. A decision in the capital to replace or discipline a governor often required enforcement by a military expedition.

In the bipolar international system that evolved after the end of World War
II, Kabul's relations with the world evolved against a Cold War background. Al-
though Afghanistan was not a significant player in the early years of U.S.-
Soviet competition, Moscow's influence in the country gradually outpaced
Washington's, beginning in the 1950s. As discussed in chapters 1 and 2, the
United States and Pakistan became strategic partners in 1954. This had the effect of raising Moscow's concerns about security along the Soviet Union's
southern frontier. In addition, Afghanistan's relationship with the new state of
Pakistan was strained and often hostile as both sides inherited the stresses and
conflicts that had long afflicted the Afghan-British relationship. Far and away
the main source of tension between Afghanistan and Pakistan was Kabul's decision to pursue an active policy of reclaiming influence over the large Pashtun
population in the loosely administered tribal area on the Pakistani side of the international border, the Durand Line that Afghans had never fully accepted.

When Afghanistan began to advocate the creation of Pashtunistan, an entity aimed at reuniting all the Pashtu-speaking peoples on both sides of the
border, presumably under Afghan control and at Pakistan's expense, the issue
deteriorated into a crisis between the two countries. As a result, Pakistan
closed its border from the late 1950s until 1963, embittering both sides and
forcing Afghanistan to seek alternative outlets to the sea and other sources of
essential products like petroleum, all of which provided an opportunity for
Moscow to expand Soviet influence in Afghanistan. Even after the border was
reopened, the relationship between Pakistan and Afghanistan remained unfriendly, with Pakistan exhibiting a constant wariness of Afghan intentions on
the never disavowed Pashtunistan issue.

In the meantime, the Soviet-Afghan relationship quietly blossomed. Soviet
aid financed large construction projects in Afghanistan, including the Bagram

military air base some twenty miles north of Kabul and the 1.7-mile-long Salang Tunnel, which was built through the Hindu Kush mountains at an altitude of more than eleven thousand feet.[5] These facilities would prove useful to the Soviets during their subsequent invasion and occupation of Afghanistan. Moscow and Kabul also collaborated on a variety of other projects in the areas of telecommunications, road building, bridge building, hydroelectric power, and river port construction.[6] Moscow also carved out a role as the exclusive supplier of military equipment and training for the Afghan armed forces. "Approximately 3,725 Afghan officers were trained in the USSR . . . from 1956 to 1977." In addition, Soviet military advisers and technicians were attached to Afghan units, and "Soviet military doctrine was adopted. Russian became Afghanistan's military language."[7]

In 1964 Afghanistan became a constitutional monarchy with a two-chamber legislature to which King Zahir Shah appointed one-third of the deputies. Although Afghanistan's so-called constitutional period was short-lived, lasting only until 1973, it gave rise to a number of new political parties. Afghanistan's first communist party was formed in 1965. The People's Democratic Party of Afghanistan (PDPA) would be wracked by chronic infighting, but all sides tended to toe the Soviet line. In 1967 the PDPA divided into two major factions, the Khalq ("masses"), led by Nur Muhammad Taraki and Hafizullah Amin, and the Parcham ("banner"), led by Babrak Karmal. The Khalq enjoyed strong support within the Afghan military.[8]

Experts date the stirrings of political Islam in Afghanistan to this period, when groups of radical Muslims and Communists often went head-to-head in their competition for the hearts and minds of the tiny, urban Afghan intelligentsia, mainly on the campus of Kabul University. One scholar writes that the "young Islamists became actively militant on the university campus from 1968 . . . against the communist penetration of the army and the university and against the Soviet infiltration of the state apparatus."[9]

In 1973 King Zahir Shah was overthrown in a military coup by his cousin Mohammed Daoud, a former prime minister. The king fled Afghanistan, eventually settling in Italy. Daoud abolished the monarchy, scrapped the constitution, and declared Afghanistan a republic in which he would be the first president and prime minister. In the coup's aftermath, the fortunes of the Communists and Islamists diverged. Because of the PDPA's strength, Daoud was forced to curry the party's favor. The Islamists, on the other hand, had no intention of working with Daoud's regime, which scorned the "backward" religious establishment. Aided by the Pakistani government, which suspected that Daoud wanted to reopen the Pashtunistan issue, the Islamists launched an unsuccessful 1975 insurgency in four Afghan provinces.

In 1978 Daoud's government was brought down by the PDPA, led by Khalq chief Nur Muhammad Taraki. The new Communist regime imposed a spate of "modernizing" reforms that Islamists viewed as subverting their own traditional leadership prerogatives in rural Afghanistan. The PDPA portrayed its coup as a "logical continuation" of the Russian Revolution.[10] Taraki himself declared that "in order to have a revolution, a past path must be established. It was on this basis that the Great October Revolution triumphed, with the help of a powerful workers' party, and we have followed that path."[11] For the Islamists, the PDPA's animosity toward Islam was symbolized by the Communists' replacement of Afghanistan's black, red, and (Islamic) green flag with an all-red one similar to those of the Soviet Central Asian republics. Perhaps most important for rural Afghans, the Khalqis instituted a number of repugnant regulations concerning marriage and other social practices by which, traditionally, alliances were made and disputes were resolved. When they protested, religious leaders were imprisoned, tortured, and executed.

The PDPA's reforms soon led to spontaneous outbursts of popular discontent. Islamist leaders began to mount violent attacks against regime targets while using Pakistani territory for sanctuary against reprisals. The violence peaked with the Herat uprising of March 1979, in which scores of Soviet advisers and thousands of Afghan Communists were killed during a local rebellion. When Taraki's former deputy, Hafizullah Amin, ousted Taraki from office, with allies of Amin murdering Taraki in the process, the Soviets searched in vain for a way to quell the disastrous civil war that was shaping up on their southern flank. But with the threat of yet a second southern neighbor undergoing an Islamic revolution, and with this neighbor, unlike Iran, an avowed member of the Communist bloc, the Soviets saw no real option but to intervene militarily in Afghanistan.

THE SOVIET ERA

With the PDPA regime crumbling under the weight of its own oppression, its factional purges and desertions, and growing Islamist resistance, the Soviet Union invaded Afghanistan in December 1979. The invading forces killed Hafizullah Amin and installed in his place Babrak Karmal, the formerly exiled leader of the PDPA's Parcham faction. The Soviet strategy was as simple as it was brutal: control the cities, the communications and supply routes, and Soviet-PDPA military garrisons in rural areas while using massive air power to empty rural Afghanistan of people and livestock and to destroy the country's fragile agricultural infrastructure.

The Islamic insurgents, now known as the mujahideen ("holy warriors"), responded with guerrilla attacks on regime targets; however, outfitted with little more than small arms in the war's early years, the resistance was woefully ill equipped to withstand the sustained Soviet air assaults. It is difficult today to imagine the carnage inflicted upon Afghanistan from 1979 to 1986. The country's prewar population was roughly fifteen million. By 1986 reliable estimates numbered Afghan casualties at over one million. Some five million Afghans had fled into squalid refugee camps in Pakistan and Iran. An additional one to two million Afghans were in internal exile, forced into Kabul and other swelling cities to escape the violence and starvation of rural Afghanistan. The United Nations's special rapporteur on human rights in Afghanistan wrote that "continuation of the military solution will . . . lead inevitably to a situation approaching genocide."[12]

But then the tide turned. By the mid-1980s, international backers of the Afghan resistance—China, Pakistan, Saudi Arabia, and the United States—had increased their support in both quantitative and qualitative terms. The mujahideen were thus able to mount more effective attacks on Soviet-Afghan positions, sometimes within miles of Kabul. Most important from the insurgents' standpoint was the provision of advanced surface-to-air weapons, including the U.S.-made Stinger missile,

[a] shoulder-fired weapon that proved durable and easy to use. Its automated heat-seeking guidance system worked uncannily. CIA-supplied Afghan rebels used Stingers to down hundreds of Soviet helicopters and transport aircraft between 1986 and 1989. The missile forced Soviet generals to change air assault tactics. Its potency sowed fear among thousands of Russian pilots and troops.[13]

By 1988 Cold War politics and Soviet military setbacks caused Moscow to give up on trying to subdue Afghanistan. Soon after his rise to power in 1985, Soviet leader Mikhail Gorbachev referred to the Afghan war as a "bleeding wound." Gorbachev was intent on saving the Soviet Union by pursuing the twin reforms of *glasnost* ("openness") and *perestroika* ("restructuring"). These reforms, in turn, depended on the implementation of Gorbachev's "new thinking" in foreign policy. Why was the Soviet Union devoting increasingly scarce resources to propping up Marxist allies in Eastern Europe, Cuba, Vietnam, or Afghanistan? From Gorbachev's perspective, these commitments sapped Soviet strength and reaped no real security benefits. Instead, the resources invested in propping up Soviet allies' unpopular governments could be rechanneled into domestic reforms. Gorbachev authorized his diplomats to negotiate the Soviet Union out of Afghanistan, and the last Soviet soldier walked over a bridge across the Amu Darya in 1989.

POST-SOVIET AFGHANISTAN

In the aftermath of the Soviet occupation, bickering Afghan factions fell upon one another in a bitter civil war, waged in fits and starts, that lasted for seven years. Early on, infighting among the resistance leaders prevented them from mounting a unified assault on the PDPA regime, led since 1986 by Najibullah (who went by only one name). As a result, and contrary to conventional expectations, the PDPA held on in Kabul until 1992. After the mujahideen finally ended fourteen years of Communist rule in Afghanistan by deposing (and murdering) Najibullah, they still could not cooperate sufficiently well to form an effective government. Afghanistan's civil war continued for another four years, as the various factions bludgeoned one another and destroyed much of Kabul in the process.

Only in 1996 did a political-military organization emerge that could control most of the country. Known as the Taliban ("students"), this predominantly Pashtun movement adhered to a strict version of Sunni Islamic law called Wahhabbism.[14] Many of the Taliban had grown up in the Afghan refugee camps of western Pakistan, where Saudi-funded madrassas (Islamic theology schools) had instilled in them the Wahhabbi creed. Assisted by Pakistan's Inter-Services Intelligence (ISI) organization, the Taliban had fought their way to power in Kabul from 1994 to 1996. Thereafter, the Taliban extended their dictatorial reign to perhaps 90 percent of Afghanistan's territory, all the while imposing upon the war-weary Afghan people a severely repressive brand of Wahhabbi rule.

In 1996 the Taliban made common cause with Osama bin Laden, the leader of al Qaeda ("the base"), a network of radical Islamic terrorist groups. Bin Laden, the wealthy son of a Yemeni bricklayer who made his fortune building roads and other infrastructure in a Saudi Arabia newly flush with oil money, had originally traveled to Afghanistan in 1979. Like many other young Muslim men from around the world, most but not all of them Arabs, bin Laden was originally drawn to South Asia by the prospect of helping the Afghan resistance fighters to oust the "infidel" Soviet occupiers from Afghanistan. As one informed account describes this influx of Muslims,

> By early 1980, the call to jihad (holy war) had reached all corners of the Islamic world, attracting Arabs young and old and with a variety of motivations to travel to Pakistan to take up arms and cross the border to fight against the Soviet invaders in Afghanistan. There were genuine volunteers on missions of humanitarian value, there were adventure seekers looking for paths to glory, and there were psychopaths. As the war dragged on, a number of Arab states discreetly emptied their prisons of homegrown troublemakers and sent them off to the jihad with the fervent hope that they might not return. Over the ten years of war as many as 25,000 Arabs may have passed through Pakistan and Afghanistan.[15]

Bin Laden reportedly spent much of the early 1980s funding Afghan resistance activities, raising money from Muslims around the world, recruiting volunteers to the cause, and helping to build training camps, tunnels, military depots, and roads that would facilitate the Islamic insurgents' military operations.[16]

In the late 1980s, as the Cold War waned and the Soviets began to disengage from Afghanistan, bin Laden's aims grew more expansive. During his anti-Soviet incarnation, bin Laden had come to be influenced by remnants of the Egyptian Islamic Jihad, a group of extremist militants who had been chased out of Egypt following their assassination of President Anwar Sadat in 1981. By 1987 bin Laden had decided to undertake a global jihad against what he viewed as the corrupt secular regimes of the Arab Middle East, as well as the infidel Western powers that perpetuated their rule, especially the United States. He established al Qaeda as a means of linking radical Muslims from around the world, training them to be terrorists, and sending them forth to fight the jihad.

From 1990 to 1996, bin Laden moved several times, all the while building al Qaeda into the transnational terror network that would ultimately carry out the September 11, 2001, attacks on the World Trade Center and the Pentagon. He initially spent time in Saudi Arabia, where he grew outraged at the deployment of U.S. military forces in the kingdom during the 1990–1991 Gulf War. Rebuffed in his efforts to gain Saudi support for a guerrilla war to repulse Iraqi forces from Kuwait,[17] bin Laden returned to Afghanistan briefly before settling in Sudan, then governed by a radical Islamic regime. For the next five years, under the cover of legitimate business interests, bin Laden oversaw the growth of al Qaeda, which developed a compartmentalized corporate structure and trained Islamic militants in Sudan and Afghanistan to use weapons, detonate explosives, kidnap adversaries, fight in urban environments, and defy Western intelligence services.

In 1996, under pressure from the United States, which was only then awakening to the scope of al Qaeda's activities, bin Laden fled Sudan. He moved back to Afghanistan as the Taliban was consolidating its rule, and a marriage of convenience was arranged: bin Laden would provide the Taliban with military assistance, build roads that would allow the regime to widen its control over the country, and buy off regional warlords opposed to the new regime; in return, the Taliban would give al Qaeda sanctuary in one of the world's most remote and inhospitable regions. It was in Afghanistan that bin Laden and his senior al Qaeda leadership plotted a series of increasingly audacious terrorist attacks against American targets. In 1998 he declared that "to kill Americans and their allies, both civil and military, is an individual duty of every Muslim who is able, in any country where this is possible."[18] Soon thereafter, explosions rocked the U.S. embassies in Kenya and Tanzania, killing more than two hundred people. Undaunted by the Clinton administration's response, which was to fire seventy-five cruise missiles at bin Laden's training camps in Afghanistan, al Qaeda–linked terrorists in 2000 bombed the USS *Cole*, a destroyer berthed in Yemen, killing seventeen.

Afghanistan's history would be profoundly transformed in the fateful year of 2001. On September 11, Muslim terrorists, most of them Saudis, believed to be part of al Qaeda flew highjacked commercial airliners into the World Trade Center in New York and the Pentagon outside of Washington, D.C. Several thousand people died in the attacks, which finally awakened Americans to the scope and severity of the threat posed by bin Laden's terrorist network. President George W. Bush responded by declaring a global war on terrorism, one that would target not only terrorist groups themselves but also the regimes harboring them.

To pave the way for military operations against the Taliban and al Qaeda in Afghanistan, Washington exerted enormous pressure on Pakistani president Pervez Musharraf, whose government was by then one of only three that still maintained diplomatic relations with the Taliban. Given that the Pakistan army, and particularly ISI, knew a vast amount about Afghanistan's complex political landscape, the Bush administration viewed Islamabad's support as vital to the antiterrorist campaign. U.S. officials also knew that if they expected Musharraf to incur the huge political risks of abandoning a cause many Pakistanis believed in, Washington would have to pay Islamabad handsomely. Faced with the prospect of Pakistan's becoming an international pariah, Musharraf acceded to U.S. demands that he give the Americans airspace rights, access to military bases, and intelligence. In return, Washington waived nuclear and prodemocracy sanctions against Pakistan; pledged more than $1 billion in economic assistance mainly in the areas of health, education, democracy promotion, counternarcotics, and law enforcement; and promised to engineer grant, loan, and debt-rescheduling programs through the major international financial institutions.

Musharraf's nationally televised speech on September 19 left no doubt as to what was at stake for Pakistan. If it did not join the U.S. war effort, the country would be marginalized and isolated. Noting that India had already offered its full cooperation to the United States, Musharraf warned that Islamabad's refusal to toe the line would result in Pakistan's being branded a terrorism-supporting state and the loss of any lingering international sympathy for the Pakistani position on Kashmir. He also implied, obliquely, that the very survival of Pakistan's hard-won nuclear-weapons capabilities were in jeopardy.[19]

Operation Enduring Freedom (OEF), the U.S.-led war against the Taliban and al Qaeda, began on October 7, 2001. U.S. and allied military forces began by launching air and cruise-missile strikes against government positions and terrorist assets. Meanwhile, the Northern Alliance, a loose collection of mainly Tajik, anti-Taliban groups who had fought in the Afghan resistance during the

Soviet war, began ground assaults extending outward from their strongholds in the Panjshir valley. Both the air and ground operations were abetted by U.S. special operations and CIA paramilitary forces, which fanned out across the country identifying regime and al Qaeda targets. Vastly overmatched by their adversaries' advantages in satellite capabilities and precision-guided munitions, the Taliban and al Qaeda armies quickly crumbled, with survivors melting away into the borderlands straddling the Afghan-Pakistani frontier. Kabul fell on November 12, 2001.

REBUILDING AFGHANISTAN

Since the Taliban's ouster, the United States, its allies, the United Nations, and the Afghans themselves have embarked on an ambitious program to completely remake Afghan society. Any analysis of this Herculean effort must begin with a realistic appreciation of its enormity. Afghanistan as of 2001 was a deeply impoverished, topographically forbidding, politically splintered entity — it was, in the blandly euphemistic jargon of the social sciences, a "failed state." In neither the Taliban- nor the Northern Alliance–controlled areas was there much of a functioning government; what passed for governance in Afghanistan was the province of regional warlords, not bureaucrats. The Afghan economy was essentially a barter system based on drug and weapons trafficking. The official currency, the afghani, was practically worthless. Although Western journalists threw around a figure of $480 a year when they described Afghan per capita income, that number was a fiction. Four years of drought and famine had brought millions of already desperately poor Afghans to the brink of extinction. Educational, medical, and other social services were exceedingly scarce.

Through all the carnage of the 1978–2001 period, the Afghan countryside remained as it had been for centuries — underdeveloped, harshly exploited, and deeply divided along regional, intra-Islamic, ethnic, and tribal lines. As discussed above, Afghanistan's political history discloses little experience with the core Western democratic traditions: popular sovereignty, regular elections, institutional checks and balances, an independent judiciary, individual rights, a free press, and so forth. Only rarely, as in their resistance to Soviet occupation, have Afghans acted together with a sufficient sense of unity and common purpose to rise above their primary loyalties as Pashtuns, Tajiks, Hazaras, Turkmen, and Uzbeks. If the country is ever to move forward with a popular and enduring representative government that serves the interests of all Afghans, it must decisively repudiate this history. From a realistic, rather than an idealized, standpoint, the best outcome that can probably be expected is a particularly Afghan form of democracy that combines a moderately strong central government with substantial provincial and local autonomy.

THE BONN POLITICAL ROADMAP

A month after the Taliban's ouster, all of Afghanistan's other political factions met in Bonn, Germany, to create a blueprint for the country's political future. The thirty-member Interim Authority was formed, with Hamid Karzai as its chairman. Karzai, a member of the Pashtun Durrani tribe with close ties to former king Zahir Shah, is widely regarded as a centrist in the Afghan political context. The Bonn delegates also decided to convene a June 2002 *loya jirga* ("grand council") in Afghanistan. The *loya jirga* would choose a two-year transitional authority charged with drafting a new constitution and governing Afghanistan until elections could be held in 2004. According to the terms agreed to at Bonn, the victorious Northern Alliance forces would withdraw from Kabul, and an international peacekeeping force would be formed to maintain security in and around the capital.

When the *loya jirga* was convened in June 2002, Karzai was selected by a large majority of delegates to lead the two-year Transitional Authority. A thirty-five-member commission set about drafting a new constitution in consultation with Afghans around the country, which was then presented to a second *loya jirga* in December 2003. In the meantime, the Transitional Authority and the United Nations Assistance Mission in Afghanistan (UNAMA) created a joint committee to organize the planned 2004 elections. After a prolonged and sometimes contentious debate, the second *loya jirga* approved the new constitution in January 2004, and it was decided that national elections would be held in June. The elections were subsequently postponed until autumn 2004, owing to widespread security problems, discussed below, and difficulties in registering Afghan voters for the first time ever.

In the future Afghan government, the president will be elected by a direct majority and serve as the head of state. In addition to being the commander in chief of the armed forces, the president will appoint cabinet ministers, the attorney general, the head of the National Security Directorate, and members of the supreme court, with the approval of a bicameral parliament. The parliament will consist of two branches. The *Wolesi Jirga* ("House of People") will be elected directly by voters in proportion to the population of each Afghan region; it will not exceed 250 members. The constitution specifies that at least two female delegates will represent each province. The *Meshrano Jirga* ("House of Elders") will consist of both elected and appointed members. The president will appoint members to this body from traditionally underrepresented groups, including women, and provincial and district councils will elect the remaining members. Afghanistan's supreme court will have nine members to be appointed by the president for ten-year terms. Matters of law with no provision in the constitution or other standing laws will be judged by the Hanifi school of Sunni jurisprudence. Afghan courts will apply the

Shia school of law in cases dealing with the personal matters of Shia Muslims. The constitution identifies Islam as the state religion of Afghanistan, saying that "no law can be contrary to the beliefs and provisions of the sacred religion of Islam," but it also specifies that followers of other religions are free to exercise their faiths.[20]

POLITICS AND SECURITY

The reconstitution and reconstruction of Afghanistan depends, first and foremost, on achieving a level of everyday security in the country that will allow political and economic development to proceed. The sad fact is that in matters of government and opposition, tearing down is easier than building up. The ultimate measure of a country's "stateness" is whether or not national leaders are able to monopolize authority over the legitimate means of coercion, namely, the police and other law enforcement agencies, the armed forces, and the intelligence services. In Afghanistan today, there is no lack of parochial interests that, due to past rivalries and fears about the future, resist the orderly ceding of these coercive powers to a nationally recognized, broadly representative authority.

Afghan politics under Karzai's Interim and Transitional authorities have been, as always, characterized by a great deal of factional squabbling, both within the government and between the government and other centers of power around the country. There are as yet no political parties in the conventional Western sense; rather, the main players tend to be fluid political-military coalitions loosely organized around ethnic, tribal, clan, and personal loyalties. As one account puts it, "The new government is composed of militarily strong Tajik, Uzbek, and Hazara factions [all previously affiliated with the Northern Alliance], and a weak Pashtun majority."[21] Karzai's writ does not extend much beyond Kabul, both because he has no personal militia and also because the nascent Afghan National Army (ANA), which is being trained by the U.S. military, has only nine thousand members to date.[22]

The core of the Transitional Authority is composed mainly of two groups: moderate-conservative Pashtun leaders aligned with Karzai and Tajiks representing different factions of the victorious Northern Alliance. Defense Minister Muhammad Fahim and Foreign Minister Abdullah (half Tajik and half Pashtun, he uses only one name) are closely aligned with Tajik Northern Alliance leader Burhannudin Rabbani. Fahim continues to command the loyalty of his own battle-hardened Tajik militia, which, contrary to the provisions of the Bonn Accord discussed above, remains garrisoned in Kabul even today. Other significant warlords affiliated with the Northern Alliance and now the Transitional Authority include Ismail Khan, a Tajik whose power is centered in Herat Province, Abdul Rashid Dostam, an Uzbek based in the northern city of Mazar-i-Sharif, and Abdul Karim Khalili, a Shiite Hazara whose supporters are located mainly in Bamiyan Province. The ultraconservative Pashtun Abdul Rasul Sayyaf is officially outside the government but commands influence in the Paghman area.

All of these competing power brokers have their own well-armed private militias, and internationally mediated negotiations over how to disarm them in the lead up to nationwide elections have proved extremely difficult.[23] As political factions jockey for favorable position in a democratizing Afghanistan, clashes between warlords and their militias remain a depressingly common phenomenon all around the country. Karzai has grown bolder in deploying the new ANA in an attempt to put a stop to regional clashes, but only with mixed results.

The most challenging security threats to the new Afghanistan emanate from the southern and eastern portions of the country (especially the provinces of Ghazni, Kandahar, Khost, Paktika, and Zabul) along and across the border with Pakistan's Northwest Frontier Province (especially the semiautonomous tribal agencies of South Wazirstan, North Wazirstan, Mohmand Agency, Khyber Agency, and Orakzai Agency). In this remote, traditionalist, Pashtun tribal belt, Taliban and al Qaeda fighters who were widely dispersed during OEF in 2001 have to a considerable extent regrouped to fight another day.

Both Osama bin Laden and Taliban leader Mullah Muhammad Omar are still at large, although it is not apparent from public sources whether they exercise effective command over their warriors or are able to collaborate with one another. It is clear that hundreds, if not thousands, of Taliban and al Qaeda militants are armed and active on both sides of the Pakistan–Afghanistan border. Over the past year, they have attacked U.S. military bases, set off explosions in crowded Afghan cities, ambushed American, Pakistani, and Afghan soldiers, and murdered and kidnapped Afghan and foreign aid workers.

Some of these Taliban and al Qaeda remnants are also believed to have aligned themselves with warlord and Soviet-era Afghan resistance leader Gulbuddin Hekmatyar and his ultraconservative Hizb-i-Islami Party, which remains powerful in the border regions of eastern Afghanistan. Hekmatyar spent much of the 1996–2001 Taliban era in Iran but returned to Afghanistan to resume the jihad in 2002, after which U.S. forces promptly tried, but failed, to kill him in a missile attack. Washington has subsequently branded Hekmatyar a "Specially Designated Global Terrorist."[24]

Battling these resurgent Taliban/al Qaeda/Hizb-i-Islami warriors on the Afghan side of the Pashtun tribal belt is a combination of U.S. Army troops, U.S. Marines, U.S. Special Forces units, and CIA paramilitary personnel. The number of U.S. military forces in Afghanistan totaled some 13,500 in the late spring of 2004. Also part of the OEF coalition have been about two thousand military personnel from France, Britain, Germany, Italy, the Netherlands, Turkey, and Denmark, although these forces are not deployed in southeastern Afghanistan. On the other side of the border, the Pakistan army has deployed some seventy thousand troops in an attempt to flush out the militants from tribal areas previously considered off-limits to the army. Its task is complicated by the fact that local tribal leaders resent the army's intrusion and provide succor to their fellow Pashtuns. Although the United States has said publicly that its forces operate only in Afghanistan, Pakistani units have coordinated their assaults with the U.S. military and been aided by U.S.-supplied intelligence.[25]

Pursuant to the 2001 Bonn Agreement and subsequent UN authorization, security in and around Kabul has been the primary responsibility of the multinational International Security and Assistance Force (ISAF). More than thirty countries have contributed some six thousand soldiers to ISAF. In August 2003 the North Atlantic Treaty Organization (NATO) assumed command of ISAF in what was the trans-Atlantic alliance's first-ever deployment of troops outside Europe or North America. ISAF's core force is the Kabul Multinational Brigade, headed by Canada and composed of three battle groups led by Canada, Germany, and France.[26] In 2002 and 2003, ISAF came under heavy criticism from UNAMA, the Transitional Authority, and humanitarian nongovernmental organizations (NGOs) for not extending its security presence outside of Kabul, where Afghan and international development specialists work every day under the threat of attack, kidnapping, and murder. Responding to these complaints, NATO in October 2003 approved the gradual expansion of ISAF's authority beyond the capital.

Over time, ISAF's mission has to an extent coalesced with that of a December 2002 U.S. initiative, also undertaken at the behest of vulnerable aid workers. The Department of Defense has spearheaded the creation of provincial reconstruction teams (PRTs) that work with local Afghan authorities to repair buildings, communications installations, bridges, dams, and roads, while creating a secure environment for reconstruction. The PRTs are essentially partnerships linking foreign soldiers, civilian affairs officers, and aid specialists with NGO and local Afghan workers. They are intended to push the reconstruction process along by drawing security-conscious NGOs into underserved areas and employing local Afghan labor in productive activities. As of March 2004, some twelve PRTs were operational.[27] So far, non-U.S. forces from Germany, Canada, and New Zealand have led three of the operational PRTs. In January 2004 ISAF/NATO personnel assumed command of the German-led PRT in Kunduz.[28] If all goes according to plan, NATO-led ISAF forces will increasingly take responsibility for leading additional PRTs.

ECONOMY AND SOCIETY

The international community is also engaged in a mammoth attempt to revitalize the Afghan economy and society. The main priorities to date have been the resettling of Afghan refugees, the rebuilding of the country's transportation infrastructure, the rehabilitation of schools and medical facilities, and, increasingly, the eradication of opium poppy production, which has skyrocketed since the Taliban's demise. Funding for these initiatives has been raised at a series of international donor conferences since 2002. The latest donor meeting, held in Berlin in the spring of 2004, resulted in pledges of $8.2 billion over the following three years, including $4.4 billion in the first year.[29]

Unilateral U.S. aid for Afghanistan has been targeted at enhancing security, including a new Afghan police force, counternarcotics programs, human rights (including women's rights) initiatives, humanitarian and development assistance, social programs, including education and health care, technical support for Afghan ministries, and infrastructure repair. Table 5.1 shows annual U.S. aid appropriations from 1990 through 2004.

Although international aid efforts have been significantly hampered by Afghanistan's precarious security environment, notable successes have been achieved. Perhaps the most important of these has been the repatriation and resettlement of some three million refugees by the United Nations High Commissioner for Refugees.[30] Aid workers have also made appreciable strides in

Table 5.1.   U.S. Aid to Afghanistan in the Post-Soviet Era (millions of dollars)

Fiscal Year	Amount
1990	88.1
1991	80.1
1992	81.4
1993	68.2
1994	42.3
1995	45.8
1996	42.5
1997	49.9
1998	52.7
1999	76.6
2000	113.2
2001	182.6
2002	815.9
2003	817.0
2004	1,565.0

Source: Congressional Research Service, U.S. Library of Congress.
Kenneth Katzman, "Afghanistan: Post-War Governance, Security, and U.S. Policy," *CRS Report for Congress*, March 24, 2004.

the area of infrastructure, crucial for a country with no functioning railroads and a road system that was in total disrepair as of the beginning of 2002. The Salang Tunnel has been repaired and reopened, restoring a vital lifeline between northern Afghanistan and the rest of the country. The three-hundred-mile Kabul-to-Kandahar highway was rebuilt and opened in December 2003 as the first leg of a planned "ring road" that will ultimately link all of Afghanistan's major cities. U.S. aid has also helped to repair more than eight hundred miles of secondary roads.[31]

Afghan schools reopened in March 2003, with girls in attendance and women teaching for the first time since the Taliban came to power in 1996. Since the war ended in 2001, the United States has constructed and rehabilitated more than two hundred schools, trained some twenty-one hundred teachers, and distributed more than ten million textbooks. U.S. aid officials plan to build 152 new schools and refurbish 255 more by September 2004. The United States has also rebuilt 140 health clinics and plans to complete work on a total of 378 new and refurbished health clinics by the end of 2004.[32]

One cause of grave concern for the Transitional Authority and its international backers is the dramatic resurgence of the Afghan drug economy, suppression of which was perhaps the Taliban regime's only decent accomplishment. Opium is Afghanistan's biggest cash crop, with the International Monetary Fund estimating that the underground opium economy is about half the size of the country's legitimate gross domestic product. Afghans produced seventy-four thousand hectares worth of opium in 2002 and another eighty thousand in 2003. Estimates for 2004 project that a record 120,000 hectares worth of opium will be produced. Some half a million—one in fifty—Afghans are believed to be involved in narcotics production and trafficking, which provides a steady stream of income for local warlords to invest in their militias.[33] Recognizing that Afghanistan is once again the leading source of heroin in the world, $170 million of U.S. aid for fiscal year 2004 is dedicated to counternarcotics programs.[34] See table 5.2 for U.S. funding priorities in Afghanistan.

CONCLUSION

Afghanistan today is a country risen from the dead. To extend the metaphor, will it walk again, gain strength, find nourishment, grow, perhaps even run one day? There is no dearth of observers predicting that if present trends continue, Afghanistan will be bedridden for a long time to come. Media accounts and expert reports are filled with grim stories about what is wrong with the country: the central government's authority is too limited; warlords and their

Table 5.2.   U.S. Aid to Afghanistan in Fiscal Year 2004 (millions of dollars)

Purpose	Amount
Disarmament, demobilization, and reintegration (of private militias)	30
Support to Afghan government	70
Elections/governance (registering voters and preparing for elections)	69
Roads	181
Schools/education	95
Health services/clinics	49
Provincial reconstruction teams	58
Private sector/power generation	95
Water projects	23
Police training/rule of law (counternarcotics training and equipment)	170
Afghan National Army (training and equipment)	287
Antiterrorism/Afghan leadership protection	35
Development/health	171
Disaster relief	35
Refugee relief	72
Economic-aid/economic-support funds (includes $5 million for Afghan women)	75
Military assistance	50
Total	**1,565**

Source: Revised, from Congressional Research Service, U.S. Library of Congress.
Katzman, "Afghanistan," 42.

militias continue to rule vast swatches of territory; the ANA is too small and too weak; reconstruction is slow going; violence is pervasive; drugs and guns fuel a black-market economy; roads, schools, health care, indeed, all the basics of a stable, modern society, are woefully inadequate.

There is no denying any of this. Measured against idealized notions of what a healthy, prosperous society looks like, Afghanistan is indeed in bad shape. But a fairer standard of measurement is to assess how Afghanistan is doing today relative to its recent past—relative to the Taliban period, when women were forbidden to work, girls were not allowed to go to school, and "criminals" were "convicted" by mullahs and stoned to death or had limbs amputated, relative to the post-Soviet civil war era, when competing warlords reduced literally to rubble a city that had survived even the Soviet onslaught, and relative to the period of Soviet occupation, when, again literally, half a nation was killed, maimed, or terrorized into flight.

By that measure, Afghanistan is in reasonably good shape. Its people are free. Men and women can work and send their children—boys and girls—to school. A process has begun that will allow Afghans, for the first time ever, to decide who will govern them. They can worship their God, sing their songs, play soccer on dusty streets. As for material well-being, Afghans are a profoundly destitute people; however, boosted by relative calm after 20 years of conflict, by good rains and by foreign money, the economy is picking up. The IMF estimates that Afghanistan's economy grew by almost 20% last year. Agriculture, which makes up over half of the legal economy and sustains 60% of the population, has started to recover from years of drought and fighting. Although Afghanistan still suffers from the destruction of its irrigation systems, the IMF reports that cereal production has gone up by 50% last year, following an 80% increase the year before. Foreign assistance has fed the construction sector, while trade has picked up. The government, which is banking on the private sector, is praised for its sound macroeconomic management, the introduction of a new currency, and new financial and investment regulations. A few foreign investors have even started to venture into the country. Two cellular telephone networks are operating, while a five-star hotel project in Kabul is betting on a continued flow of diplomats and international bureaucrats.[35]

Generalizations about a people, even positive ones, can be hazardous. But Afghans have to be counted among the hardiest, most resilient people in the world. Unfortunately, their leaders over the years have sacrificed their common good in the pursuit of personal and parochial ambitions. Among the many possible roads that lie ahead, two stand out. The first descends into political and social division, economic deprivation, and, inevitably, a new cycle of disease, death, and destruction. The second ascends into relative political and social harmony, gradual but steady economic development, and, with a lot of help from friends, an improved standard of living. If Afghan leaders can somehow find a way to bury their recent history, the Afghan people may be headed along their road less traveled. Hope springs eternal.

NOTES

1. Ahmed Rashid, *Taliban: Militant Islam, Oil and Fundamentalism in Central Asia* (New Haven, Conn.: Yale University Press, 2001), vii, 4.

2. Kenneth Katzman, "Afghanistan: Current Issues and U.S. Policy," *CRS Report for Congress*, U.S. Congressional Research Service, Washington, D.C., October 7, 2003, 29.

3. "News Focus: The United Nations and Afghanistan," UN News Centre, April 25, 2004, available at www.un.org/apps/news/infocusnews.

4. UN Development Program, "Afghanistan: Preliminary Needs Assessment for Recovery and Reconstruction," January 2002; UN Development Program, "Human Development Indicators, 2003," both available at http://hdr.undp.org/reports. The United Nations apparently cannot calculate or does not report Afghanistan's Human Development Index.

5. Henry F. Bradsher, *Afghanistan and the Soviet Union* (Durham, N.C.: Duke University Press, 1985), 9.

6, Anthony Arnold, *Afghanistan's Two-Party Communism: Parcham and Khalq* (Stanford, Calif.: Hoover Institution Press, 1983), 13.

7. Muhammad R. Azmi, "Soviet Politico-Military Penetration in Afghanistan, 1955 to 1979," *Armed Forces and Society* 12, no. 3 (Spring 1986): 335.

8. "Background Note: Afghanistan," Bureau of South Asian Affairs, U.S. Department of State, January 2004.

9. Olivier Roy, "Islam in the Afghan Resistance," *Religion in Communist Lands* 12, no. 1 (Spring 1984): 375.

10. Anthony Arnold, "The Stony Path to Afghan Socialism: Problems of Sovietization in an Alpine Muslim Society," *Orbis* 24, no. 1 (Spring 1985): 45.

11. Louis Dupree, *Leftist Movements in Afghanistan* (Hanover, N.H.: American Universities Field Staff, 1979), 2.

12. Dr. Felix Ermacora, "Report on the Situation of Human Rights in Afghanistan," UN Commission on Human Rights, February 1986, 27.

13. Steve Coll, *Ghost Wars: The Secret History of the CIA, Afghanistan, and bin Laden, from the Soviet Invasion to September 10, 2001* (New York: Penguin, 2004), 11. The helicopters referred to in this quotation were Mi-24 Hind helicopter gunships, arguably the single most significant Soviet military asset in the war.

14. Founded in the eighteenth century, Wahhabbism began in what today is Saudi Arabia. Named after Mohammed ibn Abdul Wahhab, the movement is dedicated to the purification of Islam through a return to Koranic principles.

15. Milton Bearden, "Afghanistan, Graveyard of Empires," *Foreign Affairs* 80, no. 6 (November–December 2001): 24. Bearden was the U.S. Central Intelligence Agency's station chief in Pakistan from 1986 to 1989. He was responsible for the CIA's covert action program in support of the Afghan resistance to the Soviet-supported government.

16. The oft-heard notion that the CIA trained bin Laden is apparently incorrect. As one authoritative account of this period says, "CIA archives contain no record of any direct contact between a CIA officer and bin Laden during the 1980s. CIA officers delivering sworn testimony before Congress in 2002 asserted there were no such contacts, as did multiple CIA officers and U.S. officials in interviews. The CIA became aware of bin Laden's work with Afghan rebels in Pakistan and Afghanistan later in the 1980s but did not meet with him even then, according to these record searches and interviews. If the CIA did have contact with bin Laden during the 1980s and subsequently covered it up, it has so far done an excellent job." Coll, *Ghost Wars*, 87.

17. Coll, *Ghost Wars*, 222–23.

18. Kathy Lally, "The Face of Evil, the Voice of Terrorism," *Baltimore Sun*, September 13, 2001.

19. Devin T. Hagerty, "The United States–Pakistan Entente: Third Time's a Charm?" in *Pakistan on the Brink: Politics, Economics, and Society* (Lanham, Md.: Rowman & Littlefield, 2004).

20. The constitution's full text appears on the website of the Embassy of Afghanistan in Washington, D.C., at www.embassyofafghanistan.org.

21. Kathy Gannon, "Afghanistan Unbound," *Foreign Affairs* 83, no. 3 (May–June 2004): 38.

22. Remarks by Christina B. Rocca, U.S. assistant secretary of state for South Asian affairs, as delivered to the International Conference on Afghanistan, Paris, March 26, 2004.

23. "Elections and Security in Afghanistan," *Asia Briefing*, International Crisis Group, Kabul/Brussels, March 30, 2004.

24. Katzman, "Afghanistan: Current Issues and U.S. Policy," 10.

25. Much of the information in the previous four paragraphs is from press accounts: Phil Zabriskie, "Undefeated: On the Afghanistan–Pakistan Border, the Taliban Are Regrouping, Bent on Spreading Terror," *Time Asia*, July 14, 2003, available at www.time.com/time/asia/magazine; John Lancaster and Kamran Khan, "Pakistan to Step Up Border Operations, *Washington Post*, February 23, 2004; Dana Priest and Kamran Khan, "Al Qaeda Leaders May Be Cornered," *Washington Post*, March 19, 2004.

26. Gannon, "Afghanistan Unbound," 38–39; Katzman, "Afghanistan: Current Issues and U.S. Policy," 16–17.

27. Ron Synovitz, "Afghanistan: PRTs Go beyond Humanitarian Assistance into Security Realm," Radio Free Europe/Radio Liberty, March 6, 2004.

28. "NATO Expands ISAF Peacekeeping Mission in Afghanistan," United States Mission to the European Union, January 7, 2004, available at www.useu.be/Categories/Defense/Jan0704 NATOAfghanistan.html.

29. "Berlin Declaration," International Afghanistan Conference, March 31–April 1, 2004. Overall contributions since 2002 are difficult to calculate because at any given time countries make pledges covering various future periods. Although critics claim that pledges for Afghanistan have not been completely fulfilled, the $4.5 billion pledged at the 2002 Tokyo conference has apparently been allocated in full.

30. Remarks by Christina B. Rocca, cited above.

31. "Fact Sheet: Progress in Afghanistan's Reconstruction," U.S. Department of State, March 26, 2004, available at www.state.gov.

32. "The New Afghanistan: Progress and Accomplishments," U.S. Department of State, available at www.state.gov (accessed May 1, 2004).

33. Statement of Robert B. Charles, assistant secretary of state for international narcotics and law enforcement affairs, before the U.S. House Committee on Government Reform, Subcommittee on Criminal Justice, Drug Policy, and Human Resources, April 1, 2004; Judy Aita, "Opium Cultivation Continues to Grow in World's Largest Producer, Survey Finds," Washington File, Bureau of International Information Programs, U.S. Department of State, October 29, 2003.

34. Katzman, "Afghanistan," 34.

35. "Afghanistan: Passing the Hat Round for the Rebuilders; Money Is Good, but Afghans Need Security as Well," *The Economist*, April 1, 2004.

FURTHER READING

Arnold, Anthony. *Afghanistan: The Soviet Invasion in Perspective.* Stanford, Calif.: Hoover Institution Press, 1985.

Borovik, Artyom. *The Hidden War: A Russian Journalist's Account of the Soviet War in Afghanistan.* New York: Grove Press, 2001.

Coll, Steve. *Ghost Wars: The Secret History of the CIA, Afghanistan, and bin Laden, from the Soviet Invasion to September 10, 2001.* New York: Penguin, 2004.

Dupree, Louis. *Afghanistan.* Princeton, N.J.: Princeton University Press, 1980.

Goodson, Larry P. *Afghanistan's Endless War: State Failure, Regional Politics, and the Rise of the Taliban.* Seattle: University of Washington Press, 2001.

Gunaratna, Rohan. *Inside Al Qaeda: Global Network of Terror.* New York: Berkley, 2002.

Kepel, Gilles. *Jihad: The Trail of Political Islam.* Cambridge, Mass.: Belknap, 2003.

Lamb, Christina. *The Sewing Circles of Herat: A Personal Voyage through Afghanistan.* New York: HarperCollins, 2002.

Rashid, Ahmed. *Jihad: The Rise of Militant Islam in Central Asia.* New York: Penguin, 2003.

———. *Taliban: Militant Islam, Oil and Fundamentalism in Central Asia.* New Haven, Conn.: Yale University Press, 2001.

Roy, Olivier. *Islam and Resistance in Afghanistan.* Cambridge, U.K.: Cambridge University Press, 1990.

Rubin, Barnett. *The Fragmentation of Afghanistan: State Formation and Collapse in the International System.* New Haven, Conn.: Yale University Press, 2002.

6

Great-Power Foreign Policies in South Asia

Robert Wirsing[1]

A steady accumulation of global crises since the catastrophic terrorist attacks on New York City and Washington, D.C., in September 2001 transformed what in the previous decade had remained a somewhat academic debate about the likely shape of the post–Cold War world order into an immediate and insistent matter of foreign policy. Like it or not, world leaders could no longer avoid either the question of the post–Cold War world's likely destiny or the equally imperative question of how best to fashion their nations' foreign policies in response to it.

Exactly where South Asia would fit in the emerging world order inevitably formed a subset of the questions confronting world leaders. In 2003 the region held three (India, Pakistan, Bangladesh) of the ten most populous nations on earth, and these three nations alone constituted 21.3 percent of the world's total population. Two of them (India, Pakistan) ranked among the world's nine nuclear-weapon powers. Aside from a huge share of the world's economic, political, and environmental problems, South Asia also appeared to house a disproportionate share of the world's terrorists. India and Pakistan had spent ten tension-filled months, from December 2001 to October 2002, locked in a menacing, nuclear-weapons-tinged confrontation, in which a million troops mobilized along their border. In short, South Asia could be ignored only at the policymaker's peril.

For the policymakers of the United States, Russia, and China, implicated for decades in the region's strategic development, the question of South Asia's evolving strategic role and importance in the world was especially urgent. It is on these three great powers that this chapter focuses. For each of these external actors, shaping strategic policy toward South Asia continues in the new century to present formidable difficulty. No small part of the difficulty arose from the inescapable fact of the South Asian region's premier strategic dilemma, the longstanding and seemingly intractable rivalry, now nuclear, between India and Pakistan. As in the past, this rivalry offered all three of these powers tempting opportunities for alliance, for arms sales, and for much else; at the same time it continued to impose severe limitations on the policy options open to them. The most troublesome such limitation was the zero-sum character of the India–Pakistan relationship and the consequent immense burden of framing workable policy toward one side without alienating the other. In theory, a country's policies toward India and Pakistan could be "dehyphenated" or "decoupled," as was urged upon American policymakers in the last years of the Clinton administration. In practice, pursuing discrete policy trajectories toward India and Pakistan ran up against the insuperable obstacle of their deep strategic entanglement with one another.

This chapter contends with these limitations upon great-power policies in South Asia, particularly with the handicap imposed on the foreign policy interests and objectives of the United States, Russia, and China by the deep rivalry between India and Pakistan. The discussion acknowledges important changes in the foreign policies each of the three external powers has adopted in recent years toward India and Pakistan. It maintains, however, that the stubborn persistence of the Indo-Pakistani rivalry exerts, for the most part, a profoundly conservative influence on these policies, breeding in them at least as much continuity as discontinuity and, in particular, discouraging changes in policy that would promote greater regional stability and cooperation. The discussion argues, finally, that only the world's sole superpower, the United States, appears to have the capacity to reshape fundamentally the security architecture of the region, to break the logjam in India–Pakistan relations, so to speak, and thus to set the South Asian region on a new, potentially less conflict-ridden, trajectory. Whether it has the will to do so has yet to be demonstrated.

THE UNITED STATES AND THE INDIA–PAKISTAN EQUATION

For over fifty years, India and Pakistan have been rivals, not only of one another, but also for the friendship of the United States. Pakistan has had lengthy stretches of formal alliance with Washington, in earlier decades even earning the enviable reputation as "America's most allied ally." Its reputation among Americans has been glaringly inconstant, however, slipping in the 1960s, rising swiftly during the Afghanistan War (1979–1989), falling again in the years following the Soviet Union's collapse in 1991, and then, following September 11, again rebounding.

India, apart from a brief flirtation with the idea of alliance with the United States in 1962–1963 in the immediate aftermath of China's military onslaught against India's northern borders, spent most of the first fifty years of its postindependence history in a relationship with the United States that Dennis Kux characterizes as one of "estrangement."[2] India, however, always outstripped Pakistan in real or potential economic and military weight. As a result, many Americans persisted all along in citing India as Pakistan's potential replacement. Toward the end of President Clinton's second term, just such a move appeared in Washington's policy toward South Asia. It surfaced most visibly during Clinton's much-publicized visit to the region in March 2000, in the course of which differences in Washington's attitudes toward India and Pakistan, namely, a conspicuous tilt in favor of India, were evident not only in the length of the visits to each country (five days in India, five hours in Pakistan) but in the president's public demeanor and comments.[3] During the early months of the George W. Bush administration, there were indications that the shift in India's favor would continue. The events of September 11 disturbed the shift, of course, giving an immediate and major boost to Pakistan. However, while the fact of Pakistan's current rise in stature in Washington's eyes is readily demonstrable, its permanence is not. The potential for yet another downturn in U.S. perceptions of Pakistan continues to bedevil the relationship. In contrast, sustained efforts by Washington to foster a closer strategic partnership with New Delhi seem likely.

INDIA IN WASHINGTON'S PERSPECTIVE

There is nearly uniform agreement among the subcontinent's observers that little remains of the Nehruvian weltanschauung that guided Indian foreign policy for decades after independence. The familiar beliefs that went along with it, particularly in the virtues of nonalignment, were shattered, along with much else, with the ending of the Cold War. The collapse of India's principal ally, the Soviet Union, threw India's foreign policy into disarray and left its decision makers with no option, as Sumit Ganguly puts it, but "to reassess the precepts on which the country's policies had been based and recalculate their nation's goals, options and strategies."[4] In practice, this reassessment has brought the opportunity for a fundamental redesign of Indian security policies. The possibility now looms for constructing new security partnerships. As noted above, the United States has clearly emerged as the preeminent candidate for such a partnership.

A number of factors work in favor of such a partnership. These include mounting economic ties, not only in trade and investment but in symbiotic development of information-technology industries; an increasingly large, wealthy, well-educated, and politically influential Indian diaspora community in the United States; overlapping strategic interests when it comes to China,

Central Asia, and the Middle East; and finally, though by no means least importantly, shared apprehensions in regard to global terrorism.[5] These same factors lend themselves, of course, to more than one interpretation. When it comes to two-way trade between the United States and India, for instance, there can be no doubt that it is on the rise. Merchandise exports from India to the United States rose by 21.4 percent in 2002 to $11.82 billion, the highest figure yet achieved. However, in the value of merchandise exports, India ranked only nineteenth among America's trade partners, far behind China, of course, whose exports to the United States, at $124.8 billion, ranked it fourth, but even behind tiny Israel. India's imports of merchandise from the United States were still extremely modest. At $3.7 billion in 2002, India ranked twenty-seventh among importers of U.S. goods.[6]

Just how far the Indo-U.S. relationship will or should go is thus inevitably the focus of a lively debate in both countries. While virtually everyone concedes that the relationship has taken significant strides forward in recent years, there is no consensus on what form it will take in coming years. The broad outlines of the debate have been well captured in a pair of articles published at the end of 2002 in the *Washington Quarterly*. In "A Paradigm Shift toward South Asia?" C. Raja Mohan, noted Indian commentator and strategic-affairs editor of *The Hindu,* observes, "U.S. policy toward the region since September 11 has signaled a fundamental change in both the intensity and the quality of U.S. involvement in South Asia." The United States, he says, "has begun to focus on the deeper conflicts that have long troubled the region. For its part, the region itself has been more receptive than ever before to the new U.S. engagement."[7] Boiled down to its essentials, Mohan's essay argues that September 11 "globalized" South Asian security and that this fundamental alteration in the region's geopolitical framework has opened wide the door to a qualitatively new role for the United States in the region. He points to two specific discontinuities contributing to the new globalized circumstances. The most significant of them, he claims, "has been the development of sound bilateral relations between the United States and both India and Pakistan. One year after the attacks, the Bush administration can rightfully boast of strong equities and unprecedented good relations with New Delhi and Islamabad."[8] The second of them, he says, is the shift in Washington's priorities in the region from an exaggeratedly single-minded focus on nuclear nonproliferation to a more comprehensive concern with regional peace. By this, he means that Washington, while evincing thus far no enthusiasm for direct, overt mediation of the Kashmir dispute, has discovered that its high-level political efforts at crisis management in spring and summer 2002, at the height of India–Pakistan force mobilization, were successful in helping to de-escalate tensions and might well serve as a model for the future.[9] Mohan suggests that the Bush administration, over the course of defusing the

2002 crisis, came upon three important realizations that could supply the basis for a continuing peace process in the region:

> Pakistan's sponsorship of cross-border terrorism can no longer be ignored or condoned. Conflict resolution efforts are critical to end recurrent crises between India and Pakistan. Free, fair, inclusive, and nonviolent elections to the state assembly on the Indian side of Kashmir could be the starting point of a peace process on the subcontinent.[10]

South Asia, he declares,

> is at the cusp of a historic transformation. India has begun to shed the accumulated mistrust of Washington, is seeking stronger bilateral ties, and is ready to work with the United States to promote peace and prosperity in the region. Washington will have to overcome its tendency to obsess over single issues in the region—nonproliferation in the past and the war on terrorism now—but the U.S. diplomacy since September 11 has set the stage for a more broadly based U.S. policy toward the subcontinent.[11]

In short, says Mohan, a window of opportunity has opened in South Asia, and the United States should jump through it.

In a companion piece, Satu Limaye, director of research at the Asia-Pacific Center for Security Studies in Honolulu, Hawaii, takes a far less sanguine view of developments in the subcontinent. His essay "Mediating Kashmir: A Bridge Too Far" focuses specifically on the region's premier territorial dispute. Its implicit purpose, however, is clearly to introduce greater skepticism into the Indo-U.S. equation, broadly construed, than was entertained in Mohan's essay. In particular, Limaye's essay highlights the chilling effects the deep rivalry over Kashmir has on American involvement in the region. Limaye argues that the U.S. stake in the subcontinent's affairs, even after September 11, is more ostensible than real and that calls for Washington to take a sustained interest in conflict resolution in the region are misguided. "Although greater now than in the past," he observes, "the dangers and costs of the conflict's persistence, the extent of U.S. influence, and Indian and Pakistani receptivity to U.S. mediation are all largely overstated. U.S. interests in Kashmir and the prospect of achieving a compromise are at best debatable."[12]

Limaye contends, in particular, that it is "a beguiling but illusory notion . . . that increased U.S. engagement with the subcontinent after September 11 makes sustained U.S. mediation to resolve the dispute in Kashmir more feasible."[13] In actuality, he points out, neither India nor Pakistan is especially enthusiastic about third-party intervention, Pakistan because of the fear that the Kashmir dispute has become hopelessly entangled with the war on terrorism, India because of its own deep reservations about the long-range implications of the close security relationship Washington has built with Pakistan in the wake of September 11. Limaye maintains,

> Neither the profound commitment necessary to ensure Pakistan's security, nor the efforts required to help achieve a compromise in Kashmir is justified by U.S. interests in India or Pakistan or in their amity. Episodic crisis management and behind-the-scenes facilitation, however cumbersome and unsatisfying, are feasible, effective, and more commensurate with U.S. interests.[14]

In short, he bluntly suggests, "the United States does not have a dog in the Kashmir fight."[15]

The Kashmir dispute is only one factor, of course, giving future shape to the Indo-U.S. strategic relationship. Another, potentially very powerful factor is China. Some China watchers in the United States, banking on India's inevitable resentment toward China stemming from the 1962 war and the continued festering of their unresolved border dispute, have been pressing for India's enlistment as a strategic counterweight to China. India and the United States may be laying the groundwork for just such a strategic role through the conduct recently of joint military exercises involving all branches of Indian and U.S. military forces. Indo-U.S. relations, by any yardstick, have unquestionably made dramatic advances in recent years. Nevertheless, the fact remains, as China specialist Mohan Malik comments in a recent and perceptive essay, that "Washington's preoccupations with the war on terror and Iraq have tended to push into the background the effort to fashion an overall strategic framework for advancing U.S.-Indian interests in Asia." More than that, he points out, Pakistan's renewed importance in Washington's eyes was bound to dim India's confidence in America's long-term reliability. "While 'the China factor' draws the U.S. and India closer," he says, "'the Pakistan factor' pulls them apart." When it comes to partnership with Washington, he concludes, there are both great expectations and deep skepticism on the Indian side.[16] How substantial the basis is for India's skepticism deriving from "the Pakistan factor" requires close examination.

PAKISTAN IN WASHINGTON'S PERSPECTIVE

Just how favorably Washington is disposed toward Pakistan at any given time has been shaped by many considerations, including the state of Pakistan's confrontational relationship with its Indian neighbor, the strength of its embrace of political democracy and a free market economy, the spirit in which it incorporated Islam into its state identity, and the license it took in the pursuit of nuclear weapons. More than any of these, however, Pakistan's standing in Washington was always impacted most heavily by its strategic utility or fit, in other words, whether and to what extent its leaders seemed able and willing to meld Pakistan's national interests to U.S. policy imperatives. In this transparently dependent relationship, it was always Washington's perception of strategic necessity, in company with Pakistan's capacity for adapting to it, that drove the U.S.-Pakistani relationship. Pakistan's capacity in this regard has been put to its severest test ever in the period since September 11. Washington's immediate identification of Taliban-ruled Afghanistan as state sponsor of the al Qaeda terrorist network, thus, as an active accomplice to the terrorist attacks and logical first target in the global war on terrorism (GWOT), plunged the army-ruled government of Pakistan into acute crisis. Pakistan's geographic proximity to Afghanistan made it a primary candidate for renewed alliance with the United States. Also arguing for alliance with the United States were neighboring India's prompt offer to Washington of total support in the war on Afghanistan and Pakistan's dire military and economic weaknesses. By no means least among Pakistani calculations, however, was the possibility of punishment by Washington if Islamabad made the wrong choice. Thus, Pakistan's actual choice to join the global coalition against terrorism and to offer immediate tangible aid, including military bases, in Washington's impending war on Afghanistan came as no surprise. How much longer and how fully Islamabad will continue to honor that decision, the policy implications of which clearly went well beyond the immediate rupture of Pakistan's ties with Afghanistan, will depend to a large extent on how successfully Islamabad manages to adjust its own paramount national security concerns to Washington's, particularly as these relate to the war on terrorism. In this regard, three issues stand out as crucial tests of the durability of the U.S.-Pakistani relationship: Pakistan's management of Islamic extremism, the Kashmir dispute with India, and Pakistan's nuclear-weapons program.

PAKISTAN'S MANAGEMENT OF ISLAMIC EXTREMISM

On the day following the terrorist attacks on the United States, the president of Pakistan, Gen. Pervez Musharraf, appealed for a "concerted international effort . . . to fight terrorism in all its forms and manifestations."[17] A few days later, Pakistan was formally enlisted in the global coalition against terrorism. Islamabad quickly launched a desperate effort to persuade the Taliban leadership to hand Osama bin Laden over to the West for punishment; but by the time the U.S.-led bombing campaign against Afghanistan began on October 7, Islamabad had cut its formal diplomatic ties with Kabul (the last nation in the world to do so) and was resigned to the virtually complete abandonment of its former ally. From the Pakistani point of view, there was a bright side to all of this. For one thing, Pakistan's transformation from pariah to partner on the embattled frontline against terrorism brought a welcome political boost. For another, while Musharraf was careful to describe his decision to support the international campaign against terrorism as one based on principles, the promise of relief for Pakistan's beleaguered economy brought an obvious material boost. However, there was also an unavoidable dark side to Pakistan's choice. On September 20, President George W. Bush had warned that "every nation in every region now has a decision to make: Either you are with us or you are with the terrorists. From this day forward, any nation that continues to harbor or support terrorism will be regarded by the United States as a hostile regime."[18] Musharraf had made plain in a candid address to the nation only one day earlier that taking what he called "wrong decisions" in the country's moment of crisis could have serious consequences for Pakistan's "critical concerns." These he identified as Pakistan's security against "external threat," revival of the economy, the country's "strategic nuclear and missile assets," and "the Kashmir cause." These had to be safeguarded at all costs. "Any wrong judgment on our part," he warned, "can damage all our interests."[19]

What Musharraf did not say, at least in public, was that Pakistan's avoidance of "wrong decisions" was going to be far from easy. There were several reasons for this. First, Islamic extremist forces were well entrenched in Pakistani society and would not easily be brought to heel. This was a by-product, to no small extent, of sustained and deliberate state policy. For over two decades Islam had been granted an increasingly important role not only in Pakistan's domestic politics but in its international politics, too. In the words of Islamic scholar Vali Nasr, Islamic ideology

> has become the framework through which Pakistan has defined its national interests and provided cadence between its domestic politics and regional ambitions. In fact, Islam has provided Pakistan with a powerful political language and policy-making framework to bring domestic and international interests and engagements of Pakistan into alignment. In Islam the state has found a powerful means to shore up domestic authority and to project power regionally, to make Pakistan a stronger state. Islam has also opened new foreign policy possibilities to Pakistan, most notably in Afghanistan and Kashmir.[20]

Second, Washington's conduct of the GWOT was clearly having a negative impact on public opinion in Pakistan, bringing Islamabad under increasing domestic pressure to break free of Washington's embrace. In disturbingly large numbers, Pakistanis were reported to dislike America and to be mainly unsympathetic with the GWOT. A massive Pew Global Attitudes opinion survey of over thirty-eight thousand people in forty-four nations, conducted roughly a year after September 11, reported, for instance, that only 10 percent of Pakistanis (the second lowest percentage among all the nations surveyed) had a favorable opinion of the United States; only 2 percent (the lowest figure among all the nations surveyed) had a positive impression of the spread of American ideas and customs; only 9 percent (again, the lowest figure among all nations surveyed) preferred American ideas about democracy; and while 45 percent opposed the U.S.-led war on terrorism, only 20 percent favored it.[21]

Additional evidence of anti-American feelings surfaced in the results of the October 2002 elections of Pakistan's national and provincial assemblies. In the National Assembly election, an alliance of religious parties, the Muttahida Majlis-i-Amal (MMA), won an unprecedented 52 of 272 seats (19 percent), assuring Islamists of a power-brokering role in the central government for the first time in Pakistan's history; and in the provincial elections, the alliance won outright control of the Northwest Frontier Province (NWFP) and a share of power in a coalition government in Baluchistan—like the NWFP geographically adjacent to the strategically sensitive Afghanistan border. Electoral support for the MMA was largely confined to these two provinces, and even in those there were a number of alternative explanations (among them, public disgust with the incumbents' corruption and misgovernment) for the MMA's electoral success. Nevertheless, the centrality of anti-American diatribes in its election campaign implied that anti-Americanism had had more than a minor impact on the electoral outcome. Especially hazardous for Musharraf, in any event, was the MMA's insistent demand for an end to the American military presence in Pakistan, a demand that not only ran afoul of the Pentagon's plans for forward troop deployment in a region of exceptional instability but jeopardized its capacity for tracking down remnants al Qaeda and Taliban fugitives. Pakistan had clearly been riding an extremist tiger for a long time. At a minimum, this translated in practice into what one writer describes as "Pakistan's ambivalent role in the fight against terrorism."[22] More alarmingly, it could mean that President Musharraf's disgruntled Islamic opponents might one day instigate a violent coup that could result in an extremist Pakistan.

KASHMIR'S DISPUTE WITH INDIA

President Musharraf raised the issue of Kashmir with Secretary of State Colin Powell on September 16, 2001, during the secretary's hastily arranged, post–September 11 visit to Islamabad. Musharraf emphasized to Powell that there could be no normalization of India–Pakistan relations without resolution of the Kashmir dispute and, moreover, that resolution had to be "in accordance with the wishes of the Kashmiri people."[23] This was a formulation that Musharraf knew would raise India's hackles while also reminding Washington that Pakistani collaboration with the United States would come with a political as well as an economic price. The political price asked of Washington was bound to be steep. For years, the government of India had been attempting without much success to persuade global opinion that the roots of the Kashmiri insurrection, begun in 1989, lay mainly on the Pakistani side of the border. It had increasingly emphasized not only what it claimed was Pakistani society's steady drift toward Islamic extremism and fundamentalism, its "Talibanization," in other words, but also what New Delhi claimed was Pakistan's official sponsorship of terrorism in Kashmir. The terrorist assault on the United States in September 2001 thus presented New Delhi with an opportunity to join its hitherto largely ignored concerns over the threat of radical Islam with the now hugely heightened and overlapping concerns of the United States. No less importantly, the assault significantly increased New Delhi's prospects for reframing the world's understanding of the Kashmir dispute in terms better fitted to New Delhi's strategic interests—that it was a dispute having less to do with human rights, in other words, than with the menace of global terrorism.[24]

It quickly became apparent that Washington faced a dilemma: how to balance its immediate requirement for Pakistan's seemingly irreplaceable partnership in the war on terrorism with its longer-term requirement for the goodwill of Pakistan's vastly bigger and more powerful rival? Largely to pacify India, the Department of State at the end of 2001 added to its list of designated terrorist organizations two Pakistan-based groups. Washington sent an even stronger message to Islamabad of its growing dissatisfaction with Pakistan's Kashmir policy with the dispatch to Islamabad in June 2002 of Deputy Secretary of State Richard Armitage. Armitage maintains that in his two-hour meeting with Musharraf he managed to extract from the Pakistani leader the pledge of "a permanent end" to Pakistan's support of terrorist activity in Kashmir. News accounts of the meeting suggested there was room for varied interpretation. In any event, Musharraf's apparent concession was described in the *Washington Post* as "a huge foreign-policy victory for India."[25] This seeming U-turn in Pakistan's Kashmir policy actually produced little more, however, than a suspension, rather than a permanent cessation, of Pakistan-aided cross-border infiltration. Pakistan's reluctance to cave in entirely on the matter of infiltration is understandable. In recent years, the ratio of "guest" to "indigenous" militants fighting in Kashmir had grown substantially in favor of the former, most of them Pakistanis. The fact is that the active armed element of the Kashmir insurgency had gradually been not so much Talibanized as Pakistanized. Were Pakistan to permanently sideline the Pakistani element, while also putting the militants' Pakistan army support system out to pasture, there would be no more insurgency, at least not one New Delhi couldn't easily handle. For Pakistan to help India out in this manner was just not in the cards. As Musharraf told *Newsweek* senior editor Lally Weymouth in an interview published shortly after his meeting with Armitage, Kashmir, unlike Afghanistan, "is our national interest."[26]

PAKISTAN'S NUCLEAR-WEAPONS PROGRAM

Apart from inevitable lingering suspicions in Washington stemming from Islamabad's previous close ties to the Afghan Taliban, there remained between Pakistan and the United States a host of unsettled issues relating to Pakistan's nuclear-weapons program. Pakistan was clearly vulnerable to pressure in regard to these issues, and the possibility existed that their exacerbation could at any time, notwithstanding Pakistan's cooperation in the war on terrorism, trigger a major upheaval in Islamabad's relations with Washington. High on Washington's own list of critical concerns about Pakistan's real or potential nuclear transgressions was the threat that Pakistan's nuclear weapons or fissile materials might fall into extremist hands in the event of a radical Islamist takeover of the government. Seymour Hersh's article "Watching the Warheads," published in a prominent American periodical at the height of the bombing campaign in Afghanistan, was symptomatic of the danger. In it, he made the hugely provocative allegation that joint training of American and Israeli commando teams was already underway in the United States in preparation for possible surprise raids on Pakistan's nuclear-weapons facilities. The raids were being contemplated, Hersh said, as a prophylactic measure for implementation if required to keep Pakistan's nuclear weapons from falling into extremist hands in the event of a radical Islamist takeover of the government.[27] Apart from the fact that Pakistan's nuclear program had been developed in most important respects with Beijing's illicit, but utterly crucial, assistance, there was now the startling report (denied by Pakistan) of a Chinese-facilitated nuclear barter arrangement—advanced missiles in exchange for uranium-enrichment technology—between the Pakistanis and the North Koreans, the third member of Washington's Axis of Evil.[28]

Seen from Islamabad, the South Asian region's nuclear danger sprang from an entirely different source, India primarily, and thus required a remedy tailored specifically to India. Musharraf outlined the Pakistani point of view in this regard in an address to the UN General Assembly in November 2001, not long after September 11. Reassuring his audience that Pakistan was "fully alive to the responsibilities of its nuclear status," Musharraf pointed out that "a stable South Asian security mechanism" could be achieved, but its achievement was dependent on "a peaceful resolution of disputes, preservation of nuclear and conventional balance, confidence building measures and non-use of force prescribed by the UN Charter."[29] The linkage to Kashmir was obvious in the first of these; Pakistanis' anxiety over their country's diminishing ability to keep pace with Indian military acquisitions, whether conventional or nuclear, was evident in the second. This anxiety showed up in a different context some months later in June 2002 in Weymouth's abovementioned interview with Musharraf. Speaking of the "root cause" of the Kashmir issue, the Pakistani president offered a formulation that seemed to depart from the standard interpretation of Kashmir as the single "core issue" between India and Pakistan. "If you want a guarantee of peace," he reportedly told Weymouth, "there are three ways: (1) denuclearize South Asia; (2) ensure a conventional deterrence so that war never takes place in the subcontinent; and (3) find a solution to the Kashmir problem."[30] The second of these, implying that Washington should arm Pakistan and thus be a conventional arms "balancer" in the region, rather than India's preferred military partner, hinted at Islamabad's actual strategic priorities: while sending a subtle reminder of Pakistan's unavoidable dependence on nuclear deterrence for its security, it also avowed Islamabad's conviction that an enduring regional arms balance, conventional or nuclear, could not possibly be achieved irrespective of Washington's own regional arms policy. It happened that this policy was showing increasing signs, Islamabad's apprehensions notwithstanding, of deepening military cooperation with India.

PAKISTAN AND U.S. STRATEGIC DOCTRINE

One is immediately struck, when examining current Pakistani reactions to American strategic doctrine, by the profound lack of correspondence between the way Pakistani and American leaders tend to view the emerging world order. As outlined by Richard N. Haass, director of the policy planning staff at the Department of State, in an address to the Foreign Policy Association in April 2002, what he termed the *post–post–Cold War world* would not only be one in which "American primacy was unprecedented and uncontested" but also in which "increasingly potent transnational challenges intersect with still important traditional concerns."[31] Haass explicitly cited the India–Pakistan conflict as one in which traditional (rival-nation) concerns would predominate. But the doctrine of integration, which he advanced to encompass the complexities of the new traditional/transnational era and to capture the ideas and policies of the Bush administration, left hardly any room for a conception of the world compatible with Islamabad's understanding of its national security predicament.

According to Haass, the principal aim of American foreign policy was "to integrate other countries and organizations into arrangements that will sustain a world consistent with U.S. interests and values, and thereby promote peace, prosperity, and justice as widely as possible." Integration, he said, was "about bringing nations together and then building frameworks of cooperation and, where feasible, institutions that reinforce and sustain them even more." Far from being a defensive response, integration, he said, was "a profoundly optimistic approach to international relations." "We can move from a balance of power," he said, "to a pooling of power."[32] Haass commended Pakistan in the address for having made the proper strategic choice, namely, to reorient Pakistan's foreign policy and to "stand with the United States and the rest of the international community against the Taliban and al-Qaida." Simultaneously, however, he explicitly named India among those countries slated for partnership with Washington. "This is an era of new partnerships," he advised.[33] Haass's comments did not appear to hold out any hope that the United States would bring pressure to bear on India to end what Pakistanis insisted was "state terrorism" in Kashmir or that the United States would actively mediate the Kashmir dispute. Moreover, they seemed much more likely to endorse intensified military-to-military relationships between Indian and U.S. armed forces than to license the sale of advanced military hardware to Pakistan, an interpretation of integration that would surely be favored in Islamabad. Implicit in Haass's remarks was a steadily widening world of enduring partnerships. Yet, Musharraf was bound to wonder, as he did in an interview with Larry King in October 2001, whether Pakistanis, once the moment of their country's immediate strategic utility had passed, would experience once again the sense of "betrayal and abandonment" that had been their lot in past encounters with the United States.[34] The doctrine of integration, seen from Islamabad, promised not so much a pooling of power among the world's countries as short shrift for the American-orchestrated balancing of power that Islamabad felt was essential for peace and security to thrive in the South Asian region. Pakistanis had grounds for thinking, in other words, that Haass's comments signaled not Pakistan's enduring partnership with America but rather Pakistan's far-from-commanding position in Washington's long-term strategic thinking.

RUSSIA AND THE INDIA–PAKISTAN EQUATION

China and the Soviet Union each laid down in the course of the 1960s the foundations of an "enduring entente" with one of the two South Asian rivals, China with Pakistan, the Soviet Union with India. China's alliance with Pakistan grew directly out of China's 1962 border war with India, a conflict that underscored indelibly in Chinese minds Pakistan's potential utility as a strategic counterweight to India. India's alliance with the Soviet Union was also engendered, then was hardened as a result of warfare, namely, the 1965 and

1971 clashes between India and Pakistan. The alliance rewarded both India and the Soviet Union with leverage against China, which had moved in the early 1970s toward an increasingly warm relationship with Washington.

The geopolitical furnishings of the South Asian region and its surroundings have changed in a number of fundamental ways since the Sino-Pakistani and Indo-Soviet alliances were first fashioned. The Soviet Union's demise is one of the most obvious of these changes. The emergence of both India and Pakistan as nuclear-weapons-capable states is another. Still another is the recent formation of the U.S.-led global antiterrorist coalition and the vast increase in U.S. military presence and power in Central and Southwest Asia that has resulted. Inevitably, these and other changes in the region are subjecting these two alliances to considerable strain. Observers wonder whether either one or both of them will survive the strain. They also wonder, assuming these alliances do not survive, what pattern of alignments might replace them.

India's longstanding security relationship with the Soviet Union had brought it a number of tangible benefits, including not only the above-mentioned leverage against China but also a favorable trade relationship; massive quantities of technologically advanced naval, air, and ground weaponry at concessional rates; attractive coproduction agreements that gave a boost to India's nascent indigenous defense industries; and the guarantee of a Soviet veto in the event of adverse actions in regard to Kashmir by the UN Security Council. All of these benefits were jeopardized, of course, by the Soviet Union's collapse. Virtually overnight, a comprehensive and mutually beneficial relationship was in danger of being transformed into what one observer described as "little more than a weapons-supplier nexus."[35] The Indo-Russian relationship today is unquestionably less significant than was its Indo-Soviet forerunner, and given Russia's breathtaking post-Soviet economic and military decline, there is no reason to expect restoration of the relationship to anything along the lines of what it once was—at least not in the foreseeable future. Nevertheless, there is still considerable disagreement among professional watchers of the relationship as to precisely what to make of its prospects.

On one side of the issue are those, such as Pramit Pal Chaudhuri, foreign editor of the *Hindustan Times*, who see in India's remaining links with Russia little to crow about. "[T]he shared ground between Indian and Russian interests is shrinking," Chaudhuri comments, "not expanding." First, he points out, India can contribute very little to the Russian economy, which is Prime Minister Vladimir Putin's number one priority. Nonmilitary trade between India and Russia, he notes, has shrunk to barely more than $1 billion a year. Given the geographic distance between the two countries, it is unlikely to grow very rapidly. Add to the geographic distance the presence between them of a hostile Pakistan, Chaudhuri observes, and there is equally little prospect of India's becoming a significant consumer of Russian gas and oil. Second, says Chaudhuri, Russia is simply no longer in a position either to fund the development of the smart weapons India seeks or to subsidize Indian purchases of Russian arms. Russia's bargain weapons sales are a thing of the past. Third, there are no longer grounds for Moscow and New Delhi to make common cause against China. Increasingly, Moscow sees China not as a threat but as a market. "The truth is," asserts Chaudhuri, "that on almost every economic issue, China is far more useful to Russia than India." According to Chaudhuri, "It all comes down to this: the Putin doctrine has little or no place for India. It may one day, but for now India is really just a place to make a quick buck through arms sales."[36]

On the other side of the issue are those like Nirmala Joshi, a Russian studies specialist at Jawaharlal Nehru University in New Delhi who concluded, following Putin's visit to India at the end of 2002, that Indian and Russian geopolitical and security interests, at both the global and the regional levels, continued to coincide. "India's ties with Russia," she said, "are on a firm footing; Mr. Putin's visit has added new dynamism to them."[37] However firm may be the footing on which Indo-Russian ties currently rest, one thing is certain: Moscow no longer has any good reason to remain at arms length from Pakistan. Even on the extremely volatile subject of terrorism, Pakistan's cooperation may well be more important to Moscow than is India's. "In any case, Putin clearly believes," argues Chaudhuri, "that Russia can benefit by engaging directly with Pakistan. . . . Pakistani President Pervez Musharraf is part of the solution to terrorism, not part of the problem as India believes."[38] Not wanting a hostile relationship with Pakistan is one thing. Finding a way to build a friendlier relationship with Pakistan, without at the same time driving away India, with whom Moscow continues to sustain a lucrative arms-sales relationship, is another. Not unlike the United States, Moscow today finds itself caught uncomfortably in the zero-sum rivalry between India and Pakistan.

CHINA: BALANCING INDIA AND PAKISTAN

Western watchers of the strained relationship between China and India have long been divided into two camps on the issue of the prospects of a breakthrough in Sino-Indian relations. On the more pessimistic side are those strategic analysts who consider the enmity the "natural" outgrowth of a growing clash of interests between two of Asia's largest, most populous, and most powerful continental powers. Analysts in this camp tend to argue that India's interests are better served through closer ties with the geographically "distant" United States than with "proximate" China. On the more optimistic side are those who trace the enmity to more immediate, hence removable, irritants. Analysts in this camp generally view Washington's strategic maneuvers in Asia as potentially equally threatening to India's interests as those of Beijing.

Best representing the first camp, perhaps, is China scholar John W. Garver, who points to a fundamental "security dilemma" confounding Sino-Indian relations. "China," he says,

> harbors deep suspicions about possible future Indian policies toward Tibet. India holds similar fears about possible Chinese intervention in a future India–Pakistan war. China has consistently striven to maintain a balance of power in South Asia, a region far beyond its major industrial and population centers. Since about 1998, India has launched a similar project in East Asia. India struggles to maintain control over, and China to neutralize Indian control over, strategic frontier zones in the Himalayan lands of Nepal, Bhutan, and Sikkim. The military instruments of each state pose inadvertent threats to the other. China's increasingly powerful and long-range naval forces pose challenges, intended or unintended, to Indian security in the Indian Ocean. India's maintenance of substantially ethnic Tibetan paramilitary forces . . . touches Chinese vulnerabilities associated with the huge civilizational cleavage between Beijing and the Tibetan population. And both China and India believe their international stature is at stake in interactions with the other. Each state sees small issues as tied to many other issues to make up a larger balance and, ultimately, to their status as a major power.[39]

"The primary activities that constitute the Sino-Indian security dilemma," Garver explains, "are Chinese efforts to establish and expand political and security relations with the countries of the South Asia–Indian Ocean region (SA-IOR), on the one hand, and Indian efforts to thwart the establishment of such links, on the other."[40] From the Indian perspective, China's "aggressive" activities in the SA-IOR, according to Garver, include

- Continuing nuclear, missile, and conventional arms assistance to Pakistan
- Development of a military cum intelligence relationship with Nepal
- Development of increasingly dense military relations with Myanmar
- Mounting People's Liberation Army activities in the Indian Ocean
- Formation of military relations with Bangladesh
- Efforts to establish normal diplomatic relations with Bhutan[41]

From China's perspective, Garver suggests, these activities are fully warranted by two fundamental Chinese security vulnerabilities—to both of which India is a substantial contributor. One is the stability of China's control over Tibet; the second is the safety of China's sea lines of communication across the Indian Ocean. India's close cooperation with the U.S. Central Intelligence Agency's efforts to penetrate Communist-held Tibet in the 1950s, documented in a recent study, underscores for Beijing the inherently perishable character of New Delhi's present hands-off policy toward Tibet.[42] By the same token, India's mid-2001 decision to create a Far Eastern Strategic Command at Port Blair for the Andaman and Nicobar island archipelagos, significantly enhancing India's capacity to monitor and potentially to threaten key chokepoints in the Indian Ocean, had to be looked upon apprehensively by Beijing, which was busily expanding its own military activities on islands off the coast of Myanmar. Compounding Chinese suspicions was India's Look East Policy, launched in 1995 under Prime Minister Narasimha Rao. A mix of economic and military rationales, this policy aimed at expanding India's security ties with states neighboring China in the Pacific Ocean. Alarming to Beijing, in particular, were New Delhi's efforts to deepen security dialogue and cooperation with Vietnam and Japan, both of which had long historical records of bitter enmity with China. As the Chinese saw it, the Look East Policy, more than anything, had the earmarks of a counterencirclement policy aimed against China.[43] Fundamental to China's security, viewed in the light of the foregoing, is the restraint of India, an objective that translates, in general terms, into a broadly based power-balancing strategy in the SA-IOR, and, more directly, into China's desire for both "a strong Pakistan, and a solid strategic partnership between China and Pakistan."[44]

Analysts on the pessimistic side of the debate over China's strategic relationships with the states of South Asia acknowledge both the strains that have developed in China's alliance with Pakistan as well as the powerful incentives, for both China and India, of building a closer and more cooperative relationship between the world's two most populous states. Distinguishing them from their analytical rivals, however, is the belief that the primarily conflictive relationship that now prevails between these two states is likely to endure indefinitely.[45] The reasons given for the likely persistence of Sino-Indian rivalry vary all the way from the existence of two radically opposed "strategic cultures" in India and China[46] to the prospect of a "coming showdown between China and the United States, which will further increase the significance of China's strategic ties with Pakistan."[47] A factor common to virtually all of them, however, is the strong and interdependent relationship that exists between the Sino-Indian and the Indo-Pakistani rivalries. When it comes to Sino-Indian relations, Indians' inevitable anxiety about China and the nightmare of Sino-Pakistani collusion, on the one hand, and China's huge incentive to take advantage of India's implacable rivalry with Pakistan, on the other, are powerful—for the pessimists, unbeatable—security-strategy drivers.

One of the best-known representatives of the optimist camp, Mohan readily concedes that New Delhi's handling of the relationship with China "is likely to be the biggest political challenge for Indian foreign policy in the coming decades."[48] He concedes, too, that China's dense strategic ties with

Pakistan, including active aid in building Pakistan's India-targeted nuclear-weapons and strategic-missile capability, put the Sino-Pakistani relationship "in a category of its own."[49] Nevertheless, he is adamant that "India's position is not as hopeless as Garver makes it out to be."[50]

Central to Mohan's argument is his belief that the geopolitical and geoeconomic forces released everywhere by globalization are rendering obsolete traditional Indian objectives of regional domination and economic exclusivity, while at the same time energizing new objectives of regional integration and economic cooperation with India's neighbors, including China. Rather than viewing mounting Chinese economic ties with the eastern part of the subcontinent, especially with Myanmar and Bangladesh, "as a Chinese plot to swamp the sensitive Indian North-East," says Mohan, "a confident India could in fact leverage China's growing economic presence to achieve its own objective of regional integration in South Asia."[51]

A similar but much loftier, even breathtaking, vision of the positive potential of Sino-Indian relations is that of B. G. Verghese, a versatile and prolific writer long based at New Delhi's Centre for Policy Research. In a recent book, *Reorienting India: The New Geo-Politics of Asia*, Verghese maintains that an Asian century is in the making and that an emerging "Eurasian land bridge," consisting of new or improved infrastructural architecture (including river basin, railway, and road transport routes, gas and oil pipelines, and modernized port facilities) and the trade and transit diplomatic agreements to go along with it, is already at work, reshaping fundamentally economic and political relationships among the nations of the Eurasian heartland, India and China among them.[52] He acknowledges that unsettled problems between these two Asian giants await resolution. "For the next few decades at least," however, "they should have a strong common interest in working together to build themselves and, with others, create a framework for peace and stability in Asia and a more equitable and just world order."[53] Now that "the land bridges of and to Inner Asia are redrawing the geo-political and economic map of Eurasia," he concludes, "Asia is coming together again."[54]

The contemporary South Asian geopolitical landscape is littered with developments sufficient to sustain indefinitely the argument between optimists and pessimists over the likely future trajectory of great-power involvement in the region. At practically the same moment that Pakistan's naval chief announces a visit to Beijing to nail down a contract to secure three Chinese frigates by June 2004,[55] there are reports that India–China two-way trade, having risen in 2003 by 53.6 percent over 2002, might well reach $20 billion by 2010, a development that must be reassuring to those who believe in the primacy of economic drivers.[56] For every Andrew Selth, who argues persuasively that "Beijing's influence with Rangoon has never been as strong as is sometimes portrayed . . . [and that] Indian fears of encirclement by China, with Burma being used to secure India's eastern flank, have been exaggerated,"[57] there is a Mohan Malik to suggest (also persuasively) that power-balancing still has its attractions.[58]

CONCLUSION

Geography, history, and widely disparate definitions of national interest have teamed up to ensure major differences in the strategic agendas advanced in South Asia by the United States, Russia, and China. China, sharing a lengthy and disputed border with India and with restive ethnic minorities inhabiting its own borderlands, has naturally looked upon its neighbor far differently than has Russia, which for the bulk of its long and friendly association with India could cite extensive commonality of interests. While the United States has long shared with China close (including military) ties with Pakistan, the motivation for acquiring them has sprung from profoundly different sources. For the United States, forging an alliance with Pakistan was always primarily aimed at containing an extraregional adversary (the Soviet Union). For China, the alliance with Pakistan was always largely intraregional in focus, prompted mainly by Beijing's wish to prevent India's emergence as a serious rival and, in particular, to block India from any role in China's encirclement.

Differences in the definition of these national interests naturally persist today. As India's primary arms supplier, Russia inevitably benefits from continuing tensions between India and Pakistan. So does China. While it "does not want a heightened crisis in South Asia," says Andrew Scobell, "a certain low level of tension is desirable. China seeks to thwart Indian hegemony and the emergence of a pliant or subjugated Pakistan that does India's bidding is not appealing."[59] In the absence of tensions, Pakistan would have vastly reduced incentive to seek China's friendship and, at the same time, India might show less restraint either in its border dispute with China or in dabbling in Tibetan affairs. It hardly needs mentioning that the increasing warmth in Washington's relations with New Delhi inevitably breeds distrust in Beijing. Neither Beijing nor Moscow would welcome America's undisputed dominance of the region.

Nevertheless, all of the three great powers we have dealt with in this chapter have a major interest not only in the stability of the South Asian region and the avoidance of nuclear war between India and Pakistan but also, for economic and other reasons, in simultaneous development of friendly parallel ties with both of these states. China and the United States, in particular, have striven in recent years to forge just such parallel ties. For all three of these great powers, however, this goal has thus far proven extremely elusive, demanding a balancing act none of them has yet mastered.

The only one of the three currently to have highly promising relationships with both India and Pakistan is, of course, the United States. Arguably, the United States alone has the resources and capabilities to convert its parallel and positive bilateral relationships with these two states into a sustained project of regional conflict resolution. It scarcely needs to be pointed out, however, that Washington, apart from its inevitable reticence about getting sucked into a bilateral conflict widely viewed as a tar baby, is elsewhere wholly preoccupied at the moment and most unlikely to invest the objective of improving India–Pakistan relations with the priority needed to achieve a significant breakthrough. Just such a reordering of priorities is the sine qua non, I believe, for placing India and Pakistan on a path of reconciliation firmly enough to survive the political turbulence that has come to characterize the region. Russia is clearly in no position to undo the paralysis that afflicts Indo-Pakistani relations. China's motives are yet far too mixed for it to take on the task. The task, if the political will can be found, is Washington's.

NOTES

1. The views expressed here are those of the author and do not necessarily reflect the official policy or position of the Asia-Pacific Center for Security Studies, the U.S. Pacific Command, the U.S. Department of Defense, or the U.S. government.

2. Dennis Kux, *India and the United States: Estranged Democracies* (Washington, D.C.: National Defense University Press, 1992).

3. For details, see Robert G. Wirsing, *Kashmir in the Shadow of War: Regional Rivalries in a Nuclear Age* (Armonk, N.Y.: M. E. Sharpe, Inc., 2003), 108–12.

4. Sumit Ganguly, "India's Alliances 2020," in *South Asia in 2020: Future Strategic Balances and Alliances*, ed. Michael R. Chambers (Carlisle, Pa.: Strategic Studies Institute, November 2002), 364.

5. Teresita C. Schaffer, *Rising India and U.S. Policy Options in Asia*, A Report of the CSIS South Asian Program (Washington, D.C.: Center for Strategic and International Studies, January 2002), 9–10.

6. "Indo-US Bilateral Trade Zooms in 2002," *Hindu*, March 5, 2003; and statistical table: "U.S. Trade Balance, by Partner Country 2002 in Descending Order of Trade Turnover (Imports Plus Exports)" (Washington, D.C.: U.S. International Trade Commission, 2003), available at http://dataweb.usitc.gov/scripts/cy_m3_run.asp.

7. C. Raja Mohan, "A Paradigm Shift toward South Asia?" *Washington Quarterly* 26, no. 1 (Winter 2002–2003): 141.

8. Mohan, "A Paradigm Shift," 143.

9. Mohan, "A Paradigm Shift," 150.

10. Mohan, "A Paradigm Shift," 150.

11. Mohan, "A Paradigm Shift," 155.

12. Satu P. Limaye, "Mediating Kashmir: A Bridge Too Far," *Washington Quarterly* 26, no. 1 (Winter 2002–2003): 157.

13. Limaye, "Mediating Kashmir," 161.

14. Limaye, "Mediating Kashmir," 158.

15. Limaye, "Mediating Kashmir," 164.

16. Mohan Malik, "High Hopes: India's Response to U.S. Security Policies," *Asia-Pacific Security Studies*, Asia-Pacific Center for Security Studies, Honolulu, Hawaii, March 2003.

17. Press Release, "Statement by the President of Pakistan" (Islamabad: Ministry of Foreign Affairs, September 12, 2001), available at www.forisb.org/pr/2001/PR01-161.html.

18. "Transcript of President Bush's Address," *Washington Post*, September 21, 2001, 24.

19. "Address by the President of Pakistan General Pervez Musharraf to the Nation on September 19, 2001, Islamabad" (Islamabad: Ministry of Foreign Affairs, September 19, 2001).

20. Vali Nasr, "Islamic Extremism and Regional Conflict in South Asia," paper presented to the conference on Prospects for Peace in South Asia, Asia-Pacific Research Center, Stanford University, January 21–22, 2003.

21. Pew Global Attitudes Project, *What the World Thinks in 2002* (Washington, D.C.: Pew Research Center for the People and the Press, December 2002), 53–71. The survey was conducted in Pakistan in August–September 2002. Respondents, mainly urban, numbered 2,032.

22. Joe de Courcy, "Pakistan's Impossible Dilemma," *AsiaInt Special Bulletin*, Asia Intelligence Ltd., March 7, 2003.

23. "Joint Press Conference of President of Pakistan General Pervez Musharraf and Colin Powell, U.S. Secretary of State, on September 16, 2001, Islamabad" (Islamabad: Ministry of Foreign Affairs, September 16, 2001), www.forisb.org/CE-016.html.

24. See Robert G. Wirsing, "Kashmir in the Terrorist Shadow: Impact of 9/11," *Journal of Asian Affairs* 33, no. 1 (February 2002): 91–97.

25. Glenn Kessler, "A Defining Moment in Islamabad," *Washington Post*, June 22, 2002, A1.

26. Lally Weymouth, "Voices from a Hot Zone," *Newsweek*, July 1, 2002.

27. Seymour M. Hersh, "Watching the Warheads: The Risks to Pakistan's Arsenal," *New Yorker*, November 5, 2001.

28. Glenn Kessler, "Pakistan's N. Korea Deals Stir Scrutiny," *Washington Post*, November 13, 2002, A1.

29. "Address by the President of Pakistan, General Pervez Musharraf, at the Fifty-Sixth Session of the United Nations General Assembly, 10 November 2002" (New York: Pakistan Mission to the United Nations), at www.un.int/pakistan/120011110.html.

30. Weymouth, "Voices from a Hot Zone."

31. Richard N. Haass, "Defining U.S. Foreign Policy in a Post-Post-Cold War World," Remarks to Foreign Policy Association, New York, April 22, 2002, available at www.state.gov/s/p/rem/9632pf.html.

32. Haass, "Defining U.S. Foreign Policy."

33. Haass, "Defining U.S. Foreign Policy."

34. "Live Interview of General Pervez Musharraf with Larry King of CNN on October 23, 2001" (Islamabad: Ministry of Foreign Affairs, October 23, 2001), at www.forisb.org/CE-017.html.

35. Ganguly, "India's Alliances 2020," 364.

36. Pramit Pal Chaudhuri, "Why the Indo-Russian Relationship Is Going Nowhere in a Hurry," *Hindustan Times*, December 16, 2002.

37. Nirmala Joshi, " The Putin Visit," *The Hindu*, December 11, 2002. For an earlier and also relatively upbeat comment on the Indo-Russian relationship, at least the military side of it, see P. R. Chari, "Indo-Russian Military Cooperation," *The Hindu*, June 28, 2001.

38. Chaudhuri, "Why the Indo-Russian Relationship Is Going Nowhere."

39. John W. Garver, "The Security Dilemma in Sino-Indian Relations," *India Review* 1, no. 4 (October 2002): 2–3.

40. Garver, "The Security Dilemma," 3–4.

41. Garver, "The Security Dilemma," 4–5.

42. See Kenneth J. Colby and James Morrison, *CIA's Secret War in Tibet* (Lawrence: University Press of Kansas, 2002).

43. Garver, "The Security Dilemma," 25–28.

44. Garver, "The Security Dilemma," 8–9.

45. See, e.g., Devin T. Hagerty, "China and Pakistan: Strains in the Relationship," *Current History* (September 2002): 284–89; Mohan Malik, "The China Factor in the India–Pakistan Conflict," *Parameters* 33, no. 1 (Spring 2003): 35–50; and Andrew Scobell, "Does South Asia Matter to Moscow and Beijing?" paper presented to the Conference on Prospects for Peace in South Asia, Asia-Pacific Research Center, Stanford University, January 21–22, 2003.

46. Andrew Scobell, "'Cult of Defense' and 'Great Power Dreams': The Influence of Strategic Culture on China's Relationship with India," in *South Asia in 2020*, 329–59.

47. Malik, "The China Factor," 48.

48. C. Raja Mohan, *Crossing the Rubicon: The Shaping of India's New Foreign Policy* (New Delhi: Penguin Books India, 2003), 142–43.

49. Mohan, *Crossing the Rubicon*, 158.

50. Mohan, *Crossing the Rubicon*, 155.

51. Mohan, *Crossing the Rubicon*, 156–57.

52. B. G. Verghese, *Reorienting India: The New Geo-Politics of Asia* (New Delhi: Konark Publishers, 2001), 151–214.

53. Verghese, *Reorienting India*, 255.

54. Verghese, *Reorienting India*, 265, 269.

55. "Pakistan May Get Chinese Frigates by June," *South Asian Media Net*, April 1, 2004.

56. "India, China Hold Talks on Free Trade Agreement," *Indian Express*, March 25, 2004; and "India-China Trade Pegged at US \$20b by 2010," *South Asian Media Net*, April 3, 2004.

57. Andrew Selth, *Burma's North Korean Gambit: A Challenge to Regional Security?* Canberra Papers on Strategy and Defence No. 154 (Canberra: Strategic and Defence Studies Centre, 2004), 37.

58. Mohan Malik, "Burma's Role in Regional Security," in *Burma/Myanmar: Strong Regime Weak State?* ed. Morton B. Pederson, Emily Rudland, and R. J. May (Adelaide: Crawford House Publishing, 2000), 241–77.

59. Scobell, "Does South Asia Matter?" 32.

FURTHER READING

Chambers, Michael R., ed. *South Asia in 2020: Future Strategic Balances and Alliances.* Carlisle, Pa.: Strategic Studies Institute, 2002.

Faruqui, Ahmad. *Rethinking the National Security of Pakistan: The Price of Strategic Myopia.* Aldershot, U.K.: Ashgate, 2002.

Garver, John W. "The China-India-U.S. Triangle: Strategic Relations in the Post-Cold War Era," *NBR Analysis* 13, no. 5 (October 2002).

——. "The Security Dilemma in Sino-Indian Relations," *India Review* 1, no. 4 (October 2002).

Limaye, Satu. "Mediating Kashmir: A Bridge Too Far," *Washington Quarterly* 26, no. 1 (Winter 2002–2003).

Malik, Mohan. "The China Factor in the India–Pakistan Conflict," *Occasional Paper Series*, Asia-Pacific Center for Security Studies, Honolulu, November 2002.

——. "High Hopes: India's Response to U.S. Security Policies," *Asia-Pacific Security Studies*, Asia-Pacific Center for Security Studies, Honolulu, March 2003.

Mohan, C. Raja. "A Paradigm Shift toward South Asia?" *Washington Quarterly* 26, no. 1 (Winter 2002–2003).

Schaffer, Teresita C. *Rising India and U.S. Policy Options in Asia*. Washington, D.C.: Center for Strategic and International Studies, 2002.

Wirsing, Robert G. *Kashmir in the Shadow of War: Regional Rivalries in a Nuclear Age*. Armonk, N.Y.: M. E. Sharpe, 2003.

——. "Pakistan and the Bush Administration: Precarious Partnership," *Asia-Pacific Security Studies*, Asia-Pacific Center for Security Studies, Honolulu, March 2003.

II

INTERNATIONAL ISSUE AREAS

7

Kashmir and India–Pakistan Nuclear Issues

Gaurav Kampani

South Asia is often described as the most dangerous place on earth, the likeliest place where a nuclear war might be fought in the future. Such concerns center on India and Pakistan's unabated rivalry over Kashmir and the continuing low-intensity, or subconventional, war in the region amid vertically proliferating nuclear capabilities.

As discussed in chapters 1 and 2 of this book, the Indo-Pakistani dispute over Kashmir stretches back to the founding of the states in 1947. India and Pakistan were partitioned out of the remains of the British Indian Empire on the basis of two rival ideological principles: India as a secular homeland for the Hindu majority and other religious minorities and Pakistan as a homeland for the subcontinent's Muslims. Since Partition, New Delhi has considered the successful incorporation of Kashmir, India's only Muslim-majority province, critical to affirming the success of its secular experiment. Likewise, in the absence of Kashmir's incorporation, Islamabad regards Pakistan as incomplete.

In the first two decades after Partition, India and Pakistan fought two wars to try to settle their claims over Kashmir. The first war in 1947–1948 led to Kashmir's division into Pakistani- and Indian-administered sections, with India gaining control over roughly two-thirds of the territory. In 1948 India unwittingly internationalized the dispute by seeking UN mediation. The original UN formula called for a plebiscite to grant the Kashmiri people their right to self-determination. Although India agreed in principle to a plebiscite, over time it diluted that commitment and tried to make Kashmir's accession to India permanent. Faced with a growing conventional disparity with India and frustrated by the failure of UN and U.S.-British third-party mediation efforts to resolve the dispute, in 1965 Pakistan made a military grab for Kashmir. That effort failed; subsequently, New Delhi and Islamabad reaffirmed their commitment to the status quo under the 1966 Tashkent Agreement.

Kashmir remained a marginal issue during the 1971 Bangladesh war, which resulted in Pakistan's dismemberment and the emergence of East Pakistan as the independent state of Bangladesh. However, the peace settlement that followed the aftermath of that war was significant. Under the 1972 Simla Agreement, India and Pakistan agreed to resolve the dispute bilaterally through peaceful means. From that time until the late 1980s, Kashmir receded into the background and almost became a nonissue in Indo-Pakistani relations. However, the outbreak of an insurgency in Indian-administered Kashmir (IAK) in 1989 once again gave Pakistan the opportunity to revive the dispute and seek revisions to the existing status quo.[1]

From the late 1980s, Pakistani military and intelligence agencies used their experience in the Afghan war, covered in chapter 5, to train and arm Kashmiri insurgents to wage subconventional war against the Indian government and its security agencies. Beyond the obvious goal of seeking to revise the political status quo in Kashmir, Pakistan has used this strategy to keep India off balance and draw down New Delhi's historic conventional advantage by diverting Indian military resources into a debilitating low-intensity war of attrition. In this regard, nuclear weapons have become key facilitators of Islamabad's strategy, for such weapons have induced caution in potential Indian conventional escalatory responses to Pakistani provocations. Nuclear weapons have also partially internationalized the Kashmir dispute and brought great-power attention to the region due to fears that the ongoing subconventional war could spill into a wider conventional war and possibly result in a nuclear exchange.

India's initial response to Pakistan's proxy war was defensive. But over the past decade, New Delhi has adopted a more threatening posture toward Islamabad in an attempt to bring the insurgency to an end. As a result of the intensification of the Kashmir dispute since the late 1980s, three major crises have broken out in the region. Two of them resulted in military standoffs, one of which involved military operations along a localized front in Kashmir. Nuclear weapons have assumed higher salience with the passage of each successive crisis. And international, more specifically, U.S., diplomatic efforts have been critical to resolving all of them.

The first crisis began in the winter of 1989 when India's human rights abuses and denial of democratic rights led to an insurgency in IAK. Islamabad's support for the insurgents fueled suspicions in New Delhi that the Pakistan army's prolonged deployment close to the international border after completion of its Zarb-i-Momin military exercises was a calculated attempt to support the Kashmir insurgents, divert the Indian army from counterinsurgency operations, or fight a short and sharp war to seize Kashmir from India. As a precautionary response, the Indian military reacted with counterdeployments. Mirror imaging and worst-case-scenario factoring led to mounting tensions, processes made worse by the political rhetoric of weak leaders in both countries. However, U.S. diplomats in the region helped defuse the crisis by intervening early in February 1990. U.S. military attachés carried out confidence-building inspections on both sides of the Indo-Pakistani divide to reassure the antagonists. Eventually, both the Indian and Pakistani militaries used hotlines to seek further clarifications. In May 1990 President George H. W. Bush, fearing that the crisis in South Asia could spiral out of control and involve a nuclear exchange, dispatched Deputy National Security Advisor Robert Gates to the region. The Gates mission urged both India and Pakistan to exercise restraint and offered U.S. national technical assistance to reassure both parties of each other's intent.

The 1989–1990 crisis is famous for its alleged nuclear dimensions. During the crisis, Pakistani foreign minister Sahibzada Yakub Khan obliquely threatened India with a nuclear response in the event that the latter launched a conventional war. Fears of a conventional war also probably persuaded the Pakistani military to assemble nuclear weapons as a precautionary measure. Finally, Washington's fears of a possible nuclear exchange led to the dispatch of the Gates mission. However, subsequent analysis suggests that although the 1990 crisis did have nuclear overtones, sensationalist details about Pakistan's transfer of nuclear warheads to airfields were most likely exaggerations. By the time the Gates mission reached the region in late May, the crisis was already winding down; it soon ended in June after India and Pakistan withdrew field deployments.[2]

The second crisis, or what is now commonly referred to as the Kargil war, occurred in the summer of 1999. Indian military patrols discovered that Pakistani regular and irregular forces had illegally occupied posts along mountain ridges on the Indian side of the line of control (LOC) in Kashmir. After initial localized operations to evict the intruders proved unsuccessful, Indian military commanders sought the government's permission to cross the LOC to interdict enemy supply lines in Pakistani-administered Kashmir (PAK). The Indian cabinet subsequently debated proposals to widen the war as a means of exerting additional pressure on Pakistan. Ultimately, the Indian government exercised restraint and kept military operations limited to the disputed territory. However, New Delhi used the implicit threat of widening the war to mobilize U.S. diplomatic pressure on Pakistan to vacate its aggression. During the course of the crisis, which lasted from May until the end of July 1999, both capitals traded nuclear threats. Pakistan declared that it might be compelled to resort to use nuclear arms if its existence was threatened. Likewise, Indian leaders threatened Pakistan with nuclear annihilation in the event Islamabad carried out such a threat. There is some evidence to suggest that both India and Pakistan upgraded the alert status of their nuclear forces as contingency measures. Ultimately, the crisis ended when Pakistan caved in to

U.S. diplomatic pressure, agreed to unconditionally withdraw its forces from Indian territories and return to the status quo ante.[3]

The third crisis emerged in the wake of the September 11 terrorist attacks on the United States and lasted from December 2001 until October 2002. India used the backdrop of the U.S. global war on terror to frame Pakistan's support for the low-intensity conflict (LIC) in IAK as terrorism. Subsequent suicide attacks by Islamic militants on the Srinagar state assembly and the Indian Parliament induced New Delhi to order military mobilization and threaten war against Pakistan unless the latter terminated its policy of aiding and abetting the LIC in IAK. The military standoff between India and Pakistan lasted for nine months. On at least two occasions, in January–February 2002 and May–June 2002, the Indian cabinet reportedly came close to authorizing limited conventional strikes in PAK. The threat inherent in India's compellence strategy was that a conventional war could be localized, contained in its scale and scope, and fought below the nuclear threshold. Confronted with the possibility of a larger conventional war, Pakistani president Pervez Musharraf issued an ambiguous warning that India should not expect a conventional war if its military crossed the LOC.[4] In May 2002 the Pakistani military followed up this warning by conducting ballistic-missile tests to underline its nuclear resolve.[5] However, Washington defused the crisis in June 2002 by extracting promises from Islamabad to permanently end support for the insurgency in IAK. The Indian leadership, fearing the unpredictability of a conventional war, as well as the dangers of nuclear escalation, accepted these assurances despite reservations. Finally, in October 2002, citing the decline in infiltrations along the LOC, the Indian government ordered the military to stand down, thus ending the longest military standoff in the history of Indo-Pakistani relations.[6]

The increased tensions, recurring crises, military standoffs, limited conventional war, and threats of a larger conventional war in South Asia have reignited the academic debate among so-called proliferation optimists and pessimists. The optimists cite the absence of large-scale war in South Asia as evidence that nuclear weapons keep the peace.[7] Pessimists fear that the dangers of a nuclear war in South Asia are more real than apparent because of the potential for strategic miscalculation, accident, and organizational failure, factors compounded by India and Pakistan's geographical proximity and the incipient state of their nuclear capabilities.[8]

In light of the prevailing instability in the region, this chapter analyzes how nuclear weapons have shaped India and Pakistan's security competition and strategy in Kashmir. Its primary focus is not on the military aspects of nuclear strategy, but rather on how nuclear weapons have become political tools in the furtherance of New Delhi and Islamabad's political agendas. The first section focuses on the link between nuclear weapons and Pakistan's subconventional war in Kashmir, as well as the implicit threat of a nuclear exchange in the region, to Islamabad's attempts to catalyze international intervention in the Kashmir dispute. The second section analyzes India's transition from defensive to proactive responses to Pakistani provocations in the context of nuclearization and the evolution of New Delhi's doctrine of limited conventional war under nuclear conditions. The third section links the intensified security competition in Kashmir to some of the technological, organizational, and doctrinal pressures in both New Delhi and Islamabad toward operational nuclear capabilities. Finally, the chapter concludes by making observations about the state of India and Pakistan's decade-old security competition in Kashmir in light of their acquisition of usable nuclear capabilities; the implications of India's doctrine of limited conventional war under nuclear conditions; the nature, extent, and meaning of the internationalization of the Kashmir dispute; whether nuclear-arms control or regional nuclear-disarmament regimes remain viable propositions; and why vertical proliferation in the background of unresolved ideological and political conflict makes South Asia the likeliest place in the world for a potential nuclear exchange.

PAKISTAN: THE LINK BETWEEN NUCLEAR WEAPONS AND KASHMIR

In the early 1970s, Pakistan decided to invest in a nuclear capability to avoid a repeat of the 1971 Bangladesh war, which resulted in its defeat and dismemberment. Pakistan's strategy was simple: it hoped that a nuclear deterrent would neutralize India's superiority in conventional forces and deter New Delhi from waging large-scale war in the future.[9] However, Pakistan soon discovered other creative uses for its nuclear capability. Most notably, the nuclear deterrent became a political tool with which it reopened the Kashmir dispute with India to seek a settlement on the basis of a revised status quo.[10]

Historically, Pakistan has adopted two approaches to changing the status quo in Kashmir. Successive Pakistani governments have sought to create new political and territorial faits accomplis in a bid to force New Delhi to arrive at a negotiated settlement on terms amenable to Pakistan. Equally significant, they have attempted to internationalize the dispute by lobbying in multilateral forums such as the United Nations or by seeking third-party intervention, preferably U.S. and British mediation, to offset India's larger size and strength and to level the playing field so that both countries can negotiate a political settlement from positions of relative equality.[11] Pakistan used both approaches from the late 1940s through the late 1960s, until its decisive defeat in the 1971 Bangladesh war effectively froze the Kashmir dispute and relegated it to the background.[12]

Since the late 1980s, however, nuclearization of the subcontinent has enabled Pakistan's strategic establishment to leverage Western proliferation concerns and fears of a potential nuclear exchange in the region to revive the strategies it had devised in the pre-1971 period. As part of its post-1988 strategy to change the political status quo in Kashmir and force India into negotiations to resolve what Pakistani leaders describe as the "core issue" or the "unfinished business of partition," Islamabad has used the cover of its nuclear umbrella to aid and abet a subconventional war by disaffected Muslim insurgents in IAK.[13]

The insurgency in IAK is not a Pakistani creation; its causes are diverse. Scholars have attributed the ongoing conflict to a variety of causes, which range from India's political mismanagement, human rights abuses, denial of democratic rights to the Kashmiri Muslims, ethnographic issues, socioeconomic factors, and the rise of religious extremism.[14] However, Pakistan's political, economic, and military support has been critical to sustaining it.[15]

Pakistan's nuclear deterrent has been a critical factor in shaping Indian strategy and ultimately restricting New Delhi's counterresponse to the low-intensity war. In 1965, when Pakistan launched Operation Gibraltar and infiltrated thousands of irregulars into IAK in the hope of inciting a revolt, India did the unpredictable. Instead of fighting a localized war in Kashmir as Pakistani military leaders had hoped, New Delhi widened operations by ordering the Indian army to cross the international border and carry the war into Pakistani territory.[16] Since the 1980s Pakistan's nuclear deterrent has prevented India from repeating its 1965 strategy. Fears of a wider conventional war and the inherent risks of nuclear escalation have prevented India from attacking insurgent bases, training camps, and infiltration routes in Pakistani-controlled territories. Instead, New Delhi's response has been restricted to fighting a defensive and reactive counterinsurgency campaign in Indian-controlled territories.[17]

Likewise, the acquisition of a proven nuclear capability also emboldened Islamabad to attempt minor, though illegal, changes in the territorial status quo along the Kargil mountain ridges of the LOC in late 1998 and early 1999. Given the sensitivity and secrecy surrounding the Kargil campaign in Pakistan, Islamabad's motivations can at best be inferred indirectly. Nevertheless, Pakistani operations appear to have been guided by the desire to force India into negotiations over Kashmir, to provide encouragement to insurgents battling the Indian army and paramilitary forces, to divert the Indian military's attention from counterinsurgency operations, and to highlight to the international community the urgency of resolving the Kashmir dispute.[18]

Pakistan's attempts to stoke the insurgency in IAK and its subsequent Kargil operation constitute classic examples of Glenn Snyder's stability-instability paradox.[19] The paradox lies in the strategic stability that ensues between two nuclear rivals due to mutual fears that a conventional war could turn nuclear and result in mutual destruction. At the same time, the very prevalence of such stability makes it safe for a revisionist state to apply small amounts of violence along the periphery on the assumption that the low stakes involved and the dangers of a possible nuclear exchange are likely to dampen its rival's escalatory response.[20] As a corollary to this strategy, Pakistani leaders have also sought to mount political pressure on India by seeking to internationalize the Kashmir dispute.[21] In this regard, Pakistan's efforts have benefited from Western concerns about the dangers of nuclear proliferation in South Asia. Beginning in the early 1990s, as South Asia became an important battleground in U.S. attempts to stem the global proliferation of nuclear weapons and their means of delivery, Pakistan linked the possibility of a regional nuclear-restraint regime to the successful resolution of the Kashmir dispute.[22] Pakistani leaders have since argued that Kashmir is the root cause of tensions between the two countries; its resolution is therefore a precursor to the achievement of regional nuclear disarmament or, alternatively, the creation of a restraint regime in South Asia.[23]

The above argument is certainly not without merit. However, Prime Minister Zulfikar Ali Bhutto's government first proposed the establishment of a South Asia Nuclear Weapons Free Zone (SANWFZ) in the 1970s; successive Pakistani governments reiterated their commitment to regional nuclear disarmament in the UN General Assembly during the mid-1980s.[24] As such, the proposal for a SANWFZ precedes the resurgence of the Kashmir dispute in the late 1980s. Equally significant, regional nuclear disarmament would undermine the strategic rationale for Pakistan's nuclear capability, which it ostensibly acquired to deter India. Routine statements by key Pakistani leaders also suggest that the country's nuclear capability is nonnegotiable.[25] Hence, the political linkage between regional nuclear disarmament and the resolution of the Kashmir dispute appears to be an opportunistic attempt on the part of Islamabad to create nonproliferation incentives for U.S. policymakers to intervene in the Kashmir conflict.

The achievement of some form of regional nuclear restraint in the aftermath of the resolution of the Kashmir dispute appears more plausible. However, the Pakistani military's control of the nuclear-weapons program since the early 1980s has created an in-built bias toward operability. Evidently, the Pakistani military favors continued weaponization, even as it accepts other restraints, such as the 1989 temporary cap on uranium-enrichment levels.[26] Furthermore, Pakistan's obsession with the notion of proportional parity with India, coupled with the latter's refusal to be tied down by regional arms-control arrangements and security concerns vis-à-vis China, render unlikely the idea of a strictly South Asian nuclear-restraint regime.

In a parallel tactic to internationalizing Kashmir, Pakistan has also resorted to amplifying Western concerns that South Asia constitutes a nuclear flashpoint.[27] With the passage of each Indo-Pakistani crisis, Pakistani leaders have endorsed fears expressed by Western leaders and the nonproliferation lobby that a conventionally outnumbered and outclassed Pakistani military might be compelled to resort to nuclear arms to ensure national survival, or that a nuclear war might be triggered by inadvertence, accident, or command-and-control failure.[28] To be sure, the dangers of a nuclear war in South Asia are real. But Pakistani leaders have undermined their own case for international intervention by privately dismissing Western concerns as exaggerations.[29] Furthermore, Islamabad's role in sustaining the Kashmir insurgency and the Pakistani military's policy of provoking conflict, as during the 1999 Kargil crisis, have exposed the disingenuousness of Pakistan's arguments and contributed to Western fatigue in trying to resolve the Kashmir dispute through external mediation.[30]

INDIA'S SHIFT FROM A REACTIVE TO A PROACTIVE STRATEGY

For the greater part of the 1990s, successive Indian governments responded to Pakistan's subconventional war in Kashmir in a defensive manner. New Delhi's hesitancy and defensiveness were tacit acknowledgment of the domestic roots of the insurgency, as well as of India's political mismanagement in creating it. The brutal nature of the counterinsurgency operations deeply embarrassed the Indian government, which resorted to its time-tested strategy of using a combination of military force and political and economic inducements to co-opt the insurgents in the Kashmir valley.[31] In addition, weak coalition governments, the economic crisis of the early 1990s, and serious conventional shortcomings also factored in India's response to the insurgency in Kashmir.[32]

Domestic reasons apart, nuclearization of the subcontinent in the late 1980s and early 1990s also influenced Indian policies significantly. The theoretical possibility of a large-scale conventional war culminating in a nuclear exchange induced caution in India's dealings with Pakistan. During the early 1990s, India's own weaponization program was in a rudimentary stage. Air- and ballistic-missile-deliverable nuclear warheads only became available to the Indian government in the mid-1990s.[33] To be sure, Indian government leaders were not necessarily convinced that Pakistan was further along the path of weaponization.[34] Yet, the mere possibility of the existence of a small arsenal of air-deliverable Pakistani nuclear weapons produced strategic uncertainty in New Delhi and deterred Indian leaders from taking any precipitate action.[35]

Two additional nuclear-related factors conditioned New Delhi's cautious approach toward Islamabad in the early 1990s. The first had to do with concerns that a conventional war with Pakistan and Western fears of a nuclear exchange in the region might invariably lead to the internationalization of the Kashmir dispute.[36] A second factor was that fears in the West of a nuclear holocaust in South Asia could invite international pressures on India to accept a regional disarmament initiative, which the first Clinton administration summed up as a "freeze, cap, and roll back" strategy.[37]

India's fears about international conflict-resolution efforts in Kashmir have a long history. In 1948 Prime Minister Jawaharlal Nehru's government brought the Kashmir dispute with Pakistan before the then newly formed UN Security Council. India's objective at the time was to have the United Nations uphold its legal claims over Kashmir. Much to New Delhi's chagrin, however, the Kashmir dispute became enmeshed with the wider issues raised by the partition of India and Pakistan along the Hindu-Muslim religious divide; the legitimacy and manner of the Kashmiri ruler's accession to India; and more vexingly, the issue of self-determination of the Kashmiri people in deciding whether to accede to India or Pakistan.[38] During the Cold War years, Pakistan exploited Washington's rivalry with Moscow to join U.S.-led security alliances in the Middle East and Southeast Asia. It also sought military aid and political support from the United States to challenge India in Kashmir. Although the United States never acquiesced to the Pakistani agenda in Kashmir, India's policy elites resented the U.S.-Pakistani alliance and feared that the United States was trying to contain India's regional ambitions by building up Pakistani military capabilities and imposing external mediation on Kashmir.[39]

In New Delhi's view, internationalization has the potential for diluting the legitimacy of Kashmir's legal and political union with India; Muslims in the province might vote for independence or accession to Pakistan if a plebiscite were allowed under the original UN formula. Indian leaders' sensitivity on Kashmir stems from the fact that it is India's sole Muslim-majority province. New Delhi considers the continued presence of Kashmir within the Indian Union as critical to affirming India's secular identity. Indian policymakers also fear that Kashmir's secession from India could reopen the wounds of Partition and unleash a Hindu-Muslim civil war. Kashmir's independence from India or secession to Pakistan would also create Hindu and Buddhist minorities in that province.[40]

Singed by seeking UN mediation efforts in the 1940s and 1950s and suspicious of U.S. and British third-party intervention during the 1960s, India thereafter sought to remove the Kashmir dispute from the ambit of multilateral or third-party conflict-resolution mechanisms. India temporarily succeeded in this quest after signing the Simla Agreement with Pakistan in the wake of the latter's defeat in the 1971 Bangladesh war, until Pakistan, taking advantage of the insurgency in the Kashmir valley, sought to revive the dispute in the late 1980s.[41]

From the late 1980s until 1999, there were great concerns in New Delhi about the possible internationalization of the dispute.[42] Indian fears largely stemmed from three issues. First, India's brutal counterinsurgency campaigns in the Kashmir valley created a spiral of violence, further alienated the disaffected Muslim population, and brought international attention to the human tragedy and the political volatility of the situation. India was thus clearly embarrassed. Second, with the collapse of the Soviet Union in 1991, India lost its major Cold War strategic ally.[43] At the time, New Delhi's relations with Washington were relatively cool in comparison with Pakistan's. Indian leaders were therefore distrustful of any potential U.S. mediation efforts in Kashmir. In this regard, Indian sensitivities were particularly aroused when senior officials in the first Clinton administration made statements that placed the entire status of Kashmir in doubt.[44] Third, India feared that U.S. policymakers might leverage any potential military crisis in Kashmir to pressure India into making concessions along the nonproliferation front.[45] Indeed, this last factor was critical in politically restraining India from considering more proactive military responses in the early 1990s. Although Indo-U.S. differences on proliferation stretch back to the 1960s, they reached a peak in the early and mid-1990s.[46] To a large extent, Washington's nonproliferation agenda in South Asia was driven by concerns that an Indo-Pakistani nuclear capability would encourage other aspiring proliferants; that robust technology controls would be difficult to achieve in second-tier proliferator states; and that it would be difficult if not impossible to accommodate emerging nuclear powers within the existing nuclear order.[47] Equally significant, U.S. and Western concerns were driven by fears that South Asia was the likeliest place for a nuclear war in the future.[48]

In response to Western nonproliferation pressures, New Delhi sought to portray India, and to an extent even Pakistan, as responsible nuclear powers. It dismissed the viewpoint that South Asia was the likeliest place for a nuclear war as ill informed, biased, and racist. Instead, it argued that India and Pakistan were aware of the responsibility that came with the acquisition of a nuclear capability.[49] In this regard, India and Pakistan's nonweaponized postures, in which nuclear weapons were stored unassembled and away from delivery systems, acted as natural firebreaks and inserted time and organizational barriers in the path of a nuclear exchange.[50] In a further attempt to buttress its claims to responsibility, New Delhi was careful to avoid initiating crises that could snowball into a conventional, and possibly nuclear, war with Islamabad.

By the late 1990s, as Indo-U.S. relations began to improve, Indian fears of the possible negative consequences of internationalization of the Kashmir dispute began to recede. Similarly, Washington's tacit acceptance of India's nuclear status after New Delhi's nuclear tests in May 1998 relieved concerns among Indian policy elites that a potential crisis in Kashmir might result in pressures for a "nuclear rollback."[51] These factors, in addition to India's exasperation with the mounting costs of the low-intensity war, improved political conditions in IAK, and Pakistan's growing international isolation because of its policy of using radical Islamic proxies to achieve strategic goals in Afghanistan and Kashmir, ultimately paved the way for a more muscular and proactive Indian response.[52]

In President Clinton's second term, the United States and India embarked on a major course correction in their post–Cold War foreign policy to repair relations. When confronted by India's nuclear determination in the post–May 1998 period and the political impossibility of a nuclear rollback in South Asia, the second Clinton administration changed tack and tacitly accepted New Delhi's nuclear status. Washington now sought to persuade both New Delhi and Islamabad to accept strategic restraint and participate in the nonproliferation regime by accepting the comprehensive test-ban treaty and an interim cap on fissile-material production.[53] There was also a change of tone in Washington's public diplomacy, complemented by a newfound respect and sensitivity for Indian security concerns. In contrast to the public recriminations and hectoring that had characterized Indo-U.S. nuclear diplomacy in the past, proliferation differences were now addressed quietly through private diplomacy.[54]

By the time India and Pakistan fought the Kargil war in the summer of 1999, the balance of political forces had shifted in India's favor. India successfully capitalized on Islamabad's transgression of the LOC in Kashmir to characterize it as a revisionist and irresponsible power that threatened the peace in South Asia. During the war, India also won international plaudits for restraint in the face of Pakistani provocations and for not escalating the war by crossing the LOC into PAK or by widening the war across other fronts. Indian diplomacy also succeeded in portraying Pakistan as a revisionist state bent on creating nuclear crises to change the political status quo in the region.[55] These shifting political winds were evident when the United States publicly demanded that Islamabad withdraw from occupied Indian positions and respect the sanctity of the LOC in Kashmir. By implication, Pakistan was branded as the aggressor state. U.S. pressure to withdraw also meant that Washington would no longer acquiesce to any rewriting of the status quo in Kashmir by force. Ultimately, Pakistan was forced into making a humiliating withdrawal, which resulted in an unambiguous victory for India.[56]

Kargil proved to be a turning point in the history of Indo-U.S. relations. The war allayed concerns in New Delhi that internationalization of the Kashmir dispute would invariably favor Pakistan. Instead, it opened up the new and tantalizing possibility that India could highlight Pakistan's role in fomenting Islamic militancy in Kashmir, as well as the Pakistani military's strategy of wielding its nuclear deterrent irresponsibly for political ends, to persuade Islamabad to terminate support for the insurgency in IAK.[57]

During the Kargil war, India's strategy of restraint succeeded in mobilizing international pressure to evict Pakistani forces from Indian territories. But it left open the question of how India should respond to similar Pakistani adventurism in the future. Frustrated with the decade-old low-intensity war in Kashmir, Indian political and military leaders and the strategic establishment at large reopened the debate on approaches to bringing the subconventional war in Kashmir to a successful end.[58] The central issue in this debate was whether nuclear weapons would force India to fight a war on Pakistan's terms indefinitely or whether there existed alternative means through which India could force war termination on Pakistan without significant risk of nuclear escalation. This debate reached an interim conclusion in January 2000 when India's defense minister, George Fernandes, announced a doctrine of limited conventional war under nuclear conditions. Fernandes asserted that there existed strategic space between a low-intensity and high-intensity conventional war where a limited conventional war was indeed a possibility.[59] The premise behind this doctrine was that it was possible for New Delhi to raise the costs of the subconventional war in Kashmir for Pakistan by creating local contingencies. Such contingencies, the Indian assumption went, would not threaten Pakistan's fundamental existence and, hence, could be fought below the nuclear threshold.[60] India's espousal of the doctrine of limited conventional war under nuclear conditions, just before President Clinton's March 2000 visit to New Delhi, coincided with a phase in Indo-U.S. relations when proliferation was no longer the central issue.

Proliferation receded even further into the background when President George W. Bush assumed the presidency in January 2001. The neoconservatives in the administration, eager to manage China's power transition in the twenty-first century, view India as a major stabilizing force in the Asia-Pacific region and as a country that could eventually emerge as China's peer and balance Beijing's power in the region. The Bush administration has therefore built on the Clinton administration's record to further consolidate strategic ties with New Delhi, relegating nuclear proliferation even further into the background.[61]

It was in this external political framework, where the negative consequences of internationalization of the Kashmir dispute and the risks of nuclear roll back were minimal, that India was able to threaten Pakistan with war in the wake of the September 11, 2001, terror attacks on the United States. In the immediate aftermath of those attacks, global attention focused on the links between militant Islamic groups and Pakistan's military-intelligence agencies, groups that the Pakistani state patronized to fight its proxy wars in both Afghanistan and Kashmir. Following the Bush administration's decision to wage war against al

Qaeda and its Taliban patrons in Afghanistan, Pakistan's Musharraf regime was forced to sever its ties with the Taliban. But once Islamabad made this change in its Afghan policy, it found itself in a quandary. Islamabad discovered that it could not, on the one hand, sever links with the Taliban and al Qaeda because of its alliance with the United States in the war against terror and, on the other, simultaneously support militant Islamic groups in IAK on the grounds that the latter were "freedom fighters."[62] The U.S. war on terror blurred the distinctions between "terrorists" and "freedom fighters." Once the contradictions between Pakistan's Afghan and Kashmir policies came to the fore, India seized the opportunity to pressure Pakistan militarily.[63]

The terrorist attacks on the Srinagar state assembly in October and later the Indian Parliament in November 2001 provided New Delhi with the pretext it needed to order military mobilization. Between December 2001 and July 2002, India threatened to wage a limited conventional war against Pakistan unless the latter terminated support for what the Indian government describes as cross-border terrorism. To an extent, U.S. military operations in Afghanistan and the deployment of U.S. forces in and around Pakistan created a safe space for India to exercise its policy of coercive diplomacy. New Delhi's confidence that a conventional war with Pakistan could be kept geographically localized to Kashmir and fought below the nuclear threshold was partly the result of calculations that Washington would intervene to halt such a war in its initial stages to avoid disruptions in its operations against the Taliban and al Qaeda. Another unstated Indian assumption was that the presence of U.S. forces in Pakistan and their use of Pakistani ports, air bases, and airspace would serve to reassure the Pakistani military of the limited nature of New Delhi's operations. By the same token, Pakistan would find it difficult to initiate nuclear-weapons use as the consequence of such an action would be to hold the U.S. military hostage to the risk of punitive Indian retaliatory strikes.[64]

Ultimately, India did not go to war with Pakistan. The unlikelihood of achieving limited war aims and war termination at will, coupled with the dangers of nuclear escalation and the loss of international goodwill, appear to have deterred the Indian leadership from initiating military action.[65] However, India successfully leveraged the threat of war against Pakistan and the possible disruption of the U.S. military campaign in Afghanistan to pressure Washington into confronting the duality in Islamabad's post–September 11 policies in Afghanistan and Kashmir. Subsequent U.S. diplomatic pressure led the Musharraf regime to crack down on some of the fundamentalist Islamic groups waging war against the Indian government in Kashmir.[66] India's coercive diplomacy also succeeded in mobilizing international opinion against Pakistan's policy of fighting proxy wars through radical Islamic groups. More significantly, by credibly threatening war, India forced Pakistan to admit indirectly complicity in the insurgency campaign in Kashmir and extracted public and private assurances from Islamabad that it would effectively terminate support for the insurgents waging war in IAK. However, Pakistani military leaders privately maintain that nuclear weapons deterred India from going to war during the 2001–2002 crisis, a conclusion that Indian leaders believe is overdetermined.[67]

RECURRING CRISES: THE IMPACT ON NUCLEARIZATION

The low-intensity war in Kashmir and recurring political crises, accompanied by the threat of a wider conventional war, have had a significant impact on the nuclear politics in India and Pakistan. Admittedly, New Delhi and Islamabad's nuclear-weapons programs are not rooted in the Kashmir dispute. Nonetheless, chronic instability has had a decisive impact on the pace, scope, and nature of weaponization efforts, the development of nuclear-use doctrines, and patterns of bargaining among strategic elites in both countries. Frequent crises have spurred both countries in the direction of seeking operational nuclear forces. In the late 1980s and early 1990s, New Delhi and Islamabad sought to deter one another by obliquely hinting at their existential nuclear capabilities. Observing the pattern of mutual bargaining among them, scholars inferred that the South Asian elites had perhaps discovered a new way to practice nuclear deterrence: the existence of nonweaponized capabilities shrouded in opacity might be sufficient to deter an adversary.[68] On occasions, New Delhi and Islamabad publicly parroted this latter conclusion to score propaganda points about their peaceful intent and to reinforce the notion that South Asian elites were responsible nuclear actors.

Owing to the possibility of nuclear use, however remote, policy elites in both countries have more recently concluded that nuclear deterrence cannot be anchored in phantom capabilities. Rather, the demands of credibility require that India and Pakistan at least partially replicate some of the technical and organizational models of the de jure nuclear-weapon states. Gradually, the Indo-Pakistani elites have imbibed Michael Novak's observation that greater user ease, as well as improved planning and readiness to use nuclear weapons, might lessen the political likelihood of their actual use. As such, political leaders, scientific bureaucracies, and the militaries in both countries have, at first slowly, proceeded down the path of weaponization, while each crisis has had the effect of accelerating the process.[69] This by no means implies that India and Pakistan seek to replicate the technological sophistication or redundancies built into the U.S. and former-Soviet arsenals. Nevertheless, during the past decade both countries have acquired weaponized nuclear devices; sought to develop a diversified set of reliable delivery systems; developed procedures for the safe storage, transport, and handling of nuclear weapons and their component parts; created protocols for rapid constitution of the unassembled weapons during a national emergency; and invested in command, communications, and control networks to enable their use during a contingency.[70]

However, despite the upward trend in favor of operability, there has been no change in India or Pakistan's peacetime nuclear posture. Both countries maintain their nuclear arsenals in a "recessed," or unconstituted, state. The warhead assemblies and fissile-material cores are stored separately, away from aircraft and ballistic-missile delivery systems. Control of the component parts is divided among different civilian and military agencies with protocols and procedures for reconstituting them rapidly during a crisis. But better co-ordination and training procedures have shortened deployment times and im-proved operational readiness.[71] Inherent in the thrust toward operationaliza-tion is the development of nuclear-use doctrines. This is a significant development because during the early 1990s India and Pakistan possessed nu-clear capabilities only in a purely symbolic sense. Neither government had given much serious thought to how nuclear weapons might eventually be used. For Pakistan nuclear weapons guaranteed national survival, if only in a perfunctory sense; it could in theory attack one or two major Indian urban tar-gets in a last desperate act of survival. Likewise, for India nuclear weapons constituted a symbolic reassurance against potential nuclear blackmail.

The emergence of an operational nuclear capability against the background of a subconventional war in Kashmir and increased prospects for a wider con-ventional war have created a strategic context in which India and Pakistan have seriously begun to plan for the operational use of their nuclear forces. In comparison with India, Pakistan has had less aversion in this regard. To an ex-tent, the Pakistani military's control of the nuclear effort from the early 1980s has built an operational bias into the program. Furthermore, as the weaker power, Pakistan has sought nuclear weapons to offset India's conventional su-periority. This has also created a structural imperative in favor of operability. To deter India from waging a conventional war of unlimited or limited aims, Pakistan has espoused a nuclear first-use doctrine akin to NATO's doctrine of flexible response, which envisaged the use of nuclear weapons against a So-viet attack in Europe even with conventional weapons.[72] However, the issue of how and when Pakistan might use nuclear weapons remains unclear. Be-yond vaguely stating that Pakistan would use nuclear weapons in the event that its national existence was threatened, no government in Islamabad has ever formally articulated an operational-use doctrine. The assumption among Pakistani government leaders is that any formal delineation of Pakistan's nu-clear thresholds or how it proposes to use nuclear weapons at the operational level might unwittingly create incentives for India to test those limits.[73]

Former Pakistani government leaders have suggested that Pakistan would not use nuclear weapons to fight local wars; such contingencies would be dealt with using conventional means. Nuclear-weapons use would be considered only in grave situations where Pakistan's national existence might be threatened.[74] At the operational-policy level, there is thus considerable uncertainty as to whether the Pakistani military would use nuclear weapons in a demonstrative-warning role on Pakistani territory early in any conflict with India, against massed Indian military formations to deny New Delhi its war objectives, or in graduated or massive punitive strikes against "countervalue" targets as a last resort after conventional defenses fail. Such ambiguity, Pakistani leaders believe, is necessary to enhance deterrence.[75]

India's transition toward an operational capability has been more painful. This is largely because, historically, civilians have controlled the nuclear program to the relative exclusion of the military. The civilian politicians, strategic thinkers, and nuclear-defense scientists who determine nuclear policy share an institutional aversion to sharing and transferring control of nuclear weapons to the military. This aversion partly stems from the need to ensure the institutional predominance of civilians over the military. But the biases also flow from the philosophical and moral aversion of India's civilian elites toward nuclear weapons and their view that nuclear weapons, as political instruments whose sole purpose is to deter war and nuclear coercion, are not usable instruments of war.[76] However, the multiple Indo-Pakistani crises since 1989 have starkly demonstrated the limitations of the above political view of nuclear weapons. As a result, India's civilian elites have begun to shed some of their prevailing biases against the militarization of nuclear policy.[77]

The Indian government has concluded that in the event of deterrence failure, the Indian military will have to fight and win limited conventional wars under nuclear conditions. Although some Indian military leaders and strategic thinkers believe it is possible to fight a conventional war localized in scope and geography, the prospect of fighting a limited war has also forced the Indian government to contemplate an Indian nuclear response to Pakistan's use of nuclear weapons. Some Indian observers speculate that initial Pakistani nuclear strikes might be restricted to a demonstrative-warning role on its own territories.[78] However, the Indian military believes that its Pakistani counterpart has seriously planned for the operational use of nuclear weapons on the battlefield. To prepare for such contingencies, the Indian army plans to change its equipment profile to operate in a nuclear, chemical, and biological environment. The army's plans to operate in a nuclear environment also emphasize mobility and dispersal into small units to avoid attracting nuclear firepower.[79]

At the declaratory level of policy, India subscribes to the no-first-use nuclear doctrine, but Indian leaders have threatened Islamabad with "massive" punitive retaliatory attacks were Pakistan to resort to nuclear-weapons use. For moral and strategic reasons, it is likely that an Indian operational response would be calibrated to match the nature and scale of a Pakistani attack. Likewise, any punitive Indian strikes would probably be restricted to military targets with the objective of restoring intrawar deterrence or seeking early war termination.[80]

Finally, the development of operational nuclear forces and use doctrines has changed the erstwhile pattern of implicit bargaining between the strategic elites in India and Pakistan. During the late 1980s and early 1990s, for example, rudimentary capabilities were matched by veiled allusions to existential capabilities.[81] Nuclear threats were coyly conveyed through private diplomacy. Nuclear signaling, as alleged by some during the 1990 crisis, was at best ambiguous.[82] In comparison, Indian and Pakistani leaders now openly engage in rhetorical flourishes; nuclear warnings are communicated publicly.[83] Both countries routinely resort to public displays of nuclear delivery systems. Borrowing tactics used by the superpowers in crisis situations during the Cold War, New Delhi and Islamabad have also resorted to direct nuclear signaling through ballistic-missile tests or by changing the operational status of their missile forces.[84] Such tactics underline the political volatility and mounting dangers of a potential nuclear exchange in the region.

CONCLUSION

Since the late 1980s, nuclearization of the subcontinent has facilitated the revival of the Kashmir dispute between India and Pakistan. Nuclear weapons have allowed Pakistan's military to exploit the disaffection of India's Kashmiri-Muslim population to wage a subconventional war against New Delhi. Although Pakistani military leaders privately believe that Pakistan's nuclear weapons have effectively deterred India from fighting a larger conventional war, Indian restraint is likely determined by multiple factors. Chief among them are New Delhi's fears that it might be unable to achieve its political or military objectives in any limited war, that it would be difficult to terminate such a war at will, that India might be unable to invite international intervention to end the war at a time of its choosing, that hostilities might cost India the goodwill of the international community, and that the war could not be kept limited and would carry significant risks of nuclear escalation. On balance, the evidence suggests that from the late 1990s on, nuclearization has been one of several factors that have contributed to maintaining a regime of "ugly stability" in South Asia.

No doubt, India and Pakistan's concurrent march up the ladder of vertical proliferation amid continuing conflict in Kashmir has contributed to international

perceptions that South Asia constitutes a nuclear flashpoint. However, Islamabad's hopes that global concerns about a potential nuclear exchange in the region would place Kashmir at the heart of international conflict-resolution efforts
have not materialized. Rather Pakistan, because of the role of its military in fomenting regional instability, is increasingly viewed as a "misdirected state,"
prone to wielding its nuclear deterrent irresponsibly toward dubious political
ends. Further, Islamabad's reliance on radical Islamic proxies in Kashmir has
also rebounded to its disadvantage; it has enabled New Delhi to characterize
Pakistan as the "epicenter of terrorism."

Thus, Kashmir has become internationalized, but not in the manner Pakistani leaders once imagined. International misgivings about Pakistan's strategy in Kashmir have enabled Indian diplomacy to prevent UN mediation and
restrict great-power intervention in the region. Indian leaders have also capitalized on such misgivings to portray Pakistan as a rogue state that wages terrorism from behind the security afforded by its nuclear umbrella. Washington's tacit acceptance of the new South Asian realities in the wake of India
and Pakistan's May 1998 nuclear tests have given New Delhi confidence that
the risks of Kashmir's internationalization are manageable; a future crisis
over Kashmir would not necessarily translate into international demands or
pressure for nuclear restraint or rollback. India's newfound confidence was
evident during the 2001–2002 crisis; New Delhi hijacked Pakistan's agenda
of framing South Asia as the likeliest place for a nuclear exchange by itself
threatening just such a possibility unless Washington pressured Islamabad to
end "cross-border terrorism."

Pakistan's attempts at foisting the Kashmir dispute onto the Western nonproliferation agenda have also failed. The idea that a resolution to the Kashmir dispute could pave the way for regional disarmament was never credible
to begin with. The inception of Pakistan's efforts to acquire nuclear-weapons
capability precedes the resurgence of the Kashmir dispute in the late 1980s by
nearly two decades. The motivations behind that effort lie in the strategic
logic of neutralizing India's conventional advantage and immunizing Pakistan from the risk of a large-scale war and dismemberment. Pakistan's rivalries with India are rooted in ideology and the fundamental power disparities
between the two countries. As such, the Indo-Pakistani security dialectic, and
by extension the conventional and nuclear-arms competition, would probably
transcend any resolution of the Kashmir dispute.[85] Equally significant, India's
ideological quarrel with the nonproliferation regime, espousal of universal
global norms, and unaddressed security concerns vis-à-vis China preclude the
possibility of a SANWFZ.

It is conceivable that if Pakistan's irredentist claims in Kashmir were satisfied, tensions with India might subside to the extent that Islamabad would be
willing to abide by its proposed nuclear restraint regime. But it is unlikely that

New Delhi would abide by such restraint pending the resolution of the border dispute with China, absent security guarantees to immunize India from the theoretical risk of Chinese nuclear blackmail. Further, considering Pakistan's self-image as India's peer and obsession with the notion of parity, the proposed regime is unlikely to come to fruition. However, regardless of whether nuclear restraint in South Asia is possible, a resolution to the Kashmir problem would almost certainly dampen the intensified drive in both countries toward nuclear operability. Multiple crises, military standoffs, and threats of a larger conventional war with the possibility of a nuclear exchange have created technological, organizational, and doctrinal pressures in the direction of operational nuclear forces. Pakistan has come more than ever to rely on its nuclear deterrent to bridge the widening conventional disparity with India. The Pakistani military has decided to invest in a diversified nuclear arsenal, the largest possible warhead numbers, and procedures for dispersal and activation of such forces to engage in nuclear signaling early in any potential crisis with India. Likewise, the civilians who determine nuclear policy in New Delhi are now under increasing pressure from the Indian military to replicate Islamabad's efforts and to prepare for conventional escalation and ultimately nuclear-use scenarios. Thus, the ongoing transformation in Indo-Pakistani nuclear politics from tokenism to usable capabilities has heightened risks of a nuclear exchange through deliberate choice, accident, inadvertence, or complex organizational failure.

During the last decade, Indo-Pakistani relations have alternated between troughs and plateaus. Diplomatic efforts have followed each military crisis to try to repair relations, but all have failed. The two countries are currently in the midst of another peacemaking exercise, characterized by revived government talks, summitry, and people-to-people contact. In a joint statement issued in January 2004, Prime Minister Vajpayee and President Musharraf agreed "to the resumption of a composite dialogue" on all issues "including Jammu and Kashmir to the satisfaction of both sides." Musharraf also assured the Indian government that "he will not permit any territory under Pakistan's control to be used to support terrorism in any manner."[86] Many observers have interpreted the joint statement as a tacit admission of Pakistan's past support for the LIC in Kashmir and an indication of its resolve to finally end military confrontation over the dispute. However, there is also considerable skepticism in India on the nature of change in Pakistan's policy: is it tactical or strategic? Similarly, the Pakistani government fears that India is taking unfair advantage of Islamabad's restraint to consolidate its political and military grip over Kashmir. In March 2004 President Musharraf warned Indian leaders that Kashmir was central to Indo-Pakistani differences and that the peace process would collapse in the absence of progress in resolving the dispute.[87] Musharraf's statement has raised grave doubts in New Delhi over the Pakistani government's true intentions.

A failure to sustain the current peace effort and Islamabad's return to the LIC option could gravely harm Indo-Pakistani relations. Vajpayee has made it plain that this is his third and last attempt at peace with Pakistan. In the past, Pakistani leaders have operated on the assumption that nuclear weapons will enable them to wage subconventional war against India indefinitely and to eventually force New Delhi to the negotiating table. For their part, Indian leaders are no longer prepared to fight a reactive counterinsurgency campaign on Indian territories alone; they are determined to increase the cost of the subconventional war for Pakistan. An influential section of India's political and military leadership also believes that Pakistan's nuclear bluff needs to be called and that there exist opportunities to fight a limited conventional war in PAK below the nuclear threshold.

Equally significant, the external constraints that acted to restrain India from initiating military action against Pakistan in the late 1980s and early 1990s have eroded considerably. As international opinion has swung against Pakistan's policy of fighting wars through radical Islamist proxies, New Delhi has gained confidence that the potential negative fallout of the internationalization of the Kashmir dispute can be contained. Furthermore, after the May 1998 nuclear tests, India believes that it has gained legitimacy as a responsible nuclear power. Instead, the onus is now on Pakistan to maintain the status quo during crises in light of the nuclearization of the subcontinent. Many factors in combination suggest that future crises may erupt: the low-intensity war in Kashmir, India and Pakistan's ideological antagonisms, their mutual political obstinacy, differing perceptions of past crisis outcomes, and subjective perceptions of the international environment. The next crisis could spill into a wider war and possibly involve the detonation of nuclear weapons.

NOTES

1. Sumit Ganguly, *Conflict Unending: India-Pakistan Tensions since 1947* (New York: Columbia University Press, 2001).

2. Devin T. Hagerty, "Nuclear Deterrence in South Asia: The 1990 Indo-Pakistani Crisis," *International Security* 20, no. 3 (Winter 1995/96): 79–114; P. R. Chari, Pervaiz Iqbal Cheema, and Stephen Philip Cohen eds., *Perception, Politics, and Security in South Asia: The Compound Crisis of 1990* (London: RoutledgeCurzon, 2003).

3. Ashley J. Tellis, C. Christine Fair, and Jamison Jo Medby, *Limited Conflict under the Nuclear Umbrella: Indian and Pakistani Lessons from the Kargil Crisis* (Santa Monica, Calif.: Rand, 2001); also see Bruce Reidel, "The 4th Dawns," *American Diplomacy and the 1999 Kargil Summit at Blair House* (Philadelphia: CASI, 2002), 8–14.

4. "Pakistan Was Prepared to Use Nuclear Weapons," *New York Times,* December 30, 2002.

5. Imtiaz Gul, "Pakistan Tests Ghauris, Shaheens Today," *Daily Times,* May 25, 2002.

6. Gaurav Kampani, "India's Compellence Strategy: Calling Pakistan's Nuclear Bluff Over Kashmir," *CNS Research Story of the Week,* June 10, 2002, available at http://cns.miis.edu/pubs/week/020610.htm.

7. Ganguly, "The Nuclear Dimension," *Conflict Unending,* 101–13; Scott D. Sagan and Kenneth N. Waltz, "Indian and Pakistani Nuclear Weapons: For Better or Worse?" *The Spread of Nuclear Weapons: A Debate Renewed* (New York: W. W. Norton & Company, 2003), 109–24.

8. Sagan and Waltz, "Indian and Pakistani Nuclear Weapons," *The Spread of Nuclear Weapons,* 90–108.

9. Samina Ahmed, "Pakistan's Nuclear Weapons Program," *International Security* 23, no.4 (Spring 1999): 183–85.

10. Peter R. Lavoy, "The Uses of Pakistan's Nuclear Weapons: Politics, Personalities, and Perceptions," paper presented at the Conference on Prospects for Peace in South Asia, Stanford University, Stanford, Calif., January 21–22, 2003, 8–9.

11. Ganguly, "The First Kashmir War," *Conflict Unending,* 26–27; Victoria Schofield, "Diplomacy and War," *Kashmir in Conflict: India, Pakistan and the Unfinished War* (London: I. B. Tauris Publishers, 2000), 99–103.

12. Ganguly, "The Bangladesh War," *Conflict Unending,* 69–74.

13. Lavoy, "The Uses of Pakistan's Nuclear Weapons," 10–11.

14. Chari, Cheema, and Cohen, "Kashmir: From Simla to Chaos," *Perception, Politics and Security in South Asia,* 57–64.

15. Mary Anne Weaver, "Kashmir," *Pakistan: In the Shadow of Jihad and Afghanistan* (New York: Farrar, Straus, & Giroux, 2002), 260, 262; Owen Bennett Jones, "Musharraf's Challenge," *Pakistan: Eye of the Storm* (New Haven, Conn.: Yale University Press, 2002), 26–33.

16. Bennett Jones, "Kashmir," *Pakistan: Eye of the Storm,* 74–80.

17. This view was best summed up by the famous Indian strategic analyst K. Subrahmanyam in the aftermath of the 1990 Indo-Pakistani crisis. According to Subrahmanyam, "The awareness on both sides of a nuclear capability that can enable either country to assemble nuclear weapons at short notice induces mutual caution. This caution is already evident on the part of India. In 1965, when Pakistan carried out its "Operation Gibraltar" and sent in infiltrators, India sent its army across the cease-fire line to destroy the assembly points of the infiltrators. That escalated into a full-scale war. In 1990 when Pakistan once again carried out a massive infiltration of terrorists trained in Pakistan, India tried to deal with the problem on Indian territory and did not send its army into Pakistan-occupied Kashmir." See, K. Subrahmanyam, "Capping, Managing, or Eliminating Nuclear Weapons?" in *South Asia after the Cold War,* ed. Kanti P. Bajpai and Stephen P. Cohen (Boulder, Colo.: Westview, 1993), 184.

18. Dr. Suba Chandran, "Why Kargil? Pakistan's Objectives and Motivations," in *Kargil: The Tables Turned,* ed. Maj. Gen. Ashok Krishna and P. R. Chari (New Delhi: Manohar, 2001), 30–38.

19. Glenn Snyder, "The Balance of Power and the Balance of Terror," in *The Balance of Power,* ed. Paul Seabury (San Francisco: Chandler, 1965), 184–201.

20. Robert Jervis, "The Theory of the Nuclear Revolution," *The Meaning of the Nuclear Revolution: Statecraft and the Prospect of Armageddon* (Ithaca, N.Y.: Cornell University Press, 1989), 19–22.

21. "Pakistan Urges U.N. Role in Solving Kashmir Issue," Xinhua News Agency, June 22, 1998, in Lexis-Nexis Academic Universe, June 22, 1998, available at http://web.lexis-nexis.com (accessed August 12, 2003).

22. "The Nuclear Backdrop," *From Surprise to Reckoning: The Kargil Review Committee Report* (New Delhi: Sage Publications, December 15, 1999), 194.

23. Anwar Iqbal, "Outgoing Prime Minister Says Kashmir at Root of Nuclear Arms Race," United Press International, October 18, 1993, in Lexis-Nexis Academic Universe, October 18,

61. Stephen P. Cohen and Sunil Dasgupta, "U.S.–South Asia: Relations under Bush," *Oxford Analytica*, 2001, available at www.brook.edu (accessed April 2001).

62. Ayaz Amir, "Standing a 2-Year Nexus on Its Head," *Dawn*, September 28, 2001, available at www.dawn.com (accessed September 28, 2001).

63. Pramit Pal Chaudhuri, "Why a War against Terrorism Has Pakistan Terrified," *Hindustan Times*, September 16, 2001, available at www.hindustantimes.com (accessed September 16, 2001).

64. Kampani, "India's Compellence Strategy."

65. Shishir Gupta, "When India Came Close to War," *India Today*, December 23, 2002, available at www.india-today.com (accessed December 2002).

66. Transcript of PBS interview with U.S. undersecretary of state Richard Armitage, August 30, 2002, in *OutlookIndia*, September 3, 2002, available at www.outlookindia.com (accessed September 2002).

67. Michael Krepon, "Escalator to Nowhere," *OutlookIndia*, November 11, 2002, available at www.outlookindia.com (accessed November 2002).

68. Perkovich, "A Nuclear Third Way in South Asia."

69. For an Indian perspective see, Raja Menon, "Pure Strategy and Technology," *A Nuclear Strategy for India* (New Delhi: Sage Publications, 2000), 171–73; Brahma Chellaney, "Nuclear Deterrent Posture," in *Securing India's Future in the New Millennium*, ed. Brahma Chellaney (Hyderabad: Orient Longman, 1999), 141–51. Pakistan's efforts in this direction are best summed up by Cheema, "Pakistan's Nuclear Use Doctrine," in *Planning the Unthinkable*.

70. Ashley Tellis, "Toward a Force-in-Being: Understanding India's Nuclear Doctrine and Future Force Posture," *India's Emerging Nuclear Posture: Between Recessed Deterrent and Ready Arsenal* (Santa Monica: Rand, 2001), 251–475.

71. Office of the Secretary of Defense, "South Asia," *Proliferation Threat and Response* (Washington, D.C.: U.S. Department of Defense, 2001), 21–30.

72. Lavoy, "The Uses of Pakistan's Nuclear Weapons," 13–14.

73. Agha Shahi, Zulfikar Ali Khan, and Abdul Sattar, "Securing Nuclear Peace," *News International*, October 5, 1999, available at http://jang-group.com/thenews (accessed October 1999).

74. Shahi, Khan, and Sattar, "Securing Nuclear Peace"; also see P. Cotta-Ramusino and M. Martellini, "Nuclear Safety, Nuclear Stability, and Nuclear Strategy in Pakistan," The Landau Network, Centro Volta, January 21, 2002, available at http://lxmi.mi.infn.it/~landnet/Doc/pakistan .pdf (accessed January 2002).

75. Cheema, "Pakistan's Nuclear Use Doctrine," in *Planning the Unthinkable*, 175–78.

76. Tellis, "Toward a Force-in-Being," *India's Emerging Nuclear Posture*, 261–366.

77. Tellis, Fair, and Medby, "Kargil: Lessons Learned on Both Sides," *Limited Conflicts under the Nuclear Umbrella*, 56–57.

78. Chengappa, "End the Wink and Nudge Approach," *Weapons of Peace*, 357.

79. Karnad, "The Perils of Deterrence by Half-Measures," *Nuclear Weapons and Indian Security*, 666–82.

80. Tellis, "Toward a Force-in-Being," *India's Emerging Nuclear Posture*, 341–66.

81. "Review of Events Leading up to Kargil," *Kargil Review Committee Report*, 65–66.

82. Chari, Cheema, and Cohen, "1990 as a Nuclear Crisis," *Perception, Politics, and Security in South Asia*, 115–36.

83. Vijay Datt, "Pak. Does Not Rule Out Use of N-Arms: Report," *Hindustan Times*, June 24, 1999, available at www.hindustantimes.com (accessed June 1999); "India Not Daunted by Pak. Nuke Threat: PM," *Times of India*, July 1, 1999, available at www.timesofindia.indiatimes .com (accessed July 1999).

84. "Delhi Positions Missiles on Border," *Dawn,* December 27, 2001, available at www .dawn.com (accessed December 2001); Gul, "Pakistan Tests Ghauris, Shaheens Today."

85. Tellis, *Stability in South Asia,* 8–11.

86. "Text of PM, Musharraf Statement," *Hindu,* January 6, 2004, available at www.hinduonnet .com (accessed January 2004).

87. "General Musharraf Addresses India Today Enclave, Calls for 'New Road Map for Peace,'" *Aaj Tak,* March 13, 2004, in FBIS Document SAP20040313000066, March 13, 2004.

FURTHER READING

Bennett Jones, Owen. *Pakistan: Eye of the Storm*, New Haven, Conn.: Yale University Press, 2002.

Chellaney, Brahma. "India Is Ready to Defend Itself," *New York Times*, December 28, 2001, at www.nytimes.com.

From Surprise to Reckoning: The Kargil Review Committee Report. New Delhi: Sage Publications, December 15, 1999.

Gupta, Shishir. "When India Came Close to War," *India Today*, December 23, 2002, at www .india-today.com.

Jervis, Robert. *The Meaning of the Nuclear Revolution: Statecraft and the Prospect of Armageddon*. Ithaca, N.Y.: Cornell University Press, 1989.

Krepon, Michael. "Escalator to Nowhere," *OutlookIndia*, November 11, 2002, at www.outlook india.com.

Singh, Jasjit. "Rethinking the Unthinkable: How Pakistan's Nuclear Strategy Went for a Six," *Indian Express*, June 13, 2002, at www.expressindia.com.

Tellis, Ashley. *Stability in South Asia*. Santa Monica, Calif.: Rand, 1997.

Tellis, Ashley J., C. Christine Fair, and Jamison Jo Medby, *Limited Conflict under the Nuclear Umbrella: Indian and Pakistani Lessons from the Kargil Crisis*. Santa Monica, Calif.: Rand, 2001.

Wirsing, Robert G. *Kashmir in the Shadow of War: Regional Rivalries in a Nuclear Age*. London: M. E. Sharpe, Inc., 2003.

8

International Dimensions of Ethnic Conflict

Maya Chadda

The term *ethnic conflict* may best be defined as a conflict between groups of communities that regard themselves as distinctly different from other groups on account of shared characteristics such as myths of origin, language, religion, cultural heritage, race, and clan or tribal association, and perhaps most importantly, a shared sense of history. Although there is no consensus as to why ethnic conflicts arise or to what extent they are critical in any given region, most scholars agree that such conflicts contribute significantly to the escalation of international tensions. This chapter examines the role of ethnic conflicts in the shaping of South Asia's interstate relations by outlining several cases of internationalized ethnic conflicts, exploring the conjunction of situational elements that make them a part of interstate relations in the region, and examining current debates as to why ethnic conflicts spread beyond the state to become a factor in regional relations. However, while this chapter focuses on how ethnic division is the principal setting within which conflict and cooperation occurs, two important facts must be noted: first, ethnicity is by no means the reason for all conflicts in South Asia, and second, all ethnic conflicts do not necessarily become internationalized.

There is an abundance of ethnic conflicts in South Asia, and many extend beyond the state. Here, we examine the common patterns among them to construct a broad picture of how ethnic conflicts became internationalized in South Asia. As a starting point, it might be more useful to imagine South Asia not as a subcontinent of separate sovereign states but as one of graded ethnic differences. The Pathans in the Northwest Frontier Province (NWFP) of Pakistan gradually extend into the Pashtun areas of Afghanistan; the Rajasthani language, spoken mainly in the Indian state of Rajasthan, changes only by degrees every hundred miles, depending on whether one travels toward Sindh in Pakistan or Gujarat in India. It takes on local coloration as it gains distance and moves toward the area of the next proximate language. The Indian province-state of Bengal, parts of Assam and Bihar, and what is today Bangladesh share scores of dialects derived from Bengali. South Asia's ethnolinguistic communities are concentrated in compact areas or regions. It is within such a milieu that the British colonial authorities drew the boundaries of modern South Asian states. The purpose was to legitimize conquest and facilitate colonial administration, but there is ample evidence to suggest that the colonial policies strengthened ethnic identities. The territorial boundaries that the British left behind when they departed from the subcontinent in 1947 cut across the cultural and ethnic boundaries of South Asia. The problems of territorial consolidation that bedevil the regional states today cannot be understood unless we take into account pan-Indian nationalism, narrower ethnic nationalism, and the old colonial state. Independence did not meld the disparate identities into a single whole; nor did it resolve conflict between competing identities, which now extended into the international arena.

We need to consider two additional features of South Asia. First, in size, population, and economic and military power, India dominates the region. Second, all South Asian states, with the exception of Sri Lanka, the Maldives, and Afghanistan, share borders with India, but—with the exception of Pakistan and Afghanistan—none shares them with each other. This has several immediate implications. India must contend with the problem of ethnic overlap with a large number of states. All neighboring states regard her as a hegemonic power anxious to reduce the smaller countries to a satellite status. The states that share borders with India have therefore pursued a variety of strategies to offset India's superior strength. Pakistan's reliance on the United States and Nepal's attempt to enlist China are instances of these counteracting strategies. Are South Asia's international conflicts a result of this asymmetry of power in size and military capabilities, or are they a consequence of nonconcurrence between territorial and cultural boundaries?[1] This is the overarching question that must be answered to understand the international implications of ethnic conflicts. In this chapter, I try to show that we need to consider ethnic conflict as an integral part of South Asia's security dilemma.[2]

SOUTH ASIA'S INTERNATIONALIZED ETHNIC CONFLICTS

Ethnic identities become internationalized in two ways: they may generate actors, movements, and consequences that extend beyond the claimed boundaries of a state; or events beyond the borders, such as wars, large-scale migrations and refugees, separatist agitation and militancy, political collapse or instability, might "ethnicize" a state's regional and international policy. In both instances, international boundaries become blurred and separation of domestic from foreign policy becomes difficult to maintain. In South Asia, ethnic communities that reside along international borders or those that are divided by such borders are more frequently the cause of interstate tensions than those in the interior of the country in question. Territorial concentration of an ethnic group provides greater ease in mobilizing the community behind ethnic demands than a group whose members might be geographically scattered. The three most important players in such a conflict are the host state facing ethnic dissent, the ethnic community that has the geopolitical and territorial basis to enlist support from international actors, and the neighboring state, often referred to as the ethnic kin-state, that either shares the ethnic overlap or is affected by policies of the host state. Kashmiris, Pashtuns, and Baluchis represent overlapping nationalities. The Sikhs are a case of an alienated ethnic community residing on the Indian side of the Indo-Pakistani border. India is the host state while Pakistan is an ethnic kin-state for Kashmiris and a supporting state for the Sikh separatists. Iran and Afghanistan are the ethnic kin-states for the Baluch nationalists, as is Afghanistan for the Pashtuns.

South Asia's ethnic demography provides a fertile arena for several cross-border conflicts. For the purpose of analysis here, these are grouped into three separate clusters based on their consequences for the region: (1) conflicts that have led to war, partition, rearrangement of sovereign territories, or collapse of the central state, as in East Pakistan in the 1970s and Afghanistan since the 1990s; (2) conflicts that have led to military action in which one or more extraregional states were involved but that resulted in no division of territories, as in the Baluch struggle in the 1970s and the Sikh and Naga struggles over many decades; (3) conflicts that have led to military intervention as an extension of diplomacy, as in Sri Lanka. These are not proposed as scientific categories; their purpose is mainly heuristic.

THE FIRST CLUSTER: WAR, PARTITION, STATE COLLAPSE

While there are many causes that lead to the long history of ethnic conflicts, only three events in particular have reached the status of great tragedies in South Asia: the partition of India in 1947, the partition of Pakistan in 1971, and the disintegration and collapse of Afghanistan in 1992 and beyond.[3] Each tragedy illustrates the enduring power and disintegrative potential of uncontrolled warfare between ethnic communities. No other regional conflicts in South Asia compare in the scale of killing, destruction, and human displacement with the three events mentioned above. Each represents a decisive turning point in the international relations of South Asia.

Let us take the first tragedy, the partition of India in 1947, and ask whether this was caused by a particular distribution of international power and the declining military capabilities of the British Raj or by internal factors, such as the British agenda on the eve of departure and the nature and popular base of Indian nationalism, its ideology, organization, and leadership. Most importantly, we need to ask if Partition was not primarily an outcome of rivalry, mistrust, and struggle for ascendancy between the Muslim League, claiming to represent the Muslims of the subcontinent and the Indian National Congress (INC), claiming to speak for all Hindus and Muslims. Although the British will to hold on to India had weakened greatly in the aftermath of World War II, the extensive literature on the causes of Partition suggests that while the British may have decided to leave, division of the colony was not necessarily slated in the initial plan. To understand why India came to be divided, we need to turn to political developments within the subcontinent.[4] The 1947 partition underlined the ways in which a demand for power sharing can become a demand for a separate state. It foreshadowed the enduring nature of such conflicts, which over the decades since have led to wars (between India and Pakistan), the implosion of a region (Kashmir), and continuing insurgency.

The Muslim League charged that the INC's secular claims disguised its communal (religion-based) biases. The League argued that INC provincial governments, elected under the partial representational system introduced by the British in the 1930s, had systematically discriminated against Muslims in education, jobs, and share of political office. Many in the League were convinced that by virtue of history, religion, and cultural traditions, the Muslims and Hindus constituted two separate nations, each equally needing a state to flourish without interference or domination by the other. This last rationale has given much currency to the "primordialist" explanations (based on ancient ethnic hatreds) for the communal violence that occurred in 1947. While the argument for a separate Muslim state was not prominent until the 1940s, it gained ground as the hour of freedom from the British approached. The British had promised independence in return for Indian nationalist support for Allied efforts in World War II. By the end of the war, it was clear that the British Raj had come to an end.

Historians are divided over what caused the partition and who was to blame for the communal carnage that followed.[5] Some suggest that British manipulations had sown the seeds of division between the Hindus and Muslims of the subcontinent. For evidence they point to the colonial dispensation of separate electorates during the 1930s, which had fomented Muslim ambitions and fears. If the Muslims of British India were to elect their own leaders exclusively from their community, they could concentrate only on what they wanted and avoid having to seek a larger, national consensus. Others point to the fragile and uncertain social base of the Muslim League and argue that Muhammad Ali Jinnah had no option but to demand a separate country if the Muslims were ever to have a decisive voice in the subcontinent. Yet, other scholars conclude that political and electoral considerations within the Congress Party outweighed its commitment to inclusive principles and drove the Muslim League from the fold of composite Indian nationalism. Historians are not then in agreement about whether Partition was a result of ancient hatreds, political ambitions, or expediency.

The consequences of the Partition are not, however, in doubt. In its immediate aftermath, more than twelve million people fled their homes in search of safety across the border, Hindus migrating to India and Muslims to Pakistan. This was the largest refugee migration ever experienced in the subcontinent; Punjab, Sindh, Bengal, now the border provinces, were divided. Many have described these events as an epic tragedy that cast a dark shadow over two generation of South Asians, breaking up a centuries-old social order that had set patterns of mutual ethnic tolerance and social intercourse.[6] The Partition also drowned out the voices of other ethnic nationalisms: the Bengali, Sikh, Tamil, Naga or Assamese, Singh, and Baluch. The Kashmiri and Sikh reconstruction of the events of Partition is for that reason significantly different from that of the official and national histories of India and Pakistan.[7] These were destined to surface with renewed vigor in the postindependence period.

Wary of further divisions and anxious to consolidate their rule, India and Pakistan moved to create unified sovereign nation-states. Pakistan, the more fragile of the two, opted for a centralizing viceregal model and a unitary political system, which has had a profoundly damaging impact on its history. Pakistan denied autonomy to ethnic regions and power to ethnic parties that had agreed to the creation of a separate Pakistan.[8] India, too, balked at granting political self-rule and a territorial homeland to the Sikhs, Nagas, and Assamese residing on her international borders, although the 1956 state reorganization gave ethnolinguistic homelands to other ethnic communities within India. The permanent state of conflict that marks the past fifty-eight years of Indo-Pakistani relations might have been avoided had Partition produced neat cultural and territorial divisions, but this was not possible. A large number of Muslims continue to reside in India, including Kashmiri Muslims, who constitute a majority in Indian Kashmir.

Since the Kashmir dispute is examined elsewhere in this volume, I will not discuss it here at any length. It is nevertheless important to bear in mind that the 1947 partition created an enduring ethnic conflict between India and Pakistan. This conflict has since determined their foreign and defense policies and shaped the balance of regional power. For instance, the dispute over Kashmir largely explains why Pakistan joined the military alliances led by the United States and why a nonaligned India leaned toward the Soviet Union. It explains why Pakistan forged strategic ties with China in the 1960s and developed nuclear weapons as a counter to the larger and militarily superior India. One could argue that Pakistan might have forged such ties in any event, but historians tell us that immediately after independence, Pakistan's first prime minister, Liaqat Ali Khan, was greatly attracted to the nonaligned alternative and would have opted for it had the dispute over Kashmir not compelled him to defer to the military and set Pakistan on a course of permanent rivalry with the larger India. Had there been no dispute over Kashmir, Pakistan's ties with China and the United States might have had a different focus. India might have still sought out the Soviet Union, but less as a counter to Pakistan than to America's Cold War ambitions.

These international dimensions of the Kashmir dispute had an equally profound effect on the domestic policies of each country. Scholars are divided over what occurred first, militarization of Pakistan or the conflict over Kashmir. Most would agree that the two are inextricably intertwined. India's federal design accommodated the demands of Kashmiri nationalism, but the Indian governments were never comfortable with the special status of Kashmir and sought to integrate it in contravention of the constitutional provisions of Article 370. The erosion of Kashmiri autonomy in combination with other social and economic frustrations eventually led to the insurgency in 1989, which has resulted in more than sixty thousand deaths, a large number of them of civilians, and has made Kashmir the most dangerous nuclear flash point for the past seven years

The Second Partition: The Bangladesh War

The partition of Pakistan in 1971 was a second stage replay of the first partition.[9] The uneasy integration of Bengali Muslims in East Pakistan did not survive the course of politics in West Pakistan. Bengali Muslims constituted not only a majority in Pakistan but possessed a separate landmass where they were concentrated. Most significantly, a swath of Indian territory separated East and West Pakistan. Pakistan feared that electoral democracy would empower the Bengali majority in the east and threaten the dominance of the Punjab-Pashtun ruling classes, who were ascendant in Pakistan's two important political institutions, the military and bureaucracy. Between 1947 and 1971, the Bengali nationalists confined their demands to linguistic, economic, administrative, and political autonomy for East Pakistan.[10] The West Pakistani elite feared that autonomy would set the stage for independence. In any event a grant of autonomy to its eastern part would have probably entailed a parallel grant of autonomy to other ethnically defined provinces, or so Pakistan's military bureaucracy thought. In any event, the result would be the same: a serious challenge to the dominance of the military-bureaucratic oligarchy. The elections of December 1970 brought these matters to a head. In these the East Pakistan based Awami League led by Sheik Mujibur Rehman obtained 167 seats, which gave it the majority needed to form a government. Neither the military nor the Pakistan People's Party, which had won the second largest number of seats in the National Assembly, were willing to let democracy take its course. The leaders of the Awami League were arrested, and the military struck in March 1971, unleashing a campaign of terror and killing in the months that followed. Incensed by the military's brutal response, the Awami League declared independence and mobilized the Bengali masses.[11] Pakistan was plunged into a civil war in which the Punjabi elite in the west sought to crush the revolt by its Bengali fellow Muslims in the east. Close to ten million Bengalis—Muslims and Hindus—fled across the border into India where they were granted refuge.

The Indian role, however, went well beyond humanitarian concerns. India had provided substantial support to the Bengali resistance (Mukti Bahini), extended safe sanctuaries, and trained and armed guerrilla forces under Indian military supervision.[12] The Awami League was permitted to form a government in exile in Calcutta. The flood of refugees had virtually erased the boundaries between East Pakistan and India, and the civilian suffering evoked images of the 1947 communal holocaust. India too prepared for war. During the months of March and April 1971, the Pakistani military crackdown escalated while, paralyzed by Cold War divisions, the international community did little more than criticize Pakistan for its action. In December 1971 Pakistan launched a surprise attack on the Indian airfields, officially beginning the war. The war lasted for about four weeks, at the end of which Pakistan's armed forces surrendered to India and Bangladesh became an independent country.

The Bangladesh war underlines the role of ethnic conflict in reordering the boundaries and determining interstate relations in the region. It provides insights into the mix of motives that might compel an ethnic kin-state to balance foreign policy considerations against domestic concerns. India had a compelling interest in repatriation of the refugees, who were a heavy economic burden and a potentially destabilizing presence in Bengal and Assam, where they had taken refuge. India also wanted to weaken Pakistan in order to extract from it major concessions along the line of control (LOC) in Kashmir.[13] It was anxious to calm sentiment in West Bengal, which was pressing for military action to stop the genocide of fellow Bengalis. Equally if not more compellingly, New Delhi wished to preserve the boundaries between East and West Bengal to prevent any future mobilization of pan-Bengali nationalism. A continued civil war in East Pakistan would have seriously endangered India's territorial unity. Finally, for Indira Gandhi and the Congress government, it was a highly popular war. If India won, the ruling party was certain to reap the benefits in the 1971 and 1972 elections. For the Bengali nationalists, access to safe sanctuaries, training, and arms, not to mention diplomatic support from a regionally powerful state, meant enhanced chances of liberation from Pakistan. The cultural and linguistic ties between East and West Bengal and its shared borders with India made the latter a powerful ethnic kin-state. Pakistan's vulnerability, its military weakness against both India and the Mukti Bahini, was made worse by the lack of international support.

Ethnic conflict had again led to territorial partition in South Asia, and the behavior of the state and nonstate actors, India, Pakistan, the Mukti Bahini, and the West Bengali people, was shaped by consideration of ethnic interests. Focusing only on the external elements, such as the military balance of power, in which India was obviously the superior state, offers only partial explanations as to why the Bangladesh war occurred. The popular mobilization in East Pakistan was triggered by the oppressive policies of leaders in West Pakistan, the denial of autonomy, and the growing resentment over the treatment of East Pakistani Bengalis by the Punjabi West Pakistanis, who saw themselves as a superior people. India did not intervene simply because it had the military capabilities to undertake the liberation of Bangladesh without excessive costs. Had ten million refugees not fled across the border and endangered West Bengal and the Indian northeast, New Delhi would have had far less justification for its intervention. We need therefore to integrate into our analysis the logic of ethnic mobilization and the security concerns created by South Asia's ethnic overlap. The Bangladesh war had, however, sown the seeds that were to bear a poisonous fruit in the 1990s, not in the east where the war had been fought, but in the west where nuclear-armed India and Pakistan confronted each other over the disputed Vale of Kashmir.

War, Disintegration, and Regional Reordering: The Afghan War

The collapse of Afghanistan in the early 1990s and the civil war that followed between its warring ethnic groups is the third tragedy of historic proportions whose repercussions will continue to reverberate around the region into the future. The Afghan conflict can be divided into several phases, discussed at length in chapter 5.[14] Their progression does not concern us here. What concerns us is the role of ethnic conflict in shaping these events. First of all, the Afghan civil war erased the international border that divides Afghanistan from Pakistan. The Pashtun people who reside on this border have historically possessed a sense of ethnic difference from the non-Pashtun population of British India and, later, Pakistan. Their imagined homeland stretches from Qandahar in the south and west, to the Indus River in the east, and to Dir and Swat in the north.

The Afghan civil war offered Pakistan an opportunity to settle the Pashtun question in its favor. It could do this by securing a friendly and dependent government in Kabul.[15] Pakistan hoped that such a regime in Afghanistan would permanently end the irredentist demand for Pashtunistan. In the past several governments in Kabul had denounced the Durand Line (which divides Afghanistan and Pakistan) as a colonial creation and extended support for a separate Pashtunistan or demanded that the Pashtun areas be incorporated into Afghanistan. It is against this history of Pashtun claims that Pakistan encouraged and armed pro-Pakistani Pashtuns, referred to as the Taliban, to wage a war for ascendancy in Afghanistan. The Taliban victory in the late 1990s signaled the advent of a fanatical Islamic regime in Kabul, but it also underscored the triumph of Pakistan's ethnically driven regional strategy.[16] The human toll in life and limb of the people of the region has been horrendous. The events after 1997, when the Taliban captured nearly 90 percent of Afghanistan, the international isolation that propelled them into the arms of Osama bin Laden and al Qaeda, the attack on the World Trade Center and the Pentagon, and the American intervention in Afghanistan, are the subject of other chapters in this volume. What needs stressing here is the ethnic character of these events, that the behavior of countries in the region—Pakistan, the Central Asian states, Iran, India, and Saudi Arabia—can be explained largely as an attempt to strengthen friendly ethnics or fellow ethnics to acquire influence over the course of events.

The establishment of the Taliban regime had provided a brief hiatus in the ethnic wars between 1998 and 2001, but ethnic identities were to again serve as a wedge for dislodging the Pashtun Taliban and securing Kabul for the Northern Alliance composed of the Tajiks, Hazaras, Uzbeks, and other non-Pashtuns. The Bonn Agreement in December 2001, which followed the Taliban's defeat and expulsion, tried to balance the ethnic claims and counterclaims, as did the *loya jirga*, the traditional tribal council held in June 2002. The latter was meant to legitimize the leadership of Hamid Karzai, who had emerged from the Bonn Agreement as the compromise candidate to head the proposed provisional government in Kabul. Post-Taliban Afghanistan is a place of warring ethnic regions held together by the military presence of U.S. and NATO forces. In the view of many observers, the central state has simply disappeared or is too weak to perform its conventional functions in Afghanistan. A large number of pro-Taliban ethnic Pashtuns who fled to their ethnic homeland in Pakistan have continued to regroup and attack the Karzai government and American forces from their hideouts across the border.

The history of subsequent attempts to stabilize the Karzai government and the problems encountered in nation building in Afghanistan underscore the importance of internationalized ethnicity as a factor in the shaping of war and peace in South Asia. The meddling by regional powers—Pakistan, Iran, Saudi Arabia, Russia—has not only ethnicized the nation building, but it has prevented full reintegration of disparate regions of Afghanistan. Having expelled the Taliban regime from Kabul, the United States has turned its guns toward the al Qaeda elements in order to drain the swamp and eliminate the terrorists from the Pashtun areas. That has required the United States to seek out local support. The United States is thus sucked into the vortex of domestic ethno-politics in Pakistan and Afghanistan. By many accounts Pakistan is now "Talibanized," meaning ethnic conflicts have merged with those over religious fundamentalism.[17] The immediate consequence is the intensification of cross-border infiltration from Pakistan into Indian Jammu and Kashmir. How and why the two fronts came to be connected is the subject of discussion in other chapters of this volume. It is enough to note here that the violence caused by the two sets of overlapping ethnicities, the Pashtun and Kashmiri, has escalated tensions between India and Pakistan and turned South Asia not only into a nuclear flash point but a battleground between the regular armies of states and armed insurgents that belong to no state.

It is then difficult to separate the domestic from the international issues in this situation. The interests of the United States, Russia, China, and India are at stake, but so are those of lesser powers. Indeed, proximity and ethnic affinity give those in the lesser-power category greater leverage to affect the course of events compared to those in the great-power category. What is more, the United States and China, the two great powers with important stakes in South Asia, must rely on regional states to protect their interests. The United States needs Pakistan's cooperation in hunting for al Qaeda and stabilizing Afghanistan. In return, the Bush administration is willing to ignore questions of democracy and human rights, even when Pakistan continues to support jihad in Kashmir. This is a case of reverse leverage that cannot be explained without reference to South Asia's ethnic divide.

THE SECOND CLUSTER: ETHNIC VIOLENCE AND INSURGENCY

The Indian military suppression of the Sikh separatists in Punjab during the 1980s and Nagas in the northeast since the 1950s, the use of coercion against the tribal communities in the Chittagong Hill Tracts (CHT) by the government of Bangladesh in the 1970s and 1980s, Pakistani military actions against Baluch nationalists in the early 1970s, and ethnic violence caused by large-scale migration of Nepalis into India and Bhutan over several decades do not approach the scale and impact of the three historic tragedies described above, but their effects have been intense in the areas where they occurred.[18] They outline yet another pattern in which ethnic conflicts can become internationalized. The two most important factors that shape the outcome of these conflicts is, first, the overwhelming strength of the host state in comparison to the secessionist community, as well as the ability to hold the territorial status quo, and, second, the limited and frequently episodic nature of support from ethnic kin-states for the secessionists. The cross-border ethnic linkage is then one among several factors—at times a critical one—that determines the balance of relations between states with overlapping ethnic nationalities. The intensity of conflict will depend more on the internal conditions—unity, organization, popular support, negotiating skills, and staying power—of the secessionists in question. Kin-state support certainly plays a role, but ultimately it does not determine the outcome. The response of the host state has usually depended on a whole host of factors, such as the stability of the ruling regime, election schedules, the stance of the political opposition, public opinion, relations with the ethnic kin-state such as India's with Pakistan and China, the strength and intensity of insurgency, the possibility of splitting the ethnic cohorts, and the level of international criticism for violations of human rights.

Baluchistan, the western border province of Pakistan, has been and continues to be the main obstacle in the path to greater political integration of Pakistan.[19] The conflict reached its peak in 1973 when the Baluchis tried unsuccessfully to secede from Pakistan and create an independent state of Baluchistan. About five million people of Baluch ethnic origin are located primarily in Baluchistan in southwestern Pakistan, in southeastern Iran, and at the southern tip of Afghanistan. The Baluch region is divided by the Goldsmid Line, which marks the border between Iran and Pakistan and by the Durand Line, which, as mentioned above, divides Pakistan from Afghanistan. Iran and Afghanistan are then the ethnic kin-states to the Baluch. Both these states have played opposite roles in the spread and containment of the Baluch conflict. According to Robert Wirsing, Baluch nationalists felt threatened by changing demographics that reduced them to a minority within their own homeland, socioeconomic modernization that threatened their lifestyle, and the fallout from the struggle for power in Pakistan, which led to arbitrary dismissals of provincial governments and denial of autonomy. Extensive emigration of the Baluchis and immigration of non-Baluchis, many of whom were pensioned officers in the Pakistan armed forces, produced a sense of cultural invasion. The Pakistani government's modernization policies further reinforced the Baluch fear of cultural annihilation. While Pakistani officials criticize the Baluchis for clinging to their outmoded Sardari (tribal kinship) system, the Baluchis saw Pakistani governments as exploitative and manipulative.

The immediate trigger for the confrontation of 1973 was the dismissal of the Baluch provincial assembly by Prime Minister Z. A. Bhutto, who accused the elected Baluch governor Ghaus Bux Bizenjo and Chief Minister Ataullah Mengal of plotting secession with the help of Iraq and the Soviet Union. The dismissal plunged the province into a bloody civil war. The two kin-states of the Baluch, Iran and Afghanistan, took contrasting stances on the conflict.

Afghanistan provided small amounts of material assistance to the Baluch secessionists because of its own longstanding dispute with Pakistan over the
Pashtuns, while Iran extended military assistance to Pakistan to crush the
Baluch revolt.[20] The Shah of Iran feared that the Iranian Baluchis would join
those rebelling across the border in Pakistan. He suspected that Saddam Hussein was aiding and abetting the Baluchis in retaliation for Iran's support for
the Iraqi Kurds. Although the Baluch revolt was brutally put down and drew
some international attention at the time, subsequent events in Afghanistan
took center stage. Also, Pakistan entered a period of shaky democracy in the
late 1980s. It was hoped that stabilization of democracy in Pakistan might
create new power-sharing arrangements between the dominant Punjabis and
the rest of ethnic Pakistan, but that was not to be. Pakistan's democratic experiment ended abruptly as its military and civilian leaders clashed over turf
and policy toward India, especially Kashmir. Pakistan's Baluch problem had
now merged with its problems with Islamists, whose numbers have been
greatly augmented by the Taliban and al Qaeda forces who have fled from
across Afghanistan into Baluchistan and the Northwest Frontier Province. Although the Taliban regime has been ousted, Afghanistan remains extremely
fragile and with it the bordering Baluch region of Pakistan. The memories of
the brutal oppression of the 1970s are still alive. The fall out from the Afghan
disintegration has many armed Taliban from across the boundary seeking
sanctuaries and safe havens while the government of Pakistan holds the most
tenuous control over the tribal regions. If Pakistan fails to check the growth
of fundamentalists and meet the demands of the beleaguered Baluchis, that
region may become a dangerous challenge to Pakistan's political integrity.

Internationalization of the Sikh militancy did not occur until the 1980s, although the Sikh movement for greater political autonomy dates back to the
period before 1947. This is also true of the Naga demand for an independent
Nagaland. But unlike the Sikhs, who accepted their inclusion within the Indian Union, the Naga declared an armed revolt against the government of India soon after independence.[21] The Indian government treated Sikh nationalism as an internal problem and therefore amenable to negotiated solution;
however, it deployed the army against the Naga insurgents and fought battles
to neutralize them. As the armed operations intensified, the Nagas sought support across the border from China and fellow Nagas in Myanmar. India saw
the Naga secessionism largely as a security problem and a challenge to India's
territorial unity.

The history of Sikh and Naga militancy is long and complicated. Each is
different in its particularities.[22] Similarly, the Nepalis in Bhutan and the
Chakma tribals in Bangladesh operate in very different domestic and international settings. There are, however, several common features shared by them
all. First, demographics are an important factor in each, as are social, eco-

nomic, and political inequalities. The Nagas resent the encroachment of the plains people from West Bengal and Assam into their homeland, and the Sikhs see numerical majority as a key to political power in Punjab. The Chakmas in the CHT of Bangladesh also shared with the rest of the northeast Indian tribal belt a desire to safeguard their lifestyle from Bangladeshi migrants to their tribal homeland. The mass migration of Bangladeshi Muslims into Assam, first in the aftermath of the 1947 partition, then in 1971–1972 during the Bangladesh war, and in substantial numbers since then, has created a similar sense of demographic invasion in Assam, leading to the intensified Assamese nationalism and escalated tensions between India and Bangladesh. The emergence of the militant United Liberation Front of Assam (ULFA) has further complicated the geopolitics in these regions. Over the passage of years, militant organizations of Nagas, Assamese, Mizolanders, and Tripurans have frequently collaborated to frustrate the Indian security forces and border police.

The second common reason for the internationalization of the above ethnic struggles is the strategies their respective governments have employed to contain, diffuse, and weaken ethnic nationalities. The Bhutto government dismissed the popularly elected provincial government of Bizenjo and deployed armed forces against its members. Prime Minster Indira Gandhi sought first to split the Akali Dal (which represented the Sikhs in Punjab) by supporting the religious radical priest Jairnal Singh Bhindranwale against them and later deploying the army against Bhindranwale when he demanded a separate Khalistan for the Sikhs in India. New Delhi cultivated a faction of the Nagas and sought to isolate the militants by granting a new state of Nagaland within India. The governments in South Asia have therefore employed a carrot-and-stick approach to controlling ethnic nationalities, but this has still left the fundamental grievances behind the ethnic disaffection unresolved.[23] These surface with greater ferocity each time. Indeed, Atul Kohli talks about a U-curve in the ebb and flow of ethnic conflicts: they rise to a peak, then fall in intensity, only to rise up again if the circumstances that created them in the first place resurface, namely, loss of political control and socioeconomic discrimination.[24] Use of force by the state has frequently led to guerrilla warfare and terrorist actions, as well as attacks on security forces and civilians. State coercion and enforcement of draconian laws has hardened the ethnic extremists in turn and forced them beyond the international boundaries. Many extremist groups (United Liberation Front of Assam, Khalistan Liberation Front, Liberation Tigers of Tamil Eelam) have resorted to intimidation and criminal activities to raise funds for arms. The porous nature of South Asia's international borders in the Indian northeast, along Pakistan's northwest border, as well as along sections of the Indo-Pakistan border makes the flow of arms and insurgents a routine phenomenon. Armed groups have easy access to international

bazaars in arms and weapons. Smuggling and drug dealing are the other av-
enues of raising funds. In many instances the state is very thinly represented
in the area, and its officials are often co-opted in the informal networks that
sustain ethnic violence, corruption, and crime.[25]

The third element common to these conflicts is the episodic nature of kin-
state support. When such support has been forthcoming, relations between the
host and the kin-state have invariably soured. Pakistan's support for the Sikh
separatists in the 1980s, although never very significant, generated serious
talk of military retaliation. India has been more careful in its statements linking the Naga conflict to China, but the connection is a constant reminder to
India of its vulnerability, should China resume its support of the Nagas. Indo-
Bangladesh relations have also frequently soured over illegal migration from
Bangladesh into Assam and Tripura. There have been a fair number of clashes
between their respective border police and security forces, and recently the Indian government requested that the United States supply it with monitoring
technology to seal the border. The suppression of Baluch nationalists similarly
led to deterioration in relations between Pakistan and Afghanistan in the
1970s. If Afghanistan does not stabilize under the unified national government
of Hamid Karzai, both Pakistan and Afghanistan will again face challenges
from the overlapping ethnic nationalities in Baluchistan and the Northwest
Frontier Province. Although these movements have failed so far to secure a
separate state, they have mobilized considerable international support from
human rights groups (for example, in the Baluch and Naga conflicts) and/or
from an ethnic diaspora, as in the case of the Sikh separatists.

Each case of ethnic resistance mentioned above vacillated between autonomy and independence. Insistence on separate statehood was frequently a
bargaining ploy to maximize concessions at the negotiating table. This ambivalence about goals within the ethnic group often produced factions, some
of which spun off into militancy and armed revolt. The movement for Khalistan led by Bhindranwale did not reflect the majority of Sikhs in Punjab.
Bhindranwale represented the extreme end of a broad-based Sikh disaffection.[26] Nagas are similarly split between moderates and radicals. There is a
delicate balance to be preserved between the possibility of independence and
agreement to stay within the national boundaries. Should violence escalate,
the central state can reimpose coercive control and bring the political careers
of the moderates to an end. On the other hand, the moderates can always point
to the potential escalation of violence to wrest more concessions from the
state. Broad-based ethnic movements clearly rely on the popular support of
these cohorts.

The Sikh separatist demands have evaporated since the formation of the
Akali government in Punjab in the late 1990s. Punjab has returned to the fold
of Indian electoral democracy. The recent negotiations with the Nagas may

not turn out to be as fortuitous. The demand for a greater Nagaland would mean carving out portions of Naga concentration from the adjacent states of Tripura and Manipur.[27] This is bound to unleash yet another round of ethnic violence. For the time being, however, China appears less interested in fomenting ethnic trouble in northeastern India. The potential nevertheless exists for a cascading impact of ethnic conflicts from Manipur to Assam, including Nagaland and Tripura. Internationalization of Baluch, Sikh, Naga, and Bangladeshi Muslim conflicts underscores the failure to consolidate territorial nation-states in South Asia.

THE THIRD CLUSTER: ETHNIC CONFLICT AND INTERVENTION IN SRI LANKA

Although Sri Lanka's Tamil-Sinhala conflict has a long history and shares many features with the conflicts discussed above, it is the only instance where a government invited military intervention for the purpose of settling ethnic conflict and preserving the territorial unity of the state.[28] The other two interventions, India's in East Pakistan and Pakistan's clandestine intervention in Indian Kashmir, were hardly invited. The causes of Sinhala-Tamil conflict are not dissimilar to those enumerated in ethnic conflict elsewhere in South Asia: denial of fair share in power and office, unequal access to jobs and economic opportunities, political and social discrimination, demographic aggression by a rival ethnic community backed by the central state, denial of equal cultural rights, as in language discrimination, attempt to impose hegemony of the rival ethnonationalism (in this instance Sinhala Buddhist nationalism), and use of state coercion. Most importantly, insistence on majoritarian rule within a unitary political system has linked the logic of Sri Lanka's modern democracy to illiberal rule. There is substantial literature on the causes and evolution of the Sri Lankan ethnic conflict.[29] These need not detain us here; their international dimensions, however, are important.

The political stability of Sri Lanka, located about ninety miles from the southern tip of India, is a matter of serious political concern for New Delhi. India and Sri Lanka are closely connected by history, mythology, and ethnicity. At least three separate strands can be identified in the way ethnic conflict in Sri Lanka became internationalized. The first is a result of the strong ethnic bond between Tamils in Sri Lanka and the Tamil Nadu in India. India is not only the first-order ethnic kin-state for Sri Lanka but also a large and powerful state compared to the island country. The fifty million Indian Tamils are linked by history, language, and culture, not to mention geographic proximity to the seventeen million Sri Lankan Tamils. Tamil cultural figures, entertainers, politicians, and films have natural audiences on both sides of the Palk

Strait. The cause of the Sri Lankan Tamils is a popular one in Tamil Nadu. Since the 1980s political parties in Tamil Nadu have made liberation of their Tamil brothers an election plank.[30] Family connections and kinship tie the northern part of Sri Lanka—the Jaffna and Eastern provinces—to the state of Tamil Nadu in India. The Tamil separatists on both sides of the Palk Strait envision the creation of a greater Tamil homeland, which would include northern and eastern Sri Lanka, as well as Tamil Nadu in India. After the outbreak of the civil war in 1983, the Sri Lankan Tamil militant groups were granted safe sanctuaries in Tamil Nadu and provided with small arms and training by the government of Indira Gandhi.[31] These Sri Lankan groups developed close ties to the political parties in Tamil Nadu. The latter raised huge sums of money to fund the Tamil cause. These informal networks, although weakened after the assassination of Rajiv Gandhi in 1991 and disillusionment with the militants, had managed to survive the interim period when the Liberation Tigers of Tamil Eelam (LTTE) were expelled from Tamil Nadu in 1987 and India waged a war against the LTTE in northern Sri Lanka.

The Indian involvement does not end here. Its kin-state status is only one dimension of the internationalization of the ethnic conflict. The Indian government also has great interest in preventing the Sri Lankan civil strife from fomenting Tamil separatism within India.[32] New Delhi has followed two broad strategies to prevent the emergence of a separate Tamil state of Elam: it has, on the one hand, sought to represent and own the Tamil quest for justice and equality in Sri Lanka and, on the other hand, applied alternating pressure on the disputants to shape the course of the conflict. It has failed in both these efforts. The Indian strategy nevertheless exposes the mix of motives from which ethnic kin-states may act. It shows that internationalization can make ethnic conflicts even more intractable and lethal for the civilians who get caught in the crossfire.

The alternating-pressure strategy was meant to reward or punish the disputants, the Tamil groups and the government in Colombo. The grant of safe sanctuary to the Tamil militants by Indira Gandhi and induction of the Indian Peace-Keeping Force (IPKF) into northern Sri Lanka (largely to protect the militants while they disarmed) by Rajiv Gandhi exemplified the first approach. Expulsion of the militant groups from Tamil Nadu in 1987 and subsequent military action against them by the IPKF once the disarming efforts failed were meant to punish and weaken the recalcitrant Tamil groups. India also alternated between a tough or supportive stance toward Colombo. The dispatch of combat aircraft over Sri Lanka and dropping of tons of food in 1987 was designed to breach the economic embargo imposed by Colombo and issue a warning that India would not stand aside while the Tamils in Jaffna (northern Sri Lanka) were starved and denied basic necessities. These actions contrasted with the consistently staunch support India offered to Sri

Lanka's territorial integrity. In fact, the purpose behind the dispatch of the IPKF was to help Sri Lanka do what it could not do alone: disarm the Tamils in an orderly manner, prepare the ground for negotiations that would grant provincial autonomy to the Tamil homeland, and end the conflict without jeopardizing Sri Lanka's unity. As mentioned above, a separate Tamil Elam posed a threat to India's own political integrity. While the Sri Lankan government eagerly accepted the Indian support in disarming the militants—the expulsion of the militants and induction of the IPKF came at the urging of Sri Lankan leaders—it sought to diversify international support by approaching the governments of the United States, Great Britain, and Israel. Mobilization of support from sympathetic or kin-states is then the first strand in the internationalization of the Sri Lankan civil war.

Among all the ethnic secessionists seeking independence in South Asia, no group, except perhaps the Kashmiris, has developed as large and effective an international network of support as have the Sri Lankan Tamils. They have been able to do this partly because of the existence of a large Tamil diaspora in Tamil Nadu, Europe, the United States, Australia, and Malaysia. The LTTE opened offices in London and Melbourne and created influential lobbies in Canada and European capitals. The effectiveness of the informal network is evident in that the militant groups have been able to carry on the war against the Sri Lankan forces for the past two decades without any significant state support for their cause. Their campaign to portray Colombo as a violator of human rights was highly successful until recently. The situation has changed since the mid-1990s, especially as atrocities committed by the LTTE have become public knowledge, but throughout the early 1990s the propaganda campaign put the governments in Colombo on the defensive. Since September 11 and the listing of the LTTE as a terrorist organization by the Bush administration, the former has become more receptive to peace efforts.

A third strand of international involvement is the third-party mediation by state actors. India played this role between 1983 and 1987, but since the withdrawal of India's peacekeeping forces in 1990, Norway has stepped in to mediate several rounds of talks between the LTTE and the government in Colombo.[33] Indian mediation was hardly a disinterested effort. Norway on the other hand has no evident instrumental or affective motives for extending its good offices. It has no ambitions in the region and has no ethnic affinity to the disputants. The only motive one might attribute is the honor and prestige a successful mediation might bring it in international politics.

To sum up, ethnicity is a principle mode of social and political organization of the South Asian states. It needs to be given the proper weight in any analysis of interstate relations in the region. Inadequate attention to this basic fact, evident in unitary constitutions in Pakistan and Sri Lanka and mismanagement in India, has led to instability, war, secession, and violence. This of course suggests that regional conflicts in South Asia frequently originate in ethnic overspill. No single cause, be it economic, political, or based on considerations of social status and equality, can explain why conflicts arise. More often than not, ethnic grievances are a mix of cultural, political, and economic demands. State response, whether cooperative or coercive, is equally a mix of many compulsions. A kin-state may extend support because of ethnic, religious, and ideological affinity, or it might be moved by humanitarian considerations. But frequently, the explanation for support is found in reasons of realpolitik, domestic and international political advantage, and economic and military gain. These have been evident in India's interventions in Sri Lanka and Bangladesh, Pakistan's interventions in Kashmir and Punjab, Iran's support for Pakistan against the Baluchis, and Afghanistan's support for the Baluchis against Pakistan. A kin-state may extend support to placate its own population. Consider the pressure generated by West Bengal on the Indira Gandhi government. The cause of Kashmir is similarly popular in Pakistan. One might even argue that, in some instances, involvement might not be in the larger strategic interests of the state. Pakistan is walking on a thin line by continuing its support for the Kashmir *jihadis*.

An ethnic kin-state can keep the conflict alive by extending arms and weapons and safe sanctuaries, but it may not prevail if the host state is militarily superior and willing to commit its strength to prevent secession. Indeed, a weak state may use the ethnic conflict against the host state to equalize the balance of power or to tie up the military forces of an adversary in ethnic wars. If the ethnic kin-state is more powerful than the host state, as India was in the Bangladesh war, the host state may have to seek a settlement unfavorable to its interests. Although the outcome of a conflict might be constrained by the distribution of power and capabilities between the countries involved, it cannot be explained without reference to ethnic animosities. Several factors determine whether an ethnic conflict will in fact spread: its location, the distribution of ethnics across borders, the policies of a central state toward the ethnic community, the nature of relations between the host and ethnic kin-state, and the regional political environment. Size and geopolitics have made India the dominant regional power, but they have also made it vulnerable to conflicts of ethnic overlap. The course of civil war in Sri Lanka tells us, however, that a weak state can still exercise reverse leverage against a powerful, large state if both fear secessionist demands from a shared ethnic nationality.

The internationalization of ethnic disputes can produce serious consequences for the host as well as the ethnic kin-state, depending on their ability to prevent the conflict from spreading within and beyond their national boundaries. Ethnic conflict can lead to militarization of a society if prolonged. At the minimum, it will strengthen the hard-line elements and tilt the domestic balance in favor of authoritarian forces within that society. The fear of a Bengali majority in Pakistan strengthened the arguments in favor of military regimes over democratic rule. The example of the Taliban, a fundamentalist Islamic ethnocracy, underlines the devastating consequences of ethnic wars for a society and people.

DEBATING THE INTERNATIONALIZATION OF ETHNIC CONFLICTS

The above examples of ethnic conflicts, partitions, and wars tell us that they are a frequent occurrence in South Asia. But there is no agreement among scholars about how to fit such conflicts into the mainstream theories of international relations. Some scholars view ethnic identities as primordial and unchanging; others see them as a tool used by individuals, groups, and elites to obtain some larger material end.[34] We might do better to see ethnic identities as products of enduring social construction forged by human action and choice, instead of as primordial accidents of birth. Similarly, ethnic solidarity does not evaporate when the political or material ends of leaders and political elites are fulfilled. The establishment of the Akali Dal government in Punjab might have ended the violence for the time being, but there is no assurance that violence will not resurface should the balance of economic and political power shift in Punjab. The sense of collectively belonging to a group usually endures beyond the immediate calculations of gain and loss. Indeed, one of the hard lessons leaders of postindependence India had to learn was that ethnic loyalties could not be modernized out of existence. India would have to build its democracy within a deeply divided social context.

Each of the three perspectives, primordial, instrumental, and constructivist, has distinctly different implications for the internationalization of ethnic identities. The notion of primordiality leads to the thesis of ancient hatred and the inevitability of war and violence, hence permanent separation of the warring ethnics. The partition of India in 1947 and then Pakistan in 1971 are cases in point. In both instances, the primordialists would argue that the departure of the British from India and a weak central state in Pakistan led to large-scale violence and a resurfacing of ancient hatreds. Pakistan insisted on a two-nation solution. In 1971 the Bengali Muslims turned the two-nation thesis against Pakistan by asserting their own right to a separate nation-state. Instrumentalist interpretations tend to focus on calculations of political gain, but they frequently ignore the social and economic causes of ethnic conflict. In this perspective, preventive strategies usually focus on building incentives for leaders to abandon ethnic vote banks and seek broader representation from among competing ethnic communities. Such a remedy will not, however, remove the root causes of ethnic conflict; nor will it diminish the sense of accumulated injustices. The continued turmoil in the seven states of India's northeast (created in response to demands for ethnic homelands) provides ample evidence for this. To prevent internationalization of ethnic conflict, alienated ethnic communities must be reintegrated into the larger body politic in which they can live with a renewed sense of confidence. This requires changes in the social and economic structures that breed ethnic inequality. The constructivist approach points to historically accumulated conditions that produce the divide, but it also points to socially relevant models of ethnic co-existence.[35] A constructivist perspective alerts policymakers to the dangers of pursuing homogenous nationalism, European-style states, and hardened boundaries. I explained earlier why we might do better to see South Asia as a society of graded ethnic differences. In light of that and the accumulated history of conflict since 1947, a condominium solution with soft international boundaries and shared or overlapping political regions might be a solution for the Kashmir and Pashtun areas. The Sri Lankan conflict might be more amenable to solution within a federalized Sri Lanka and a larger Indo–Sri Lankan common market.

A second set of controversies revolves around preventive strategies. A majority of South Asian scholars argue that denial of political and economic autonomy, use of coercion, and attempts to forge monolithic nationalism lead to conflict and violence. Others point to institutional decay.[36] There is a great deal of evidence supporting these arguments. The mobilization of Tamil, Kashmiri, Assamese, Naga, and Baluch nationalism occurred around the themes of oppression, exploitation, and loss of autonomy. Several have therefore endorsed the solution of consociational democracies to distribute power and office proportionally among competing ethnic groups.[37] Others, however, point to the danger of disintegration via ethnic self-determination. Examples of the Soviet Union, Yugoslavia, and Afghanistan are often cited to show how privileging ethnicity can lead to violence, chaos, and collapse. Choices of strategy to contain or settle conflict depend largely on how one perceives the conflict, its causes, and the mechanisms required to contain or settle them.

A majority of realist and neorealist perspectives define conflicts mainly as conflicts between states. A state is assumed to be a self-interested, rational, unitary entity that engages in conflict or cooperation because of external compulsions, such as anarchy, power distribution, and the presence or absence of factors that inhibit or exonerate the conflictual consequences of international anarchy.[38] Critics of neorealism, however, argue that this is essentially a Eurocentric perspective and is, for that reason, limited in its ability to explain ethnic conflicts in the Third World. If we concretize this criticism in the context of South Asia, we might ask if the India–Pakistan conflict is entirely a result of asymmetrical distribution of power between them. Why did India not move to partition Pakistan before 1971 when it had a military advantage in

East Pakistan? Why did India withdraw from Sri Lanka, and why might it again intervene should the Tamil-Sinhala conflict escalate to envelope Tamil Nadu? Is distribution of power and international anarchy a sufficient explanation for these anomalies? As we have seen in the foregoing pages, India and Pakistan are not fully consolidated nation-states. The process of state formation in each shapes their national-interest agenda. Similarly, their regime types—democratic, quasidemocratic authoritarian—have profound implications for the prospects of war and negotiations between them. Similarly, the neorealists are likely to explain the war and collapse in Afghanistan in at least two ways: as a result of the Cold War competition (international anarchy) during the 1980s and the jockeying for influence among the regional states after 1992. As argued in a previous section, such an explanation is both insufficient and misleading. Afghanistan's collapse cannot be understood separately from its ethnic divide. One could debate whether its ethnic divisions are primordial or instrumental. We still need to explain how Afghanistan became an arena of proxy wars waged by foreign intelligence agencies, such as the Inter-Services Intelligence and the Central Intelligence Agency, and regional political leaders, such as Nawaz Sharif and Musharraf. Nor is the story of collapse and chaos complete without explaining how Afghanistan and Kashmir became issues in the domestic struggle for power in Pakistan. A perspective that ignores the nature of the state and its internal dimensions fails to explain adequately the wars and violence in South Asia. Reversing the argument of anarchy, Steven David suggests that it might be more accurate to "assume a world of international order and domestic anarchy" in explaining wars and violence in the Third World.[39] While realism and neorealism have yet to collapse the bifurcation of the internal and external factors into a theoretically empowering framework, the other genre of international-relations theories, economic underdevelopment and dependency theory, ignores issues of war within and between Third World states.

How do we then construct a broad conceptual frame that will link domestic to international dimensions and accommodate the peculiarities of ethnic conflicts in South Asia? First, we need to understand the nature of relationships between the South Asian state and its ethnic groups and nationalities. Since their inception, states in South Asia have sought to achieve coherence and territorial unity. Their failures and successes in this regard can provide clues to at least three sets of key questions: What accounts for failures and what convergence of factors produced the successes? What kind of operational mechanisms has the state evolved? What capacity does the state have to learn from its failures? In other words, can it alter the operational logic that underlies the mechanism of integration? Second, we need to analyze the internal political and economic conditions of the ethnic community. Is it unified? Is it diasporic or territorial, dispersed or concentrated in what it considers a homeland? What are its grievances? A third set of questions must deal with the impact of ethnic conflict on reordering a state's international objectives (i.e., security, development, and legitimacy).

I have constructed such a conceptual frame for analyzing India's regional policy and found that conventional analysis of India's role in the region has focused too much on the external pressures on foreign policy making. India's relations with South Asian states, its insistence on bilateralism and desire for preeminence in the region, is explained in large part by the lack of congruence between the boundaries of the Indian state and its ethnic nations. India seeks relational control, that is, the ability to structure interstate relations so as to insulate itself from the fall out from overlapping ethnic conflicts in the region. The ultimate purpose of relational control is internal, namely, building a consolidated modern nation-state. Given India's enormous diversity, this task can be accomplished only within a democratic framework. But democracy is not a panacea for ethnic conflict.[40] The decades since independence show that party competition and electoral logic in fact exacerbated ethnic polarization. Darini Rajasingham-Senanayake comes to a similar conclusion about Sri Lanka's ethnic conflict.[41] It is then not enough to define India as a developing democracy, assume its state to be unified, and move on to analyzing India's international relations in terms of the balance of regional power. We need to factor in the failures of ethnic integration within India's democracy.

These failures point to the second paradox that challenges conventional wisdom. Ethnic diversity suggests decentralization as a solution, but my analysis of India's ethnic relations shows decentralization alone will not resolve ethnic conflict, especially when the central state's capacity to diffuse, negotiate, and contain conflicts is declining. The debates about centralization and decentralization that have so preoccupied India scholars are largely misleading. Abdication of the central government's role in negotiations and, hence, power to punish or reward ethnic parties did not make for a quick solution. We need to separate the quantum of power defined as an ability to successfully negotiate conflicts and to centralize decision making. These are conversely related. Critics of Indira Gandhi's government are not wrong in pointing to centralization as the cause of ethnic conflict, but they are wrong in arguing that centralization is a sign of a muscular and strong Indian state. The rise of authoritarian tendencies at the center can reflect the weakening, not strengthening, of the state. The study of ethnic conflicts in India shows that the state cannot delegate power and abandon the task of building consensus to ethnic communities. It needs to stay in the process and use its power (to punish and reward) to forge an agreement. Ethnic differences need to be resolved before they transgress international boundaries. South Asian states have a poor record of ethnic accommodation, although arguably India has done better than most other states in institutionalizing ethnic accommodation. What is important for the purpose of international-relations theory is the presence or absence of such domestic accommodations as they shape the state and its relations with overlapping ethnic communities. To build a predictive and prescriptive model of international relations in South Asia, we need to take into account domestic compulsions, particularly those that arise from the evolution and spread of ethnic conflicts.

The comparative experiences within the region suggest that ethnic accommodation is a key to building democracy and forging a viable nation-state. If the Kashmiris had been content to live within India, Pakistan would have had a hard time fomenting separatism. In this sense, India's failure in Kashmir is the failure of the Indian state to accommodate its ethnic nationalities. Pakistan's drift into military rule is partly a consequence of failing to build just such a mechanism for ethnic integration. Sri Lanka needs similarly to provide autonomy and political self-rule to its large Tamil minority, but that can be done only within some form of a federal democracy with self-rule for the Sri Lankan Tamils. For Afghanistan the process of national consolidation will require establishing conditions that will prevent fragmentation and ethnic wars, but that also means setting up political institutions that are ethnically neutral. Current international theories do not therefore adequately capture the origin or nature of conflicts in South Asia. For that, we need a theory sensitive to the domestic and international problems created by the diverse nationalities of the subcontinent.

NOTES

1. T. V. Paul and John Hall, eds., *International Order and the Future of World Politics* (Cambridge: Cambridge University Press, 1999), chapters 13 and 14.

2. Barry Posen, "The Security Dilemma and Ethnic Conflict," *Survival* 35, no. 1 (Spring 1993); I. William Zartman, "Introduction: Posing the Problem of State Collapse," *Collapsed States: The Disintegration and Restoration of Legitimate Authority* (Boulder, Colo.: Lynne Rienner, 1995), 1.

3. Thomas Kuhn argues for a fundamental distinction between normal and extraordinary events. In the latter, all rules of social life are violated. See *The Structure of Scientific Revolutions* (Chicago: University of Chicago Press, 1962).

4. A short list will consist of C. H. Phillips and M. D. Wainwright, eds., *The Partition of India, Politics and Perspectives, 1935–47* (London: Allen and Unwin, 1970); W. H. Morris-Jones, "The Transfer of Power: A View from the Sidelines," *Modern Asian Studies* 16, no. 1 (1982): 1–32; C. M. Ali, *The Emergence of Pakistan* (New York: Columbia University Press, 1967); R. J. Moor, "Towards Partition and Independence in India," *Journal of Commonwealth and Comparative Politics* 20, no. 2 (July 1983): 189–99; A. Roy, "The High Politics of India's Partition: The Revisionist Perspective," *Modern Asian Studies* 24, no. 2 (1990): 385–415.

5. Tai Young Tan and Gyanesh Kudaisya, *The Aftermath of Partition in South Asia* (London: Routledge, 2002), 9–28.

6. Tan and Kudaisya, *Aftermath*, 8.

7. Maya Chadda, *Ethnicity, Security and Separatism in India* (New York: Columbia University Press, 1997), 49–77.

8. Iftikhar Malik, *State and Civil Society in Pakistan* (London: Macmillan Press, 1997); Maya Chadda, "Pakistan's Road to Military Dictatorship," in *Ethnicity and Polity in South Asia*, ed. Giri Phukon (New Delhi: South Asia Publishers, 2002), 35–58.

9. Chadda, *Ethnicity, Security*, 84–97; Richard Sisson, *War and Secession: Pakistan, India and the Creation of Bangladesh* (Berkeley: University of California Press, 1990).

10. M. Rashiduzzamn, "The Awami League in Political Development of Pakistan," *Asian Survey* 10, no. 7 (July 1990): 574–87.

11. Anthony Mascarenhas, *The Rape of Bangladesh* (New Delhi: Vikas Publications, 1972).

12. Rajat Ganguly, *Kin State Intervention in Ethnic Conflicts* (New Delhi: Sage Publications, 1998), 123–24.

13. Maya Chadda, *Ethnicity, Security*, 97.

14. Larry Goodson, *Afghanistan's Endless War* (Seattle: University of Washington Press, 2001).

15. Amin Saikal, "The Rabbani Government 1992–1996," in *Fundamentalism Reborn? Afghanistan and the Taliban*, ed. William Maley (New York University Press, 1998), 37.

16. Ahmed Rashid, "Pakistan and the Taliban," in *Fundamentalism Reborn?* 85–89.

17. For a detailed analysis of how Pakistan's Taliban strategy emerged from domestic imperatives, see Maya Chadda, "Talibanization of Pakistan's Afghan Policy," *World Affairs* 3, no. 3 (July–September 1999): 98–116.

18. For the evolution of these movements see Rajiv Kapur, *Sikh Separatism: The Politics of Faith* (London: Allen and Unwin, 1986); Al Sinha, *Bhutan: Ethnic Identity and National Dilemma* (New Delhi: Reliance Publication House, 1991); Jaswant Singh, "Assam's Errors," *Asian Survey* 24, no. 10 (October 1984): 1,056–68; Amena Mohsin, *The Politics of Nationalism: The Case of Chittagong Hill Tracts, Bangladesh* (Dhaka: The University Press Ltd, 1997); Subir Bhaumik, *Insurgent Crossfire: Northeast India* (New Delhi: Lancer Publishers, 1996).

19. Selig Harrison, *In Afghanistan's Shadow: Baluch Nationalism and Soviet Temptation* (New York: Carnegie Endowment for International Peace, 1981); Robert Wirsing, "South Asia: The Baluch Frontier Tribes of Pakistan," in *Protection of Ethnic Minorities: Comparative Perspective*, ed. Robert Wirsing (New York: Pergamon, 1981).

20. Ganguly, *Kin State Intervention*, 154–55.

21. Sanjib Baruah, "Generals as Governors," in *Ethnicity and Polity in South Asia*, 191.

22. Yogendra Malik, "The Akali Party and Sikh Militancy: Move for Greater Autonomy or Secession in Punjab," *Asian Survey* 26, no. 3 (March 1996): 345–62; Sanjib Baruah, *India against Itself: Assam and Politics of Nationality* (Philadelphia: University of Pennsylvania Press, 1999), 144–72.

23. Partha Ghosh, "Ethnic Conflict and Conflict Management," in *Ethnicity and Constitutional Reform in South Asia*, ed. Iftekharuzzamn (New Delhi: Manohar, 1998), 49–84.

24. Atul Kohli, "Can Democracy Accommodate Ethnic Nationalism? The rise and Decline of Self-Determination Movements in India," *Journal of Asian Studies* 56, no. 2 (May 1997): 326.

25. Sanjib Baruah, "Generals as Governors," in *Ethnicity and Polity in South Asia*, 188–89.

26. Maya Chadda, *Ethnicity, Security*, 123–39.

27. Wasbir Hussain, "Northeast Polls: Bullets and Ballots," *South Asia Intelligence Review, Weekly Assessment and Briefings*, 1, no. 32 (February 24,2003), available at www.satp.org.

28. On November 3, 1988, at the request of President Gayoom, India sent its forces to help foil a coup attempt by Sri Lankan mercenaries in the Maldives, but this was not of the same order as the Sri Lanka intervention.

29. S. D. Muni, *Pangs of Proximity: India and Sri Lanka's Ethnic Crisis* (New Delhi: Sage Publications, 1993); Dayan Jeyatileka, *Sri Lanka: Travails of a Democracy: Unfinished War, Protracted Crisis* (New Delhi: Vikas, 1995); Robert Oberst, "Federalism and Ethnic Conflict in Sri Lanka," *Publius* 18 (Summer 1988): 175–94; Wilson Jeyaratnam, *The Break Up of Sri Lanka: The Sinhalese Tamil Conflict* (London: C. Hurst 1988); S. Ponnampalam, *Sri Lanka: The National Question and Tamil Liberation Struggle* (London: Zed Books,1983); David Little, *Sri Lanka: The Invention of Ethnicity* (Washington, D.C.: United Institute of Peace Press, 1994).

30. Salamat Ali, "The Dravidian Factor," *Far Eastern Economic Review* (February 4, 1988): 20.

31. Maya Chadda, *Ethnicity, Security*, 153.

32. Maya Chadda, *Ethnicity, Security*, 145–74.

33. "Norway Opens Sri Lanka Talks," *BBC News*, January 10, 2002, available at http://news.bbc.co.uk/1/w/world/south asia/1753534.stm (accessed March 6, 2003).

34. For the primordialist view see Walker Connor, "Nation-Building or Nation Destroying," *World Politics* 24, no. 3 (April 1972): 319–55; Cynthia Enloe, *Ethnic Conflict and Political Development* (Boston: Little Brown, 1973); Anthony Smith, *The Ethnic Origins of Nations* (Oxford: Blackwell, 1986). For the instrumentalist view, see David Lake and Donald Rothchild, "Spreading Fear: The Genesis of Transnational Ethnic Conflict," in *The International Spread of Ethnic Conflict: Fear Diffusion and Escalation*, ed. Lake and Rothchild (Princeton, N.J.: Princeton University Press, 1998), 5.

35. Sudipta Kaviraj, "Religion, Politics and Modernity," in *Crisis and Change in Contemporary India*, ed. Bhiku Parekh and Upendra Baxi (New Delhi: Sage Publications, 1996), 30.

36. Atul Kohli, "Interpreting India's Democracy," *India's Democracy: An Analysis of Changing State-Society Relations*, ed. Atul Kohli (Princeton, N.J.: Princeton University Press, 1988), 16.

37. Arend Lijphart, *Democracy in Plural Societies: A Comparative Explanation* (New Heaven, Conn.: Yale University Press, 1977); E. A. Nordlinger, *Conflict Regulation in Divided Societies* (Cambridge, Mass.: Harvard Center for International Affairs, 1972).

38. Stephanie Neuman, ed., *International Relations Theory and the Third World* (New York: St. Martin's Press, 1998), 1–31.

39. Steven David, "The Primacy of Internal Wars," in *International Relations Theory and the Third World*, 78.

40. Maya Chadda, *Ethnicity, Security*, 1–26.

41. Darini Rajasingham-Senanayake, "Democracy and the Problem of Representation: The Making of Bi-Polar Ethnic Identity in Post-Colonial Sri Lanka," in *Ethnic Futures: The State and Identity in Asia*, ed. Joanne Pfaff-Czarnecka et al. (New Delhi: Sage Publications, 1999), 99–135.

FURTHER READING

Ali, Mahmud S. *The Fearful State: Power, People and Internal War in South Asia*. London: Zed Books, 1993.

Basu, Amrita, and Atul Kohli, eds. *Community Conflict and State in India*. New Delhi: Oxford University Press, 1998.

Brass, Paul. *Ethnicity and Nationalism: Theory and Comparison*. New Delhi: Sage, 1991.

Chadda, Maya. *Ethnicity, Security, and Separatism in India*. New York: Columbia University Press, 1997.

———. *Building Democracy in South Asia: India, Pakistan and Nepal*. Boulder, Colo.: Lynne Rienner, 2000.

Ganguly, Sumit. *The Crisis in Kashmir: Portents of War, Hopes of Peace*. Cambridge, U.K.:
    Cambridge University Press, 1997.
Gurr, Ted R. *Minorities at Risk: A Global View of Ethnopolitical Conflicts*. Washington, D.C.:
    United States Institute of Peace Press, 1993.
Hazarika, Sanjoy. *Strangers of the Mist: Tales of War and Peace from India's Northeast*. New
    Delhi: Viking, 1994.
Kapur, Rajiv. *Sikh Separatism: The Politics of Faith*. London: Allen Unwin, 1986.
Mitra, Subrata, and Alison Lewis, eds. *Subnational Movements in South Asia*. Boulder, Colo.:
    Westview Press, 1996.
Phadnis, Urmila. *Ethnicity and Nation-Building in South Asia*. New Delhi: Sage, 1989.
Taras, Raymond, and Rajat Ganguly. *Understanding Ethnic Conflict: The International Dimen-
    sion*. New York: Longman, 2002.

9

Religion and Politics

David Taylor

Why is religion such a problem for the countries of South Asia? In the decade or so leading up to 2005, there have been major clashes on the streets of many Indian towns and cities in which people have been brutally killed simply for belonging to the "wrong" religious community, and certain members of the leading party in the ruling coalition in Delhi, the Bharatiya Janata Party (BJP) or of its ally, the Shiv Sena, have been complicit in attacks on religious minorities, such as those that erupted in Gujarat in the first few months of 2002.[1] In Pakistan and Bangladesh, clashes over the extent to which Islamic injunctions on issues of blasphemy or sexual morality should be enforced by the state have led to fierce political battles and to the victimization of individuals, very often women or members of small and vulnerable religious minorities.

The implications of these conflicts for South Asian states in the global context are very significant. First of all, there is the question of perception. Despite the postmodern turn in the academy, Western imaginings of societies in South Asia as somehow defined and determined by religion appear to be reinforced by the images that constantly emerge from the region and are distributed through the global media. Second, decisions on matters such as investment and trade relations reflect these perceptions so that the region as a whole and individual countries, such as Pakistan in particular, risk being ignored in the globalization of the world economy that is currently taking place. Third, internal differences within the region, expressed in some respects in terms of religious difference, most notably between India and Pakistan, inhibit the ability of South Asia as a whole to make its full contribution to global affairs. India, currently the world's second most populous country and at some point in the next half-century the world's largest, is still without a permanent seat on the UN Security Council, in large part because of external perception.

Conflict between adherents of different religious traditions in South Asia is often referred to within the region as communal conflict, and this term brings out the inherently social and political context within which it takes place. Religious belief, in the conventional sense, plays only a limited role, and indeed some of those most heavily involved in communal violence may be people with little religious sensibility. It is equally important to note that communal conflict is a relatively recent phenomenon, dating back to the second half of the nineteenth century.[2] Different religious groups or communities have lived together in South Asia for many centuries in social and economic interdependence (although often in some sort of hierarchical relationship). What is critical, therefore, is the way that the notion of community has changed radically in the region over the last two hundred years, first under the impact of colonialism and second in response to the compulsions of political competition under conditions of universal franchise.

This chapter begins by setting out some general considerations about religion and society and the way their interrelationship changed during the colonial period. It then discusses the experiences of the three largest South Asian countries, India, Pakistan, and Bangladesh, since they achieved independence in 1947 (with Bangladesh separating from Pakistan in 1971) to demonstrate the complex interaction of religion and politics within the domestic, regional, and international spheres.[3]

THE COLONIAL PERIOD

Like all premodern societies, South Asia had seen no sharp dividing lines between religion, social structure, and political power. While this was seen in the past as a recipe for stasis and fatalism, in fact the evidence shows that men and women have always had some scope for making conscious choices both in religious and social matters, even if the power structures have restricted the means by which they can be expressed. One important way, in fact, of approaching South Asian history over the very long term is to study the ebb and flow of religious reform movements and to link them to political and social change in the same period. The political rise of Buddhism in the third century BCE, the penetration of Islam into many parts of the subcontinent, not by forced conversion but by the actions and examples of Sufi saints, the devotional sects within Hinduism at different times, and the growth of a distinct Sikh community in the eighteenth and nineteenth centuries are all examples of ways in which social and religious change were interconnected.[4] Changes in the way local communities of farmers or artisans chose to articulate their religious beliefs were linked, on the one hand, to changes in the political balance at the regional level and, on the other, to the continual revitalization of regional religious traditions through charismatic preachers or holy men.[5]

It is significant that throughout the subcontinent the hierarchical social ranking implicit in the Hindu caste system was capable of embracing groups that were not in the religious sense Hindu. Even in areas where Muslims were in a majority, such as the western parts of the Punjab, social institutions developed that had close parallels to caste. The *biradari*, or brotherhood, was, like the individual caste, generally an endogamous group and acted collectively to defend and advance its members' interests. Rulers such as the Mughals recognized these blurred lines and made use of them in their strategies of government.

During the colonial period, the British rulers adopted a policy, subject always to the needs of imperial power, that recognized the rights of the individual, for example in the courts or in some cases as a voter, but which simultaneously embedded that individual, whether he or she liked it or not, in a web of prescriptive identities, the most important of which were religious community and caste (or in some areas, tribe). Whether it was in the decennial census forms that had to be completed from the late nineteenth century or in legislation about who was entitled to hold agricultural land or in the writings of colonial administrators, the assumption was made that individuals acquired a large part of their social identity from the primordial group into which they had been born. Much scholarly work was undertaken by colonial officials, Christian missionaries, and others to delineate the minutest details of such identities through works on individual castes and tribes.[6] Despite the recognition of the rights of the individual in some areas, the direction of colonial policy was very strongly to emphasise a coincidence between the different aspects of an individual's social being. In the language of Sudipta Kaviraj, the fuzzy identities that had characterized the precolonial period were replaced by enumerated identities.[7] The political implications of the British analysis were clear: India could never form a united society, and imperial rule, recognizing the due rights of all the groups, was valid and legitimate.

Although the process described above was dominated by colonial concerns and perspectives, countermovements began to assert a single identity for all Hindus or all Muslims. Among Hindus, Swami Vivekananda in Bengal stands out for his ability to inspire young men to spread the universal message of Hinduism, as does Swami Dayanand Saraswati in Punjab, who preached a message of Hindu solidarity in the face of perceived challenges from Christianity and Islam alike.[8] Among Muslim communities Syed Amir Ali wrote about the glorious history of Islam, while in several different parts of the country, Muslim reform movements, such as the one based around the seminary in the town of Deoband, preached the importance of purifying Islam of its local accretions.[9] Ironically, the assumptions about identity that underlay these movements were often derived from colonial models, even as they strove to reject the colonial presence.

The assumptions that the British had made about Indian society provided some basis for government and political activity. Entitlements to land, for example, were linked to caste status in the Punjab, while certain low-status seminomadic groups were collectively identified as "criminal tribes," subject to special regulation.[10] The census process itself brought into existence large numbers of groups claiming separate recognition for themselves, while from the beginning of the twentieth century, political organizations such as the Hindu Mahasabha and the Muslim League began to lobby for the interests of their constituents and to do so within the framework that the British had created. Some of their demands had to do with access to government-controlled resources, jobs in particular, while others were symbolic, for example claims to disputed religious sites. In the 1920s determined efforts were made to claim additional converts or to reclaim those who had earlier shifted from Hinduism to Islam. At the same time local clashes between members of the main communities became more common, mainly in the larger cities. In the light of the hardening of identities described above, these clashes were generally described as communal, although responsibility for their occurrence was hotly disputed.

The Indian National Congress, led and inspired by Mahatma Gandhi, tried hard to find inclusive ways of representing the nation, but it was difficult to achieve this on a reliable basis. Gandhi himself, whose strength came from his ability to move from one political idiom to another while remaining firmly rooted in his personal Hindu identity, attempted to reach out on a basis of equality to all sections of the population but had only limited success. His message was rejected not only by many Muslims but among Hindus by significant sections of the lowest caste groups, the so-called Untouchables, whose leader B. R. Ambedkar accused Gandhi of trying to deprive them of the right to independent action and who eventually in the 1950s led many of his followers out of Hinduism into the Buddhist faith.[11] In 1925 a representative from the opposite end of the caste hierarchy, K. B. Hedgewar, who felt that Congress under Gandhi's leadership did not recognize the importance of the Brahminical core of Hinduism, founded the Rashtriya Swayamsevak Sangh (RSS), an organization devoted to recruiting young boys and offering them physical training alongside indoctrination in the RSS view of India.

With the decision of the British in the early 1930s to cede some local power to elected governments, then the pressure during World War II to announce its intention to grant full independence, the use of "community" for political advantage became overwhelming. The Muslim League under the leadership of Muhammad Ali Jinnah, a successful lawyer and at one time an advocate of joint political action between the Congress and the League to achieve independence, articulated the two-nation theory, in which Islam was seen as the basis of a fundamentally different way of life from Hinduism. This in turn authorized a claim for a separate state.[12] From 1940 on, when this goal was adopted as official Muslim League policy, Jinnah waged a highly effective campaign to bring most of the other Muslim leadership groups under the wing of the Muslim League and then in 1946 to conduct an election campaign on the slogan, "Islam in danger." With help from some, but by no means all, of the religious leaders of the community, the established Muslim political leaderships of the various provinces, reinforced by a new generation of enthusiasts for the cause, achieved a sweeping victory in most parts of the country (the sole major exception was the Northwest Frontier Province [NWFP]). The Congress achieved a similar degree of success in the "general" constituencies,[13] and for the next few months the three-way negotiations between the outgoing British and the two main political blocs made little progress. On the streets, however, the level of communal violence began to rise alarmingly. A new viceroy, Lord Mountbatten, who arrived in February 1947, made the decision shortly after he arrived that partition as demanded by the Muslim League was an inevitable accompaniment of independence.

The months that followed Mountbatten's announcement of partition in June saw an eruption of communal violence in which hundreds of thousands of people on both sides lost their lives and in which millions became refugees. The position was especially bad in the Punjab, where there was a virtually complete expulsion of Hindus and Sikhs from the Muslim-dominated areas and vice versa. The position in Delhi and other parts of North India was hardly any better. At the same time, the two new states quickly came to blows over the fate of the princely state of Jammu and Kashmir, a Muslim-majority area ruled by a Hindu dynasty. Whether, given the constraints of the colonial period, a political formula could have been found that preserved the unity of India while giving all religious groups a proportionate share of power and resources is problematic. Comparative experience in other multiconfessional situations suggest that ultimately such power-sharing formulae tend to fall apart and that tensions between religious communities, as in the Balkans, tend to survive state-imposed attempts to reduce them to the purely private sphere or to eliminate them altogether in favor of secular identities.

INDIA SINCE 1947

Although British India was partitioned in 1947 into two successor states, the Republic of India was able to claim continuity with the British Raj. This included the ambiguous legacy of a government that claimed to be impartial while ruling over a people defined in terms of multiple religious communities.

Jawaharlal Nehru, the first prime minister, made a conscious decision to break from this by moving toward a model of secularism in which the spheres of religion and of social and political life were decisively separated and the institutions of democratic participation were open to all citizens equally. In Nehru's view, a state that could achieve rapid economic development and a massive improvement in the living standards of the poor would at the same time have removed the conditions in which religious identifications were relevant for political action. Economic and social development, including the development of national consciousness, had to take place in parallel, with the state acting as benevolent mentor and facilitator. In the mid-1950s, for example, Nehru introduced major reforms to personal law, including the abolition of polygamy, the possibility of divorce, and greater freedom for individuals to will their property. But ironically, the scope of the reforms had to be restricted to the Hindu population, as short-term political considerations, namely, the risk of losing the electoral support of prominent, but socially conservative, Muslim leaders, led to the exclusion of the Muslim minority, despite the injunction in the Indian constitution, which had had Nehru's full backing, to move toward a uniform system of personal law for all Indian citizens.

Until Nehru's death in 1964, and for some time thereafter, the official discourse on secularism appeared to be gaining some ground. In particular, once the immediate partition violence was over, there were no major clashes until a riot in Ahmedabad in 1969, which cost nearly a thousand lives. The institutions of Indian democracy appeared to be able to accommodate a variety of group interests and religious identifications without allowing any one of them to dominate. The diversity of India, in which no individual group could dominate and in which broad class interests linked otherwise divergent sections, seemed to be a guarantor of a broadly secular democracy. In fact, the Gandhian approach to secularism, in which the state was expected to give equal respect to all religions rather than to ignore religion, was just as important as the Nehruvian in providing its underpinnings.[14] What could not be achieved under colonial conditions could be achieved in a state of freedom.

Political developments in the Punjab, for example, gave weight to theories that argued that allowing space for the articulation of group interest but laying down certain ground rules would lead to the blurring of lines and to the re-creation of the fuzzy identities mentioned above. The part of Punjab that had remained in India had been characterized immediately after independence by sharp conflicts between different groups, one of whose characteristics was religious difference. The demand for a reconstituted state that was forcefully articulated in the 1950s, although expressed in linguistic terms, could easily, and in some respects correctly, be construed as a Hindu-Sikh conflict. Initially the Congress had aimed at a political coalition representing all religious groups in the state, but by a series of steps and manoeuvres it eventually permitted in 1966 the division of Punjab into two states, one a truncated Punjab with a Sikh majority and the other the new state of Haryana, which was predominantly Hindu. This was achieved without major violence and with the apparent end to demands for secession.

Two aspects of the Punjab case need to be emphasized. First, the Sikhs who had taken the lead in the demand for Punjabi statehood were predominantly rural farmers from one particular caste group. Although there were no doubt cultural motives in their demand for separation, there were equally powerful economic interests at work. The post-1966 success of the Green Revolution in Punjab undoubtedly owes much to this fact. Second, although the Sikh-based Akali Dal Party has always made much of its special association with the achievement of separation, the Congress and, indeed, other parties have also been able to maintain their strength in the Punjab. Governments in the state are typically coalitions between one or another element of the Akali Dal and one of the national parties.[15]

In contrast to the picture sketched above, the last quarter-century in India has seen a much more explicit expression of religion in public life. Two major examples are presented here. In the Punjab itself, the balance described above was upset at the end of the 1970s by the rise of a movement led by a Sikh preacher called Jarnail Singh Bhindranwale. Using targeted assassinations of Hindu and Sikh opponents, he led a demand for Khalistan, an independent or autonomous region within South Asia, where Sikhs would hold power and Sikhism would set the dominant values. After a series of clashes with the government, he eventually took refuge in the Golden Temple in Amritsar, from where he directed further militant actions. In June 1984 Indira Gandhi, who had succeeded her father Jawaharlal Nehru as prime minister in 1966 (except for a brief interlude from 1977 to 1980), sent the Indian army in to take control of the temple. In the ensuing battle, Bhindranwale and some hundreds of his followers were killed. On October 31 of the same year, Mrs. Gandhi was assassinated by two Sikhs from her personal protection group, and in the following week large-scale rioting broke out in Delhi in which up to two thousand Sikhs were massacred.[16]

At around the same time, the position of the Muslim minority in India became much more problematic. Partition had led to large-scale movements of population, especially in the Punjab, and to a very substantial movement of businessmen, professionals, and senior government officials and army officers from across the whole of India. What was left behind was a demoralized community, with a proportionately much smaller middle and professional class than the majority community. For many years it chose to trade its electoral support for a measure of protection and symbolic representation. In practice, this meant supporting the Congress. Yet, even within the Congress, and certainly outside it, there were political leaders who deeply distrusted the

Muslims and doubted their commitment to the Indian state. Pakistan's constant campaign to gain control of the state of Kashmir was proof in their eyes that Indian Muslims were potential fifth columnists.

Building on themes and organizations that had existed from the late nineteenth century, certain political parties had constructed narratives of Indian history in which the Muslim was always cast as the invader and enemy of true Indian (*Bharatiya*) culture. The most prominent of these was the Bharatiya Jana Sangh, founded in 1951. In so doing it had the ideological and organizational support of the RSS. Until the 1970s the Jana Sangh had enjoyed some support in the Hindi-speaking northern states of the country, especially among the Hindu refugees who had been forced to migrate from Pakistan. But beyond inclusion in coalition governments at state level, it had never come close to power nationally. At the end of the 1970s, it was included in the non-Congress government formed after Mrs. Gandhi's electoral defeat in 1977. The party's defeat in the 1980 election led it to regroup under a new name, the BJP, and briefly to experiment with a politics of class interest, attempting to create a coalition of farmers and small businessmen. However, the failure of this tactic led to a reconsideration of its strategy. Under the leadership of Lal Krishna Advani (at the time of writing, India's home minister), the party linked hands with the RSS and its daughter organization, the Vishwa Hindu Parishad (VHP) to launch a nationwide campaign around the theme of *Hindutva* (approximately translated as Hinduness). *Hindutva*, according to its advocates, was an inclusive umbrella under which all those who recognized India as their homeland could find shelter. The only groups that were excluded were those with alleged foreign connections, that is, Muslims and Christians.[17]

The themes around which the BJP and VHP were able to mobilize support in the 1980s were in some respects presented to them by the Congress itself. In 1985, for example, a court case over an issue of Muslim divorce law and a subsequent attempt by the Congress to pass legislation to gain support among some Muslim groups allowed the BJP and VHP to raise the issue of a uniform civil code for all Indian citizens. Crude stereotypes of Muslims were propagated; for example, the allegation was made that they recklessly had large families so as to increase their proportion of the population. Above all, however, the main focus of the BJP and VHP's joint campaign during the late 1980s was a smouldering dispute over control of a sacred site at Ayodhya in northern India, where a mosque, the Babri Masjid, was built on what some Hindus believed was the site of the birthplace of Lord Ram, one of the incarnations of Vishnu. The Congress had attempted to gain some mileage out of the same issue but had easily been outplayed by their opponents. The conflict over the mosque played itself out over several years until a VHP-led mob stormed the building in December 1992 and demolished it by hand. The act was followed by communal riots in a number of cities in which the victims were largely Muslim. The worst such event occurred in Bombay (now Mumbai) in January the following year. With the active connivance of the state government, a local ally of the BJP, thousands of Muslims were massacred.

The BJP did not make immediate electoral gains from the demolition of the mosque; in fact, they lost ground among some sections of the population otherwise sympathetic to their emphasis on the Hindu basis of Indian culture. By 1998, however, the BJP was in power at the national level (and in a number of states) as the dominant partner in a coalition government and has remained so under Atal Behari Vajpayee's leadership to the time of this writing. It would be wrong, however, to link this success directly to the communal mobilization that took place during the 1980s and early 1990s. The BJP more accurately can stay in power only if it does not follow the logic of its earlier actions. Thus, the commitment to build a temple on the site of the mosque has yet to be fulfilled, with the Indian courts being used as a means of staving off a decision. At a more general level, rather than harping on a narrow *Hindutva* agenda, the government has tried to emphasize its economic policies, which have begun to bear fruit for some sections of the electorate, as well as its success in raising India's international profile as a mature member of the international community.

Since 1998 it has been difficult to assess precisely the direction in which the electorate has moved and the way the political parties have interpreted the popular mood. Elements within the BJP have encouraged continuing campaigns by the VHP to build a temple at Ayodhya, even though officially the policy appeared to be to allow the status quo to persist. On February 27, 2002, a group of VHP members returning by train from a demonstration at Ayodhya were attacked at a station in Gujarat with many deaths and injuries. This attack was very probably the result of action by a group of Muslims.[18] Its aftermath was a sustained pogrom against the Muslim population of the state in which a thousand or more were killed and in which there was clear evidence of the direct involvement of the state chief minister and the state apparatus. Although the chief minister was eventually forced to resign, the resultant elections at the end of the year brought the BJP back to power with an increased majority, demonstrating the popular support in some quarters for a purely communal appeal to anti-Muslim sentiment.

But although there were important elements in the BJP outside Gujarat who shared the same strong anti-Muslim elements, the emphasis of central government policy and of the prime minister personally was to continue its broad-based, economically focused policies. Linked to this have been Prime Minister Atal Behari Vajpayee's efforts to secure an improvement in Indo-Pakistani relations with a view to a final settlement of the Kashmir dispute.

As the general election scheduled for 2004 approached, the BJP's strategy was evidently to send a dual message: that it understood the feelings of the Hindu majority but that it wanted to limit the role of the state to sympathetic encouragement while pursuing a vigorous agenda of economic and social development.

A significant dimension of recent developments in India (as elsewhere in South Asia) has been the role of the diaspora. Emigrants from India who have settled in North America and Europe and have often done very well economically have at the same time had to face issues of discrimination and exclusion in their new countries of residence, as well as more personal issues of identity. Responses to these dilemmas have been very diverse, but for some people transnational identities and networks that link them back to their regions of origin have been very important. Untempered by the constant interaction of different spheres of life, which make up the political world within the region, people in the diaspora have often given moral and material support to exclusivist movements "at home." In both the cases outlined above, this has clearly been the case. Supporters of the Khalistan movement in Britain and North America sent material and moral aid to the militant groups in the Punjab. So, too, did many Hindu groups in the same countries support the campaign to build a temple at Ayodhya. The leaders in India readily received this support, and they made regular trips abroad to enhance the flow. As well as providing bilateral support to their fellows in India, members of the diaspora acted as lobbies for Sikh and Hindu nationalism in their countries of adoption, often translating the issues at stake into idioms that made sense in local political discourse.[19]

PAKISTAN SINCE 1947

Pakistan is the country of South Asia where over an extended period of time religion appears to have played the highest-profile role, but the situation is a great deal more complicated than it might appear at first sight. The leaders of the movement for the creation of a separate Muslim state adopted, by and large, a modernist view of religion, which sat easily enough with a secular state.[20] Many (although not all) of the religious leaders of the community in the years before 1947 had, by contrast, been opposed to the idea of Pakistan, in part precisely because it meant the ascendancy of men like Jinnah. More recently, the so-called religious parties, the three most important of which are aligned, broadly speaking, with different sectarian traditions within South Asian Islam, have not been able to win more than a small fraction of the total votes cast in a general election. Even in October 2002, when the parties came together on a common platform and were able to appeal to anti-Western sentiment expressed in terms of religious conflict (Muslims under threat from a Christian- and Jewish-dominated United States), they only won 11 percent of the vote and forty-five seats in the National Assembly. Today, Pakistan is stalemated as far as religion and politics are concerned. While, as indicated above, religious parties are unlikely ever to win a majority of the popular vote, they can obstruct change in critical areas such as gender equity. This power of veto can extend beyond the social to the key area of relationships with India and the question of Kashmir.

Although there had been opposition from religious leaders to the creation of Pakistan, once it was an accomplished fact, they began to see the new state as an opportunity to pursue their own specific agendas. Political parties were formed with close links to particular religious tendencies, notably the Jamaat-i-Islami, founded by Maulana Abul Maududi. In 1953 the Jamaat led a major agitation aimed at the small Ahmadi sect. Members of this group had elevated their own founder, Mirza Ghulam Ahmad, to a position close to that of the prophet and were thus accused of rejecting one of the basic tenets of Islam, namely, the finality of Muhammad's prophethood. The agitation became violent, especially in Lahore, and was only brought under control by the declaration of martial law in the city. Yet, although some participants felt strongly about the central issue, others were venting their opposition to the autocratic politician who ran the Punjab at that time. The chief justice of Pakistan, Muhammad Munir, held an official inquiry into the disturbances, part of which restates in clear terms the official understanding that religion and politics belonged to two separate spheres, despite the opinions of some that Islamic belief led necessarily to an Islamic state.[21] This issue was further discussed in the lengthy debates that led to the framing of the first constitution in 1956 (although it was never implemented). The Objectives Resolution passed in 1949 had stated clearly that Pakistan was to be a state where "Muslims shall be enabled to order their lives in the individual and collective spheres in accord with the teachings and requirements of Islam as set out in the Holy Quran and the Sunna," but it also explicitly recognized the rights of minorities and the sovereignty of Parliament. The 1956 constitution, which incorporated the Objectives Resolution, designated Pakistan as an Islamic republic and stated that no law should contravene Islamic beliefs, but it also reaffirmed the sovereignty of Parliament (although there was provision for an advisory body to advise on the compatibility of legislation with the teachings of Islam).[22]

For nearly two decades the relationship between religion and politics remained stable. Popular religious feeling and practice continued largely unaltered, while the bureaucracy, the army, and the political parties pursued their own agendas. In 1961 the first military ruler of Pakistan, Ayub Khan, introduced the Muslim Family Laws Ordinance. This was a substantial attempt (comparable to the legal reforms in India mentioned above) to align marriage and inheritance laws with the requirements of a progressive society and introduced significant improvements in the status of women. But while the ordinance was welcomed by those who were actively committed to the separation of religious and political spheres of life, it was only very patchily implemented in the rural areas where the majority of the population lived.[23]

Pakistan faced a major crisis at the end of the 1960s and, in 1971, following a civil war and military intervention from India, broke into two states. Politically, this resulted in Zulfikar Ali Bhutto's coming to power. While Bhutto presented himself as a radical populist committed to social justice and reform, he chose to describe his goal as "Islamic socialism." Whether this made much difference to his electoral success is doubtful, given that there was a great deal of popular support for a new beginning after the failures of previous regimes to make progress in dealing with issues of poverty and social exclusion. However, as the immediate surge of support for him began to decline, Bhutto saw the possibility of using religious sentiment to bolster his position. In 1973 he declared the Ahmadis to be a non-Islamic sect, thus conceding what had been refused in 1953. Immediately after the disputed 1977 elections, when he was fighting to survive in power, he declared a complete ban on alcohol consumption and moved the weekly holiday from Sunday to Friday.

While Bhutto was merely using whatever political tools were at hand, and although he was, of course, toppled in 1977 and executed for alleged complicity in the murder of the father of a political opponent, there was nevertheless clearly a constituency in the country that would respond to religious appeals. Bhutto's successor, Gen. Zia ul-Haq, a man of strong religious conviction, decided to attempt a thoroughgoing reform of Pakistan's institutions with the intention of thereby encouraging, if not compelling, the individual citizen to live his or her life in accordance with the strict provisions of religious law as interpreted by the dominant Hanafi school of interpretation. Changes were introduced into the legal system: the boundaries between the private and the public were altered, women's equal legal status was challenged, and a blasphemy law was introduced that gave special protection to Islam. In the economic sphere efforts were made to eliminate interest (*riba*) as a principle of borrowing and lending, and *zakat*, a levy on wealth traditionally used for charitable purposes, was made obligatory for all Sunni Muslims. Parties were denigrated as un-Islamic, and committees were set up to discuss what a truly Islamic form of government would look like. One of the last actions that Zia took before his death in August 1988 was to insist that Pakistan's existing legal framework should be entirely subordinated to sharia, or Islamic law.

Since 1988 Pakistan has seen an extended period of instability. Four short-lived civilian governments, two led by Benazir Bhutto from the Pakistan People's Party and two by Nawaz Sharif from the Pakistan Muslim League, failed to sustain themselves in power, not least because of the unresolved tensions between the army leadership, the president, and the party leaders. In 1999 the army again intervened, this time with an avowed modernist at its head, Gen. Pervez Musharraf. Like Ayub Khan and other military rulers before, he saw the way forward as being to revitalize local government and to promote a new generation of political leadership free from the encumbrances of the past. Having declared himself president in June 2001, he then held elections in September 2002. A breakaway group from Nawaz Sharif's party, which was the clear favorite of Musharraf, eventually succeeded in cobbling together a government. In the meantime, however, the situation had been substantially affected by the World Trade Center and Pentagon attacks on September 11, 2001, and by the U.S. invasion of Afghanistan. Musharraf had chosen to offer full support to the United States and its allies, largely for pragmatic reasons. On the one hand, the United States offered economic and diplomatic incentives and, on the other, he must have been aware that opposition to the United States would have weakened his own internal position. However, the consequence was to promote strong anti-American feeling in the areas bordering Afghanistan. This translated into support for the Muttahida Majlis-i-Amal (MMA), a grouping of Islamic parties that gained their best-ever result in the 2002 elections and control of the provincial government in the NWFP. Members of this government made a number of strong statements in favor of Islam and passed a measure that in principle introduced sharia law into the province.[24] At the same time the MMA played an active role in the maneuverings for and against Musharraf. In an apparent volte-face, it concluded a political deal with the president at the end of 2003, which permitted him to pass key constitutional changes. The quid pro quo was not specified but appears to have been linked to the requirements of provincial politics and the maintenance of MMA strength in NWFP and Baluchistan.

The personal preferences of the key political players in Pakistan are clear enough. Musharraf himself supports a separation between religion and the public sphere.[25] The MMA is working toward a political system that would use state power to enforce an orthodox Sunni set of norms and values, for example, in the way women dress and behave. But while the constraints of politics force both sides into deals and compromises, the potential power of religion at the street level makes it very difficult for there to be an open debate on such questions as women's rights, the position of minorities, and the rigid law on blasphemy. Nor has the government been able to find effective ways of restraining the growth in violence between different Muslim groups, notably between the Sunni and Shia.

BANGLADESH SINCE 1971

Bangladesh came into existence in 1971 on the basis of what appeared to be a forthright assertion of the importance of language as the basis of national identity. Bengali had been systematically downplayed during the Pakistan period, and the first confrontations with the Pakistani state in 1952 had come as a result of protests over language policy. Yet, there was no rush to reunite with Bengali-speakers across the border in India, despite the role that India had played in defeating Pakistan during the civil war that preceded independence. Indeed, since 1975 if not earlier, relations with India assumed an ambiguous quality that persists to the present day, while normal relations with Pakistan were established sooner than might have been expected, given the mass murders and other atrocities that occurred in 1971. This points to the complex relationship that has existed in East Bengal between language, religious identity, and politics since at least the nineteenth century.

Islam in the delta area of Bengal had not been imported by force, even though for some centuries the region's rulers had been Muslim. Rather, it had gradually taken hold in the rural areas; it had in the process become particularly associated with the small peasantry of the region, tenants for the most part of Hindu *zamindars*, or landlords, although a few Muslim *zamindars*, descendants of non-Bengali migrants, also existed. Local accommodations developed between inherited beliefs and practices and those that had been imported, in many cases by Sufi saints. But although in some respects Islam appeared to have assumed a quietist form in Bengal, the message of equality that was implicit in Islamic belief was potentially a powerful political resource. This first manifested itself in religious reform movements in the nineteenth century, which simultaneously targeted exploitative (Hindu) landlords, as well as calling for stricter adherence to orthodox practice. During the course of the century, Muslims in the remote villages of the delta region were brought into closer contact with Muslims and the practice of Islam in the wider Islamic world.[26] Yet, some political leaders were conscious of the importance of maintaining a Bengali identity as well, not least because of the way that official Muslim leadership in India was closely identified with the Urdu-speaking elites of northern India. At the first major test of Muslim sentiment in the elections of 1937,[27] the Krishak Praja Party (KPP) of Fazlul Huq, rather than the Muslim League, won the day, even though the latter won a number of seats by allying with a local group of landlords. The KPP in practice represented principally the Muslim peasantry, but it was in theory open to all, and its platform was one of land reform and social justice. Yet, only three years later Huq joined hands with Jinnah to move the so-called Pakistan Resolution.

This ambivalence toward the idea of Pakistan and therefore to a political role for religion has persisted to the present day. During the period when East

Bengal was part of a united state, the overweening arrogance of the West Pakistani ruling elites meant that religious identity as a basis for political action was replaced by linguistic affinity. Many sections of the country, especially the educated, felt that they had been permanently relegated to second-class citizenship, despite forming a majority of the population. Their religious status itself was undermined by casual references to their convert status and to the continuing presence in East Bengal of a significant Hindu minority. At independence in 1971, therefore, the initial decision was to emphasize the Bengali identity of the country's citizens and their commitment to a secular political system. But taken to its logical conclusion, this would have meant reunification with West Bengal under the Indian Union, something that would have been difficult to fit with other aspects of East Bengal's modern history.[28] Even the close relationship with India that Sheikh Mujib pursued was unacceptable to many.

Following Mujib's assassination in August 1975 for reasons that had in part to do with his failure to establish a stable relationship between the elements that had taken part in the liberation struggle and those that had not, power eventually devolved to the army, and in particular to Gen. Zia-ur Rahman. A major figure in the liberation struggle, he understood that for both internal and external reasons, a new Bangladeshi identity had to be constructed that recognized both dimensions of its history. In 1977 a new constitution deleted the references to secularism that had been there initially and replaced them with a specific reference to Islam. However, his policies emphasized economic progress and development, and there was little attempt to change the practices of everyday life. In 1988 Zia's successor, General Ershad, who had also come to power through a military coup, changed the constitution again to declare Islam as the country's state religion. More significantly, he allowed the Jamat-e Islami, which had been discredited after the creation of Bangladesh, to reemerge. In 1993 and 1994 writings and interviews by a feminist author, Taslima Nasreen, provoked large-scale demonstrations demanding her arrest and execution, orchestrated by religious groups. These in turn led to widespread concern among human rights groups internationally. As in Pakistan, the government did not tackle the problem head-on, but found ways of circumventing it. Eventually, Nasreen found refuge in Sweden.

Since 1990 Bangladesh has returned to civilian rule, and both the main parties, the Awami League and the Bangladesh Nationalist Party (BNP), have been concerned primarily with maintaining themselves in power. The personal rivalry between the two leaders has been a major factor. While neither party has seen religious appeals as of immediate political value, the BNP was prepared to enter into a coalition with the Jamat-e Islami in order to come to power in 2001. The price of this was a marked increase in some areas in pressure on the country's Hindu minority. Bangladesh has not, however, had to face the same international and regional pressures as Pakistan, such as, for example, the backwash from Afghanistan both before and after the fall of the Taliban regime, and the dynamics of politics have been somewhat different.

CONCLUSION

Current modes of religious identification, born in the colonial period, continue to emphasize the link between the individual and the group in ways that often emphasize and heighten difference and at particular moments give concrete form to some elements of individual identity in ways that sideline others. The democratic political process plays an ambivalent role in perpetuating these identifications. Religiously defined groups (in the same way as other groups) may create their own leaders, who then enter formal political institutions with clearly articulated objectives, as happened with certain Hindu figures at the time of the Ayodhya agitation. Bolstered by their support on the street, such leaders can make an immediate impact and obtain some of their goals. Yet, at the same time the constraints of politics in terms of coalition building and compromise soon take effect as well. In most cases, in fact, the mainstream political parties themselves bring religiously defined groups into politics, so these processes are in operation from the very beginning.

Internationally, there seems to be a contrast between Pakistan and the other two countries discussed above. While India and Bangladesh have been able to keep their domestic disputes over the place of religion more or less to themselves, except for the diaspora involvement in the Punjab, Pakistan's Islamist groups have attracted considerable, generally negative attention, at least outside the Muslim world. This reflects both the strategic location of the country in the present world situation, as well as features of Islamic assertion there.

NOTES

1. Arguments about the rights of the majority are often used as code to condone such attacks. There is now a large literature on the Indian case. For a sample, see David Ludden, ed., *Making India Hindu: Religion, Community and the Politics of Democracy in India* (Philadelphia: University of Pennsylvania Press, 1996); Manjari Katju, *Vishva Hindu Parishad and Indian Politics* (Delhi: Orient Longman, 2003).

2. A standard expression of this view can be found in G. Pandey, *The Construction of Communalism in Colonial North India* (Delhi: Oxford University Press, 1990). Note, however, the important caveat entered by C. A. Bayly, "The Prehistory of 'Communalism': Religious Conflict in India, 1700–1860," *Modern Asian Studies* 19, no. 2 (1985): 177–203.

3. Sri Lanka has been excluded for reasons of space, but much of the argument that follows would apply. The case of Nepal is rather different, in part because it was never formally colo-

nized. Officially a Hindu kingdom, it nevertheless has a significant Buddhist population living symbiotically with the Hindu.

4. Romila Thapar, *Early India: From the Origins to AD 1300* (Berkeley: University of California Press, 2003), is a standard history of South Asia. See also Burton Stein, *A History of India* (Oxford: Blackwell, 1998).

5. A particularly instructive example of these processes is that of East Bengal. In this remote delta region, where Buddhism had survived longer than almost anywhere else in the subcontinent, Islam did not arrive in a rush; nor was it imposed by force. Rather, it was adopted through the gradual influence of Sufis, or holy men, whose shrines became the focus of popular religious enthusiasm. Islam in this area, therefore, developed organically out of the previous patterns of religious belief and practice and did not mark a sharp break. See especially Asim Roy, *The Islamic Syncretistic Tradition in Bengal* (Princeton, N.J.: Princeton University Press, 1983). In the early nineteenth century, Islamic reform movements emerged that were closely linked to political and social protest against (Hindu) landlords and other exploitative elements. They are covered in the introductory chapter of Rafiuddin Ahmed, *The Bengal Muslims, 1871–1906: A Quest for Identity*, 2nd ed. (Delhi: Oxford University Press, 1996).

6. Among many others, see the seven volumes of Edgar Thurston, *Castes and Tribes of Southern India* (Madras: Government Press, 1909). Thurston was superintendent of the Madras Government Museum.

7. Sudipta Kaviraj, "The Imaginary Institution of India," in *Subaltern Studies,* vol. 7, ed. Partha Chatterjee and Gyanendra Pandey (Delhi: Oxford University Press, 1992), 1–39.

8. William Radice, ed., *Swami Vivekananda and the Modernization of Hinduism* (Delhi: Oxford University Press, 1998); Gwilym Beckerlegge, *The Ramakrishna Mission: The Making of a Modern Hindu Movement* (Delhi: Oxford University Press, 2000); J. E. Llewellyn, *The Arya Samaj as a Fundamentalist Movement: A Study in Comparative Fundamentalism* (Delhi: Manohar, 1993).

9. Martin Forward, *The Failure of Islamic Modernism? Syed Ameer Alé's Interpretation of Islam* (Bern: Peter Lang, 1999); Barbara Metcalf, *Islamic Revival in British India: Deoband, 1860–1900* (Princeton, N.J.: Princeton University Press, 1982).

10. For the Punjab, see Norman Barrier; for the "criminal tribes," see Anand Yang, ed., *Crime and Criminality in India* (Tucson: University of Arizona Press, 1985); Sanjay Nigam, "Disciplining and Policing the 'Criminals' by Birth," *Indian Economic and Social History Review* 27, nos. 2 and 3 (1990): 131–64, 257–88.

11. Eleanor Zelliott, *From Untouchable to Dalit: Essays on the Ambedkar Movement* (Delhi: Manohar, 1992).

12. Initially, the claim was for two Muslim states, one in the west and the other in the Bengali-speaking areas of the east.

13. This is a euphemism for Hindu constituencies.

14. For a discussion of the different meanings of secularism in India, see Rajeev Bhargava, ed., *Secularism and Its Critics* (Delhi: Oxford University Press, 1998).

15. The Punjab case is well covered in the literature. See, e.g., Paul R. Brass, *Language, Religion and Politics in North India* (Cambridge: Cambridge University Press, 1974); Baldev Raj Nayar, *Minority Politics in Punjab* (Princeton, N.J.: Princeton University Press, 1966).

16. People's Union for Civil Liberties, *Who Are the Guilty?—Report of a Joint Inquiry into the Causes and Impact of the Anti-Sikh Violence in Delhi from 31 October to 10 November, 1984* (Delhi: PUCL, 1984).

17. Katju, *Vishva Hindu Parishad*; Walter Andersen and Shridhar Damle, *Brotherhood in Saffron: A Study of Hindu Revivalism* (Boulder, Colo.: Westview, 1987); Christophe Jaffrelot, *The Hindu Nationalist Movement in India* (New York: Columbia University Press, 1998).

18. The argument has been made that the fire that destroyed the train was accidentally ignited, although most of the evidence points in the opposite direction. For further comment, see

BBC World Service story, July 3, 2002, available at http://news.bbc.co.uk/2/hi/south_asia/
2087709.stm.

19. Katju, *Vishva Hindu Parishad.*

20. On the eve of independence, Jinnah made a much-quoted speech setting out a vision of
Pakistan that was entirely compatible with the European notion of a secular state, with religion
operating entirely in the personal sphere.

21. *Report of the Court of Inquiry . . . into the Punjab Disturbances of 1953* (Lahore: Superintendent of Government Printing, 1954).

22. Rubya Mehdi, *Islamisation of the Law in Pakistan* (London: Curzon Press, 1994).

23. Mehdi, *Islamisation of the Law.*

24. The act that was passed was in fact a virtual carbon copy of an earlier bill passed at the
national level in 1991, although it was never implemented.

25. General Pervez Musharraf, "Personal Liberties and Freedoms Should Be Respected. No-
body Has Any Right by Virtue of Being in Power to Tell Others Who Is a Good Muslim and
Who Is Not," *Dawn,* June 9, 2003.

26. Ahmed, *The Bengal Muslims.*

27. These were held on a restricted franchise, and only around a third of the adult population
had the right to vote, but this was a much higher proportion than in previous elections under
colonial rule. The British had taken care to ensure that rural, as well as urban, voters were en-
franchised, so the results can be taken as a not-wholly-unreliable test of opinion at that time.

28. In practice the Indian government would have been most unwilling to take on the burden
of coping with East Bengal's economic problems, as well as coping with a doubling in size of
the Muslim minority.

FURTHER READING

Andersen, Walter, and Shridhar Damle. *Brotherhood in Saffron: A Study of Hindu Revivalism.*
  Boulder, Colo.: Westview, 1987.
Beckerlegge, Gwilym. *The Ramakrishna Mission: The Making of a Modern Hindu Movement.*
  Delhi: Oxford University Press, 2000.
Bondurant, Joan Valerie. *Conquest of Violence: The Gandhian Philosophy of Conflict.* Prince-
  ton, N.J.: Princeton University Press, 1988.
Fuller, Graham E. *The Future of Political Islam.* New York: Palgrave Macmillan, 2003.
Jaffrelot, Christophe. *The Hindu Nationalist Movement in India.* New York: Columbia Univer-
  sity Press, 1998.
Katju, Manjari. *Vishva Hindu Parishad and Indian Politics.* Delhi: Orient Longman, 2003.
Ludden, David, ed. *Making India Hindu: Religion, Community and the Politics of Democracy
  in India.* Philadelphia: University of Pennsylvania Press, 1996.
Mitchell, Richard P. *The Society of the Muslim Brothers.* Oxford: Oxford University Press,
  1993.
Nasr, Seyyed Vali Reza. *The Islamic Leviathan: Islam and the Making of State Power.* Oxford:
  Oxford University Press, 2001.
Pandey, G. *The Construction of Communalism in Colonial North India.* Delhi: Oxford Univer-
  sity Press, 1990.
Roy, Asim. *The Islamic Syncretistic Tradition in Bengal.* Princeton, N.J.: Princeton University
  Press, 1983.

10

Democratization and Development

Jonah Blank

Democracy (as Winston Churchill famously noted) is the worst form of government ever devised—except for all the others. To many twenty-first-century readers this proposition may seem obvious, but the real test of a political system is whether or not it delivers the goods. Does democracy? The postcolonial history of South Asia provides evidence both for and against.

The five largest countries of South Asia have all experimented with democratization, and the results have been decidedly mixed.[1] Democratic norms have taken firm root in India and Sri Lanka but at present are struggling to implant themselves in Bangladesh and are observed mainly in the breach in Pakistan and Nepal. If democratization led inevitably to economic and social development, the question as to which form of governance to follow would be a matter of dogma rather than discussion. And discussion is an integral part of democracy; how ironic if the end sought should be an end of political debate, or even (as some theorists would have it) an end of history.[2] Democratization must be seen as a process, not as a mere destination.

Economists and political scientists are often given to grand comparisons: the trade figures posted by China compared with those of Russia over the past decade demonstrate the ascendancy of economic reforms over political ones; the trade figures posted by Thailand compared with those of Vietnam demonstrate just the opposite. But any such comparison is necessarily apples to oranges: no two countries are exactly alike, so the basis for evaluation is inherently speculative. Even comparisons of development in the same nation during periods of democratization and authoritarianism must be somewhat hypothetical—an economy can grow or shrink for any number of reasons (drought, worldwide recession, regional warfare) that may have little to do with the way political leaders make their decisions. In order to be truly meaningful, a country's performance should be judged not against that of its neighbors, or even within the context of its own history, but according to where the state would be if a different system had been in place. Such a question is, by its very nature, unanswerable.

Further complicating the issue is the matter of definitions. Democratization means far more than the mere exercise of periodically holding elections; if that were the only requirement, the Democratic People's Republic of Korea would be deserving of its name. But where can a line be drawn between a less-than-perfectly-democratic democracy and a less-than-perfectly-oligarchic oligarchy? The threads from which a democracy can be woven may include rule of law, civil-society groups independent of state control, freedom of speech, and a wide range of others. But the precise pattern of the weave, let alone its component threads, are duplicated inexactly.

Moreover, development must be understood in more than merely economic terms. The standard of living in a particular country cannot be fully captured in an array of figures or ratios. Such indices as gross national product (GNP) per person are very useful, but they do not present the whole picture. If we know that the average annual income in a particular country is $400, what does that tell us? What can be bought for that sum of money in country x, as opposed to county y?[3] What social mechanisms are in place to make life worth living in the absence of material abundance? To put development in its proper perspective, one must consider a wide range of indices, from literacy to caloric intake to gender equality to social mobility. Even then, any comparisons will be far from objective: whatever human beings may be, they are more than the sum of the figures by which they may be measured.

Further complicating the equation is the interaction between any given society and the wider world. How do democratization and development affect a country's relations with neighboring states, with traditional rivals, and with the rest of the global community? How do external forces, in turn, affect a country's democratization and development? It is often assumed that democracies will inevitably enjoy more harmonious international relationships and present fewer challenges to global peace than nondemocratic states, but there are plenty of counterexamples. Saber rattling and war mongering have been effective electoral tools for more than a few politicians, be they in India, Pakistan, or the United States of America.

With all of these caveats, however, South Asia provides a relatively good means of examining the interplay of democracy and development. Four of the major countries of the region share a common colonial history up to the mid-twentieth century. (The fifth, Nepal, was under the thumb of the British Raj, but not actually a part of it). The history of these countries prior to European domination had been closely linked, and there are innumerable ties of language, ethnicity, religion, and social strata that run from one nation to the next. How, then, to explain the different political paths tread by the South

Asian states over the past fifty-odd years? Perhaps the only generalization one can safely make is to avoid generalizations. Any attempt to situate a propensity for democratization in religious values is, at best, highly doubtful. Max Weber's identification of the spirit of capitalism with a supposed Protestant ethic today seems (in light of, say, the entrepreneurial Muslim, Hindu, and Parsi bania communities of Gujarat) as if it were written in 1905.[4]

India is home to most of the world's Hindus, but an attempt to postulate links between that faith and democracy founders on the fact that the world's only constitutionally Hindu nation, Nepal, is an old-fashioned monarchy. Sri Lanka's success with democracy can hardly be chalked up to its Buddhist roots, at least, not without taking into account the counterexamples of traditionally Buddhist China, Burma, Vietnam, Cambodia, Laos, and North Korea. And attempts to portray Islam as a faith inherently inimical to democracy must somehow deal with the examples of fledgling democracies in Turkey, Indonesia, and Bangladesh, nations that, together with the 140 million Muslims in India and a similar number in occasionally democratic Pakistan, contain a solid majority of the world's Muslim population.

Both democratization and development are slow processes, unfolding over the course of decades rather than years. Nor is the order of the two preordained: economic development can lead to democracy, as it has in Taiwan, South Korea, and Thailand. The counterexamples, including countries like the People's Republic of China, Malaysia, or Singapore in which economic reforms have not yet led to political ones, may simply have a longer road to travel. On the other side of the ledger are those countries that have undertaken democratization prior to, or in tandem with, rapid economic development. The foremost example in South Asia would be India, but this pattern has been seen throughout Europe and the Americas.[5] Whether the effect had anything to do with the supposed cause must remain unprovable. The examples of the five major nations of South Asia provide some basis for believing, however, that while democracy isn't the only path to development, it may well be the most reliable one.

INDIA

From 1947–1991 economic development in India took a back seat to democratization. Economists and businessmen have criticized this decision by India's first prime minister, Jawaharlal Nehru (particularly in recent decades), but the slow process of solidifying democratic norms established a firm foundation for more rapid economic development in the 1990s and the new century. Seen from the vantage point of the present, the stifling economic restrictions placed on the Indian economy during its first four decades strike many observers as thoroughly misguided. The so-called license permit raj suppressed innovation and entrepreneurial experimentation, and lazy state-supported enterprises were guaranteed market domination without the threat of domestic or foreign competitors. But at the time this system was instituted, many Western economists were lauding the supposed efficiencies of a Soviet-model centralized economy, particularly for a nation such as India that was early in its development curve. Much of the criticism leveled at Nehru has been based on the only type of economic analysis to stand the test of time: hindsight.

Nehru's economic model subsidized staples such as rice, flour, and cooking oil: this did not steer production in the most cost-effective directions, and it required families to waste time standing in line with their ration-books, but it insured that after the wait, they would not go home empty-handed. Inefficient factories and government offices kept vast numbers of unproductive employees on the books, often maintaining a dozen workers to do a job that could be better performed by one. This practice (still a hallmark of the Indian economy) hurt the financial balance sheet: productivity figures were poor and remain far below those of industrialized countries.

The social balance sheet, however, is a different story: bloated job rolls meant relatively little unemployment, which avoided the creation of a discontented urban underclass that could have been easy tinder for antidemocratic firebrands.[6] Under the license permit raj, very few got rich, but almost everyone got fed. The system was not a formula for rapid economic growth of the type enjoyed by Japan, South Korea, Taiwan, and the Southeast Asian "Tigers," which were averaging 8 to 15 percent annual growth during the same period. India's growth rate between 1950 and 1980 averaged a mere 3.5 percent per year, a figure that economist Raj Krishna termed (tongue only partially in cheek) the *Hindu rate of growth*.[7] But it was a system designed to insure social stability, and without social stability, the slow, steady institutionalization of democratic norms would probably have been impossible.

What norms were instituted? One of the most important was land reform, without which many others might have been strangled in their cribs. Nehru abolished the feudal zamindari system, which had concentrated land and wealth in the hands of a tiny class of rich noblemen for centuries. The compensation paid to the former zamindars insured that the reform would not be blocked outright, and by separating the feudals from their traditional power bases, India was able to mitigate their dominance of democratic politics.[8]

Civilian control over the military was institutionalized as a bedrock value, a value so deeply engrained in the Indian officer corps that there has never been a serious threat of military coup d'état. Even when Prime Minister Indira Gandhi set aside democratic governance during the 1975–1977 Emergency, the army refrained from stepping in. This decision was very good for both the professional standing of the military and for the future of democratization: the Indian people were able to see that even the most dire threat to democratic rule could be overcome without breaking the fundamental taboo against military intervention in political affairs.

This taboo had an important ancillary benefit to both India and to the region: the solidification of democratic norms and the prohibition against military veto of civilian initiatives, served to cushion India's foreign policy from the adventurism that has plagued many quasidemocratic and nondemocratic regimes. Despite India's military supremacy over any South Asian rival,[9] New Delhi has never sought to conquer the territory of a neighboring state. Since independence India has fought three and a half wars against Pakistan (with the 1999 Kargil conflict counting as the "half"), and despite at least one crushing victory in 1971, it has not sought significant territorial expansion.[10]

In the 1980s India sent peacekeeping troops to Sri Lanka and was quite happy to withdraw them as quickly as possible. Military involvement in Nepal and Bhutan has been covert and never designed to alter the boundaries of either state. As for Bangladesh, India's principal involvement took place during the 1971 war, when Indian troops engaged those of Pakistan to help usher Bangladesh into existence and safeguard its newly won independence. In brief, then, democracy has not guaranteed India a uniformly placid relationship with its neighbors, but it has served (at least to some degree) to keep the country from embarking upon wars of territorial conquest. None of these decisions were preordained by the political structure of the Indian state: there is no way of proving that a nondemocratic India would have made different choices regarding military policy. But the record of engagement—a series of limited wars, several of them resulting in clear Indian victories, none of them leading to significant shifts in boundaries—is at least highly suggestive.

Perhaps most important for the purpose of the current discussion, four decades of economic inertia gave Indian politicians a free hand to work out the kinks of an electoral system encompassing a greater variety of languages, ethnicities, religions, and competing social interests than perhaps any other democratic country in existence. The creative turmoil characteristic of free-market capitalism may unleash productivity, but it also unleashes an unruly array of challenges to any newly developing country. Open economies create winners, but they also create losers, and every loser may be tempted to turn his anger against the entire political system responsible for his loss. Between 1947 and 1991, India established itself as a secular state in which Hindus, Muslims, and practitioners of at least half a dozen other faiths are all equal citizens. This was by no means a foregone conclusion at independence (and is not necessarily an inevitable condition of the future), so the institutionalization of a secular norm must rank as a key aspect of India's democratization. In the 1950s Nehru forged a lasting compromise between subnational ethnic aspirations and the need for national unity. The reorganization of India's states along linguistic lines largely satisfied the demands of Tamil, Gujarati, Punjabi, and other groups agitating for increased recognition of their unique identities. By making the basis for reorganization linguistic rather than religious or ethnic, Nehru avoided the legitimization of communal schisms, which had already caused unspeakable bloodshed during Partition and at other times in India's history. This did not prevent such schisms from coming to the fore: Kashmir's insurgency is now in its second decade and shows few signs of burning out; Punjab was in a state of near rebellion for much of the 1980s and early 1990s; and several northeastern states are periodically shaken by separatist movements with varying degrees of grassroots support. But the political decisions made during India's first few decades have firmly established a national identity for India that is strong enough to survive any centrifugal pressures of the past, present, and foreseeable future.

Moreover, the breathing space provided by economic order (as opposed to more-productive economic activity) helped India solidify the workings of the democratic process. Unlike many leaders of independence movements who found themselves suddenly in control of their nations during the postcolonial period, Nehru nurtured the mechanisms of democracy rather than fostering a cult of personality or subverting democratic processes to attain his favored political outcomes. Despite a legacy of one-party rule lasting well into the 1980s and despite an abrupt (albeit temporary) setback to democratization under the administration of Nehru's daughter Indira Gandhi, the various aspects of democratization appear firmly embedded in the Indian body politic. Free elections, an independent judiciary, a critical press, freedom of expression: all are practiced at least as zealously as in democratic states elsewhere in the world.[11]

In 1991 the shortcomings of the Indian economy were brought into embarrassing highlight: much of the nation's gold reserves had to be put forward as collateral to secure a loan from the International Monetary Fund. The prospect of defaulting on international obligations shocked Indian decision makers into action: Congress prime minister Narasimha Rao undertook reforms to liberalize the Indian economy, and all other Indian governments since have maintained the program. The license permit raj, which carved up the economy into a patchwork of inefficient, de facto monopolies, has largely been dismantled. Many burdensome regulations still exist, and many enterprises (private and state-owned alike) still keep large numbers of unproductive workers on the books, but India is no longer a place wholly insulated from the business practices of the outside world. Tariffs protecting Indian products from external competition are still very high compared with those of most industrialized countries, but by 2002 they had dropped to an average 32 percent; ten years earlier, the average Indian tariff was 128 percent.[12]

In response, the Hindu rate of growth nearly doubled: India's gross domestic product (GDP) averaged 6.6 percent growth per year between 1992 and 1997, and even since the Asian financial crisis of 1997, it has been outpacing not only the rates of its own prereform past but also those of several Southeast Asian "Tiger" economies. Total flows of foreign direct investment rose from $133 million in 1991/1992 to $4.8 billion in 1997/1998.[13] Indian cities that once looked like overgrown villages are now sprouting skyscrapers. But how much of this economic development is due to democratization? Indeed, how much more impressive might India's economic performance figures be without democracy's burdens? The case of China is sufficient to put a damper on any enthusiasm. India's economic growth rate may be twice what it used to be, but it is only half that of China. India's GDP per capita was slightly higher than that of China in 1990, but in 2002 (after both countries had instituted economic reforms) it was barely half that of its rival.[14] Whatever the benefits of democratization, it has not caused India to outpace an avowedly communist dictatorship in the sphere of pure capitalism. Moreover, the World Bank estimates that 44.2 percent of the Indian population lives below the international poverty indicator level of $1 per day.[15] While the Chinese government has not delivered its people into a workers' paradise, at least since the end of the Cultural Revolution, it seems to have done a better job of tending to its citizens' most basic material needs.

But basic material needs are only one part of the development equation. Many of the core elements of social uplift, the things that make life worth living, are bought more easily with nonmaterial capital. The economists Jean Dreze and Amartya Sen make a valuable point when they add the Indian state of Kerala to the standard India–China comparison. In real GNP per capita for 1992, based on purchasing-power parity (a scale in which the United States forms the benchmark at 100), China scored 9.1, India 5.2, and the state of Kerala a mere 4.6. The annual growth rate of per capita GNP between 1980 and 1992 for China was 7.6 percent, for India 3.1 percent, and for Kerala a stagnant 0.3 percent.[16] But when one moves from macroeconomic statistics to numbers that measure true quality of life, the tables (quite literally) are turned. The 1992 rates for life expectancy at birth were fifty-nine years for India, sixty-nine for China, and seventy-two for Kerala. Infant mortality the same year was seventy-nine per thousand live births for India, thirty-one for China, and seventeen for Kerala. India's fertility rate (one indicator of both female disempowerment and general poverty) was 3.7, China's (due to draconian forced-abortion policies) a nationally mandated 2.0, and Kerala's a voluntary 1.8. Perhaps most noteworthy are the literacy figures: India's rate for 1990–1991 was 39 percent for women, 64 percent for men; China's was 68 percent for women, 87 percent for men. Kerala's literacy rate was an astounding 86 percent for women and 94 percent for men.[17] Nor are these numbers a

statistical fluke: the social development indicators for Kerala are widely recognized to have been far superior to those of India as a whole both prior to and
since the 1991 economic reforms, despite Kerala's persistently poor overall
economic performance. These numbers indicate that social development may
well outstrip economic development and that the intangibles of a society that
places a high value on social equity (as the Marxist state governments of Kerala have ever since independence) can improve the daily lives of its citizens
more effectively than any accountant's balance sheet might suggest.

With India poised to become a regional superpower in the twenty-first
century, democratization may well provide the needed edge. Lacking vast
deposits of oil, valuable minerals, or excess acreage of agricultural land, India's greatest natural resource might well be its people. Southern states such
as Andhra Pradesh, Karnataka, and Tamil Nadu are already discovering this:
since the Asian financial crisis, India's economic engine has been kept
primed largely by the information-technology sector centered in Hyderabad,
Bangalore, and Chennai. For such knowledge-based sectors to succeed,
however, India will need to nurture its human capital. As the Keralan example indicates, it is possible to do this in a cost-effective manner, but only if
the government is firmly committed to such a program. In Kerala the advances in social development were directly due to the impact of democratization: in colonial times, Brahmins and ritually impure, but locally powerful, "dominant castes" joined with the British to put the brake on moves for
universal education or social uplift of the lower *Shudra* or *Dalit jatis*. With
democracy, however, the majority has ruled and legislated its own development. In the years to come, perhaps the lesson will spread northward to the
rest of the country.

PAKISTAN

Throughout the past half-century, Pakistan's experience of both democracy
and development has been sketchy at best. This confluence may not be a coincidence: lack of representative government has enabled the military-led
regimes to avoid delivering on promises of development. For all of Pakistan's
changes of leadership, whether by coup d'état, executive order, or back-room
handover of power, the citizens of the country have never been involved in the
decisions. Five governments (led by three prime ministers) have been voted
into office, and all five have been removed through nondemocratic means.

Pakistan's failure to institutionalize democratic norms owes much to the
unique circumstances of the nation's founding: Muhammad Ali Jinnah, the
towering leader of the movement for creating Pakistan as a state independent
of India, died barely a year after seeing his vision achieved. India's new gov-

ernment was able to survive the political shock caused by the assassination around the same time of Mahatma Gandhi: the nation-building movement was well-stocked with strong political figures in addition to Prime Minister Jawaharlal Nehru, such as Sardar Vallabhbhai Patel, Maulana Abul Kalam Azad, and Dr. B. R. Ambedkar, all firm advocates of democratization, albeit from different viewpoints. In Pakistan, however, the burdens of political leadership had been tightly concentrated with Jinnah alone, both before and after independence. When he passed away, the country lacked a ready-made cadre of political leaders to carry on his work.

The first decade of Pakistan's existence was an untidy display of would-be leaders jockeying for authority, with the only enduring source of power remaining the military's top brass. Liaquat Ali Khan, Jinnah's ally and successor, was assassinated after three years in office, and no other civilian of stature emerged from the fray. In 1958 President Iskander Mirza, a former major general, suspended the newly written constitution and declared martial law. Almost immediately, his prime minister and army commander, Gen. Muhammad Ayub Khan, forced Mirza to resign and stepped into the presidency. Ayub continued martial law for three and half years, then instituted a pseudodemocratic form of government based on an easily rigged assembly. His leadership was confirmed in 1962 and 1965, but these polls are commonly regarded as window-dressing for a de facto military regime rather than a genuine example of democratic rule. Following a drubbing at the hands of the Indian military in an ill-considered 1965 war over Kashmir, Ayub fired his foreign minister, a rising star named Zulfiqar Ali Bhutto, and imprisoned East Pakistan's Bengali nationalist leader Sheikh Mujibur Rahman. In 1970 an ailing Ayub turned power over to his army chief of staff, Gen. Agha Muhammad Yahya Khan, who declared martial law and announced free multiparty elections. He would not, however, prove willing to abide by the results.

Two decades of denial of political power and economic development to the half of the Pakistani population who lived in the eastern wing would not have been sustainable under a democratic form of government; any regime attempting to maintain such policies would have been voted out of office. And in Pakistan's first democratic elections in 1970, that is exactly what happened. As discussed below, the election of 1970 was a turning point for East Pakistan, directly leading to its independence as Bangladesh. It was also a turning point for West Pakistan. After a humiliating defeat by India and the loss of half of the nation's territory, Pakistan's military was thoroughly discredited in the eyes of the people. Gen. Yahya Khan permitted Zulfiqar Bhutto to take over control of the wreckage.

Bhutto negotiated the 1972 Simla Agreement with India, returned Pakistan to parliamentary democracy in 1973, and recognized Bangladesh as an independent state in 1974. But in the elections of 1977, accusations of fraud on

the part of his Pakistan People's Party (PPP) led to street protests and the im-
position of martial law. Shortly thereafter, Bhutto's army chief, Gen. Muhammad Zia ul-Haq, staged a coup d'état. Despite worldwide outcry, under Zia's
rule Zulfiqar Bhutto was hanged on widely discredited charges of murder. Zia
promised free elections within three months, but until 1988 Zia governed by
virtual fiat. He banned political parties, kept martial law in place until 1986,
and pushed forward a program of Islamizing the Pakistani military, government, and society. While Pakistan had been notionally an Islamic republic
since the short-lived constitution of 1956, it was only under Zia's rule that
sharia (Islamic law) became institutionalized as a key component of the legal
framework. In 1988 Zia unexpectedly dismissed his prime minister and announced open, multiparty elections. On August 17 of that year, he and several
of his closest allies within the military echelon died when their jet crashed under circumstances that remain cloaked in mystery.

The elections brought to power Zulfiqar Ali Bhutto's daughter, Benazir,
who at the tender age of thirty-six became the first woman ever elected to lead
a Muslim nation. The military establishment had much residual hatred for the
long-dead Zulfi and little affection for Benazir; after less than two years, the
generals pressed President Ghulam Ishaq Khan to dismiss Benazir's government on charges of corruption and abuse of power. In new elections Mian
Nawaz Sharif, who owed his political rise to the patronage of Gen. Zia during the 1980s, emerged victorious. For a decade, from 1988 to 1999, Pakistani
politics consisted largely of a duel between Benazir's PPP and Nawaz's Pakistan Muslim League (PML). Both prime ministers were elected twice, and
both were twice evicted from office on similar charges when they ran afoul
of the military establishment. Despite stirring populist rhetoric since the days
of Zulfiqar Ali Bhutto, both parties allied themselves with the powerful zamindars, whose control over most of the country (particularly the rural areas)
has never been broken. In India Nehru's land reforms of the 1950s set the
stage for genuinely popular political parties, but in Pakistan the absence of
such reforms insured that politics (when permitted to be practiced at all)
would remain a family affair. The bitter contests between Benazir and Nawaz
were not so much a battle between two competing ideologies, or even between Sindh (the PPP heartland) and Punjab (the base of the PML). As the
1990s wore on, Pakistani politics seemed little more than a duel, at both the
local and national levels, between rival feudal clans loosely disguised as political parties, with all participants well aware that the real power would remain in the hands of the military brass.

Well aware, that is, until 1999. Following a humiliating Kargil conflict (a
Pakistani incursion across the line of control in Kashmir was driven back by
Indian forces, while the rest of the world watched), Nawaz tried to pin all
blame for the fiasco on his generals. Army chief of staff Pervez Musharraf,

one step ahead of Nawaz's clumsy attempt to remove him, staged a bloodless coup and declared himself chief executive (later president). The move was initially popular with a citizenry disillusioned by years of failed democratic government, but in the subsequent years Musharraf has not done a noticeably better job of providing effective governance or material development than his civilian predecessors.

The Kargil conflict illustrates the dangers to international order of weak (or nonexistent) democratic standards. While the legitimately elected civilian government appears to have been informed (at least in vague terms) of the Kargil project beforehand, there is considerable evidence that the operation was planned and executed by the military, with little detailed knowledge or input from civilian authorities. According to documents released subsequent to the coup that deposed Nawaz Sharif, at the height of the crisis the Pakistani prime minister seemed genuinely unaware of nuclear preparations set in motion by his own general staff.[18] One school of thought among students of Pakistan's political history notes that military regimes have been more likely than civilian ones to initiate conflict with India. They point to the army's dominance over inchoate civilian political systems during the 1947–1948 Kashmir war and to military adventurism in 1965 and 1971. On the other side of the ledger, however, a plausible case can be made that army leaders have greater power, should they choose to exercise it, to exert the necessary control over their military colleagues and deliver the sacrifices necessary to solidify any long-term peace agreement. Thus far, neither military nor democratic leaders of Pakistan have proven themselves willing or able to establish a durable peace. Perhaps one or the other will eventually demonstrate the power of its respective system, but at the time of this writing, the case remains unproven. If an edge can be given to either camp, it would have to go to the advocates of democracy: Even during periods of democratic rule, the military has exercized power of veto over any important government decisions. In such a context, democratic regimes in Pakistan can legitimately argue that they haven't actually failed, but rather that they've never truly been given the chance to succeed.

The economic picture is similarly shaded. After half a century of governments controlled by the military (whether directly or thinly concealed behind an elected prime minister), Pakistan has a gross national income per capita far below that of India: $1,860 versus $2,820 (when measured by purchasing-power parity).[19] Its poverty rate is four percentage points higher than that of India, and only one point below that of desperately poor Bangladesh.[20] Infant mortality is eighty-three per thousand live births, ten higher than the South Asia average. Literacy is a mere 46 percent, well below the regional mean. Moreover, Pakistan's economy has barely kept pace with the growth of its population, and civilians seem to have done at least as bad a job as the generals at managing the nation's finances: GDP per capita grew at 3.3 percent annually from 1981 to 1991 and a mere 1.0 percent between 1991 and 2001. In 2001 the growth rate approached the point of total stagnation, clocking in at only 0.3 percent.[21] But the military itself may be the greatest drag on Pakistan's material development. Whether openly running the government or controlling affairs from behind the scenes, Pakistan's military has eaten up a disproportionate share of the country's resources. It has pushed the nation into three self-destructive wars with India (and one miniwar, Kargil, that ran the risk of escalation to the nuclear level), and despite losing all of these conflicts, it continues to support an insurgency in Kashmir, which makes future warfare virtually inevitable.

The cause of democratization in Pakistan has been seriously damaged by the poor performance of duly elected governments. None of Pakistan's democratically elected prime ministers could credibly claim to have delivered the goods: the best that either of the two living former premiers can assert is that their terms were cut short unfairly and that their successors were worse. Neither claim, justified or not, constitutes a ringing endorsement for the project of democratization. Yet, the Pakistani people remain generally supportive of democratization. The most authoritative current polling data suggests that a decade of bad experience with elected leaders has not soured Pakistanis on the experiment. According to the Pew Global Attitudes Project, 57 percent of Pakistanis surveyed in 2003 said that Western-style democracy could work in their country, up from 44 percent the previous year. This figure is markedly higher than those posted in Muslim countries like Turkey and Indonesia that are also making the slow transition from military to civilian rule. Almost two-thirds of the respondents said it was very important to live in a country where people can criticize their government, and when asked whether a democratic government was more important than strong leadership, 42 percent of Pakistanis opted for democracy while only 32 percent favored a strong leader instead.[22] Having seen bad governance both in and out of uniform, Pakistanis seem to prefer (all things being equal) inept civilians over inept generals.

SRI LANKA

An island known until 1972 as Ceylon, Sri Lanka highlights both the weaknesses and the strengths of democratization. As is the case for any nation ravaged by decades of warfare, the weaknesses are more visible. But on closer examination, it is the strengths that seem most notable. Ever since gaining independence in 1948, Sri Lanka has been governed by politicians rather than generals. The shortsightedness of democratically elected leaders, however, was perhaps the key cause of the country's long civil war. In a democracy the majority rules, but if the rights of the minority population are not respected, the wheels of governance grind to a halt.

Prior to independence, Sri Lanka's Tamil minority (currently 18 percent of the population and predominantly Hindu) had enjoyed a privileged position in the British colonial regime. Since 1948 the Sinhalese majority (now 74 percent of the populace and predominantly Buddhist) has controlled the government. It is only natural that a people shut out of power in their own homeland might exercise it too freely when they finally win the opportunity. But if the majority treats democracy as a winner-takes-all sport, it is also only natural for the minority to make "all" seem more like nothing.

In 1983 after a quarter-century of feeling shut out of the circles of power and being treated like second-class citizens, Tamils in the northern and eastern portions of the country started a rebellion that continues to this day. The Liberation Tigers of Tamil Eelam (LTTE) were only one of the militias to spring up during the 1980s, but they are now the only one left standing. Led by the reclusive Vellupillai Prabhakaran, they battled government troops to a standstill, governed a quarter of the country as their virtual fief during the early 1990s, and pioneered terrorist techniques (suicide bombings being only the most dramatic) that have paralyzed most of the nation for a whole generation.

Sri Lanka's two major political parties have highlighted the uglier side of democracy: for most of their history, they have been more interested in partisan wrangling than in solving the problems of the nation. Both parties have engaged in shameless nepotism. The United National Party (UNP) has so thoroughly entrenched the practice that Sri Lankans joke that its initials stand for the Uncle-Nephew Party. The Sri Lanka Freedom Party has blazed a new trail in old terrain: current president Chandrika Bandaranaike Kumaratunga is the daughter of Sri Lanka's first prime minister, S. W. R. D Bandaranaike, and of its (and the world's) first female prime minister, Sirimavo Bandaranaike. In 1978 a constitutional reconfiguration moved the country from a Westminster-style government to a model based on that of France, greatly increasing the power of the president vis-à-vis the prime minister. When Kumaratunga won the presidency in 1994, she established what may have been a landmark in the annals of nepotism: a daughter appointing her mother to their nation's second-highest office.[23]

Politics as a family affair has not discredited democracy in the eyes of its Sri Lankan practitioners, but the inability of the two major parties to set aside their rivalry for the sake of the common good just might. Throughout the mid-1990s, Kumaratunga's attempts to negotiate an end to the civil war were impeded by backbiting from the UNP. In 2003, on the verge of what appeared to be a breakthrough, UNP prime minister Ranil Wickremesinghe found his own efforts to negotiate peace with the Tamil Tigers subjected to harsh criticism and legislative roadblocks cast up by President Kumaratunga herself.

The civil war is clearly the greatest failure of the Sri Lankan government: any regime that permits widespread bloodshed to continue for twenty years can hardly be called a success. In this context, democracy has shown itself to be no magic cure for the chronic ailments of religious or ethnic conflict. Not only have the parties to the civil war had access to the political process, but they have availed themselves of this opportunity while still maintaining military capabilities. In the parliamentary elections of April 2004, the Tamil National Alliance (a proxy party for the dominant faction of the rebel LTTE) won twenty-two seats and 7 percent of the vote. With Kumaratunga's party dominant but unable to gain an absolute majority, this outcome put the representatives of the insurgents, composing the third largest party, in a fairly powerful position. It has not, however, brought the civil war any closer to a long-term resolution. And, as the Indian intervention of 1987–1990 made clear, Sri Lanka's internal warfare has a way of spilling over to affect its regional neighbors.

Since the outbreak of hostilities, it is believed that sixty-four thousand Sri Lankans have been killed. Sri Lanka's economy is expected to grow 4 to 5 percent over each of the next two years, but this rate would be an estimated three percentage points higher in the absence of civil strife. As it is, the growth rate is overshadowed by inflation (9.6 percent in 2002 and expected to remain high for the near future), and the country has only begun to recover from a recession in which the economy shrank by 1.4 percent in 2001.[24]

On the other hand, Sri Lanka's success in economic and social development is all the more remarkable considering the challenges presented. The first South Asian nation to liberalize its economy (as far back as 1977), Sri Lanka has had nearly a fifteen-year head start on its neighbors. The GNP per capital for 2001 was $3,260 in purchasing-power-parity terms, well above that of India or Pakistan, and more than double that of Bangladesh or Nepal; in the Atlas model, Sri Lanka's figure is $880, about twice that of India, Pakistan, and Bangladesh and more than triple that of Nepal.[25] Peace talks between the government and the LTTE are underway, and for the first time the rebels have agreed to accept autonomy rather than full independence. The World Bank has pledged "unconditional support" to the tune of $800 million in grants and no-interest loans over the next four years. In the realm of social development, the gains are even more impressive than those in the economic sphere. Life expectancy at birth is seventy-three years. Literacy is an astounding 89.3 percent for women, 94.5 percent for men, about double the figures for India or Pakistan and approaching those of Western Europe and the United States.[26] Democratization may not be able to deliver all of the goods, but it can clearly deliver some of them.

NEPAL

The only major South Asian nation never to have fallen under colonialist domination, Nepal is also the poorest country in the region and the one with the least success in democratization. The lack of democratic norms seems to be impeding Nepal's social and economic development: decades of unresponsive monarchical rule have given rise to a powerful grassroots rebellion that has stifled the Nepali economy and poses a very real danger to the government itself.

Since its consolidation as an independent country in 1768, a monarch enjoying more or less absolute power has governed Nepal. In 1959 King Mahendra decided to set his country on a democratic path and held open parliamentary elections; the following year, however, he reconsidered the experiment, suspended the newborn constitution, and banned all political parties. Democratization remained on hold for another thirty years.[27] In 1990, following similar ferment throughout the Soviet bloc, and particularly in neighboring China and Tibet, Nepali students and political activists began to stage increasingly vociferous protests. After first attempting to suppress the movement by force, King Birendra decided to accede to their requests and declare his nation a constitutional monarchy. The next decade showcased the wide range of ideas and viewpoints that democracy can set free, as well as the dangers of too much politics and too little governance.

Corruption, never distant from official dealings, became omnipresent. Governments waltzed in and out of office like changing seasons: eleven years of democratic rule saw eleven different parliamentary governments. There was endless talk, but all too little real action. For the second half of the decade, the struggling democracy faced a new challenge: a civil war launched by two communist parties that had previously been successful participants in the electoral process. The Communist Party of Nepal (Maoist) and the United People's Front had been part of a left-wing coalition that had actually won power through the ballot in 1994, but two years later they abandoned their more mainstream comrades in the Nepal Communist Party (united Marxist and Leninist) to go underground and launch a people's war. The fact that this guerrilla movement could be conducted so successfully without the backing of any foreign state, relying purely on grassroots support (be it willing or not) and limited material assistance from ideological soul mates among the Naxalites of India, is testament to the depth of democratization's failure in Nepal. In the latter half of the 1990s, the Maoists established de facto governments in remote rural areas and by many accounts did a better job of providing basic government services than the authorities appointed by Kathmandu. The Nepali army was a ceremonial force, unprepared for actual combat, and therefore kept out of the fight. Police were overextended, underpaid, underequipped, and compelled by circumstances to rely on brutal abuses of human rights instead of professional counterinsurgency campaigns. Every attempt to terrify the populace into cutting off support for the guerrillas merely deepened the alienation of the embattled villagers.

This dynamic—an antidemocratic government strengthening the appeal of an antidemocratic rebel army—has had a deleterious impact on the nations of the region. Instability and lack of governmental control has led to an upswing in international terrorist activity in Nepal. India's Research and Intelligence Wing (RAW) and Pakistan's Inter-Services Intelligence (ISI) bureau have staged a low-intensity espionage war in Kathmandu. It is widely believed that RAW supplies the Royal Nepalese Army with arms and training, and in recent years this role has expanded beyond India to such states as Great Britain and the United States.

The stakes are particularly high for India: the Maoist rebels are widely believed to get arms and financial support from ideological soul mates based in India, such as the Naxalites and the People's War Group. The Nepali insurgents, in turn, send battle-hardened cadres back to India to help train and indoctrinate their comrades to the south. In brief, therefore, Nepal's civil war, fed and perpetuated by a lack of responsive democratic government, has both stoked and been stoked by external forces of varying political hues.

The moral standing of the Nepali state was shaken to its core on the evening of June 1, 2001, in a tragedy almost too bizarre to be credited. Crown Prince Dipendra, in the grip of narcotics and alcohol, distraught over his inability to gain permission to marry the woman of his choice, burst into a family gathering in the royal palace armed with a shotgun, a pistol, and two automatic rifles. Within minutes he had killed both his parents and seven other relatives, before firing his last bullet into his own head. Two years later, Nepalis still refuse to believe that their popular crown prince could have killed their beloved king—there must be some other explanation. But none of the rumors are at all flattering to the parliamentary officials, the rebels, the generals, the few royals lucky enough to survive the massacre, or to anyone else on the political stage.

Prince Gyanendra, the former king's brother, assumed the throne. Gyanendra was widely regarded as being very close to the army—an army that had thus far been kept out of combat against the Maoist rebels, but was quite able to exert its authority over the streets of Kathmandu. In November after the Maoists broke a cease-fire, Gyanendra issued a state of emergency and let the military join in the civil war for the first time. The results have not been a cause for pride: of the seventy-two hundred deaths recorded since the insurgency began in 1996, roughly 60 percent have occurred since Gyanendra's state of emergency. The bulk of these have been killings of civilians (whether

Maoists or bystanders; the figures cannot be reliably broken down) by military and police. This crackdown, however, did little to weaken the insurgency's power. If anything, it may have strengthened the movement by turning yet more of the populace against the government.[28]

Nepal's experiment with democratization was suspended on October 3, 2002. Prime Minister Sher Bahadur Deuba, having rashly asked the king to declare new elections, was forced to admit that his government didn't have the military means of conducting open polling in vast areas of the country. King Gyanendra dismissed parliament and assumed the unfettered monarchical powers of his forefathers. He has opened peace talks with the Maoists, but little progress has been made: the rebels appear to believe they have reached the phase of revolution known in Maoist terminology as strategic stalemate. Their goal, say former comrades and mainstream Communists within the political sphere, is to consolidate their gains in the countryside while preparing for the final strategic offensive against the capital itself. Ironically, the Maoists' grip on the rural areas is itself contingent on the government's failure to democratize. If the palace were able to provide genuine grassroots support to the people, to address their concerns, provide them with basic services, and empower them to take control of their own political, social, and economic fortunes, it is unlikely that the Maoists would find such a widely responsive audience.

As it is, Nepal is a fertile recruiting ground for revolutionary ideas. It is by far the poorest nation in South Asia and one of the dozen poorest nations in the world. The country's GNP per capita is a mere $1,360 (by the purchasing-power-parity model; $250 by the traditional model), barely half the average for the region or the global average for low-income countries. Nearly half the population (42 percent) lives below the poverty line. Life expectancy at birth is a mere fifty-nine years, and literacy is only 43 percent.[29] Even compared with chronically impoverished neighbors like Bangladesh, Nepal seems mired in exceptional destitution. Neither half-hearted stabs at democratization nor the long-term practice of authoritarian monarchical rule has succeeded in bring economic or social development to Nepal. The country is heavily dependent on foreign capital merely to stay afloat: not only is Nepal heavily reliant on direct foreign assistance from governments and international financial institutions, but it depends on international nongovernmental organizations to provide many basic services to the population. Tourism is a crucial part of the domestic economy and is highly vulnerable to upswings in civil unrest.

All of these elements suggest that Nepal's hope may lie in more democratization rather than less: a country able to wall itself off from the outside world can afford to play by its own rules, but a state like Nepal (landlocked, sandwiched between three enormous neighbors, possessing few readily exploitable natural resources other than its beautiful scenery) will remain dependent on the goodwill and support of the wealthy aid-giving nations. Even a more competent display of democratization than that Nepal experienced during the 1990s would not cure the ills of the country quickly, but it might entice the deep-pocketed countries of Western Europe, the United States, and Japan to provide more desperately needed financial medicine.

BANGLADESH

As the only country in South Asia to experience a one-way postcolonial journey from authoritarianism to democratization, Bangladesh might come closer than its neighbors to providing lessons about the interplay of representative government and material development. But any lessons one might draw depend on what point one wishes to demonstrate: is Bangladesh proof of democracy's success or its failure?

From 1947 to 1971, the nation now called Bangladesh was an integral part of Pakistan. During this period the inhabitants of East Pakistan often complained that the government in Islamabad (before that, Karachi) treated them as second-class citizens. They were separated from the center of power not merely by sixteen hundred kilometers of Indian territory but also by the chasms of language, ethnicity, and history. Nearly all of the citizens of East Pakistan were Bengali, while the top ranks of the Pakistani military and political elite were dominated by Punjabis and Urdu-speaking *mohajirs* (migrants from India) of the Western wing. During Pakistan's limited forays into representative government, Bengali politicians failed to mobilize their followers along East–West lines in sufficient numbers to stake a claim at the center; that is, until the election of 1970. The polling of December 7, 1970, Pakistan's first nationwide election, caused a political crisis. The Bengali nationalist Awami League, led by Sheikh Mujibur Rahman, won 160 of the 162 seats assigned to the eastern wing. It was an overwhelming victory: the next-largest party nationwide was Zulfiqar Ali Bhutto's PPP, which won a majority of seats assigned to the west, but barely half (81) as many as the Awami League overall. Neither Bhutto nor military commander Gen. Yahya Khan were willing to shift Pakistan's center of gravity east, and in March of the following year Mujib (as Sheikh Mujibur Rahman was called) declared Bangladesh independent. He was promptly thrown into jail, and the nation began to unravel. Bengali rebels, often armed and equipped by India, staged attacks on government institutions, and the Pakistani military suppressed popular dissent in the east with extreme brutality.

By December ten million Bengali refugees had fled to India. The financial burden ($200 million per month[30]), combined with the strategic opportunity to truncate an enemy against which it had already fought two wars, impelled India to prepare for invasion. Fighting on the western front was inconclusive, but in the eastern theater Indian troops and their Bengali allies routed the Pakistani military. Mujib was released from prison and became Bangladesh's first prime minister. Bangladesh may be the only nation in the world to experience a free election prior to independence but not again for two decades afterward. Mujib was assassinated in 1975, before his party would have to face the electorate. The following sixteen years were a time of military rule and a period characterized by material hardship, political repression, and economic stagnation.

During this period military tensions with neighboring states (especially India) ebbed and flowed but never burst into full-fledged conflict. It would be difficult, however, to attribute this to the form of government in place. A fledgling state greatly indebted to its vastly more powerful neighbor to the west, Bangladesh lacked the military capabilities to challenge India in a meaningful way. With a host of more pressing problems on its plate (floods, poverty, the creation of a national identity distinct from both Pakistan and from Bengalis across the border in the Indian state of West Bengal), the government of Bangladesh had little incentive to embark on foreign adventurism.

In 1991 the country held its first democratic elections. Since then the prime minister's office has been battled over by the two dominant figures of Bangladeshi politics: Khaleda Zia, the daughter of assassinated military leader Gen. Zia-ur Rahman, who won the elections of 1991 and 2001, and Sheikh Hasina Wajed, the daughter of Mujib, who won the election of 1996. Zia's Bangladesh National Party is sometimes described as right-wing and Sheikh Hasina's Awami League as left-wing, but the ideological differences between the two parties are negligible. For more than a decade, the scions of two murdered leaders have used the realm of politics to engage in a bitter contest for the spoils of rule.

It is sometimes said that Bangladesh is a democracy, but only for one day out of every five years. Leaders from both parties have been freely elected and have voluntarily turned power over when voted out of office, but between elections both parties have behaved with scant regard for democratic norms. When in power the ruling party (be it the Awami League or BNP) has treated government as a resource to be exploited to the fullest. When out of power the opposition party has sought to undermine the political process through street protests, strikes, and boycotts of Parliament.

Has democratization led to greater development in Bangladesh? Both democratically elected prime ministers have pursued a program of economic reform, and this has had a generally beneficial effect on the Bangladeshi economy. The country is still very poor: nearly half of the nation's population lives in poverty, and in 2001 a UN report ranked Bangladesh's foreign direct investment 122nd out of 128 countries listed.[31] But the glass can more accurately be described as half-full than half-empty. The economic figures are less gloomy looking forward than backward. The GDP per capita ($1,600 for 2001) is projected to grow nearly 4 percent for the next two years. The country is nearly self-sufficient in rice, the staple food. The rate of population growth has fallen from over 3 percent per year at independence to less than 2 percent at the time of this writing.[32]

Moreover, Bangladesh has made significant strides in indices of social, as opposed to strictly economic, development. Literacy is higher today in the (democratizing) former East Pakistan than in the (nondemocratizing) former West Pakistan: 63 percent versus 55 percent for men, and 49 percent versus 29 percent for women. Bangladesh and Pakistan have nearly identical rates for life expectancy at birth (about 61 years), but this figure hides a telling disparity: Bangladesh has lower rates of both birth and death (25 births and 8.5 deaths per thousand, compared with 30 births and 9 deaths for Pakistan).[33]

Bangladesh's success in microenterprise is a good example of development in both the economic and the social sphere. Grameen Bank has made small loans to over 2.4 million clients, and boasts a recovery rate of 99 percent. Other microenterprises have replicated the formula on a somewhat more modest scale. A common feature of this mode of lending is that it is explicitly geared toward the women of the community: by enabling women (many of them from traditionally conservative rural areas) to start their own businesses, microenterprises advance the causes of economic uplift and female empowerment at the same time.

Elections may check the temperature of the populace only once every half decade, but polling data indicates Bangladeshis see the democratic experiment as one eminently worth pursuing. In the Pew Global Attitudes Project, more than two-thirds of Bangladeshi respondents favored a good democracy over a strong economy and a democratic government over a strong leadership. These percentages are significantly higher than those of Indian and Pakistani respondents or of respondents from the other five Asian countries cited.[34] Moreover, Bangladeshi respondents to the survey topped the Asia list when it came to valuing many of the specific elements of democratization. In enumerating the essential norms of good governance, 71 percent of Bangladeshis cited honest elections, 89 percent a fair judiciary, 93 percent religious freedom, 81 percent free speech, and 64 percent a free press. The figures for Indian respondents were between eight and twenty-three percentage points lower in all categories.[35] The large majority of the Bangladeshi respondents noted that they lacked the very democratic norms that they valued,[36] indicating that Bangladeshis recognize both the promise of democracy and the fact that their own democracy is very much a work in progress.

Has Bangladesh been better served by democracy than military rule? Bangladeshis seem to think so. Despite the slow pace of material development, they want more democratization, not less. Democracy isn't a magical potion; Bangladesh is still a poor country and, deposits of natural gas notwithstanding, will remain one for the foreseeable future. But the flawed, unsteady, democratizing government seems to provide more to its citizens than the prior military governments, be they Bangladeshi or Pakistani, could deliver.

CONCLUSION

Amartya Sen has observed that democracies in South Asia may not always be effective at lifting their populations from poverty and hunger, but they are extremely effective at preventing these social ills from turning into disaster. He notes particularly the case of famine: during (nondemocratic) British colonial rule, India suffered several localized famines in the twentieth century, in which millions of people died, despite the presence of sufficient quantities of food elsewhere in the country. The same can be said of (nondemocratic) Communist China: during the Great Leap Forward, the death toll from unnecessary, man-made famines is reckoned in the tens of millions. No democratic government, Sen argues, could survive such epic mismanagement, and for this reason, he writes, "no substantial famine has ever occurred in a country with a democratic form of government and a relatively free press."[37]

Sen's argument is reinforced by the record of nondemocratic authorities in the other portion of his native Bengal. In 1970 East Pakistan was ravaged by a cyclone of almost apocalyptic proportions; the callous indifference of the government, a military regime dominated by officers from the Western portion of the country, was a key factor in driving the population of the east into first voting overwhelmingly for the Awami League, and then, when their votes were rendered meaningless, to rising in open rebellion. Throughout the 1970s, other cyclones, floods, and natural disasters turned the newly independent Bangladesh into a virtual synonym for developing-world misery, a country known internationally largely for misfortune. It is, perhaps, no coincidence that during this period none of the underperforming, out-of-touch, woefully derelict leaders ever had to subject himself to a democratic election.

Contrast this with the situation in 1998. In that year, Bangladesh, by this time under democratic rule, suffered its worst flooding of the entire twentieth century. Monsoon rains lashed the country for three solid months and left two-thirds of the nation's landmass under water. The extent of the human tragedy was enormous, but the death toll was only about one thousand.[38] The government knew it would have to face the voters and that it stood no chance of retaining office unless it did everything in its power to mitigate the impact of the floods.

Democracy's results are unpredictable: Sheikh Hasina, the Bangladeshi prime minister who ordered massive flood relief, lost badly in the elections of 2001. Indira Gandhi, after leading her nation to overwhelming victory in the 1971 war against Pakistan, saw her popularity plummet after she staged an unnecessary power-grab during the Emergency of 1975–1977 and was voted out of office at the first available opportunity. But the results of democratization almost always provide a more accurate reflection of popular sentiment than other systems. Democracy doesn't automatically produce economic or social development, but it lays a foundation that may well be essential for such development to take place.

Can democratization deliver the goods? Not always, not all the goods, and not to all people, but a democratizing government, even one wracked by corruption and incompetence, may deliver one thing that few military regimes have the ability to conjure up: hope for better performance in the future. Winston Churchill never applied his own maxim to Britain's colonial possessions in South Asia. A champion of democracy at home, he was ironically blind to the inconsistency of denying this form of government to the countries that would soon become modern India, Pakistan, Bangladesh, and Sri Lanka. But democracy tosses up its share of surprises: immediately after winning a war for Britain's (and democracy's) very survival, Churchill was unceremoniously voted out of office. By 1948 he could no longer call himself prime minister (he'd later return for a brief swansong), but Jawaharlal Nehru, Muhammad Ali Jinnah, and S. W. R. D. Bandaranaike could.

The worst form of government, indeed—except for all the rest.

NOTES

1. Of the countries not discussed in this chapter, the Himalayan kingdoms of Bhutan and (until its absorption into India in 1974) Sikkim never ventured down the democratic path. The Maldives took a few minor steps toward representative government in the late 1990s but still forbid the existence of political parties. These states are too small to be considered good test cases: The population of Bhutan and the Maldives together is probably less than one million. The World Bank figures for 2001 list the Maldives as having 280,000 citizens and Bhutan as having 830,000 (World Bank Development Indicators Database, at www.worldbank.org, World Bank, April 2003), but the latter figure includes 100,000 Bhutanese refugees in Nepal and an unspecified number of residents of Bhutan whose citizenship is in dispute. In personal conversations in Thimpu in December 2002, top-ranking officials of the Bhutanese government quoted to me the figure of 600,000 as their best estimate of their country's population.

2. See Francis Fukuyama, *The End of History and the Last Man* (New York: Avon Books, 1993).

3. To help overcome this definitional problem, economists at the World Bank and elsewhere have begun using models based on purchasing-power parity. This method uses as its benchmark not the U.S. dollar but the local purchasing-power equivalent to what a U.S. dollar would have bought in the United States.

4. Max Weber, *The Protestant Ethic and the Spirit of Capitalism*, trans. Talcott Parsons (New York: Charles Scribners' Sons, 1958; original German edition, 1905).

5. Not that it has been universal even in these spheres. Spain, Portugal, Greece, and the states of the former Soviet bloc have only recently democratized, as have most of the countries of Latin America. And as the 2000 election demonstrated, democracy in the United States is still very far from a finished product.

6. India has experienced a great deal of underemployment but less unemployment than it would have if millions of nonproductive workers were cut from the employment rolls. The argument here is not that it makes economic sense to provide ten workers with a pittance instead of one worker with a healthy wage; it is that keeping ten workers on the payroll creates greater social stability than turning nine of them out into the street.

7. Shashi Tharoor, *India: From Midnight to the Millennium* (New York: Arcade, 1997), 166. For a discussion of the economic failings (and modest successes) of India from 1947–1991, see pp. 159–99.

8. For details of Nehruvian land reform, see Lloyd I. Rudolph and Susanne Hoeber Rudolph, *In Pursuit of Lakshmi: The Political Economy of the Indian State* (Chicago: University of Chicago Press, 1987), 109–10, 354–56.

9. The only one of India's neighbors that boasts greater military resources, the Peoples' Republic of China, is beyond the ambit of South Asia.

10. One of the very few instances in which Indian forces took and held any significant amount of territory occurred in the mid-1980s when Indian troops seized possession of much of the Siachen Glacier straddling the poorly demarcated line of actual control between the two countries. This barren patch of land, the world's highest-altitude battleground, is utterly uninhabitable and contested purely for reasons of military and political advantage. For further discussion of conditions on the Pakistani portion of the glacier, see Jonah Blank, "Kashmir: All Tactics, No Strategy," in *The Kashmir Question: Retrospect and Prospect*, ed. Sumit Ganguly (London: Frank Cass, 2003), 193–94.

11. One might attach a number of asterisks to this statement, the most notable indicating the state of Jammu and Kashmir.

12. For a more detailed discussion, see Jeffrey D. Sachs, Ashutosh Varshney, and Nirupam Bajpai, eds., *India in the Era of Economic Reforms* (New Delhi: Oxford University Press, 1999). Tariff figures: Wayne Morrison and K. Alan Krondstadt, "India-US Economic Relations," *Congressional Research Service Report for Congress* (Washington, D.C.: Congressional Research Service, April 22, 2003), 3.

13. Montek Ahluwalia, "India's Economic Reforms: An Appraisal," in *India in the Era,* 33, 55. The World Bank puts India's GDP growth rate for 1992–2002, a period including both the high-growth 1990s and the lower rate after 1997, at an annual average of 6.1 percent (World Bank Development Indicators Database, at www.worldbank.org, World Bank, April 2, 2003).

14. Morrison and Krondstadt, "India-US Economic Relations," 3. India: 1990, $1,400; 2002, $2,610. China: 1990, $1,390; 2002, $4,700. All rates given are calculated on the basis of purchasing-power parity.

15. This rate is slightly down from a 50 percent measure estimated by the World Bank for the 1970s. The Indian government uses a different scale, measuring its poverty rate at 26 percent of the population at the end of the 1990s (versus 36 percent in 1993–1994).

16. Jean Dreze and Amartya Sen, *India: Economic Development and Social Opportunity* (New Delhi: Oxford University Press, 1996), 60.

17. Dreze and Sen, *India*, 60.

18. Bruce Riedel, "American Diplomacy and the 1999 Kargil Summit at Blair House," Center for the Advanced Study of India, Philadelphia, University of Pennsylvania, 2002.

19. World Development Indicators Database, World Bank, at www.worldbank.org, April 2003. The figures are for 2001. By the Atlas method of calculation, Pakistan's GNI per capita was $420, while India's was $460.

20. World Development Indicators Database, World Bank, at www.worldbank.org: Pakistan: 33 percent; India: 29 percent; Bangladesh: 34 percent. These figures are for 2001 and vary from higher poverty figures listed by the World Bank in other documents since they use a different method of calculation. I employ the lower figures here in the interest of transnational comparability.

21. World Development Indicators Database, World Bank, at www.worldbank.org, September 30, 2002.

22. The Pew Global Attitudes Project, "Views of a Changing World." (Washington, D.C.: Pew Research Center, 2003), 7, 37, 41. The survey size for Pakistani respondents was 2,032 in the 2002 poll and 999 in the 2003 one. For polls conducted in Bangladesh and India in 2002, the survey size was 689 and 2,189, respectively.

23. For a more extensive discussion of the political framework of Sri Lanka, including the impact of the civil war on the political system, see Jonah Blank, *Arrow of the Blue-Skinned God: Retracing the Ramayana through India*, 2nd ed. (New York: Grove Press, 2000), 277–300, 360–64.

24. Teresita Schaffer and Nisala Rodrigo, "Sri Lanka: Finding the Start of a Long Road," *South Asia Monitor* 54, Center for Strategic and International Studies, January 1, 2003; World Bank press release, April 1, 2003; "Sri Lanka: Executive Summary," *Global Insight*, May 14, 2003; K. Alan Kronstadt, "Sri Lanka: Background and U.S. Relations," Congressional Research Service Report to Congress (Washington, D.C.: Congressional Research Service, May 30, 2003), 1, 9.

25. Figures from the World Bank, using Atlas method of calculation: Sri Lanka: $880; India: $460; Pakistan: $420; Bangladesh: $360; Nepal: $250. World Bank figures using the purchasing-power-parity method of calculation also put Sri Lanka on top: Sri Lanka: $3,260; India: $2,820; Pakistan: $1,860; Bangladesh: $1,600; Nepal: $1,360. World Bank Development Indicators Database, at www.worldbank.org, World Bank, April 2003.

26. "Sri Lanka at a Glance," World Bank Development Indicators Database, at www.world bank.org, World Bank, September 18, 2002. Kronstadt, "Sri Lanka," 1; The World Bank estimates overall literacy for India at 58 percent and Pakistan at 44 percent (World Bank database at www.worldbank.com, March 28, 2003). In both countries it is widely accepted that the rate for male literacy is significantly higher than the rate for female literacy.

27. In the interests of full disclosure, I should note that my father-in-law served as Nepal's foreign secretary and ambassador to the United Nations during this period. The analysis laid out here is mine alone—and most certainly not his.

28. This view was expressed to me in December 2002 by high-ranking Kathmandu-based Western diplomats and by top officials of the Nepali government.

29. "Nepal at a Glance," World Bank Development Indicators Database, at www.world bank.org, World Bank, November 2002. Dozen poorest countries: K. Alan Kronstadt, "Nepal: Background and U.S. Relations," CRS Report for Congress (Washington, D.C.: Congressional Research Service, 2003), 11.

30. Stanley Wolpert, *A New History of India* (New York: Oxford University Press), 389.

31. K. Alan Kronstadt, "Bangladesh: Background and U.S. Relations," CRS Report to Congress (Washington, D.C.: Congressional Research Service, April 29, 2003), 3–4. The total amount of Bangladesh's foreign direct investment was listed as a mere $78 million for 2001.

32. "Bangladesh at a Glance," World Bank Development Indicators Database, at www .worldbank.org, World Bank, May 22, 2003. Kronstadt, "Bangladesh," 1, 3, 4.

33. *World Factbook, 2002* (Washington, D.C.: Central Intelligence Agency, 2002), 43, 397.

34. Bangladesh figures: 73 percent favor good democracy versus 19 percent for strong economy; 70 percent favor democratic leadership versus 24 percent for strong leadership. By contrast, 56 percent of Indian respondents favored good democracy versus 31 percent for strong economy, and 54 percent of Indians favored democratic leadership versus 34 percent for strong leadership. Results for Pakistani respondents are noted only for the second question, and the comparison is revealing: 42 percent for democratic leadership versus 32 percent for strong leadership. Pew Global Attitudes Project, "Views of a Changing World," 41, 65.

35. Pew Global Attitudes Project, "Views of a Changing World," 62–63.

36. Only 6 percent of Bangladeshi respondents said they had a fair judiciary, 19 percent free speech, 17 percent honest elections, and 13 percent a free press. Pew Global Attitudes Project, "Views of a Changing World," 62–63.

37. Amartya Sen, "Freedoms and Needs: Why Political Rights Are Primary, Even in the Face of Dire Economic Need," *The New Republic*, January 10, 1994, 31. Sen outlines his theory in greater detail in his book *Democracy as Freedom* (New York: Anchor Books, 1999). Among the most notable colonial-era famines was that which hit Bengal in 1943–1944.

38. Kronstadt, "Bangladesh," 4.

FURTHER READING

Bhagwati, Jagdish. *India in Transition*. Oxford: Clarendon Press, 1993.

Bhattachan, Krishna B., and Chaitanya Mishra, eds. *Development Practices in Nepal*. Kathmandu: Tribhuvan University, 1997.

Blank, Jonah. *Mullahs on the Mainframe: Islam and Modernity among the Daudi Bohras*. Chicago: University of Chicago Press, 2001.

Brass, Paul R. *Ethnicity and Nationalism: Theory and Comparison*. New Delhi: Sage Books, 1991.

Cohen, Stephen P. *India: Emerging Power*. Washington, D.C.: Brookings Institution Press, 2001.

Dreze, Jean, and Amartya Sen. *India: Economic Development and Social Opportunity*. New Delhi: Oxford University Press, 1996.

Ganguly, Sumit. *The Origins of War in South Asia*. Boulder, Colo.: Westview Press, 1994.

Jalal, Ayesha. *The State of Martial Rule*. Lahore: Vanguard Press, 1991.

Kux, Dennis. *Disenchanted Allies: The United States and Pakistan, 1947–2000*. Washington, D.C.: Woodrow Wilson Center Press, 2001.

Lodhi, Maleeha. *Pakistan's Encounter with Democracy*. Lahore: Vanguard Press, 1994.

Pandey, Devendra Raj, and Anand Aditya, eds. *Democracy and Empowerment in South Asia*. Kathmandu: Nepal South Asia Center, 1995.

Rudolph, Lloyd, and Susanne Hoeber Rudolph. *In Pursuit of Lakshmi: The Political Economy of the Indian State*. Chicago: University of Chicago Press, 1987.

Scott, James C., and Nina Bhatt, eds. *Agrarian Studies: Synthetic Work at the Cutting Edge*. New Haven, Conn.: Yale University Press, 2001.

Sen, Amartya. *Inequality Reexamined*. Oxford: Clarendon Press, 1992.

Sisson, Richard, and Leo E. Rose. *War and Secession: Pakistan, India, and the Creation of Bangladesh*. Berkeley: University of California Press, 1990.

11

Globalization and Economic Liberalization

Anupam Srivastava

This chapter discusses the state of the economy in the countries of South Asia and examines the impact of globalization and economic liberalization on their economies. In an increasingly interconnected world of instant communications, rising popular expectations, and relentless scrutiny, the national leadership in the relatively impoverished countries of South Asia is struggling to balance the competing demands for enhanced security, economic growth, and environmental safety, among others. This task has been made more complicated with the intensification of the forces of globalization that present greater opportunities as well as greater perils. This challenge is reminiscent of the difficult economic choices that Britain faced at the end of World War II. Sir Winston Churchill, then the prime minister, is said to have remarked, "I would like to appoint a Finance Minister who has only one hand . . . so that his policy advice does not begin with . . . on the one hand we should do this, and on the other do that."

This chapter examines the state of the national economy in the seven countries of South Asia (excluding Afghanistan, whose war-ravaged economy is treated to the extent possible in chapter 5), including how globalization has influenced their policy choices and might impact their future. It proceeds in three sections. The opening section describes the terms *globalization* and *economic liberalization* and provides the overall context within which to examine their roles and influence in South Asia. The second section provides a succinct portrayal of the contemporary state of the economy in each of the seven countries and their principal strengths and weaknesses. The bulk of this discussion focuses on the last decade of the twentieth century since it was in 1991 that the Soviet Union disintegrated, signaling the end of the Cold War. The consequent end to the East–West confrontation also marked the start of the process to dismantle technology embargoes, provided greater latitude and impetus for countries to undertake political and economic reforms, and witnessed an overall intensification of the forces of globalization. The third section assesses the role and relevance of regional organizations and other models that might assist in improving the overall economic performance of the South Asian states.

GLOBALIZATION AND ECONOMIC LIBERALIZATION

The true meaning of the term *globalization*, its core contents, and its impact on the economies and societies of developed versus developing countries have been vigorously contested for a long time now. This debate reminds one of the story of the elephant and the seven blind men. Each person touched a separate part of the pachyderm's anatomy, and depending upon the contours of that part, described the complete animal, with his imagination taking over where his visual faculty left off. The message of this allegory is not that the narratives were inherently flawed in their analytical conception. It is rather that globalization is a complex dynamic that is still unfolding and one account of it could be at significant variance with another; yet, both might offer true but partial accounts of the overall phenomenon.[1]

Indeed, in contemporary international discourse this term is often bandied about as a new phenomenon. In reality, globalization has long been a feature of the international system, whether it relates to transmigration of people, cross-fertilization of ideas, or even transmutation of technologies. What has changed distinctively in recent decades is the pace and scope of globalization, and as its most powerful manifestation, advanced technology runs through the increasingly complex jigsaw of the international system as a lubricant, imparting to it liquidity as well as dynamism. Thus, the distinctive aspect of contemporary globalization is the increase in its liquidity, which makes it a diabolical phenomenon, capable of tremendous progress but also considerable harm.

Most experts agree that at its core, globalization denotes the international integration of the basic factors of production (i.e., labor, capital, technology, and entrepreneurship) and their output (i.e., goods and services).[2] As national economies become increasingly integrated into the global economic matrix, this blurs the traditional boundaries between the local, national, and transnational and impinges crucially upon the latitude, jurisdiction, and sovereignty of state actors in the international system. For instance, the volume of total capital flows across international markets often exceeds $100 billion a day, which is greater than the size of the national economies of over half the countries in the world! Clearly, adverse capital flows, that is, foreign investment flowing out of an important sector of a country's economy, could prove disastrous, at least in the short-term. On the other hand, if the fundamentals of an economy are strong and the government has helped create a favorable climate for foreign investment, massive infusions of foreign capital can occur within weeks, dramatically improving capital availability in the relevant sectors of the domestic economy.[3]

Similarly, when a multinational company (MNC) seeks to reduce its costs of production, it can elect to outsource production of a product to its subsidiary unit in a foreign country (say, *A*).[4] This is likely to substantially increase the aggregate demand for (and supply of) labor in the new host country *A* and to depress the demand for labor in the parent country. Over time, because of increased production and sales, wages are likely to rise in *A* in the sector where the MNC is operating, eroding the latter's profit margins. The MNC might then elect to shift its production of that product to another country (say, *B*), where it finds the relevant labor skills and other enabling conditions (i.e., availability of the other factors of production at competitive prices). This movement of production is captured in the economics literature as the product-cycle theory. This movement does not necessarily imply that the MNC will shift all of its production from country *A* to *B*. It is often the case that the skill-sets of the relevant labor force in *A* have improved sufficiently such that the MNC can now start producing greater value-added products from *A* that require a higher degree of labor specialization. Alternately, domestic entrepreneurs in *A* might step into the void created by the departing MNC and produce specialized goods that might be competitive in the domestic as well as international markets.

On the other hand, a negative and all-too-familiar outcome could be that the government of country *A*, in its eagerness to retain the business of the MNC, permits it to keep wages artificially low or ignores the use of environmentally polluting technologies by the MNC. Such actions can seriously distort the factor market in *A*, thwart the rise of indigenous businesses, and degrade the environment in the country or even beyond its borders. An ill-conceived wooing of the business of the MNC in *A*, or in *B*, or as they compete with each other, often leads to a "race to the bottom" in terms of the overall economic and environmental health of the two countries. This is often the result of self-serving motives and opportunistic behavior on the part of government officials in *A* or *B*. On the flip side, sound strategies by government officials could leverage the presence of the MNC as a dynamo to invigorate the indigenous industrial base and promote equitable economic development.

Finally, globalization connotes several noninvestment and noneconomic changes as well. For instance, the Globalization Index developed by *A. T. Kearny/Foreign Policy Magazine* includes rankings of sixty-two countries for thirteen variables grouped in four baskets: economic integration, personal contact, technology, and political engagement.[5] Other yardsticks of globalization include percentage of trade to gross domestic product (GDP), technology flows (especially intangible or knowledge-based technologies), levels of telephone density, per capita usage of personal computers, and access to the Internet, among others. In sum, the forces of globalization and their impact are neither uniformly positive nor negative. Instead, this dynamic, which is almost technologically deterministic in nature, must be conceptualized in value-neutral terms. Globalization signals a logical progression of the free-market capitalist ideology, and embracing it proactively can assist in devising a policy and regulatory framework that optimizes the gains from this powerful force. At the international level, it underlines the need for policy coordination among the community of nations and principal substate or parastate economic actors, including the MNCs. And at the domestic level, it underscores the need for generating wider clarity and subsequent consensus on proactive policy making where significant national actors and interests act in concert to pursue realistic goals within the permissible domain of enlightened self-interest.

By comparison, the term *economic liberalization* is relatively simpler to comprehend, even if not easy for governments to implement and sustain over time. In essence, economic liberalization denotes an attitudinal change along with changes in the structures and processes of an economy that was hitherto closed to the international markets. In attitudinal terms, this means change in the role of the government from chief controller to facilitator and arbiter of competing economic groups and interests within a country. The structural and procedural derivatives of liberalization signify the entire gamut of changes that result from the deliberate policies of governments to permit a greater role for market forces in the functioning of the economy. It includes, for example, reduced regulations in the labor market concerning the setting of wages, conditions for hiring and firing of workers, compensation, medical and retirement benefits, and laws governing the operation of labor unions. More broadly, in the factor market, it means a greater role for market forces to determine resource allocation in different sectors of production, as well as in the mobility of labor and capital. Further, the government lowers the overall levels of tariffs on imports and exports, desists from an overly protectionist use of nontariff barriers (NTBs) and quotas that infringe on free trade, and simplifies the rules for the entry, exit, and functioning of domestic and international firms, among others. Along with the above are a host of policy changes that a government enacts to implement economic liberalization. This includes changing the regulatory framework of the economy, strengthening the rule of law, securing intellectual property rights, reforming the banking sector, and taking active membership in regional organizations and multilateral institutions.

COUNTRY ASSESSMENTS

India's relative scores on almost all indices of measurement accord it the predominant position among the seven South Asian countries examined here, although this does not ipso facto imply that it is the most successful of them. To an extent this preponderance is natural, given that the remaining six countries were formally or otherwise a part of the ancient Indian Empire or a protectorate of it, as in the case of Ceylon (now Sri Lanka), until their independence at varying times during the twentieth century. Thus, India's economy is nearly 80 percent of South Asia, its population over 65 percent, and its landmass over 55 percent, and it is the only country that shares land or sea borders with all of the other six countries.

After securing its independence from the British on August 15, 1947, the government of India (GOI) pursued a conscious policy of welfare socialism until at least the mid-1980s, when the first hesitant blush of reforms appeared on the Indian economic horizon. Prior to that, partly buoyed by the early successes of the Soviet planning model (including the Gos Plan and Pyatiletki), the GOI launched its five-year plans. During the 1950s and 1960s, the plans emphasized development of agriculture, heavy engineering, and the need to locate major industrial centers in the strategic hinterland of the four metropolises (New Delhi, Mumbai, Kolkatta, and Chennai) so as to prevent inordinate population pressure over any one area. This industrial-dispersal strategy has worked up to a point (in contrast to Mexico City, Taipei, or Tokyo), although the enormous population still puts an onerous burden on domestic resources and strategies to avoid urban congestion.

Further, in the years after independence, the GOI enacted the Industrial Development and Regulation Act (1951), the Monopolies and Restrictive Trade Practices Act (1969), and the Foreign Exchange Regulation Act (1973) to deliberately restrict growth of the domestic private sector and limit the scope for foreign participation in Indian firms. Sadly, the government did not progressively roll back its overly protectionist policies. One consequence was the birth of the infamous "license raj" (or "license rule"), a moniker suggestive of the cumbersome procedures for obtaining licenses and government clearances and a host of operational constraints. Over time, this created an unhealthy collusion of political-bureaucratic-economic interests, and this entrenched troika effectively thwarted the enterprise of all but the strongest, wealthiest, and politically best connected.[6] The inevitable outcome was that the inefficiencies of the production process, including high costs and low quality, were passed on to the consumers in an economy insulated from competition by high protective tariff walls.

An acute balance-of-payments crisis in July 1991[7] was in part the catalyst for the GOI decision to initiate a bold and systematic process of economic reforms. One of the more heartening developments today is a grudging consensus among the major political parties that reforms must be continued and deepened, although differences remain regarding their center of gravity along the growth-versus-redistribution axes. This is crucial for the pursuit of the second generation of reforms, which will be easier for those who have embraced the reforms but harder for many others. A succinct review of the first-generation reforms reveals that the GOI has undertaken a series of progressive measures in fiscal policy, trade- and exchange-rate policy, industrial policy, and foreign-investment policy. Thus, tariffs have been successively lowered from a high of 200 to 300 percent in 1991 to below 25 percent in 2004, although these rates are still among the highest in Asia (a comparative tariff in the advanced industrialized countries is 10 percent). As a founding member of the General Agreement on Tariffs and Trade (GATT) and its successor body, the World Trade Organization (WTO), India is obligated to reduce its median tariffs to 15 percent by 2005.

Other indices measuring the openness of the Indian economy and the influence of globalization reveal a mixed picture. On the positive side, foreign exchange ("forex") reserves have grown from near zero to $110 billion.[8] The average GDP growth for the period from 1991 to 2000 is 6.5 percent and is sustainable at this rate in the medium term. The size of the economy has more than doubled during this period to over $500 billion, making India the tenth-largest economy in the world and the fourth largest in terms of purchasing-power parity (PPP). Exports grew from a low of $9 billion to $58 billion in 2004, while imports during the same period grew from $10 billion to $65 billion. Even more significant, both the export and import baskets have shown a positive diversification of product-country mix during this period. The relative weight of traditional export earners (gems, jewelry, textiles, handicrafts, tea, minerals, etc.) has declined in favor of newer items (chemicals, pharmaceuticals, engineering goods, marine products, petroleum derivatives, software and IT-enabled services, etc.). International estimates of software and IT-enabled exports alone will top $50 billion by 2008, and biotechnology-related exports are expected to net $25 to $50 billion by 2010. The import basket too has changed significantly over this period and now includes a larger share of capital goods and equipment to stimulate domestic export-oriented production. This diversification in the export and import profiles is indicative of the conscious policy to pursue modernization and a broad export-led growth (XLG) strategy.[9] The import-substitution-industrialization (ISI) strategy, which yielded partial dividends as India briefly experimented with it through the 1960s and 1970s, as did much of Latin America and parts of Africa, has been given a quiet burial.[10] On the negative side, a consistent criticism offered by both international and domestic experts is the consistently high level of fiscal deficit (4 to 5 percent of GDP), which left unchecked might constrain rapid economic growth in the future.

Clearly, the macroindicators at the close of the previous decade reveal an encouraging trend. To wit, India's middle class has become a rapidly growing consumer market that by international standards of disposable income is over 150 million strong. However, even accounting for the lower prices in the domestic market that swell the actual size of the Indian middle class, the country is still home to a staggering population below the poverty level (25 percent of the total population of over one billion). At the same time, since 1991, poverty has declined both in percentage terms (from 36 percent to 25 percent) and in absolute numbers. This negates the popular myth propagated in Indian domestic politics that economic liberalization favors the rich and powerful at the expense of the poor. On the other hand, although the rate of population growth has been brought down to 1.47 percent, India's sheer population (nearly one-sixth of the world's population) renders the scale and scope of the remaining task of eliminating poverty and promoting balanced development a formidable one. Yet, the strong fundamentals of its economy and the ongoing reforms have consistently merited a significant portion of developmental aid from the World Bank. In recent years India has considerably reduced its foreign indebtedness (its percentage of external debt to GDP is now about 4.5 percent), especially the share of short-term borrowings. This, and the fact that forex reserves are above $110 billion, have prompted the International Monetary Fund (IMF) to take India off its list of countries in need of borrowings in the foreseeable future.

Another significant impact of the reforms process has been the declining role of state-owned enterprises (SOEs) in India: the private sector now accounts for almost 75 percent of the national GDP. Similarly, life expectancy has improved to sixty-four years and literacy levels to 60 percent, although regionwide data remain highly skewed in favor of the economically progressive southern states. Finally, India has one of the largest technical manpower pools in the world, a well-developed banking system, an extensive commercial banking network of over sixty-three thousand branches, and a vibrant capital market comprising twenty-two stock exchanges with over nine thousand listed companies. A well-established rule of law, an independent (though tardy) judiciary, English as the preferred language of business, and entrenched democratic institutions complete the picture.

The country is now embarked upon the second generation of economic reforms. One of its most important features is the attempt to make individual state governments partner with the federal government in an "alliance for progress." For instance, until 2000, foreign trade had remained part of the central government's jurisdiction such that state governments could not tax the exports generated in their territory; nor would the revenue return directly to their exchequer. But starting in 2000, the GOI allocated $60 million, to be renewed annually, to assist states in the development of their export-related infrastructure based upon their export performance. States would spend this sum on building roads that connect production centers to commercial ports, research and development of state-specific ethnic products, development of cold chains for agroproducts, development of market infrastructure, and so forth. Another crucial feature is the emphasis on developing special economic zones (SEZs) and upgrading the export-processing zones (EPZs) to SEZ status. This approach, analogous to the Chinese Shenzen model, includes tax breaks for firms exporting over 50 percent of their outputs, a modern and reliable infrastructure, and a host of measures to attract domestic and foreign industry.

The automotive industry adequately represents the pains and gains of the Indian experience with economic reforms and globalization. India's bigger and paternalistically oriented automotive houses, as well as several inefficient, smaller firms, closed down or suffered under the stiff competition, especially from Japan, South Korea, Germany, and Italy. Within a few years of painful restructuring and investment in the latest capital equipment and production techniques, however, the Indian automotive industry recovered to emerge at par with the competition. Further, a number of major Indian cities now employ compressed natural gas (CNG) as an alternate fuel, and all cars produced since 2000 require the installation of catalytic converters that comply with Euro-2 emission standards. Equally significant, when the labor union of a government-owned automobile company (Maruti Udyog Limited) staged a protest to demand a hike in wages, the government refused to cave in, stating that salaries of workers in private firms with higher productivity remained lower than those of workers in the government ones. The automotive industry clearly serves as a microcosm of the Indian experience with economic reforms and coping with the forces of globalization.

On a broader plane, the increased pragmatism and growing success of the economy has gradually influenced India's foreign and security policy trajectories as well. Rapid economic growth is seen not just as reducing poverty and addressing developmental imperatives but also as a means to elevate the country beyond the confines of South Asia. As such, growing economic ties are being leveraged to secure better outcomes in foreign policy negotiations. Thus, while the European Union and the United States remain the largest bilateral trade partners, India has steadily increased economic ties with China and with East and Southeast Asia.[11] Similarly, in 2003 India made available a small, but highly symbolic, grant (of $250 million) to the "least developed countries." The message was that India is no longer merely a recipient, but now also a donor, country. Overt comparisons with China and the adroit use of economics in China's foreign policy negotiations are becoming common in

Indian strategic discourse. Both domestic and foreign participation are increasingly permitted in defense production, while the government and industry are coordinating strategies to offset the growing backlash in the United States against the outsourcing of white-collar jobs to India. Thus, India's ongoing economic reforms are instructive of how this large, diverse, and relatively poor country in South Asia has sought to harness, as well as cope with, the forces of globalization.

The economy of Pakistan is characterized by a relatively well-developed agrarian sector and a manufacturing sector primarily engaged in the production of goods that embody modest levels of labor and technology specialization. The same is true for the service sector, which in 2003 contributed about 51 percent to the national GDP while employing 39 percent of the labor force, with outputs embodying modest levels of specialization. The overall GDP for Pakistan recorded a moderate-to-high growth rate of 4 to 6 percent after its independence until the mid-1990s, making it one of the faster growing economies in South Asia. The subsequent dramatic slowdown in its growth rate is attributable in part to the international sanctions imposed on Pakistan after it (and India) conducted a series of subterranean nuclear explosions in May 1998.

Following the attacks on the United States on September 11, 2001, Washington enlisted the support of Pakistan in its global war on terrorism, restoring the frontline status of that country in the U.S. strategic calculus. This has resulted in the U.S. waiver of economic sanctions, fresh aid exceeding $3 billion, help in renegotiating longer payment terms for prior international loans, and fresh allotment of multilateral loans with an extended payment window (over $3 billion from the World Bank, IMF, and Asian Development Bank). This period has also seen most advanced industrial countries lifting their sanctions and renewing economic aid to Pakistan. The net result has been that Pakistan has secured valuable breathing room to implement much-needed reforms and put its economic house back in order.

Pakistan briefly attempted economic reforms in the early 1990s, but its momentum and scope were constrained by longer-standing structural problems and the adverse role of entrenched politico-economic forces. The unfinished agenda of land reforms from the early decades after the country's creation in 1947 set this stage, resulting in distortions of the size of individual land holdings and uprooting peasants and sharecroppers from their ancestral lands without offering them viable employment in the formal agrarian sector. Over the years the landowning elite with political patronage consolidated their hold over economic decision making and extended their influence on the industrial sector as well, with the military controlling the majority of national economic assets. Income inequality in Pakistan has worsened to the point where over 80 percent of the national wealth is controlled by the top 10 percent of the population, severely limiting the rise of the middle class and the voice of progressive forces in economic agenda setting.

In spite of sectoral and structural distortions, Pakistan's economy has never been completely insulated from international influence. A private consortium called the Independent Power Producers has made Pakistan an electricity-surplus country since the mid-1990s, while a host of MNCs in the apparel and textile industry continue to operate from Pakistan to service their global markets. The pathology of the malady that has plagued Pakistan's economy over the decades is the monopolistic stranglehold of entrenched domestic interests that resist opening the economy to free competition, both from within and without. A revealing example is the refusal to export surplus electricity to India and to remove quantitative restrictions and quotas on imports from India. Worse, Pakistan has refused to grant most-favored nation (MFN) status to India, although as a member of the WTO (and GATT before that), it is obligated to do so.

A brief review of the principal challenges facing the Pakistani economy enables us to make an objective assessment of its longer-term viability.[12] The GDP of Pakistan in 2000 was approximately $67 billion in constant 1997 U.S. dollar terms. When one adds up the total debt, interest payments on the debt, and the defense budget, the sum nearly equals the total GDP for the country! This leaves precious few resources in the hands of the government to allocate for economic development or investments in education, infrastructure, or other targeted spending to stimulate growth. One possible avenue to generate additional resources for the government would be to enhance its tax receipts, an endeavor that has had limited success so far. Other revenue could come from enhanced domestic investments, given the relatively modest per capita domestic-savings rate (about 25 percent), but this in turn is limited by two factors. One, the disposable income in the hands of the average Pakistani for medium-to-longer term investment is relatively modest. Two, given the uncertainties of return on investment in the national market, a majority of Pakistanis instead opt to invest their money abroad. This changed somewhat between 2001 and 2003 because U.S. and EU efforts at tracking and freezing financial networks suspected of supporting al Qaeda have scared many expatriate Pakistanis, who have started to remit their savings, causing a sharp rally of the Karachi Stock Exchange.[13] But this phenomenon is not expected to last long and, in any case, does not provide sufficient capital to finance the enormous developmental requirements of the country. In the absence of genuine banking reforms, the investment prospects are unlikely to improve drastically. A case in point is the March 2004 report by the auditor general of Pakistan, which states that foreign exchange reserves had been shored up using irregular speculation that cost the State Bank of Pakistan, the apex bank of the country, $109 million.[14]

A third avenue to stimulate domestic growth, especially in the high-end manufacturing and services sector, would be to attract foreign investment. However, an external investor bases his decision on, among other things, the political stability of the country and its macroeconomic policies. Inflamed rhetoric about Kashmir and war with India, plus very high levels of defense spending, do not generate the requisite investor confidence. Equally, refusal to join international-security regimes means restrictions on access to advanced technology even for the civilian sector. Since Pakistan does not have much of an indigenous industrial base to begin with, its ability to generate and sustain high levels of economic growth on its own remains severely limited. Soon after Gen. Pervez Musharraf overthrew the civilian government to take power in a bloodless coup on October 17, 1999, his administration outlined a series of priorities for the government.[15] These included rebuilding investor confidence through stability and consistency in economic policy, increasing domestic savings, carrying out tax reforms, restructuring state enterprises, developing the information-technology sector, and reducing corruption. These priorities mirror the principal prescriptions of the World Bank economic report on Pakistan issued in April 1999,[16] which detailed the country's adroit economic and diplomatic management to tide over the adverse conditions created following the nuclear tests of May 1998. It stated that by these actions, the country had "gained a window of opportunity to . . . refocus on the key structural constraints while putting macroeconomic stabilization on a sustainable footing."

A generic challenge faced by regimes in such situations is that a crash program of economic revival presents two inescapable problems. One, it involves economywide belt tightening, which includes restructuring, cloture, and shedding of inefficiencies. Since much of the inefficiency obtains in the SOEs, which in addition to being close to the center of power also provide large-scale employment, such decisions generate widespread discontent. Thus, proceeding with this belt-tightening gets mired in politically embedded bargains for the favored few. Two, economic-stimulation measures require emphasizing growth over redistribution in the short run, briefly widening income inequality. For a country with widespread poverty, such measures unleash mass discontent, making the disadvantaged especially susceptible to opportunistic political mobilization. Apart from growing disillusionment with the ruling establishment, if and when Musharraf cedes power to civilian rule (not the return to limited civilian rule, as at present), conditions would be ripe for a return to populist economic policies that could neutralize any gains that his administration might have made. On the other hand, if Musharraf succeeds in steering the economy toward a balanced profile and higher trajectory of growth and stays in power long enough to cleanse state and private institutions, the Pakistani economy could yet turn a healthy corner. Failure will mean a revisitation of the nonvirtuous cycle of military and civilian rule that has scoured the economic landscape of many a country in Latin America and Africa.

Sri Lanka was the first country in South Asia to have initiated economic reforms in a process that started as early as 1977. Indeed, during the initial period after its independence in 1948, Sri Lanka (or Ceylon as the country was called until 1972) pursued a liberal trade regime until growing balance-of-payments (BOP) problems induced a policy shift toward the protectionist ISI approach in the early 1960s. By the mid-1970s, Sri Lanka had become one of the most inward-oriented economies outside the group of centrally planned, Soviet-style economies. In 1977 it responded to the dismal economic outcome of the protectionist era by embarking on an extensive economic liberalization process, making it the first South Asian state to pursue this course of action.[17] In spite of major macroeconomic problems and political turmoil, the trajectory of reforms has been maintained, making it one of only four countries outside of East Asia (together with Argentina, Uruguay, and Chile) to have achieved a clear policy shift from ISI to XLG.[18]

The lessons from the earliest attempts at reforms (1948–1965) and the adverse outcomes of the protectionist era (1965–1976) proved instructive in initiating the first generation of reforms in 1977. Significant trade reforms were enacted wherein quantitative restrictions were replaced by tariffs, and tariff structures were simplified and streamlined. Similarly, restrictions on foreign investment were reduced and attractive norms provided to stimulate investment in export-oriented firms operating in the free-trade zones (FTZs). Other changes included substantial financial- and banking-sector reforms, realignment of exchange rates, and limits placed on the role of SOEs, especially in determining resource allocation, output, and employment outcomes in the national economy.[19] To a great extent, the trajectory and momentum of these reforms suffered during the 1980s with a partial return to populist government schemes and the rising toll of the raging ethnic violence between the majority Sinhalas and the secessionist Tamil movement. However, in 1990 the government responded by initiating the second generation of reforms designed to carry forward the liberalization program. This included the promotion of privatization, further tariff cuts, removal of exchange controls on current account transactions, and broader changes to the foreign-investment policy. In the late 1990s the economy stumbled, and GDP growth has slowed down considerably, partly on account of the Asian financial crisis (1997) and later with the surge in domestic separatist violence.[20]

Nevertheless, cumulative assessment of the two generations of economic liberalization reveals a modest, but wholesome, impact on the national economy, factor productivity, employment, foreign investment, and export orientation of the national economy. The government has also permitted market forces a greater influence in the domestic labor market. This has resulted in a reduced number of work hours lost to labor disputes, flexible wages, a rise in labor productivity, and an increase in its mobility and skill levels in response to the aggregate demand in the more productive sectors of the domestic economy. One heartening aspect of the reforms is the growing bipartisan political consensus to continue with this process and trajectory. For instance, the long rule (1977–1994) of the United National Party (UNP) ended when it lost power to its main opposition party, the People's Alliance (PA), in the 1994 general elections. Contrary to popular fears, the PA continued and to an extent accelerated the reforms, particularly toward privatization. Similarly, in 1997 an important policy report commissioned by the National Development Council recommended greater, albeit selective, state intervention to enhance domestic technological capability and improve coordination between SOEs and the private sector.[21] The central bureaucracy declined to implement these guidelines, persisting with a more laissez-faire approach, a decision that is perhaps a reflection of their growing experience in economic management and recognition of limits on the utility of state intervention.

It is clear from the preceding analysis that the Sri Lankan economy has been exposed to international economic forces since 1977, including during the last decade of the twentieth century, which coincided with the intensification of the impact of globalization. It is further evident that on balance the economy has performed better when it has not been completely insulated from international competition. On the contrary, external technological and capital investments have improved the capacity utilization of Sri Lankan firms, increased factor productivity and brought it closer to international standards, enhanced the share of exports and the role of the private sector in national output, and made the economy more resilient to international competition.

Finally, the operation of foreign-owned export-oriented firms alongside domestic ones has improved business performance and factor productivity to the point where the prices of Sri Lanka's major exports (especially textiles, engineering goods, and electronics) have increasingly converged with international prices, a clear pointer to their longer-term viability. This is significant, given that the benefits from the quota-based Multi-Fiber Agreement (MFA) will now erode for a small country such as Sri Lanka as the MFA gets folded into the WTO by 2005. This is in addition to the wider set of WTO obligations that Sri Lanka must adhere to in terms of tariffs, nontariff barriers, and other restrictions.

On balance, a longer-term projection of the economic performance of Sri Lanka reveals a cautiously positive picture.[22] On the other hand, significant impediments to this salutary outcome reside in the political arena. The economic costs of the long civil war on Sri Lanka's economy have been significant, especially during its worst phase, when the country's military budget jumped from 1 to 7 percent (it is now back to about 4 percent). It is notable that the government has managed to adequately insulate the conflict from destroying the larger economic landscape, although economic disparity across the region has certainly grown over time. Moreover, the conflict has kept foreign investors away from making any longer-term investments and locating their export-oriented businesses in Sri Lanka. Thus, the country's ability to fully realize its economic potential (beyond its current plateau) will remain impaired until its longer-term political and macroeconomic stability is assured.

The economic landscape of Bangladesh bears the mark of its creation and political history. When Britain granted independence to India in 1947, it partitioned the country into two, in the process creating Pakistan, with East Pakistan separated from its western part by over one thousand miles of Indian territory. The mechanism for sharing seats and power in the unified Pakistani Parliament, located in West Pakistan, never reached an optimal stage, with the center of gravity of political and military powers heavily skewed in favor of the west. The landslide victory of the Awami League party led by Mujib-ur Rehman in East Pakistan during the 1971 general elections stipulated that he form the government to oversee both parts of the country. This was unacceptable to the military and the political leadership of West Pakistan, triggering a major political crisis that rapidly escalated into a war of independence. The Bengali separatists requested that India intervene, and the ensuing war ultimately resulted in East Pakistan becoming the independent state of Bangladesh in 1971.

The political landscape of Bangladesh and the country's economic decision making continue to bear the imprint of its turbulent past. Thus, Mujib's insurgents morphed into the Bangladesh Krishak (farmer) Shramik (laborer) Awami League party, which he used as a vehicle to centralize power and amend the constitution. His daughter, Sheikh Hasina Wajed, is now the leader of the Awami League ("party of the masses") in the personality-dominated politics of Bangladesh. The rival, Bangladesh Nationalist Party (BNP), took power in the October 2001 elections and is led by Begum Khaleda Zia, widow of the former president, Gen. Zia-ur Rehman. General Zia had seized power in a coup (in 1976) a few months after Mujib's assassination in 1975, while his own assassination in 1981 brought General Ershad to power and a prolonged military rule (1982–1990). And although democratic governance has not been interrupted since 1990, the military continues to wield enormous power over national decisions, including in the economic arena.

Agriculture has been the mainstay of Bangladesh's economy, although the country took notable steps during the 1990s to diversify its agrarian output, enhance factor productivity, and improve the share of agrobased products in national exports. It is now largely self-sufficient in rice production, with jute and wheat production improving in recent years. The dependence on monsoons for irrigation remains high, with the annual variation in rains affecting agro-output. The destructive impact of cyclones and ocean tides has been managed to a large extent with the use of satellite-generated weather-forecasting data, while technology-embedded capital investments have improved cropping patterns, yield, storage, distribution, and exports. Since 1975 Bangladesh has demonstrated an episodic progression toward a greater role and market share for the private sector, although inefficient and overemployed SOEs continue to be propped up by government doles. This familiar malaise began to be eradicated with more vigor in the 1990s, including the government's successfully implementing the enhanced structural adjustment facility (ESAF) recommendations of the IMF during 1989 to 1993. The BNP government (1991–1996) initiated tax reforms and permitted greater foreign direct investment (FDI) into the gas and power sectors. The Awami League (1996–2001) had opposed the steps of the previous regime, but once in power essentially continued the reforms trajectory, although privatization has been stunted by periodic worker unrest and intervention by entrenched politico-economic interests.[23]

Banking-sector reforms are a major priority to catalyze the manufacturing and services sectors. State-owned banks are largely dysfunctional, control almost 75 percent of total deposits and loans, carry an unhealthy burden of nonperforming loans, and show other related symptoms of "crony capitalism." In this context, the most refreshing change has come from the novel concept of grameen banks that issue microcredits to a village or a group rather than an individual. Rural women have led this transformation, and their sense of group pride in repaying the loans has meant that grameen banks have a track record of over 95 percent of loan repayment, and on schedule![24] Micro-credit has spurred the growth of cottage and small-scale industries in textiles and jute-derivative products that are able to compete in the international market. Another imaginative use of micro-credit has been in individual villagers purchasing cellular telephones, and making their use commercially available to entire villages, bypassing the problem of land-phone connectivity.

In sum, Bangladesh embarked on an arduous path toward economic liberalization and harnessing the positive forces of globalization during the 1990s, although significant hurdles remain. It still ranks among the least-developed countries (LDCs) with very high and worsening population density, poverty (35 percent), and unemployment (38 percent). On the positive side, the GDP has grown consistently around 5 percent, and inflation remained in single digits throughout the 1990s. The country has considerable natural gas (and some oil) reserves that will well surpass its domestic demand for at least fifty years. This is a good case where the military and political leadership must explore a strategic decision as to whether to export gas via overland pipelines (to an energy-deficient India[25]) or as liquefied natural gas (LNG) via ships to distant markets. In either case, sound economic decisions would persuade foreign companies to invest in longer-term exploration and exports and in the process augment national capacity to accelerate the task of economic growth and its equitable distribution.

Nepal is the only country in the world with Hinduism as its official state religion. Nestled in the Himalayas, it is linked by arduous mountain passes to China in the north, and its only viable land access to the outside world is through India to the south. India's assistance was crucial in 1951 when this landlocked country established a constitutional monarchy whose governance is aided by a parliamentary democracy. While India remains the predominant factor in Nepal's economic and strategic calculus, the country has diversified its economic profile and policy options to engage other states in the region and outside.

Agriculture remains the mainstay, employing 80 percent of the population, contributing 40 percent to the GDP, and comprising 70 percent of total exports. Rice and wheat are the staple crops for both domestic consumption and exports, with carpets, garments, jute goods, and basket weaving as the other principal contributors to exports. Average GDP growth during the 1990s was between 4 to 6 percent, but unemployment remains very high at over 45 percent, and foreign aid contributes over 50 percent to the total development budget.[26] The Nepalese economy displays the familiar pattern of the entrenched role of inefficient SOEs in the production process, capital and labor markets, and banking and financial sectors. During the 1990s the government took hesitant strides to enhance the role of the private sector, made the currency (Nepalese rupee) convertible on the current account, and privatized seventeen SOEs.

Trade with India constitutes over 40 percent of Nepal's total exports and imports and received a big boost with the 1996 signing of a bilateral trade treaty. This treaty, which has been renewed to run until March 2007, permits zero-duty access of Nepalese exports to Indian markets, in addition to providing other preferential measures. Hydroelectricity represents a major potential for boosting export revenues, with India as the principal market. India has partially or wholly financed several hydel projects, and bigger ones are in the pipeline with funding from diverse international sources.

In 2000 the Asian Development Bank signed a partnership agreement on poverty reduction (PAPR) with Nepal to bring poverty down from over 40 percent to below 10 percent by 2017. In 1998 Nepal submitted its memorandum of understanding (MoU) on foreign trade to the WTO and in May 2000 began direct negotiations regarding its entry into this international body. Tourism is another major source of foreign exchange, although terrorist strikes on U.S. targets on September 11, 2001, and subsequent crises have drastically reduced tourist influx and revenues. By far the greatest threat to longer-term economic viability, however, is the pitched battle that the five-thousand-strong Maoist rebels have fought against the government since 1996, estimated to have cost about $300 million to the national exchequer so far. In 2003 the government and the Communist Party of Nepal–Maoist (CPN-M) agreed to a cease-fire and a code of conduct to guide their negotiations. CPN-M recognizes that political parties, whose role was suspended following the national emergency of 2002 when most members of the royal family were massacred, will have a central role in the future governance of Nepal. However, this will be determined within the framework of an amended constitution that rectifies the balance of power that is currently heavily skewed in favor of the monarchy. A pragmatic and durable resolution of this impasse will permit Nepal the latitude and resources to respond favorably to the challenges and opportunities presented by globalization.

Bhutan, a Buddhist kingdom with a population under seven hundred thousand, presents a wholesome variation from the traditional developmental models for small LDCs. King Jigme Singye Wangshuk, whose long rule (over twenty-seven years) has provided political stability, stresses that "gross national happiness" is more important than GNP. Pursuant to this goal, the country's developmental strategy emphasizes health, education and environment, and blending new technology and a cash economy with spirituality and ancient Buddhist values, particularly the famous "median path." The impact of this approach on the socioeconomic health of the country, as measured by major indicators of the Human Development Index (HDI), has been remarkable. State investment has revolutionized health and patient care, achieving near-universal child immunization and a high life expectancy of sixty-six years. Primary and secondary education is free, and medical care is virtually free. Similarly, strategic investments in agriculture, including terraced farming and modern methods, have enhanced productivity such that agro-outputs contributed nearly 36 percent to the national GDP during the 1990s, even though arable land is scarce (only 7 percent of total land area) and employs nearly 95 percent of the population.

During the 1990s GDP grew by 6 to 8 percent, with the government focus on boosting exports by increased sale of hydroelectricity to India, which already imports 80 percent of the country's surplus power and has financed several hydel projects.[27] Broadly, India's influence remains writ large on Bhutan's economic landscape, with its currency (ngultrum) tied to India's rupee. India is by far the largest source of trade and largest donor of external aid. India entirely financed the first two five-year economic development plans (1962–1967, 1967–1972) of Bhutan, contributed $215 million to the eighth plan (1997–2002), and closely coordinates the country's security affairs. During December 2003 the Bhutanese Royal Army mounted a successful operation, with tactical and logistical assistance from India, to drive out separatist guerrillas from India's province of Assam who for years had taken refuge in southern Bhutan. The rebel leadership is now seeking political reconciliation, while some of their cadres have moved into neighboring Bangladesh. Maoist rebels from Nepal also continue periodically to seek refuge in Bhutan, and that problem will require greater political accommodation and resource coordination between the various stakeholders.

Another major challenge facing Bhutan is that at the current growth rate of 3 percent, its population will double in eighteen years, putting a severe strain on national resources and developmental targets. The government is devising strategies to cope with future changes.[28] Thus, in June 2000 the king permitted the entry of satellite TV and the Internet into Bhutan, while the first Internet café opened in March 2001, and two online newspapers began to operate. The Center for Bhutan Studies is the country's only think tank and is increasingly tasked to provide policy briefs to the government on various social and economic priorities.[29] Bhutan is also working with the Asian Development Bank to corporatize its power sector and created the Bhutan Power Corporation in 2001.[30] Other priorities include measures to liberalize investment, foreign-trade, and exchange regulations.[31] In sum, the country's leadership is sensitive to the myriad challenges and is formulating policies to sustain and enhance national development without loosening the spiritual moorings of Buddhist values.

The island nation of the Maldives in the Indian Ocean presents another variation of economic policies to cope with the limits of size, natural resources, and the external environment. Its economy is based on tourism and fishing, while severe limits on potable water and arable land have meant that only 198 of the Maldives' 1,900 islands are inhabited. Tourism constitutes about 33 percent of the national GDP, with the share of agriculture being 6 percent, industry 7 percent, and fishing another 10 percent. The bulk of the domestic industry and service sectors is designed to support earnings from tourism and fishing. GDP growth during the 1990s fluctuated from 10 percent to 3 percent but averaged around 7.5 percent, while inflation remained in single digits. The government has permitted the private sector, which manages the bulk of commercial shipping, to play a strong role. Further, the government is working with the Asian Development Bank to reform the telecommunications and energy sectors and open them up to foreign competition, improve infrastructure and capacity utilization, and develop an information-and-communication network in the atolls.[32]

Foreign aid has come to the country from multilateral sources (United Nations Development Program, Asian Development Bank, and World Bank) and from India, Japan, Australia, and some European and Arab countries (as well as the Islamic Development Bank and the Kuwaiti Fund). Piracy on the high seas represents a significant threat to the Maldives' maritime commerce, and so it remains engaged in efforts to secure sea-lanes of communication (SLOC) and other dimensions of maritime security. In November 1988 the Indian navy foiled a serious threat to the political leadership of the Maldives, and bilateral cooperation now includes augmenting the Maldives' national capability against such threats in the future. Similarly, the U.S. government has recently funded training in airport management and narcotics interdiction and provided laptop computers for customs and immigration officials.[33] Finally, global warming represents another serious threat to the survival of the island group if ocean water rises more than two meters beyond current levels. In sum, the economic policies of the Maldives indicate serious attempts at structural, financial, and other reforms and greater sensitivity to calibrate resource allocation to optimize gains from the international environment. The immutable limits of size, location, and resource endowment obviously influence the pursuit of its policy options, and on balance the country appears to have modestly succeeded in its developmental endeavors.

REGIONAL AND WIDER IMPLICATIONS

The South Asian Association for Regional Cooperation (SAARC) is the principal regional organization, created in 1985 to promote economic, scientific, technological, and cultural cooperation among the seven South Asian countries discussed in this chapter. Keeping in mind the sensitivities of India and Pakistan, the SAARC mandate was revised to exclude security matters from its ambit of deliberation and adjudication. Since the first summit meeting on December 7–8, 1985, SAARC has evolved gradually in terms of both its institutions and its programs. It appeared to have taken a major step forward when the seven states ratified the South Asian Preferential Trading Agreement (SAPTA) in December 1995 and decided to create a South Asian Free Trade Area (SAFTA) "at the earliest possible date."

On balance, however, SAARC has failed to realize its potential, as well as the enormous expectations vested in it, especially by the smaller states of the region. The principal impediment from the outset was the difference in perception of the leadership in the various countries about the true purpose behind creating this body. India, as the predominant country in the region, would like to make SAARC a vibrant and viable entity, especially if investing in it would not heighten the suspicions of smaller states that India is pursuing its hegemonic agenda in South Asia via this multilateral mechanism. On the other hand, the Indian leadership has a lingering suspicion that SAARC could become the vehicle for smaller states to bandwagon against it on issues where they felt less confident of securing favorable terms in a bilateral negotiation with India.

The empirical outcomes of subsequent SAARC negotiations reveal that both the above scenarios proved correct at different points, with Pakistan and Bangladesh in particular withholding cooperation due to concern about India's hegemonic designs. This was illustrated again in 2004, when, during the January summit meeting of SAARC in Islamabad, Bangladesh remained the only country not to endorse the commitment to a speedy implementation of SAFTA. In February 2004 Bangladesh withheld its signature to the creation of a free-trade area between the member countries of an economic group still known by its erstwhile designation Bangladesh, India, Myanmar, Sri Lanka and Thailand—Economic Cooperation (or BIMST-EC). Nepal and Bhutan joined this group and signed the agreement, which seeks to bridge South and Southeast Asian economies.[34]

On the other hand, India has also been selective in investing its resources and political will to strengthen SAARC and has remained distant when it seemed inconvenient to pursue the matter within SAARC. Thus, the gains from SAARC have been limited to two spheres. One, it has provided a platform for regular interaction of officials from the member states and the growing confidence to pursue a pragmatic and incremental agenda of cooperation. Two, it has led to extensive data creation of the comparative economic advantages of each country, identifying sectors in which national exports will complement and not compete with each other, and to modest reductions in tariffs and regulations to boost intraregional trade and facilitate factor movement (especially labor) across the region. The ratification of SAFTA has aided the above process, but doubts remain about its actual performance, although preparatory work at national levels has begun for its phased implementation from 2008.

The most voluble indicator of this pessimistic assessment is that intra–South Asian trade has scarcely increased over the past decade and still constitutes less than 5 percent of the overall trade by these countries with the rest of the world. Another serious impediment to SAARC's longer-term economic viability comes from evaluating the experience of other regional organizations, including the Asia Pacific Economic Cooperation (APEC), the Association of Southeast Asian Nations (ASEAN), the European Union (EU), and the North American Free Trade Agreement (NAFTA). This assumes added relevance given the oft-expressed wishes of South Asian leaders to build trans-regional bridges with ASEAN and APEC and to emulate the positive lessons of the EU.

To an extent policy coordination on security issues has acted as a cementing factor or facilitator of economic cooperation in the other regions. Broadly speaking, the United States, China, and Japan expect positive security derivatives from an economically stronger and integrated APEC and have accordingly invested in this organization. To an extent the same is true about ASEAN and is further reflected in the dynamism of the ASEAN Regional Forum (ARF) that coordinates policy on a growing list of security issues. In recent years, issues that bear on economic security have become more prominent, including international terrorism, piracy on the high seas, transshipment of contraband, precursors or components of weapons-of-mass-destruction programs, export controls, enforcement, and interdiction. India is a member of ARF and a "dialogue partner" of ASEAN, while its request for entry into APEC is pending since the organization has decided to freeze its membership level until a suitable future date. But India's growing trade and contact with these bodies reflects its domestic decision to reinvigorate its *Ostpolitik* ("look east") policy and is not driven by its intent to leverage these ties to facilitate closer SAARC ties with East and Southeast Asia.

Similarly, on the economic side, the institutional and programmatic development of the EU has taken place in stages and over several decades, aided by the participation of major European countries within the Organization for Economic Cooperation and Development (OECD). On the security side, their participation in NATO and a host of multilateral regimes that regulate the production and export of dual-use goods and technologies has forged a closer sense of collective security.[35] Over time, the notion of shared security has helped to keep detractors in check and forge greater economic cooperation. The formalization of NAFTA also followed the establishment of strong economic linkages between the United States, Canada, and Mexico, as well as the conscious U.S. decision to invest considerable financial and policy resources to make NAFTA a viable entity. This is certainly not to suggest any direct comparison between Indian and U.S. leadership capabilities but that such a facilitating role by India remains bitterly contested in South Asia, primarily by Pakistan but also by Bangladesh.

An appraisal of these intraregional organizations brings into sharper focus two interrelated variables that stymie the progress of SAARC. One, states in South Asia were partitioned or created such that the ethnic, communal, or linguistic identity of groups is divided by international boundaries. Two, the process of nation building has not been completed, wherein ethnic, religious, or other identities are submerged to forge a national identity. As a consequence of the interplay of the above factors, high levels of mistrust, even antagonism, prevent the states from participating fully and voluntarily in the process of economic cooperation and the building of institutions to pursue shared prosperity. Finally, and partly a result of the above, the depressed economic condition and lack of strong institutions in these countries denies them the capacity and will to face external competition. This impedes regional cooperation and economic interpenetration out of fear that the stronger economic actors in the other states would dominate the indigenous actors in the host country. And it also limits the resolve, and ultimately the capacity, to forge regional links to gainfully harness the forces of globalization.

NOTES

1. Gene Sperling, national economic advisor to former U.S. president Bill Clinton, provides a good account of the political prism through which this debate often plays out. See Gene Sperling, "How to Be a Free Trade Democrat," *Foreign Policy* (March–April 2004), at www.foreign policy.com/story.

2. For a good analysis, see Matthew J. Slaughter and Philip Swagel, "Does Globalization Lower Wages and Export Jobs?" *Economic Issues No.11, International Monetary Fund,* September 1997, available at www.imf.org. For a broader analysis, see Thomas L. Friedman, *The Lexus and the Olive Tree: Understanding Globalization*, rev. ed. (New York: Anchor Books, 2000), 512. See also Jan Aart Scholte, *Globalization: A Critical Introduction* (London: Palgrave Macmillan, 2000), 304.

3. "Foreign Investment, Remittances Outpace Debt as Sources of Finance for Developing Countries," *World Bank*, Washington, D.C., April 2, 2003.

4. The issue of outsourcing has recently attracted much attention in the United States. For a concise account, see Vivek Agrawal and Diana Farrell, "Who Wins in Offshoring?: By Moving Service Industry Work to Countries with Lower Labor Costs, US Companies Can Focus on Creating Higher-Value Jobs," *The McKinsey Quarterly*, no. 4 (2003).

5. "Measuring Globalization: Economic Reversals, Forward Momentum?" *Foreign Policy* (March–April 2004). As per the 2003–2004 rankings, Pakistan comes in at number 46, Sri Lanka at 51, Bangladesh at 56, and India at 61, while the remaining three South Asian countries fall outside the range of measurement.

6. For a good historical account, see B. R. Tomlinson, "Historical Roots of Economic Policy," in *Foundations of India's Political Economy*, ed. Subroto Roy and William E. James (New Delhi: Sage, 1992), 274–302.

7. It is estimated that in July 1991, the forex reserves of around $600 million were barely sufficient to service two to three weeks of India's external debt.

8. The receipts of $5.5 billion from the Indian Millennium Deposits pushed forex reserves in January 2001 past the $40 billion mark. In April 2004 forex reserves crossed $110 billion, growing at about $3 billion per month.

9. The economic manifesto of the ruling National Democratic Alliance, unveiled during the election campaign in April 2004, proposed to create a Ministry of International Trade to "capture opportunities in global trade, promote Special Economic Zones and multicommodities exchanges, and remove internal trade barriers" (see, "NDA Pledges 8–10 pc Growth in Next Five Years," *The Hindu*, April 8, 2004, available at www.hindu.com/thehindu/holnus). Since 1996 successive ministers of finance and of commerce and industry have made greater export-orientation a core element of India's economic policy, stressing this theme while addressing both domestic and foreign audiences.

10. For a survey of dependency theory, world systems theory, and related scholarly work on models of economic development, see the works of authors such as Andre Gunder Frank, Raul Prebisch, Oswaldo Sunkel, Samir Amin, Paul Baran, Celso Furtado, Immanuel Wallerstein, and Gunnar Myrdal.

11. Despite outstanding border-dispute and mutual-security concerns, Sino-Indian bilateral trade grew from $1 billion in 1999 to $7.5 billion in 2003 and is projected to reach $20 billion by 2010. Economic ties with East and Southeast Asia have deepened, where some smaller

states, leery of Chinese power preponderance in the region, welcome the growing Indian presence as promoting a soft balance of power.

12. For a detailed treatment on this subject, see Anupam Srivastava and Seema Gahlaut, "A New Policy for Pakistan," in *Kargil and After: Challenges for Indian Policy*, ed. Kanti Bajpai, Afsir Karim, and Amitabh Mattoo (New Delhi: Har Anand Publishers, 2000), 164–90.

13. "FBI Fuels Pakistan's Share Boom," *British Broadcasting Corporation*, July 23, 2002, available at http://news.bbc.co.uk/s/hi/business.

14. Maryam Hussain, "Musharraf Sitting on Multi-Billion Dollar Scandal Reported by Auditor General," *South Asia Tribune*, no. 85 (March 28–April 3, 2004): available at www.satribune.com.

15. "Address to the Nation by Chief Executive of Pakistan General Pervez Musharraf," *The Dawn*, December 15, 1999.

16. *The World Bank Group: Pakistan Economic Report*, April 7, 1999, available at www.worldbank.org.

17. For an incisive account, see Prema-Chandra Athukorala and Sarath Rajapatirana, "Liberalization and Industrial Transformation: Lessons from the Sri Lankan Experience," in *Economic Development and Cultural Change* 48, no. 3 (April 2002): 543–72.

18. John Williamson, "Sri Lanka's Search for the Right Economic Policies," keynote address delivered at the conference "Independent Sri Lanka: Economic Development (1948–1998) and Prospects," Kalutara, Sri Lanka, March 1998.

19. See, e.g., Don K. Embuldeniya, "Economic Reforms and the Corporate Sector in Sri Lanka," *Contemporary South Asia* 9, no. 2 (July 2000): 165–79.

20. Manik de Silva, "The Peace Dividend," *Far Eastern Economic Review* (Hong Kong), July 4, 2002.

21. Sanjaya Lall, Kishore Sharma, Ganeshan Wignaraja, Sabrina Di Addario, and Gokhan Akinci, *"Building Sri Lankan Competitiveness: A Strategy for Manufactured Export Growth"* (Colombo: National Development Council, 1996).

22. For a more critical assessment of the Sri Lankan economy, see, e.g., V. Nithyanadam, "Ethnic Politics and Third World Development: Some Lessons from Sri Lanka's Experience," *Third World Quarterly* (London) 21, no. 2 (April 2000): 283–311.

23. "Bangladesh: Economic Performance," *Annual Report 2002*, Asian Development Bank, available at www.adb.org/Documents/Reports/Annual_Report/2002/BAN.asp.

24. Muhammad Yunus, "The Grameen Bank," *Scientific American* (November 1999).

25. Bangladesh has had a high trade surplus with India (over $700 million in 2001), which the latter permits in search of a broader economic engagement, but persistent political differences prevent a consensus in Bangladesh regarding expanded trade with India. In April 2004, the American oil and natural gas company UNOCAL, which is operating in Bangladesh, was once again rebuffed when the Bangladeshi parliament overturned the proposal to sell natural gas to India.

26. Babu Ram Shreshtha, *Managing External Assistance in Nepal* (Kathmandu: Jamuna Shrestha, 1990).

27. Report of the Central Statistical Organization, Royal Government of Bhutan, 2000.

28. Thierry Mathou, "Bhutan in 2001: At the Crossroad," *Asian Survey* 42, no. 1 (January–February 2002): 192–97.

29. David L. Wheeler, "Blending Buddhism and Technology: Bhutan Develops on Its Own Terms," *Chronicle of Higher Education* 46, no. 33 (April 21, 2000): A54–A56.

30. Editorial, "The Cost of Necessities," *Kuensel* (Bhutan's only public online newspaper), April 8, 2003, available at www.kuenselonline.com/article.php.

31. "Bhutan: Economic Performance," *Annual Report 2001*, Asian Development Bank, available at www.adb.org/Documents/Reports/Annual_Report/2001/bhu.asp.

32. "Maldives: Economic Performance," *Annual Report 2001*, Asian Development Bank, available at www.adb.org/Documents/Reports/Annual_Report/2001/mld.asp.

33. "Background Notes: Maldives," Bureau of South Asian Affairs, U.S. Department of State, October 2001, available at www.state.gov/r/pa/ei/bgn/5467pf.htm.

34. "Bimstec Nations, Barring Bangladesh, Sign Trade Pact," *The Financial Express*, February 9, 2004, available at www.financialexpress.com.

35. The principal multilateral security regimes in this context are the Nuclear Suppliers' Group, the Missile Technology Control Regime, the Australia Group, the Chemical Weapons Convention, and the Wassenaar Arrangement.

FURTHER READING

Banerjee, Parthasasathi, and Frank-Jurgen Richter, eds. *Economic Institutions in India: Sustainability under Liberalization and Globalization*. New Delhi: Palgrave Macmillan, 2003.

Dreze, Jean, and Amartya Sen. *India: Development and Participation*. New York: Oxford University Press, 2002.

Hossain, Moazzem, Iyanatul Islam, and Reza Kibria, eds. *South Asian Economic Development: Transformation, Opportunities and Challenges*. London: Routledge, 1999.

Looney, Robert E. *The Pakistani Economy: Economic Growth and Structural Reform*. New York: Praeger, 1997.

Scholte, Jan Aart. *Globalization: A Critical Introduction*. New York: Palgrave Macmillan, 2000.

Sen, Amartya. *Development as Freedom*. New York: Anchor Books, 2000.

Stiglitz, Joseph E. *Globalization and Its Discontents*. New York: W. W. Norton, 2003.

ul Haq, Mahbub. *Human Development in South Asia 2001: Globalisation and Human Development*. Karachi: Oxford University Press, 2003.

Vanaik, Achin, ed. *Globalization and South Asia: Multidimensional Perspectives*. New Delhi: Manohar, 2004.

Weiss, Linda, ed. *States in the Global Economy: Bringing Domestic Institutions Back In*. Cambridge: Cambridge University Press, 2003.

Zaidi, S. Akbar. *Issues in Pakistan's Economy*. Karachi: Oxford University Press, 1999.

12

The War on Terrorism: Implications for South Asia

Timothy D. Hoyt[1]

The September 11, 2001, terrorist attacks on the World Trade Center and Pentagon prompted fundamental changes in the foreign and security policies of the United States. These changes affected security and stability throughout the international system and redefined the U.S. relationship with many states and regions. South Asian security, in particular, is now evolving in a significantly different direction, due at least in part to the new U.S. "terrorismcentric" strategy.

Using terrorism as a defining concept in U.S. relations with South Asian states complicates an already historically difficult relationship. Definitions of terrorism abound, and the concept can be shaped to fit any particular policy. In an effort to reduce these complications, I focus on terrorism from an American perspective, using speeches and publications from U.S. government agencies as the defining tool. This chapter is organized into three sections. First, I briefly discuss and analyze terrorism in South Asia, examining in particular the relationship between regional terrorism and extraregional states and nonstate actors. Next, I analyze the impact of U.S. actions on regional states, focusing in particular on India, Pakistan, Afghanistan, and, to a lesser extent, Nepal, Sri Lanka, and Bangladesh. Each of these states has been affected by, and has attempted to exploit, the new U.S. focus on terrorism. Finally, I assess the U.S. war on terrorism's long-term implications, which are mixed: while smaller states like Nepal, Sri Lanka, and Afghanistan may benefit significantly from the war on terrorism, the larger states (India, Pakistan, and perhaps even Bangladesh) may find U.S. involvement confusing, contradictory, and even destabilizing.

WHAT IS TERRORISM?

No single definition of terrorism is commonly accepted by the international community. As a result, any analysis of the terrorism issue causes disagreement. As elsewhere, multiple definitions of terrorism compete for acceptance in South Asia, based on one's support for or rejection of the political objectives of a given group. The U.S. State Department defines terrorism this way: "The term 'terrorism' means premeditated, politically motivated violence perpetrated against noncombatant targets by subnational groups or clandestine agents, usually intended to influence an audience."[2] This definition does not address some types of incidents that many analysts consider to be terrorism. The attack on the USS *Cole*, for example, would not be considered terrorism under this definition.

The U.S. government refines this definition slightly to distinguish between international terrorists and other terrorist groups. Again, using the State Department definition, "The term 'international terrorism' means terrorism involving citizens or the territory of more than one country," and "the term 'terrorist group' means any group practicing, or that has significant subgroups that practice, international terrorism."[3] This definition, again, creates difficulties for assessing terrorism in South Asia. Terrorism exists in various forms throughout the region. It can be based on local conditions, a response to political oppression, social injustice, economic disparity, or caste, religious, or ethnic differences. Many terrorist groups in the region benefit from state support in the form of intelligence sharing and support, training facilities, arms supplies, or territorial sanctuary. This support ranges from tacit to deliberate and varies in scope from minor to massive. For the purposes of my analysis in this chapter, a "state-supported" terrorist group lies at the tacit/minor end of the spectrum, while a "state-sponsored" group lies at the deliberate/massive end of the spectrum.[4]

A brief examination of the major terrorist groups in South Asia, from a pre–September 11 perspective, suggests that these three categories, local, state-supported, and state-sponsored, roughly describe most of the terrorist activity in the region. Local terrorist groups include the Maoist United People's Liberation Front (UPLF) in Nepal, which arose in the 1990s as a result of failure in democratic elections, ideological fervor, exploitation of social deprivation, and policy failures on the part of the Nepalese government.[5] The UPLF accelerated its military activities in the summer of 2001, after the tragic massacre of Nepal's King Berendra and his family in June, and formed the People's Liberation Army in November 2001.[6] This organization benefits, according to regional reports, from tacit Indian support in the form of territorial sanctuary, but it must also be recognized that this region of the world is extremely difficult to police.[7]

Other local terrorist groups can be found in Pakistan and Bangladesh, where political, sectarian, and ethnic conflicts have fueled domestic terrorism. Among these groups are the Sipah-e-Sahaba, Pakistan (SSP), a violently anti-Shia Sunni sectarian group, and its offshoot Lashkar-I-Jhangvi, which has been linked to attacks on Pakistani Christian communities and an assassination attempt against then prime minister Nawaz Sharif in 1999.[8] In Bangladesh, Harakut ul-Jihad-I-Islami/Bangladesh (HUJI-B) aims to establish an Islamic regime in that country, and infighting between the two major political parties raises the possibility that it or other domestic terrorist organizations could play a destabilizing role in the future.[9] Another local group, but one with substantial international connections, is the Liberation Tigers of Tamil Eelam (LTTE, or Tamil Tigers), founded in 1976.[10] The LTTE's objectives are independence or substantial regional autonomy for the Tamil minority in Sri Lanka. The group has waged war in Sri Lanka since 1983 and is the de facto inventor of the suicide bomb. It benefited early in its existence from modest Indian state support and has created a formidable extortion network for coercing resources from the Tamil diaspora.[11] The LTTE has targeted non–Sri Lankans, most notably in the assassination by suicide bomb of former Indian prime minister Rajiv Gandhi in 1991. The United States designated LTTE a Foreign Terrorist Organization in 1997, reflecting its international links and connections.[12]

State-supported groups were also abundant before September 11 and were often difficult to distinguish from state-sponsored groups. The Kashmir conflict, for example, spawned a series of groups whose objectives varied from independence to absorption into the Pakistani state, whose personnel were composed of different proportions of Indian Kashmiris, Pakistani Kashmiris, and foreign nationals, and whose reliance on and support from Pakistani authorities ranged from minimal to almost total.[13] The decline of the Jammu and Kashmir Liberation Front, the most autonomous Kashmiri group, can be traced directly to Pakistani efforts to isolate it and promote alternative groups with objectives closer to Pakistan's.[14] An umbrella political organization, the All Parties Hurriyat Conference (APHC), was formed in 1993 to represent a common political front for Kashmiri separatist movements.

Other ethnic and religious separatist groups exist in the northeast of India, including the United Liberation Front of Assam (ULFA), the National Democratic Front for Bodoland (NDFB), and the United People's Democratic Solidarity (UPDS) in Assam, the most troubled of India's northeastern states. In Manipur, Tripura, Nagaland, and Mizoram, separatist groups utilize low-level violence, and the violent Naxalite movement also remains a problem.

The most important terrorist organization in the region, however, is al Qaeda, a group that created a close alliance with the Taliban regime in Afghanistan.[15] Led by Osama bin Laden, al Qaeda consists of a loose alliance of Islamic extremist groups. Originally assembled and financed by bin Laden for jihad (holy war) against the Soviet occupation forces in Afghanistan, al Qaeda evolved into a pivotal force in anti-American terrorism in the 1990s.[16] The organization has been blamed for an attack on the World Trade Center (1993), the Khobar Barracks assault (1996), the bombing of two U.S. embassies in Africa (1998), and the attack on the USS *Cole* (2000). Al Qaeda moved its headquarters from Sudan to Afghanistan in early 1997.[17]

In Afghanistan, al Qaeda received significant support from the Taliban regime. The Taliban, an unusually extremist Islamic regime, came to power in Afghanistan in the mid-1990s. It found in al Qaeda a close ally, as well as a source of scarce hard currency. Al Qaeda benefited from Afghan bases for training and logistics and provided the 055 Brigade, a force of several thousand volunteers that constituted the spearhead of the Taliban's conventional fighting forces.[18] In turn, the Taliban received substantial support from Pakistan, particularly from Inter-Services Intelligence (ISI), Pakistan's powerful and highly independent intelligence service.[19] Pakistan saw a friendly Afghanistan as crucial to its security, both as a source of strategic depth versus India and also as a means of minimizing tensions from a porous and politically disputed border in the northwest. Pakistan first provided the Taliban with military equipment and advisers in August 1994.[20] After the Taliban took control of Kabul and most of the countryside, ISI used Afghanistan as a training facility for militants preparing to fight in Kashmir.

The rise of the Taliban and al Qaeda's increasing influence in Afghanistan severely complicated regional politics. Bin Laden had twice attempted to assassinate then prime minister Benazir Bhutto in Pakistan.[21] But Pakistan's eccentric civil-military relationship and its commitment to a secure relationship with Afghanistan in order to obtain strategic depth trumped any reservations about the Taliban–al Qaeda relationship. By 1997 regular Pakistan army troops fought with Taliban forces against the Northern Alliance, which still controlled some of the more distant northern provinces in Afghanistan. India provided financial and logistic support to the Northern Alliance, increasing Pakistan's concern and providing incentives to assist a friendly Taliban regime.[22] As one analyst writes, "Increasingly, the Kashmir issue became the prime mover behind Pakistan's Afghan policy and its support to the Taliban. The Taliban exploited this adroitly, refusing to accept other Pakistani demands knowing that Pakistan could deny them nothing, as long as they provided bases for Kashmiri and Pakistani militants."[23]

The potential difficulties this relationship posed for U.S. relations with the region were first demonstrated on August 20, 1998, when U.S. naval ships fired cruise missiles against al Qaeda installations in Afghanistan in response to the bombing of U.S. embassies in Africa. The missiles had to fly over Pakistani air space, nearly causing a diplomatic incident.[24] The al Qaeda bases they struck reportedly housed both Pakistani citizens ("volunteers" in the Kashmir struggle) and ISI trainers. According to Western reports, two ISI facilities were destroyed in the attack, killing five ISI officers and twenty trainees.[25] The deteriorating U.S. relationship with Pakistan—the result first of Pakistan's nuclear program, then accelerated by the South Asian nuclear tests of May 1998, Pakistan's military incursions across the line of control (LOC) in Kashmir in May–July 1999, and General Musharraf's coup of October 1999 overthrowing Prime Minister Nawaz Sharif—impeded efforts to undermine al Qaeda or the Taliban.

SEPTEMBER 11, 2001: THE WAR ON TERRORISM BEGINS

Shortly after the stunning terrorist attacks of September 11, 2001, the United States began a campaign against the forces of international terrorism. In his speech of September 20, 2001, President Geroge W. Bush referred specifically to the forces of international terror and declared that the United States would wage war against them wherever they were found:

> Our enemy is a radical network of terrorists, and every government that supports them. . . . Our war on terror begins with Al Qaeda, but it does not end there. It will not end until every terrorist group of global reach has been found, stopped, and defeated. . . . Every nation, in every region, now has a decision to make. Either you are with U.S. or you are with the terrorists.[26]

In the attack's immediate aftermath, the United States approached General Musharraf about Pakistan's role in the coming conflict. The initial conversation between ISI chief Gen. Mahmoud Ahmad and Deputy Secretary of State Richard Armitage was confrontational. Armitage reportedly told Mahmoud that "the future begins today" and that Pakistan needed to decide whether it was with the United States or against it.[27] The next day, Mahmoud was summoned to the State Department, where Armitage provided a list of seven demands and stated that the list was nonnegotiable. To the administration's surprise, General Musharraf agreed to support the United States in all seven actions.[28]

Reports from the subcontinent suggest that this decision was not an easy one for Pakistan. According to Lt. Gen. Javed Ashraf Qazi, minister of communications, the cabinet unanimously supported acceptance of the U.S. demands.[29] A September 14, 2001, meeting of the Pakistani army's corps commanders, generally acknowledged as a key element in Pakistani national policy, demonstrated significant divisions in this crucial group. At least two key commanders, Lieutenant Generals Mahmoud and Usmani, were reluctant to overturn Pakistan's Afghan policy, and it reportedly took six hours of debate before

Musharraf was able to gain support for the policy change.[30] The result was that Musharraf made a groundbreaking speech in which Pakistan completely reversed direction, removing its support for the Taliban and pledging cooperation with the United States. Musharraf stated that this decision was necessary to obtain four key objectives for Pakistan: security, long-term economic development, the protection of Pakistan's nuclear assets, and a settlement of the Kashmir dispute. Pakistan's concerns about its nuclear assets stemmed, in part, from an article claiming that the United States was training with Israeli special forces to seize the Pakistani nuclear arsenal, an issue on which Musharraf reportedly received very direct assurances from President Bush.[31] Pakistani assistance to the United States eventually included logistical support, base rights in western Pakistan, and vital intelligence collaboration. Without this assistance, the campaign in Afghanistan, Operation Enduring Freedom, would have been very difficult.

India also offered unexpected assistance. Immediately after the attack, India sent formal condolences and offered the United States Indian air bases for use in military operations against Afghanistan. Indian intelligence also offered unprecedented cooperation, including substantial information about al Qaeda and the Taliban, information that India had been collecting both through sources focused on Pakistan and through its connections with the Afghan Northern Alliance. This assistance was unprecedented and reflected an Indian effort to capitalize on the changing international environment to create a deeper strategic relationship with the United States. U.S. delays in responding to Indian offers and prompt reestablishment of a close relationship with Pakistan dashed Indian hopes and caused great disappointment in policy circles.[32]

The end result of this cooperation from the two most powerful states in the subcontinent was that the United States carried out an enormously successful military operation in one of the most foreboding environments on the planet. Operation Enduring Freedom began on October 7, 2001, with the support of a coalition of ninety nations, the largest coalition in world history.[33] The Taliban were routed in a little over a month. Al Qaeda has been battered and harassed; more than three thousand al Qaeda operatives and associates have been detained in over one hundred countries.[34] A new government, headed by Hamid Karzai, took power and reasserted control, supported by an international military force and substantial international-development aid.[35] In the course of just a few months, the U.S. war on terrorism had substantial and significant results.

Operation Enduring Freedom did not, of course, result in an end to all terrorism in the region. On October 1, 2001, terrorists in Kashmir attacked the state legislative assembly in Srinagar, killing over thirty people.[36] India, not surprisingly, viewed this incident as a direct attack on the legitimacy of its government in the state of Jammu and Kashmir, the area Pakistan still disputes. Even more audacious was the December 13, 2001, five-person suicide attack on the Indian parliament building in Delhi. Several of the terrorists nearly made it inside the building, which at the time contained hundreds of members of Parliament and much of the cabinet. India swiftly attributed responsibility to two Pakistan-based insurgent groups with links to al Qaeda—Jaish-e-Mohammad (JeM) and Lashkar-e-Tayyiba (LeT).[37]

India responded with an unprecedented military mobilization, ultimately reaching over seven hundred thousand men.[38] Entire "strike corps," mechanized forces based around India's three armored divisions, were moved to forward positions on the Indo-Pakistani border, and mountain infantry divisions were moved from the border with China into Jammu and Kashmir.[39] The crisis peaked in early January 2002 when Indian officials spoke publicly of the possibility of nuclear-weapons use, stating bluntly that if war broke out and Pakistan used nuclear weapons, its continued existence would be jeopardized.[40] According to reports from the region, India was prepared to launch a cross-border conventional strike that risked escalating to a broader regional conflict.[41]

Faced with a more serious threat of regional war than at any time since 1971, the United States responded by sending Secretary of State Colin Powell to the region in an effort to avert a calamity. India's demands were simple: the extradition of twenty suspected terrorists and an end to infiltration of combatants from Pakistan across the LOC into Jammu and Kashmir.[42] On January 12, 2002, President Musharraf dramatically announced to the nation that Pakistan would no longer be used as a base for terrorism of any kind, stated that the government would crack down on madrassas (religious schools) suspected of aiding terrorist groups, and banned several terrorist groups including JeM and LeT. The demand for extradition of terrorist suspects was not met. These dramatic statements sufficed to calm the crisis, and at the State of the Union address on January 29, 2002, President Bush specifically praised President Musharraf for his courageous acts. However, President Musharraf's address was made in the winter, when infiltration across the LOC is historically constrained. As the weather warmed, infiltration across the LOC became evident.[43] The brutal slaughter of women and children at an Indian military barracks in Kaluchak in early May 2002 reinvigorated the crisis.[44]

Indian troops, which had remained in place rather than retiring to their usual peacetime cantonments, conspicuously began preparations for military operations, laying mines and moving reserve ammunition to forward depots.[45] The Pakistani ambassador to the United Nations bluntly threatened the use of nuclear weapons in the event that Pakistan's existence was jeopardized by an Indian assault.[46] The United States again intervened diplomatically with a parade of high-ranking officials in May and June and recommended the evacuation of all American civilians from India. The crisis was defused in mid-July, again with Pakistani promises to rein in infiltration across the LOC, but as of this writing U.S. officials admit that infiltration has not ceased. India has heightened patrols on the LOC and is improving surveillance measures.[47] The war on terror thus created opportunities for changing relationships between India, Pakistan, and the United States, but cooperation against international terrorism has not resulted in fundamental breakthroughs in Indo-Pakistani relations. Terrorism remains a powerful force in the region, and U.S., Pakistani, and Indian perceptions of regional terrorism differ considerably, which impedes triangular cooperation. For example, during the Kaluchak crisis of 2002, Pakistan drew forces away from the Afghan border (where they operated against al Qaeda and Taliban remnants) to the west for possible deployment against India.[48]

In Sri Lanka and Nepal trends are somewhat more positive. In each case, terrorist groups have reached a cease-fire with the government in the aftermath of the September 11 attacks and increased U.S. presence in the region. It is reasonable to assume that an increased U.S. military presence, U.S. support for governments fighting terrorist threats, and the spectacular pulverization of al Qaeda and the Taliban may have prompted some reconsideration on the part of terrorist leaders. In the case of Sri Lanka, the LTTE ceased hostilities with the government on December 23, 2001. It reached a memorandum of understanding with the government in February 2002, has accepted the concept of considerable autonomy within a federalized state, and has engaged in six rounds of talks with the government, using Norway as an intermediary.[49] Negotiations have failed in the past, in 1981, 1983, 1989, and 1994, but the current cease-fire is considered promising.

In Nepal talks were held between the Maoists in July, September, and November of 2001, but the monarchy refused to accept the three main demands of the Maoist leadership: abolishing the monarchy, establishing an interim government, and forming a constitutional assembly. As a result, on November 24, 2001, the Maoists declared the formation of the Peoples Liberation Army and launched a new wave of attacks on government forces and installations. In May 2002 the United States provided $20 million in assistance to help the government fight the insurgency. U.S., Indian, and British support to the Royal Nepal Army played a crucial role in forcing the Maoists in 2002 to accept first a cease-fire and then a code of conduct, perhaps a stepping-stone to genuine negotiations.[50] Continued conflict appears likely in the near term, however, due to the fundamental discrepancies between Maoist demands and the government's position.

FUTURE TRENDS?

The war on terrorism changed the terms of U.S. engagement in South Asia. Most of the states in the region saw opportunities created by a U.S. decision to engage in a global war against international terrorism. Some of the more astute nonstate actors in the region also perceived a distinct threat emerging from new U.S. policy and adapted their political positions accordingly. In the cases of the largest and most important actors in the regional balance of power, India, Pakistan, and the United States, these new opportunities have not resulted in fundamental changes in policy toward or within the region. Both India and Pakistan hoped to leverage the terrorism issue to their benefit and to the detriment of the other. Judged by this standard, both states have been frustrated.

India sought to use this opportunity to fundamentally alter a traditionally problematic relationship with the United States.[51] India hoped to emphasize Pakistan's links with the Taliban and al Qaeda and its support for groups staging terrorist attacks across the LOC into the Indian state of Jammu and Kashmir.[52] A greater U.S. awareness of terrorism, it was hoped, would accelerate the tilt toward India evident from President Clinton's 2000 visit and increase U.S. sympathy for India's position on Kashmir, sympathy already evident in the Clinton administration's vocal defense of the sanctity of the LOC during the 1999 Kargil war. The war on terrorism, therefore, could be used to move the United States even further away from Pakistan and relatively closer to India. A more positive Indo-U.S. relationship would, it was hoped, lead to tangible benefits, including the lifting of sanctions imposed after the May 1998 nuclear tests and greater openness to the transfer of both military and civilian technologies.

In most of these objectives, India was ultimately frustrated. Pakistan's links with the Taliban were emphasized, but those very links meant that Pakistan also provided the best intelligence on the Taliban, an issue of great importance as the United States committed itself to the Taliban's overthrow.[53] U.S. concerns about Pakistani support for terror did emerge, particularly in the 2001–2002 crisis, but never resulted in wholehearted support for the Indian position on Kashmir or, in fact, for India's efforts during the crisis. The order for evacuation of American civilians from India at the height of the Kaluchak crisis was viewed by some Indians as an act of economic coercion. Despite India's best efforts, the United States maintains a close relationship with Pakistan. Indo-U.S. strategic partnership, perhaps always an unrealistic near-term objective, has been compromised in favor of the short-term advantage of Pakistani cooperation in the war on terror, while the China factor has, at least temporarily, receded from the forefront of U.S. policy concerns. Technology transfer, while forthcoming, remains at a much more limited level than India would prefer. In short, India's hopes for a rapid transformation of its relationship with the United States have not been achieved.[54] This does not mean that the relationship is not evolving in a favorable manner, with high-level meetings, military cooperation, joint terrorism task forces, and intelligence cooperation.[55] India hoped that the war on terror would spark rapid, almost revolutionary change in the relationship. Instead, it continues to mature in a more evolutionary fashion.

Pakistan also hoped to revitalize a traditional relationship with the United States—renewing a Cold War alliance.[56] Pakistani leaders viewed the United States as a critical, but unpredictable, perhaps unreliable, partner. Musharraf's rejection of the alliance with the Taliban and Pakistan's continuing efforts to cooperate with the United States in pursuing al Qaeda and Taliban leaders come at a high cost domestically.[57] Pakistani unrest during the Afghan conflict, while manageable, indicated substantial opposition to government policy. More recently, the surprising strength of the alliance of Islamist parties after the fall 2002 elections and the public uproar when the United States published details of Pakistani cooperation in the Afghan campaign suggest that the government's policies have substantial opposition.[58]

Pakistan also hoped for substantial U.S. concessions in both the economic and the military spheres. Although the administration recently announced a five-year, $3-billion aid package for Pakistan, many Pakistanis are critical about what they see as a lack of reciprocity in the relationship. Two items of particular concern, the transfer of F-16 fighter aircraft and Pakistani textile imports to the United States, are matters of constant comment. The U.S. decision to allow India to purchase the Israeli PHALCON aerial warning and control aircraft will, over the course of several years, substantially add to India's already formidable advantages in air power. Pakistan, by contrast, cannot get the United States to release F-16 aircraft, now over a decade old, which are already built and paid for. The Pakistani economy, in relatively dire straits after decades of mismanagement and institutionalized corruption, would benefit enormously from the opportunity to export more textiles into the U.S. market.

Both India and Pakistan, to some extent, view their relationships with the United States as a zero-sum game, where one state improves its relationship at the expense of the other. The United States, on the other hand, continues to follow a long policy of attempting to maintain good relations with both states. This policy has been difficult to manage in the past and remains highly problematic as the subcontinent enters a new era of nuclear confrontation. Due to shifts in domestic politics in both India and Pakistan, religion has become politicized to a greater and more dangerous extent than at time since Partition. Sectarian killings in Pakistan, cries for jihad against both Westerners and Hindus by extremist Islamic groups, and the emergence of Hindu nationalism as a powerful force in India—not always a benign force as demonstrated by the massacre of Muslims in Gujarat in early 2003—do not contribute to regional stability.[59]

Competing policy priorities further complicate the U.S. predicament. These include terrorism, nonproliferation, human rights, and democracy. Because the United States has publicly declared its intention to wage war against international terrorists, the issues of terrorism, its definition, and its condemnation represent a focal policy concern in both the United States and the region. The U.S. definition has not remained constant—an issue of some concern to both India and Pakistan. The same war on terrorism that prompted a preemptive strike on the Taliban, clearly linked to al Qaeda, has also been used to justify the conquest of Iraq, an American policy priority, but one that has not, as of this writing, been reliably linked with al Qaeda or other international terrorist groups of concern.[60] India argues that Pakistan is the epicenter of international terrorism, but the United States refuses to treat Pakistan in the same way it treats other state supporters of terrorism, including Iran, Syria, or even North Korea, whose links with international terrorism are minimal.[61] Instead, the United States reassures Pakistan but recently has put the Hizb ul-Mujaheddin on the Other Terrorist Organizations list, suggesting that the largest (and least overtly Islamic extremist) Kashmiri insurgent group is now on watch and perhaps signaling to Pakistan that the Kashmir insurgency needs to be shut down.[62] Indian sources note, however, that even banned Pakistani groups are now reorganizing to continue operations in Kashmir.[63] U.S. leaders vacillate on whether al Qaeda is active in Kashmir, although clearly at some point al Qaeda had significant contact with various Kashmiri groups through the complex of Afghan training camps.[64]

The United States also faces a double standard on nonproliferation. On the one hand, nonproliferation was a major element of U.S. policy from 1990 to 1998, when the objective was to halt and, if possible, roll back the Indian and Pakistani nuclear programs. After the 1998 tests, U.S. nonproliferation policy unwound but continues to influence policy in the region. Pakistani use of nuclear weapons as cover for a limited invasion of Indian territory, exploiting the stability-instability paradox,[65] caused a regional crisis in 1999. India's threat of a massive invasion in 2001–2002 led to another crisis. Neither crisis has resulted in significant U.S. penalties against either state, in a major effort to cap or reduce nuclear weapons in the region, or in significant U.S. pressure to end the Kashmir impasse and eliminate the most likely cause of a future, possibly nuclear, conflict.[66] The United States has instead opted to live with a nuclearized region—President Bush's reassurances to President Musharraf on the security of Pakistan's strategic arsenal are now a matter of anecdotal record—and has not undertaken any significant diplomatic efforts outside of crisis management.

Human rights are also a matter of some confusion. It is a tragic truth that India's human rights violations in Kashmir, a matter of record with multiple independent observers and reports, have been widely ignored by the international community.[67] Ethnic and religious separatist tendencies in India have only been exacerbated by the rise of extremist Hindu nationalism, which has manifested itself in the destruction of the Ayodhya Mosque, the Gujarat riots of 2002 and other sectarian attacks, and occasional murders of Christian missionaries. Pakistan's support for Kashmiri separatists, whose brutal attacks on Hindu pandits and innocent women and children are also a matter of record, has drawn no formal U.S. condemnation, only the condemnation of the groups involved, and only after the September 11 attacks. Sectarian attacks within Pakistan were also generally ignored until after the war on terrorism was declared. In fact, the U.S. internment without trial of Pakistani nationals at a facility in Guántanamo, Cuba, could be condemned as a violation of the rights of those citizens. The contradictions in American human rights policy in the subcontinent have only been exacerbated, and not resolved, by the war against terrorism.

Finally, the U.S. commitment to democracy remains an issue, particularly regarding Pakistan. President Musharraf took power in a military coup, overthrowing a democratically elected, but extraordinarily corrupt, government in October 1999. After several years of attempted economic and political reforms, Musharraf held nationwide elections in October 2002.[68] The list of possible candidates for election was deliberately limited in hopes of minimizing the possibility that supporters of former prime ministers Nawaz Sharif and Benazir Bhutto would gain substantial representation. The result, however, was that an alliance of Islamist parties became the primary opposition force in government. This alliance now controls the Northwest Frontier Province/tribal areas, where it has implemented Taliban-style codes of conduct, and is a partner in the government of Baluchistan. These two regions border Afghanistan and are believed to house large numbers of Taliban and al Qaeda refugees.[69] While a new prime minister has been selected, central authority remains in the hands of President Musharraf, and the current U.S. policy appears to be to accept Musharraf as the lesser of a range of possible evils, even if his commitment to democracy appears selective at best.[70]

Elsewhere in the region, terrorism remains a simmering threat. In Afghanistan the Taliban has reestablished a presence despite the new regime and a force of international peacekeepers.[71] Gulbuddin Hekmatyar, former leader of Afghanistan, has joined forces with the Taliban and al Qaeda.[72] The new Karzai regime still has unresolved border issues with Pakistan as well.[73] Despite generous U.S. and international assistance, stability in Afghanistan is far from assured, and a resurgence of the Taliban remains a possibility.[74] Nepal and Sri Lanka face similar problems. Negotiations with terrorists and insurgents are a notoriously difficult problem. As mentioned above, the LTTE has already engaged in numerous talks with various Sri Lankan governments, and Nepal has also attempted to negotiate with its Maoist opponents in the past. The looming threat of U.S. intervention or enhanced U.S. assistance may have played a role in the decision of these groups to negotiate. A key factor in defusing these conflicts will be the willingness and ability of the United States to provide diplomatic, economic, and military assistance to the governments of both countries. Bangladesh also remains an area of concern for the U.S. government. While it is not a sanctuary for al Qaeda, the U.S. government believes that Bangladesh acts as a conduit for illicit financial flows to terrorist organizations.[75] Deep divisions between the country's two major parties and abundant corruption threaten economic growth and create obstacles for cooperation against terrorism. In fact, the U.S. government fears that these factors may endanger long-term Bangladeshi stability and perhaps even make it vulnerable to an outbreak of terrorism.[76]

CONCLUSION

The September 11, 2001, terrorist attacks fundamentally changed U.S. policy in South Asia because of the physical presence of al Qaeda in Afghanistan. The renewed American presence and interest in the region offered new opportunities for both of the major regional players (India and Pakistan) and also many of the smaller states (Nepal, Sri Lanka, Afghanistan, and Bangladesh). A more robust American military and diplomatic posture also forced nonstate actors, from the relatively friendly Northern Alliance in Afghanistan to the more hostile LTTE and Nepalese Maoists, to reexamine their policies and objectives and to adapt to a far more threatening U.S. presence. It would appear, at least in the short term, that the smaller states in the region have been more successful in leveraging the new U.S. role to their advantage. Sri Lanka and Nepal are now both engaged in promising negotiations with local terrorist and insurgent groups. Afghanistan has been freed of the repressive and bizarre Taliban regime and has an opportunity for the first time since the Soviet invasion in 1979 to rebuild and restore itself with strong international support.

The larger players in the region are less satisfied with the new U.S. role, and for good reason. India truly hoped to leverage a war on terrorism to its advantage and Pakistan's detriment. India had much to offer a business-oriented Republican administration that saw China as a likely adversary, voiced a strong preference for democracies, and saw India as a natural counterweight both to radical Islamic movements and to Chinese expansion. India's disappointment is due, in large part, to differing definitions of terrorism. India perceived the epicenter of radical Islam to be moving east from Afghanistan into Pakistan. International terrorism, from an Indian standpoint, began in the Khyber Pass and threatened the east, a viewpoint reinforced by the fifteen-year conflict in Kashmir that has resulted in tens of thousands of deaths. Although it is clear that the United States recognized the shift of the political and religious center of radical Islam from Iran to Afghanistan and South Asia, U.S. concern over terrorist activity remains focused on points west, on the threat to the U.S. homeland, its allies in Europe, the Middle East and the Persian Gulf, and most especially to the global supply of oil. As a result of these differing definitions, based on different national interests, India was disappointed when the United States renewed its relationship with Pakistan. What India saw as the major threat, the United States saw as the major asset: Pakistan was the one state that best understood the Taliban and al Qaeda and whose support was absolutely critical in the waging of perhaps the most geographically difficult military campaign in American history.

Pakistan, however, has also been deeply disappointed by the U.S. role in the region. Pakistan's military remains technologically backward and suffers from a significant qualitative disadvantage compared to the Indian military, particularly the air force. The United States has not attempted, as it did in the past, to redress that disadvantage with high-technology arms transfers to Pakistan. In fact, it has permitted the transfer of PHALCON aircraft that will significantly increase the Indian air force's capabilities over time. In addition, Pakistan now has an Afghan neighbor that is distinctly less friendly than Pakistan's former Taliban friends. Although Pakistani leaders complain about inadequate economic compensation for their sacrifices, the Pakistani economy has benefited enormously from U.S. and international assistance. Pakistan's intelligence services apparently continue to cooperate closely with their U.S. and Western counterparts, creating an atmosphere where al Qaeda and its associates cannot move freely about the region or pose a significant threat to the Musharraf regime. While Pakistan was widely viewed as a failing state before September 11, 2001, it now has a temporary window for reform and renewal. Whether it can take advantage of that opportunity remains to be seen.[77]

The new U.S. role in the region remains fragmented and unclear. As soon as Operation Enduring Freedom deposed the Taliban, the primary focus of U.S. policy shifted to Iraq. This resulted in embarrassing mistakes, including neglecting to ask for funding for Afghan aid in a budget request, as well as a series of ad hoc crisis interventions by increasingly high-ranking government officials in the 2001–2002 Indo-Pakistani crisis. The international wrangling over intervention in Iraq and the U.S. decision to undertake operations without UN authorization did nothing to stabilize relations with the region. Neither India nor Pakistan supported the U.S. intervention, and India recently refused to supply a division of seventeen thousand troops for post-war peacekeeping and reconstruction without a UN mandate and command structure.[78]

The war on terrorism provided the opportunity for a fundamental reassessment of U.S. interests and opportunities in the region. It provided a motive to engage all of the states in the region in a more productive manner on issues of mutual concern and for the United States to intervene to promote stability and security. The United States had an opportunity to redress mistakes and neglect stemming from the Cold War and to forge new relationships with states in a region of increasing importance to the global economy and international security system. As of this writing, it is not clear that the United States is truly capitalizing on this opportunity. Repeating the errors of past administrations, the United States is focusing on crisis avoidance in the region, rather than taking the risky alternative of attempting to negotiate a solution to the region's most intractable problems. This hands-off posture has not harmed negotiations in the smaller states, but it will not and cannot help resolve the fundamental issue in the region that represents the greatest threat to both U.S. and regional interests, the ongoing Indo-Pakistani conflict, which is exacerbated by the presence of nuclear weapons on both sides.

The Bush administration came into office hoping to back away from the Middle East conflict, only to be dragged back into the fray because it is the only state with sufficient power and gravitas to help solve such an intractable problem. The same is almost certainly true in South Asia as well. In the absence of a concerted effort by the United States to help create the conditions for a solution, it will continue to be dragged into the region as a crisis manager as each successive Indo-Pakistani crisis gets a little more dangerous. Resolving the Kashmir issue, the fundamental stumbling block in Indo-Pakistani relations and in regional stability, will not be easy. But it will not happen by accident, and it will not happen as long as each state sees the United States as a tool to use against the other. The United States has the ability to play a leadership role in the region. It remains to be seen whether it has the will and the stamina.

NOTES

1. The views expressed in this chapter are those of the author, and do not reflect the official policy of the United States Navy, the Department of Defense, or any other agency of the United States government.

2. *Patterns of Global Terrorism 2002* (Washington, D.C.: U.S. Department of State, April 2003), xiii. This definition has been used in this report since the mid-1980s. For purposes of this definition, "noncombatant" is interpreted to include, in addition to civilians, military personnel who at the time of the incident are unarmed and/or not on duty.

3. *Patterns of Global Terrorism 2002*, xiii.

4. This distinction is not reflected in U.S. policy, but is simply a convenience used by the author.

5. See "Nepal" in *Country Reports on Human Rights Practices—2002,* Bureau of Democracy, Human Rights, and Labor, U.S. Department of State, March 21, 2003, available at www .state.gov/g/drl/rls/hrrpt/2002.

6. Ahmad Abbas, "Impact of 9/11 on Smaller States of South Asia," *Strategic Studies* 22, no. 3 (Autumn 2002): 78.

7. Shireen Mazari, "Comments," *Strategic Studies* 22, no. 3 (Autumn 2002): 13.

8. *Patterns of Global Terrorism 2002*, 114, 143. The United States has declared Lashkar-I-Jhangvi a Foreign Terrorist Organization because of its link to the murder of journalist Daniel Pearl in early 2002. SSP is considered an Other Terrorist Group by the United States and was banned by Pakistani president Pervez Musharraf in January 2002.

9. *Patterns of Global Terrorism 2003*, 133–34; "United States Relations with South Asia," Christina Rocca, assistant secretary for South Asian affairs, testimony before the House International Relations Subcommittee on Asia and the Pacific, March 20, 2003. HUJI-B is classed an Other Terrorist Organization by the United States but has financial links to Pakistan-based groups. According to other sources, HUJI-B was established with financial backing from Osama bin Laden.

10. *Patterns of Global Terrorism 2002*, 114–15.

11. India's Research and Analysis Wing (RAW) trained and armed the LTTE in the early 1980s and reportedly failed to warn Indian officials of this when India intervened in Sri Lanka in 1987. Stephen Philip Cohen, *India: Emerging Power* (Washington, D.C.: Brookings Institution Press, 2001), 150.

12. "Foreign Assistance Programs in South Asia," Christina Rocca, assistant secretary for South Asian affairs, testimony before the Senate Committee on Foreign Relations, March 26, 2003. Al Qaeda reportedly maintained connections with both LTTE and Hezbollah in order to learn about suicide tactics. Rohan Gunaratna, *Inside Al Qaeda: Global Network of Terror* (updated with new material) (New York: Columbia University Press, May 2003), 98.

13. For brevity's sake, these groups will be listed here and discussed in more detail below. According to *Patterns of Global Terrorism 2002*, foreign and other terrorist groups engaged in Kashmir include Harakut-ul-Mujaheddin (HUM), Jaish-e-Mohammed (JeM), Lashkar-e-Tayyiba (LeT), Harakut ul-Jihad-I-Islami (HUJI), Hizb ul-Mujahiddin (HM), and Jamiat ul-Mujahidin (JUM). Other groups exist, and some groups have changed their names. Prior to September 11, 2001, the only Pakistani group listed by the State Department as a Foreign Terrorist Organization was HUM, formerly known as Harakut ul-Ansar, for its kidnapping of five Westerners in Kashmir in 1995. Owen Bennett Jones, *Pakistan: Eye of the Storm* (New Haven, Conn.: Yale University Press, 2002), 27.

14. Bennett Jones, *Pakistan*, 83.

15. The best works on this relationship are Gunaratna, *Inside Al Qaeda,* and Ahmed Rashid, *Taliban* (New Haven, Conn.: Yale University Press, 2000).

16. *Patterns of Global Terrorism 2002*, 118–19.

17. Rashid, *Taliban*, 133.

18. Gunaratna, *Inside Al Qaeda*, 78–80.

19. Rashid, *Taliban*, 184

20. Gunaratna, *Inside Al Qaeda*, 53.

21. Gunaratna, *Inside Al Qaeda*, 40.

22. Gunaratna, *Inside Al Qaeda*, 57.

23. Rashid, *Taliban*, 186.

24. See Mary Anne Weaver, *Pakistan: In the Shadow of Jihad and Afghanistan* (New York: Farrar, Straus & Giroux, 2002), 32–33.

25. Bennett Jones, *Pakistan*, 27; Weaver, *Pakistan*, 32–33.

26. President George W. Bush, "Address to a Joint Session of Congress and the American People," September 20, 2001.

27. Bob Woodward, *Bush at War* (New York: Simon & Schuster, 2002), 47.

28. Woodward, *Bush*, 58–59. The demands included stopping any and all support for al Qaeda, either official or unofficial; overflight and landing rights; access to Pakistan, including basing and possibly use of the borders; intelligence and immigration information; Pakistani condemnation of the September 11 attacks and curbing all domestic expressions of support for attacks against the United States and the West; cutting off shipments of fuel and volunteers to the Taliban; and breaking diplomatic relations and ending support for the Taliban if Afghanistan continued to harbor bin Laden and al Qaeda. The last demand amounted to a complete reversal of almost a decade of Pakistani foreign policy.

29. Isabel Hilton, "The General in His Labyrinth," *The New Yorker*, August 12, 2002.

30. To complicate matters further, Generals Mahmoud and Usmani were key Musharraf supporters, who had played critical roles in the coup that brought him to power in October 1999. According to one report, Mahmoud was sent to Afghanistan in an effort to persuade Mullah Omar, leader of the Taliban, to hand bin Laden over to the United States but instead assured Omar that he could continue to count on ISI support! In October 2001 Musharraf removed both Mahmoud and Usmani from positions of power. Bennett Jones, *Pakistan*, 3, 25–26.

31. See Seymour Hersh, "Watching the Warheads: The Risks to Pakistan's Nuclear Arsenal," *The New Yorker*, November 5, 2001. According to Bob Woodward, President Bush told Musharraf bluntly in a phone conversation that "Seymour Hersh is a liar." Woodward, *Bush*, 303.

32. Juli A. MacDonald, *The Indo-U.S. Military Relationship: Expectations and Perceptions* (Washington, D.C.: Office of Net Assessment, October 2002), 52.

33. *Patterns of Global Terrorism 2002*, ix.

34. *Patterns of Global Terrorism 2002*, iv.

35. Karzai was elected leader of Afghanistan in July 2002. *Patterns of Global Terrorism 2002*, 9.

36. Indian sources attest that JeM carried out this attack. See *Patterns of Global Terrorism 2002*, 109.

37. See *Patterns of Global Terrorism 2002*, 10, 109–10, 113.

38. This total includes members of official paramilitary formations that carry out counterinsurgency and policing operations in Kashmir. "India Builds Up Forces as Bush Urges Calm," *New York Times*, December 30, 2001. This report cites Pakistani intelligence officials as having identified twenty-three Indian divisions on the border, in addition to 600 aircraft. India moved troops from the border with China (III Corps) as well.

39. "India Fully Prepared to Meet Exigencies, Says Jaswant," *The Hindu*, December 24, 2001.

40. "Pak Would Be Wiped Out if It Uses Nuclear Bomb: BJP," *Hindustan Times*, December 26, 2001; "Military Option if Diplomacy Fails," *The Hindu*, January 4, 2002; Army Ready for War, Says Chief," *The Statesman* (India), January 12, 2002. According to reports, Chief of Army Staff general Padmanabhan remarked that if Pakistan used nuclear weapons against Indian soldiers on the battlefield, "the continuation of the existence of Pakistan as a nation would be in doubt."

41. Rahul Bedi, "A Strike Staunched," *Frontline* 19, no. 12 (June 8–21, 2002); "India Had Planned Offensive," *Dawn*, December 24, 2002. The latter noted that according to Indian chief of army staff designate Lt. Gen. N. C. Vij, the army planned a joint army/IAF mission with paratroopers, pushing a brigade of army commandos to capture key infiltration routes like Haji Pir Pass in January 2002 to hit and seal off major terrorist bases in Pakistan-administered Kashmir. This attack was called off at the last moment.

42. "India's Leader Continues Accusing Pakistan of Terror," *New York Times*, December 30, 2001.

43. "Militants Still Entering India, Says Musharraf," *London Daily Telegraph*, August 21, 2002.

44. India claimed that the attack had been carried out by LeT. *Patterns of Global Terrorism 2002*, 10, 113.

45. A former Pakistani chief of staff insists that the crisis proved that India could not win a war against Pakistan and that Pakistan's conventional forces deterred India. See General Mirza Aslam Beg, "Converging Interests on Kashmir," *The News International* (Pakistan), May 18, 2003. In this article, Beg asserts that 50 percent of the insurgents in Kashmir are local, and the other 50 percent are foreign volunteers, Pakistani, or from the Pakistani-held section of Kashmir. The notion that India's forces were inadequate for rapid, decisive victory was supported by the testimony of Indian army leaders in 2003. According to defense sources, the Indian conventional combat ratio advantage declined from 1.75:1 in 1971 to 1.56:1 in 1990 and is now only 1.22:1. "Army Seeks Swift Modernisation to Counter Pak," *Times of India*, April 3, 2003.

46. "Pakistan Won't Rule Out Use of Nuclear Arms if Attacked," *Media Corporation of Singapore Pte Ltd.* (Channel News Asia), May 29, 2002 (accessed through Lexis-Nexis); "At UN, Pakistan Defends First-Strike Nuclear Policy," *Agence France Presse*, May 29, 2002.

47. "India Starts Blocking Infiltration Routes," *The Hindu*, May 21, 2003.

48. K. Alan Kronstadt "Pakistan–U.S. Relations" (Washington, D.C.: Congressional Research Service, Library of Congress, September 24, 2002), 9.

49. *Patterns of Global Terrorism 2002*, 8, 12.

50. "Foreign Assistance Programs in South Asia," Christina Rocca, assistant secretary for South Asian affairs, testimony before the Senate Committee on Foreign Relations, March 26, 2003.

51. The most comprehensive study of the Indo-U.S. relationship is Dennis Kux, *Estranged Democracies: India and the United States* (Washington, D.C.: National Defense University Press, 1993).

52. "US Refusal to Admit Iraq-Pak Similarities Unacceptable," *Times of India*, April 14, 2003. External Affairs Minister Yashwant Sinha said Pakistan was the "epicentre and exporter of terrorism."

53. Indians, for example, were furious at the reported "Kunduz airlift," in which Pakistani aircraft moved Pakistanis and, perhaps, Taliban and al Qaeda leaders from the Afghan city of Kunduz shortly before it fell to the Northern Alliance in late 2001. See Seymour Hersh, "The Getaway," *The New Yorker*, January 28, 2002.

54. According to Indian and U.S. interviewees, three areas of difference may prevent long-term Indo-U.S. strategic convergence: different definition of threat (international versus regional focus), different views on the roots of terrorism (Pakistan as root of problem or part of solution), and Indian concerns about the impact U.S. campaigns on terrorism (especially Iraq) may have on destabilizing the Persian Gulf or other regions. McDonald, *Indo-U.S. Military Relationship*, xxiv.

55. For example, a U.S.–India Counterterrorism Joint Working Group met twice in 2002. *Patterns of Global Terrorism 2002*, 10. See also McDonald, *Indo-U.S. Military Relationship*.

56. The most comprehensive study of the U.S.-Pakistani relationship is Dennis Kux, *Disenchanted Allies: The United States and Pakistan 1947–2000* (Baltimore: Johns Hopkins University Press, 2001).

57. Pakistan arrested and transferred into U.S. custody nearly 500 al Qaeda suspects and associates in January 2001 and ranked third behind the United States and Switzerland in seized terrorist assets. *Patterns of Global Terrorism 2002*, 11. Key al Qaeda leaders have been arrested in Pakistan, including Abu Zubaydah (March 2002), Ramzi Binalshibh (September 2002), Khalid Sheikh Mohammed (March 2003), and Walid Ba'Attash (April 2003).

58. "U.S. Report on Aid From Pakistan Angers Islamists," *Philadelphia Inquirer*, May 21, 2003. According to a report from U.S. Central Command, 57,800 air missions over Afghanistan crossed Pakistani air space, and 800 U.S. Marines used a Pakistan port to transit to the war zone.

59. According to *India: Country Reports on Human Rights Practices—2002* (Washington, D.C.: Bureau of Democracy, Human Rights, and Labor, U.S. Department of State, March 31, 2003), "NGOs [non-governmental organizations] reported that police were implicated directly in many of the attacks against Muslims in Gujarat, and in some cases, NGOs contended, police officials encouraged the mob."

60. Iraq was listed, along with Syria, Iran, Cuba, North Korea, Sudan, and Libya, as a state sponsor of terrorism in *Patterns of Global Terrorism 2002*, xi.

61. "US Refusal to Admit Iraq-Pak Similarities Unacceptable," *Times of India*, April 14, 2003. External Affairs Minister Yashwant Sinha said Pakistan was the "epicentre and exporter of terrorism." This statement occurred just a few days after the Indian parliament (*Lok Sabha*) condemned the U.S. invasion of Iraq and called for immediate withdrawal—on the same day U.S. military forces entered Baghdad. "Irrelevant India," *India Today International*, April 21, 2003, 6.

62. "Terror Label Upsets Kashmiris," *Washington Post*, May 24, 2003. After the State Department classified HM as an Other Terrorist Group in late April, Pakistan followed suit in mid-May by announcing a ban on the group. Analysts in South Asia have described HM as the group "most likely to put down its weapons and pursue peace" if India and Pakistan start serious talks.

63. "Pak Has Revamped Kashmir Terror Strategy: BSF," *Times of India*, April 2, 2003. According to this report, JeM, LeT, Al Badr, and HUJI have formed a Joint Command Council to coordinate operations and infiltration. The latter two groups are on the State Department Other Terrorist Organization List, and President Musharraf formally proscribed both JeM and LeT in his January 2002 speech.

64. See Weaver, *Pakistan*, 261, for an account of Secretary of Defense Donald Rumsfeld's contradictory remarks on the presence of al Qaeda in Kashmir during the June 2002 crisis.

65. The stability-instability paradox, essentially the idea that nuclear deterrence created opportunities for low-intensity conflict because neither participant would want to escalate fighting to a level where nuclear use was possible, was first identified in by Glenn Snyder, "The Balance of Power and the Balance of Terror," in *The Balance of Power*, ed. Paul Seabury (San Francisco: Chandler, 1964), 184–201, and is discussed in Robert Jervis, *The Meaning of the Nuclear Revolution* (Ithaca, N.Y.: Cornell University Press, 1989), 19–22. See also Michael Krepon and Chris Gagne, eds. *The Stability-Instability Paradox: Nuclear Weapons and Brinkmanship in South Asia* (Washington, D.C.: Henry L. Stimson Center, June 2001).

66. See the dedicated issue of *India Review* (Summer 2002) on the Kashmir problem.

67. See, e.g., Bennett Jones, *Pakistan*, 83.

68. The United States officially views these elections as flawed. "Foreign Assistance Programs in South Asia," Christina Rocca, assistant secretary for South Asian affairs, testimony before the Senate Committee on Foreign Relations, March 26, 2003.

69. The Muttahida Majlis-I-Amal (MMA), an alliance of six religious parties, won 11 percent of the votes cast but a total of 45 of 268 directly elected seats (18 percent). See "Two Elections: New Hopes and Old Frustrations," *South Asia Monitor* 52 (November 1, 2002). By January 2003, after additional by-elections, the MMA held 83 of 342 seats and had become the biggest opposition block. "Right, Pro-Military Big Winners in Pakistan By-elections," *Sydney Morning Herald*, January 17, 2003.

70. A recent article noted that "of all of Pakistan's leaders, Musharraf has most explicitly and forcefully reiterated [Pakistani founding father Muhammad Ali] Jinnah's vision of a liberal, secular, and democratic Pakistan." Stephen Philip Cohen, "The Nation and the State of Pakistan," *Washington Quarterly* 25, no. 3 (Summer 2002): 111.

71. "Taliban Appears to Be Regrouped and Well-Funded," *Christian Science Monitor,* May 8, 2003. According to this report, the Taliban has appointed regional commanders in all of the regions of Afghanistan and is receiving cross-border support from supporters in Pakistan, including members of Pakistan's MMA.

72. See "Designation of Gulbuddin Hekmatyar as a Terrorist"—Press Statement, Richard Boucher, U.S. Department of State, February 19, 2003.

73. "Border Issue with Pakistan Raises Concern in Afghanistan" *New York Times,* April 21, 2003.

74. The United States pledged $897 million in assistance in 2002. "Foreign Assistance Programs in South Asia," Christina Rocca, assistant secretary for South Asian affairs, testimony before the Senate Committee on Foreign Relations, March 26, 2003.

75. "United States Relations with South Asia," Christina Rocca, assistant secretary for South Asian affairs, testimony before the House International Relations Subcommittee on Asia and the Pacific, March 20, 2003.

76. "Foreign Assistance Programs in South Asia" and "United States Relations with South Asia."

77. An ominous note is sounded in "Musharraf Mulls Options for Reasserting Authority," *Wall Street Journal*, July 21, 2003. According to the article, the MMA can combine with other factions to create a 160-seat opposition in the current 360-seat government, one that has refused to enact Musharraf's policies or grant him the constitutional amendments and sweeping powers he desires. This may bode poorly for Prime Minister Zafarullah Jamali. The article also notes a recent surge in sectarian murders of Shiites and Christians in Pakistan.

78. "U.S. Downplays India's Choice of Not Sending Troops to Iraq," *Washington Times*, July 15, 2003.

FURTHER READING

Clarke, Richard A. *Against All Enemies: Inside America's War on Terror*. New York: Free Press, 2004.

Coll, Steve. *Ghost Wars: The Secret History of the CIA, Afghanistan, and bin Laden, from the Soviet Invasion to September 10, 2001*. New York: Penguin, 2004.

Hoffman, Bruce. *Inside Terrorism*. New York: Columbia University Press, 1999.

Laqueur, Walter. *No End to War: Terrorism in the Twenty-First Century*. New York: Continuum, 2003.

Margolis, Eric S. *War at the Top of the World: The Struggle for Afghanistan, Kashmir and Tibet*. New York: Routledge, 2002.

Santhanam, K., et al. *Jihadis in Jammu and Kashmir: A Portrait Gallery*. New Delhi: Sage, 2003.

Stern, Jessica. *Terror in the Name of God: Why Religious Militants Kill*. New York: Ecco Press, 2003.

———. *The Ultimate Terrorists*. Cambridge: Harvard University Press, 2001.

Talbott, Strobe, and Nayan Chanda. *The Age of Terror: America and the World after September 11*. New York: Basic Books, 2002.

Weaver, Mary Anne. *Pakistan in the Shadow of Jihad and Afghanistan*. New York: Farrar, Strauss, & Giroux, 2002.

Index

301

About the Contributors

Craig Baxter, a retired Foreign Service officer, is professor emeritus of politics and history at Juniata College in Pennsylvania. He received a Ph.D. from the University of Pennsylvania. His books include *Bangladesh: From a Nation to a State* (1997). Baxter is also coauthor with Syedur Rahman of *Historical Dictionary of Bangladesh* (2003). He was the founder and first president of the American Institute of Bangladesh Studies.

Jonah Blank is chief policy advisor for South Asia to the Democratic staff of the Senate Foreign Relations Committee. Concurrently with his government service, he has taught anthropology and South Asian studies at Georgetown University and the Johns Hopkins University School of Advanced International Studies. He is author of *Mullahs on the Mainframe: Islam and Modernity among the Daudi Bohras* (2001) and *Arrow of the Blue-Skinned God: Retracing the Ramayana through India* (2000).

Maya Chadda is professor of political science at William Paterson University of New Jersey and author of *Building Democracy in South Asia: India, Pakistan, Nepal* (2000); *Ethnicity, Security, and Separatism in South Asia* (1997); and *Paradox of Power: The United States Policy in Southwest Asia* (1987). Chadda is the U.S. editor of *Global Review of Ethnopolitics* (UK) and is currently working on a volume to be entitled *Ethnicity and Economic Development in India and Sri Lanka*.

Devin T. Hagerty is an associate professor of political science at the University of Maryland, Baltimore County. He was previously a senior lecturer in government and international relations at the University of Sydney in Australia.

Hagerty was awarded a Ph.D. by the University of Pennsylvania, an M.A.L.D. by the Fletcher School of Law and Diplomacy, and a B.A. by Rutgers University. He is the author of *The Consequences of Nuclear Proliferation: Lessons from South Asia* (1998), as well as (with Sumit Ganguly) the forthcoming *Fearful Symmetry: Indo-Pakistani Crises in the Shadow of Nuclear Weapons.* Hagerty is also the founding managing editor of a new Taylor and Francis journal, *Asian Security.*

Herbert G. Hagerty is a member of the Senior Foreign Service (Ret.) and a graduate of the National War College. He has a B.A. from Columbia College and an M.A. in South Asia regional studies from the University of Pennsylvania. Hagerty served in New Delhi and Oslo as a political officer, in Islamabad as political counselor, in London as political advisor to the commander in chief of U.S. Naval Forces, Europe, and in Colombo as deputy chief of mission. His State Department assignments included country officer for India; director of the Office of Pakistan, Afghanistan, and Bangladesh Affairs; and director for Intelligence Liaison. Among other publications, Hagerty has written a first-person account of the 1979 attack on the U.S. embassy in Pakistan for *Embassies under Siege* (1995) published by the Institute for the Study of Diplomacy at Georgetown University.

Timothy D. Hoyt is an associate professor of strategy and policy at the U.S. Naval War College, teaching about strategy, terrorism, contemporary conflict, and South Asian security. In October 2003 he testified before two subcommittees of the House Committee on International Relations regarding terrorism in South Asia. He is the author of *Military Industries and Regional Power* (forthcoming), in addition to numerous chapters and articles on terrorism, nuclear proliferation, and security in the developing world. Hoyt is beginning work on technology and international security and a coauthored volume on strategy and the global war on terrorism.

Gaurav Kampani is a senior research associate at the Center for Nonproliferation Studies in Monterey, California. Kampani is an expert on South Asian affairs. His publications span a wide range of media and locales, including articles in numerous U.S. academic journals and periodicals. He has been commissioned by the Department of Defense's Defense Threat Reduction Agency to conduct research on South Asian political stability and relations between India and Pakistan, and he is a frequent commentator and analyst for the news media. Kampani was previously a research assistant at the United States Institute of Peace and a Herbert Scoville Jr. Peace Fellow at the Natural Resources Defense Council in Washington, D.C.

Peter R. Lavoy is director of the Center for Contemporary Conflict at the Naval Postgraduate School. He coedited *Planning the Unthinkable: How New Powers Will Use Nuclear, Biological and Chemical Weapons* (2000). His forthcoming books are *Learning to Live with the Bomb: India and Nuclear Weapons, 1947–2002* and an edited volume titled *Asymmetric Warfare in South Asia: Causes and Consequences of the Kargil Conflict.* During 1998 to 2000 he worked in the Office of the Secretary of Defense, serving as director for counterproliferation policy and then principal director for requirements, plans and counterproliferation policy. He holds a Ph.D. in political science from the University of California, Berkeley, and a B.A. in government from Oberlin College.

Swarna Rajagopalan is a Chennai, India–based analyst of South Asian politics and security interested in the intersection of security, governance, and identity politics, in addition to women in politics and security. She has written *State and Nation in South Asia* (2001) and coedited *Re-distribution of Authority: A Cross-Regional Perspective* (2000). Her forthcoming book is titled *A Clearing in the Thicket: Women, Security, South Asia.* Educated at the University of Bombay, Syracuse University, and the University of Illinois, Rajagopalan has taught at Michigan State University, Yale University, and the University of Illinois, Urbana-Champaign.

Anupam Srivastava is the codirector of the South Asia Program at the Center for International Trade and Security, University of Georgia. Srivastava teaches courses on Asian and South Asian security and political economy within the university's School of Public and International Affairs. He has provided briefings on U.S.–South Asia technology-security issues to various government agencies and presented his research at numerous international academic and policy forums. He has published widely in books and policy journals, appears regularly on the BBC and Voice of America, and is quoted in several mainline U.S. and international newspapers.

David Taylor has been vice provost (academic development) at the Aga Khan University in Karachi since 2002. Before that, he was for thirty-two years on the faculty of the School of Oriental and African Studies, University of London. A political scientist and historian, he was educated at the Universities of Cambridge and London. He has spent extended periods in South Asia and has been a visiting scholar at Panjab University (Chandigarh) and Jawaharlal Nehru University (New Delhi). He has published regularly on the history and politics of India and Pakistan.

Robert Wirsing is a member of the faculty of the Asia-Pacific Center for Security Studies, Honolulu, Hawaii. A specialist on South Asian politics and international relations, he has made over thirty research trips to the South Asian region since 1965. His publications include *Kashmir in the Shadow of War* (2002); *India, Pakistan, and the Kashmir Dispute* (1994); and *Pakistan's Security under Zia, 1977–1988* (1991).